CINEMA 4D

The Artist's Project Sourcebook

Anne Powers

CMP **Books**

San Francisco

This book is dedicated to the mystery and joy of creation in all its forms, and to all the members of my family who have fueled my life with patience and love.

Published by CMP Books
an imprint of CMP Media LLC
600 Harrison Street, San Francisco, CA 94107 USA
Tel: 415-947-6615; FAX: 415-947-6015
www.cmpbooks.com
email: books@cmp.com

Managing editor: Gail Saari
Copyeditor: Dawn Adams
Interior design and composition: Leigh McLellan
Cover design: Damien Castaneda

Distributed to the book trade in the U.S. by:

Publishers Group
1700 Fourth Street
Berkeley, CA 94710
1-800-788-3123

Distributed in Canada through:

Jaguar Book Group
100 Armstrong Avenue
Georgetown, Ontario M6K 3E7 Canada
905-877-4483

For individual orders and for information on special discounts for quantity orders, please contact:

CMP Books Distribution Center, 6600 Silacci Way, Gilroy, CA 95020
Tel: 1-800-500-6875 or 408-848-3854; Fax: 408-848-5784
Email: cmp@rushorder.com; Web: www.cmpbooks.com

Library of Congress Cataloging-in-Publication Data

Powers, Anne.
   CINEMA 4D : the artist's project sourcebook / Anne Powers.
     p. cm. — (Digital media academy)
   Includes index.
   ISBN 1-57820-242-6 (alk. paper)
1. Computer animation. 2. Three-dimensional display systems. 3. Cinema 4D XL. 4. Computer graphics. I. Title. II. Series.
   TR897.7.P69 2004
   776'.6—dc22   2004012754

Printed in the United States of America
04 05 06 07   5 4 3 2 1
ISBN: 1-57820-242-6

Contents

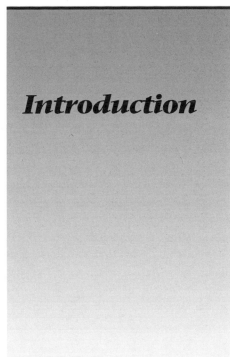

Introduction

Figure I.1

Close your eyes! Imagine you are once again nine years old. It's early Saturday morning, and the radio says that rain has set in for the day. (The TV is on the blink.) Whatever toy you reach for will have to entertain you a long, long time. Maybe it's an Erector Set, a dollhouse, a train set, or Legos. Whatever it is, chances are it has lots of fascinating widgets that will keep you immersed in building a world where your imagination is king.

Now that you're older, welcome to CINEMA 4D, a powerful and seriously professional tool with all the fun and engaging appeal of the ultimate toy. With C4D, you'll explore the definitive creative high—the adventure of inventing 3D worlds. C4D provides you with access to a massive arsenal of tools for modeling and animation without bogging you down with years of learning curve. Because this application is so intuitive, you can get to work (and fun) sooner.

No other media lets you "wear so many hats" and exercise so many skills simultaneously. In the creation of exciting and vibrant 3D worlds, the very essence of childhood play will be present in the most serious of work. Have fun!

Who This Book Is for and How It's Different

This book is about creating all kinds of artistic imagery using CINEMA 4D as a tool. It is intended to be an enjoyable, attainable, and thorough introduction to the creatively fluent use of C4D. In addition to being a great start for beginners, it will encourage new ways of working and thinking for more seasoned C4D users. It is especially suited for the visual dreamer who may feel overwhelmed by the technical complexities of 3D and who may have had a hard time making the creative leap using digital tools. In spite of its playful and artistic nature, the text introduces a wide range of skills for using C4D as a serious production tool for almost any purpose.

Artists of all kinds—illustrators, motion graphics and print graphic designers, and those who wish to animate goofy characters or solemn scientific data—will find many engaging step-by-step examples that can be easily fit to their purposes. Whether in film, TV, the web, or an instructional QuickTime movie in a classroom, 3D is unsurpassed for adding comprehension and visual enhancement. In today's world, anyone in any field can benefit from using 3D as a clear and compelling visual communication tool.

The design of this book and the projects inside are perfectly suited for classroom use, as well as for the learner at home. Busy teachers (probably with more than just 3D on their educational plate) will find this text and the massive collection of instructional goodies on the DVD a great helper.

By using project-based instruction that quickly rewards the reader with results, the text and DVD examples introduce the important concepts of CINEMA 4D without restating the manual. This book should be used in conjunction with the manual, so that involved explanations will come straight from those who know the software at its very core. The focus of this text is more about artistic possibilities of CINEMA 4D, and how anyone can use C4D creatively.

The 3D Environment and Workflow

When you open CINEMA 4D and begin to work, the GUI (Graphical User Interface) lets you create and manipulate objects in a virtual working environment which has three spatial dimensions and the element of time. Within this environment there is a collection of virtual tools with which you can create and animate virtual objects. Because you have the freedom to move your view of the 3D world, objects can be looked at and edited from any viewpoint or perspective. The workspace is infinite in size and can be configured with any units of measurement.

The 3D environment is not the finished product but the virtual workshop in which you are creating objects, scenes, and worlds. The final output is produced by rendering. In layman's terms, a flat picture is digitally "painted" from a chosen view of the 3D scene. This may be a still picture or a frame of animation. It may be highly realistic or manipulated so the final pictures are stylized and have more of a painterly or illustrative look.

The Animation Pipeline

In large animation studios, individuals usually perform very specialized tasks and their piece of the puzzle then feeds into the big picture. The Animation Pipeline is the sequence of stages in the development of an animation project, often broken down into character development, modeling, materials and textures, lights, cameras, animation, effects, rendering, and compositing. Even if you plan to specialize in just one of these areas, it's important that you know something about everything. Decisions made in each of these stages have the power to greatly enhance or destroy the success of all the other stages.

If you bought this book, chances are that you are either home alone or in a classroom situation and want to learn the basics of the entire 3D creation process. You may end up specializing at some point, but then again many 3D artists work independently or in small companies where they perform many parts of the pipeline. Artists working alone in a more linear fashion often refer to their pipeline as workflow.

Thinking Holistically

The order in which tasks are performed varies from person to person. Typically, the animator working alone sketches and develops ideas or characters, creates models, designs and applies texture, sets up cameras for the scene, works out the composition, introduces lighting, and then creates the animation. Many times, things will have to be done in a different order because one aspect of the process is drastically affecting the outcome of another. As impossible as it may seem, you'll have to think holistically about the project, or about many of the aspects of the project at once.

Acknowledgements

To these individuals I owe gratitude:

To Dorothy Cox, Gail Saari, Paul Temme, Dawn Adams, Meg McCalmon, and Sachie Jones of CMP books for their aid and patience.

To Leigh McLellan of Leigh McLellan Design.

To Kevin Aguirre, Jamie Aronson, Paul Babb, Rick Barrett, Chad Hofteig, Diana Lee, Joan Marks, and especially Josh Miller of MAXON, who all remained kind through my endless questions.

To Tom Wolsky, Beth Corwin, and Phil Gibson for their encouragement.

To my parents, Peggy and Hershel Scandlyn, for never suggesting I abandon art for a "real job."

To my children, Maggie, Patrick and Charlene, who often wonder if their artist mother came from Mars but love me anyway.

To Tom Krewson, a master of technology with an understanding of art.

An Animator's Hats

This digital world awaits your creative decisions about everything in it. Forms, personalities, scale, choreography of motion, colors, textures, mood and atmosphere, lighting, music and sound effects, and special effects are only some of the choices that will be yours to make. These are just a few of the hats you'll be wearing:

- Sculptor
- Choreographer
- Lighting Designer
- Set Designer
- Painter
- Architect
- Director
- Business Manager
- Illustrator
- Music Director
- Musician
- Cinematographer
- Animator

Credits and Contributions

Frédéric Berti, Essania Design
Tim Borgmann
Doug Chezm, Acme Pixel
Tim Clapham, Hypa TV
Chris Cousins, Grafficc
Paul Debevec, Institute of Creative
    Technologies
Gerald Double
Robert Drozd
Joel Dubin, Betatron Studios
Per-Anders Edwards, The Third Party
Paul Everett, Tools4D, The Third Party
David Farmer, Cidertank
Phillip Gray
Ryan Jack
Anders Kjellberg, Dept. of Historical
    Studies, Umeå University
Patrick Landry
Ray Larabie, Larabie Fonts
Stephen Leworthy
Tycho Luyken (Kirl)
MAXON

Jim McCampbell, Department Head,
    Computer Animation, Ringling
    School of Art & Design
Kent McQuilken
Josh Miller
Naam, Happyship
Eni Oken, Oken3d
Jeremy Pulcifer
Matt Riveccie, Ozone
Brucie Rosch
Matthieu Roussel
Mikael Sterner, Xlent
Adam Trachtenberg
Neil Vaughan
Bryan Wilkerson
Darrin Woods
Michael Young, WeWorkForThem,
    YouWorkForThem
Pjer Zanchi, Onyx Computing

Illustrations or model designs not
credited to other individuals were created
by Anne Powers.

Using This Book

The goal of this book is to get right down to the fun and productivity of using
CINEMA 4D as a creative power tool. Pronto! All the dry reference information
has been placed in the Appendix in the back of the book. If you have never used
CINEMA 4D before and need to familiarize yourself with the general geography
of CINEMA 4D's work environment, interface workings, basic 3D world navigation, and other overall skills, head right back to the Appendix before you start
the tutorials. Only instructions specific to each project are included in the project steps, and most general things, such as rendering a preview or a QuickTime
movie of the project, are in the Appendix.

Refer to the CINEMA 4D manual for advanced explanations of the theory
behind processes and tools in C4D.

In the interest of packing as much information as possible into the book, the
tutorials gradually repeat less and less of the basic information in the early chapters. Therefore, if you skip around through the book you will probably bump into
words and tools you aren't familiar with! Likewise, repetitive instructions like "Click
OK" and "Press Return (Enter)" will gradually disappear after you've had a chance
to make the habits. If you just can't wait to try a certain advanced tutorial, be forewarned that you may have to check the index for beginning skills you may have
missed.

8.5 Overview

In Version 8.5, the methods and interface for building materials have undergone substantial changes. 8.5 users should print out the R8.5 Addendum document and keep it close by for detailed reference. This document shipped with your 8.5 update and can be downloaded from www.maxoncomputer.com in the Downloads>Documentation section. Anything you've "lost" from the previous version is still around (just renamed or moved) and the Addendum document will help you find them. In addition, 8.5 symbols throughout the book will alert you with notes regarding version differences or refer you to the 8.5 Update PDF on the DVD.

In Version 8.5, shaders formerly named BhodiNUT or SLA have now been intergrated into CINEMA 4D (So those names are no longer used.) All the parameters for these shaders are now no longer in the SLA editor but are available in the Material Editor. BhodiNUT volume shaders formerly accessed in the Materials Manager by choosing File>BhodiNUT Volume are now under File>Shader.

In the Material Editor, the small black triangle on the parameter page houses shaders, the long button in the middle lets you edit the current shader, and the small button on the right (which we may refer to as the Image button) lets you navigate to images. (The black triangle and Image button have swapped places from former versions.) Materials may also be edited in the Attributes Manager. Naturally, you'll have an adjustment period as you get used to the new way of working.

The good news is, all this change is definitely worth the price. The building of Materials in C4D has been artistically supercharged! See the 8.5 Update on the DVD (Chapter 01>EXTRA!EXTRA!>InDepth) for expanded information on using these new features to enhance your work creatively, and consult MAXON's 8.5 Addendum PDF for technical information.

Be sure to take advantage of the many learning opportunites beyond the printed text in this book. On the DVD, there are legions of C4D example files, instructional movies, PDF files, and goodies which support and expand on projects in the book. In addition, the EXTRA!EXTRA! folder in every chapter section is packed with example models and working methods. Rambling through the C4D files and analyzing them is a great way to learn how things are done. For example, you can figure out exactly how a selected material was made by browsing through the panes of the Material Editor. Open any file's Animation Layout and inspect the Timeline and F-Curves for a quicker understanding of animation.

Version 8.5

There are updates to Version 8.5 at appropriate spots in the text and a more complete 8.5 update PDF on the DVD. The 8.5 update symbol will let you know when to refer to updated information. It's important to note that because of inherent differences in the file format of this release of CINEMA 4D, that files created in 8.5 will lose certain features (including materials) if opened in earlier versions.

Setting Up Your Work Space

Before you begin your journey through the book, get organized! Create a folder titled Models and place it on your hard drive. Save every C4D file you create into this folder so they will be easy to find.

Mac or PC: Ode to a Three-Button Mouse

If you don't have a three-button mouse, get one now, before your work habits become ingrained. Whether you work on a PC or a Mac, the multiple button mouse works great on both platforms and make life so much easier! Right-clicking is ever so much more intuitive than pressing the Cmd key and clicking. C4D files move back and forth between platforms easily, and with the exception of the usual Opt/Alt, Command-click/Right-click, and Command/Control substitutions CINEMA 4D works very much the same on either platform.

Windows commands have been placed in parentheses after the corresponding Mac commands. If there is no command in parentheses, the command works for both platforms. Windows users wishing to play rendered previews and movies in Windows Media Player should choose AVI as the format.

A Note about Tools

When you are first learning to use the toolset in CINEMA 4D, it's easy to confuse one tool with another. Roll the mouse over a palette icon and you'll see a handy cue at the bottom left of the screen reminding you of the tool's name. Notice that a tool named "Use Polygons Tool" in the cue may be streamlined to Polygons tool in the text.

Symbols

◆*Tip:* Tips, tricks, and "Gotchas" to watch out for.

On The DVD: Related material, libraries of goodies, extra projects, pointers to resources, and examples on the DVD.

Connect: Connect to another location in the book, the DVD, or go to the web for more information.

● *Springboard!* Off you go on your own. When you see the Springboard symbol, it's time to take what you just learned and make some creative leaps.

■ *Shortcut:* Standard Keyboard shortcuts for more efficient workflow.

8.5 Update Notes that update the instruction to CINEMA 4D v8.5.

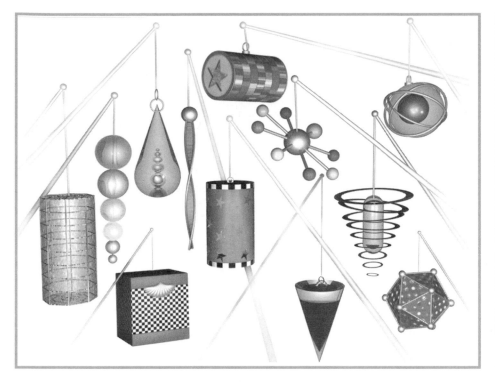

Figure 1.1

A Dynamic Dozen

Step right up! You'll be amazed at the creative impact a humble primitive has to offer! In this section, you will craft a dozen finished objects that derive their "Wow!" factor from inventive arrangements of forms, artistic materials, and dynamic motion. Preview the finished models in Chapter 01>MOVIES/STILLS>STILLS on the DVD.

What Is a Parametric Primitive?

Like most 3D programs, CINEMA 4D has a set of primitive building blocks which are parametric. Basic parameters of a primitive, or critical dimensions such as height and radius, are defined mathematically. Because the program only has to remember a few bits of information, parametric primitives are very efficient. The parametric values for an object may be manipulated live in the editor window using the orange parametric handles, but the object's surface has no points, polygons, or edges that may be pushed and pulled into more complex or organic forms. In the parametric state, the surface and axes of an object are not editable. Notice that every time you choose a primitive, it appears at the same place in the center of the 3D world (coordinates 0, 0, 0) and it has a set of red (X), green (Y), and blue (Z) object axes that show how the object is oriented.

Getting to Know Managers

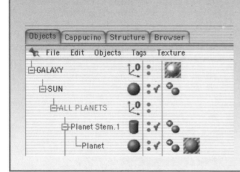

Managers are specialized windows for different work processes in CINEMA 4D. When you create an object, its name appears in red in the Objects Manager at the top right of the screen. Objects with red titles are currently selected. In this window, you can keep an inventory list of all the objects in a scene and see important information about their relationship to each other. This list is called a hierarchy.

Figure 1.2 Objects Manager

In the Attributes Manager, important information about the selected object can be viewed and edited. Values may be entered into the Attributes Manager's input boxes by dragging over text and retyping, by dragging up and down on the small black arrows on the right of input box, or by using the wheel of a multiple-button mouse in the input box. Use the panels across the top of the Attributes Manager to access pages of different information about an object.

Figure 1.3 Attributes Manager

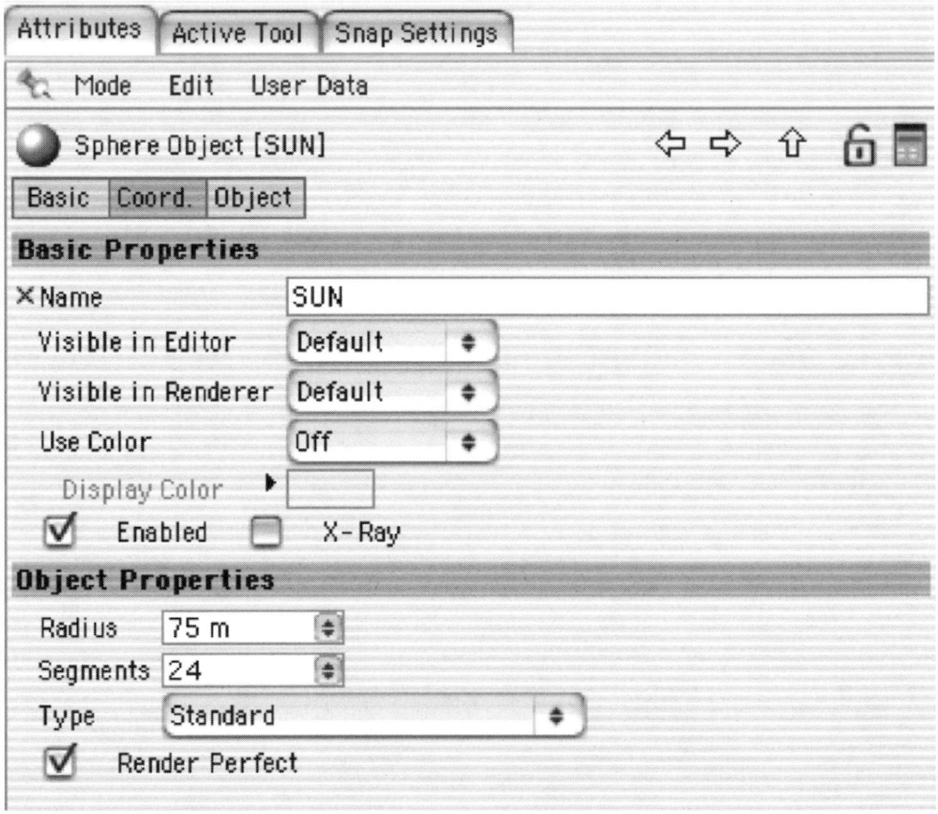

Renaming Objects

Rename objects as you create them. Even though it may seem slower at first, properly named objects in the Objects Manager will speed up your workflow. You can rename in the Objects Manager by double-clicking an object name and typing the new name.

The new title may also be entered in the Attributes Manager Basic panel.

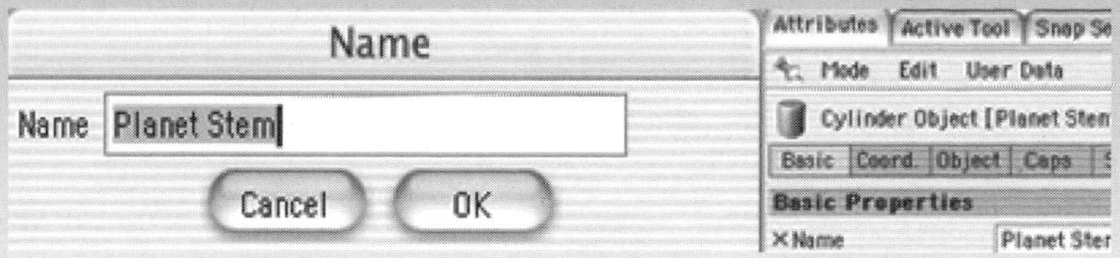

Figure 1.4 Renaming Objects

The Galaxy Ball

Assembling the Model

Step 1 From the top menu, choose File>New to open a new scene. Choose File>Save or Cmd+S (Ctrl+S) to save the file under the name Galaxy Ball into your Models Folder. Be sure to save frequently while you work by pressing Cmd+S (Ctrl+S).

Step 2 Choose Objects>Primitive>Cylinder from the top menu. In the Objects Manager, rename the Cylinder as Planet Stem.

Step 3 In the Attributes Manager (its default position is beneath the Objects Manager) under Object Properties, enter a value of 8 in the box next to Radius and press the Return (Enter) key. Choose +Z from the Orientation pulldown menu.

Step 4 This time, choose a Sphere from the primitives palette icon across the top of the view window. Rename the Sphere as Planet.

Figure 1.5 Attributes Manager Object ParametersProperties

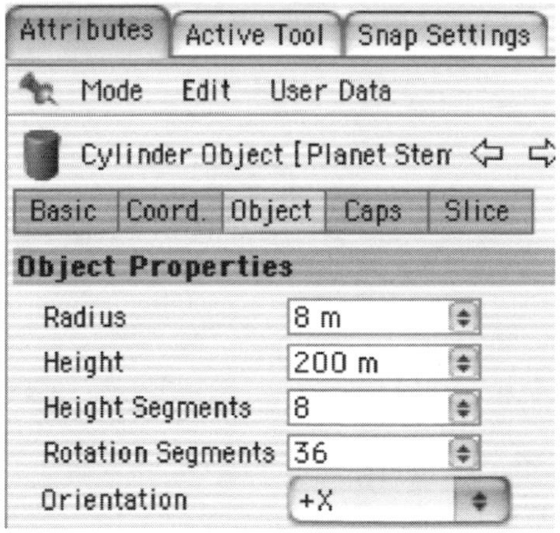

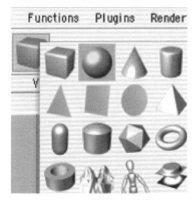

Figure 1.6 Choosing a Sphere

Toolbars

The default icon for all primitives is a blue cube. A quick click on the cube will create a cube. To access all the other primitives, move your mouse down on the cube icon and slide over to your choice. Primitives may also be chosen from the top menu under Objects>Primitive. All the Toolbar palettes work the same: a quick click produces an object like the icon you see in the palette, while moving the mouse down with a sideways slide accesses other choices in the palette.

Figure 1.7 Primitives Palette on the Top Toolbar

Step 5 In the Attributes Manager under Object Properties, enter a value of 35 for Radius and press Return (Enter).

Figure 1.8 Model Tool

Figure 1.9 Move Tool

Step 6 Choose the Model tool from the left toolbar and the Move tool from the top toolbar. In the Editor window, drag the blue Move handle until the planet is covering the front end of the stem. Check the Coordinates Manager at the lower right of the Editor window. The Z Position value should be about 125. If you wanted to, you could send the sphere there by entering the value and pressing Return (Enter).

Figure 1.10 Blue Move Handle

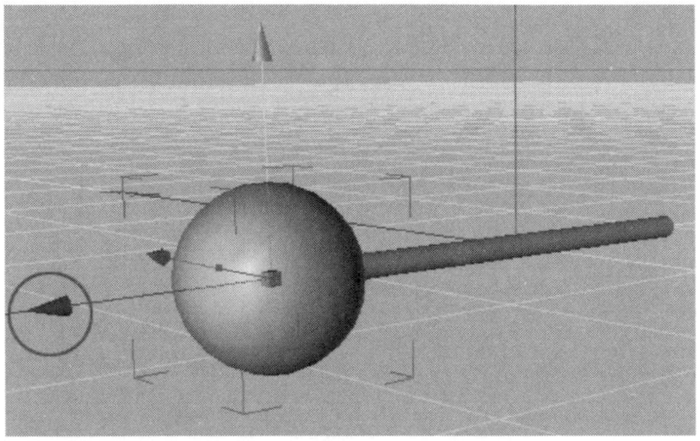

Figure 1.11 Coordinates Manager

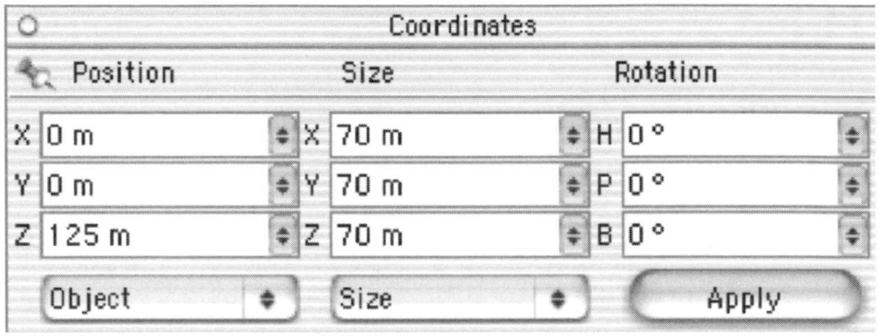

The Model tool versus the Object tool

Figure 1.12 Object Tool

Figure 1.13 Model Tool

When you are manipulating objects in the modeling process, the Model tool should always be chosen from the left toolbar. When you are animating an object, the Object tool should be chosen. If you need a reminder of a tool's identity, roll the mouse over a tool and check the prompt at the lower left of the screen.

Step 7 In the Objects Manager, drag the name Planet and drop it onto the name Planet Stem.

Figure 1.14 Parent and Child

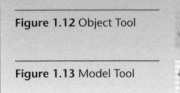

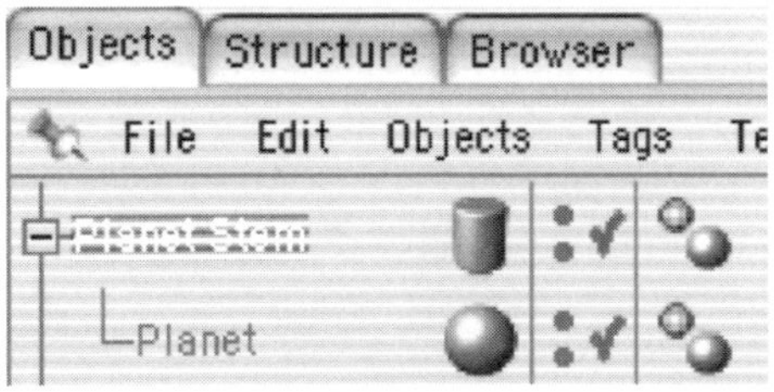

You just made Planet a child of Planet Stem. Notice how Planet is now on a line indented under the Planet Stem, indicating dependency. The Planet will now follow and inherit any transformations to Planet Stem. In the Objects Manager, notice how the Planet Stem now has a small minus sign to its left. Click on the minus symbol to temporarily hide the child and then click on the plus sign to bring it out of hiding. When you successfully make an object a child of another, a downward arrow cue appears. A left-facing arrow means the object will be dropped on the same hierarchal level as the target object.

Step 8 In the top toolbar, click on the Array. In the Attributes Manager under Object Properties, enter a Radius of 150 and press Return (Enter). Drag the name Planet Stem onto the name Array, then rename the Array as All Planets. (If you can no longer see the entire object, choose Edit> Frame Scene from the top menu.)

Figure 1.15 Array Icon

Figure 1.16 All Planets

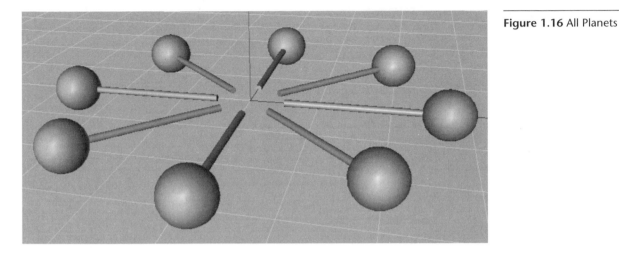

Step 9 Choose Primitive>Sphere. In the Attributes Manager under Object Properties, give the Sphere a Radius of 75 and press Return (Enter). Rename the Sphere as Sun.

Step 10 Drag the All Planets object onto the Sun object. Select the Sun object, and press the G key. Rename the resulting Null Object as GALAXY.

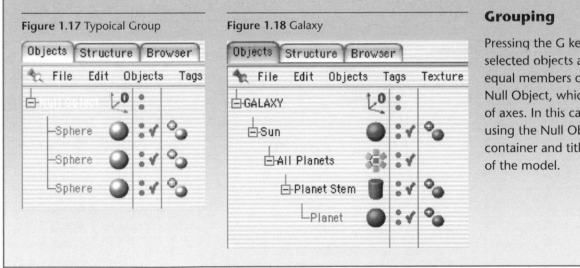

Figure 1.17 Typoical Group

Figure 1.18 Galaxy

Grouping

Pressing the G key collects any selected objects and makes them equal members of a Group titled Null Object, which has its own set of axes. In this case, we are simply using the Null Object *GALAXY* as a container and title for all the parts of the model.

Figure 1.19 The Materials Manager

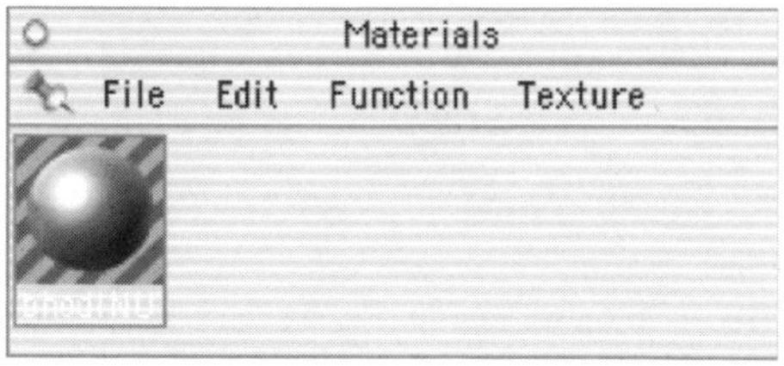

Copying Materials or Objects

To copy materials in the Materials Manager, press the Control key and drag the material thumbnail to an empty space in the manager window.

To copy objects in the Objects Manager, press the Control key and drag the name of the object to an empty space below or above the original in the Object Manager's Hierarchy (the list of objects).

Figure 1.20 SLA Window

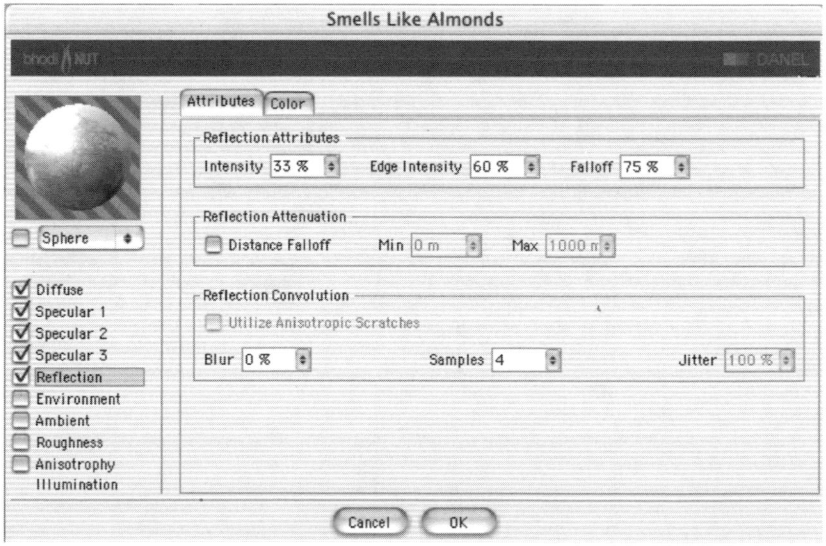

Choosing Materials

Step 1   From the Materials Manager at the bottom left of the screen, choose File> BhodiNUT Volume>BhodiNUT Danel. Double-click on the material thumbnail that appears. In the Smells Like Almonds window, make sure the gray selection band is over the word Diffuse.
8.5 Update   Instead of File>BhodiNUT Volume>BhodiNUT Danel, choose File>Shader>Danel. Double-click the material thumbnail.

Step 2   Click the vertical color rectangle in the upper lefthand corner of the Diffuse page and choose a golden yellow from the color picker. Alternately, you can drag the RGB sliders to create a color. (R255, G218, and B107 at 100 percent brightness will do fine.)
8.5 Update   Edit the Diffuse color by double-clicking the horizontal rectangle in the Material Editor.

Step 3   On the left side of the Smells Like Almonds editor window, click on Specular 2 to access its parameters and edit the color to be a pale light blue. Then choose Specular 3 and make its color a pale green.
8.5 Update   These parameters are now in the Material Editor rather than the SLA editor.

Step 4   Now select the Reflection parameter. On the page for Reflection, turn the value for Intensity up to 33 percent. Click OK to close the box. Double-click the name of the material thumbnail (currently BhodiNUT Danel in red) in the Materials Manager and in the name box, type Gold, and Click OK.
8.5 Update   Click the small red close button on the top left of the window to exit the Material Editor. The current name in red is now Danel.

Step 5   Place the gold material on the entire model by dragging the Gold material thumbnail from the Materials Manager onto the object GALAXY in the Objects Manager.

You can also drop the material thumbnail directly onto the object in the Editor window, but in the case of complex objects, dropping materials to the Objects Manager gives you more specific control.

Step 6   In the Materials Manager, choose File>New Material.

Step 7   Double-click the Material Preview Thumbnail. On the left of the Material Editor, make sure the gray selection band is on the word Color in the list of parameters. On the Color page in the righthand area of the Material Editor, create a red using the R, G, B, and Brightness sliders. (Drag G and B to the left.) Click on Luminance and check its checkbox. On the parameter page drag the Brightness slider down to 10 percent.

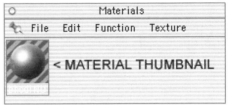

Figure 1.21 Material thumbnail

Step 8   In the Materials Manager, Ctrl-drag enough copies of the red material for the rest of the planets. Double-click each material thumbnail and edit only the color, until you have enough different colors for all the planets. Adjust the Brightness of each color to your liking.

Figure 1.22 Color parameter

Figure 1.23 Luminance parameter

Figure 1.24 Planet Materials

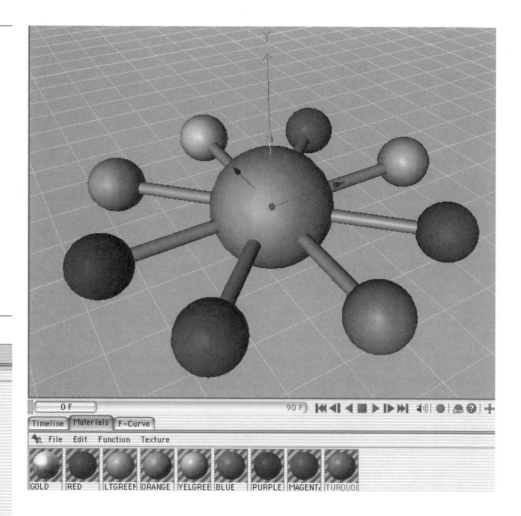

Figure 1.25 GALAXY Hierarchy

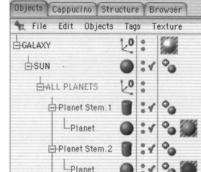

Notice that you can keep the Material Editor open as you move from material to material, and the parameters of the currently selected icon are displayed. *8.5 Update* Clicking from material to material will display different materials in the Attributes Manager. In the Material Editor, the arrows at top of the screen navigate through shader levels and material to material.

Step 9 In the Objects Manager hierarchy, click the small + to the left of the word GALAXY, and select the All Planets object inside it. Press the C key. (This is the shortcut for Make Editable, and will let you work with the individual planets in the All Planets array.)

Step 10 Place a different colored material on each Planet object in the Objects Manager. Choose File>Save from the top menu.

Manipulating Objects

Now that you've made a complex object, it's a good time to stop and try out the basic tools for manipulating objects. Before you begin experimenting, choose File>Save or press Cmd+S (Ctrl+S) from the top menu so that you have a saved version of the GALAXY with no changes to return to afterward. You have already used the Move tool, but let's try out Scale and Rotate. Make sure the Model tool on the left toolbar is chosen. Choose the GALAXY object in the Objects Manager, and select the Scale tool. Drag the mouse anywhere in the open gray area of the editor window to scale the object. Now choose the Rotate tool from the top toolbar. Notice that the axes handles become spheres, and if you drag the mouse onto any one of the sphere handles the rotation is constrained to that axis. Alternately, you could make sure the axis is unlocked by clicking an outline around it in the Top toolbar.

Try it. Click the X,Y, and Z symbols on the top toolbar so the X has an outline and the Y and Z don't. Now drag the mouse anywhere in the open gray area of the editor window and note how the rotation is occurring only around the X axis. Now, choose the Move tool and see that the axis handles have changed to cones. Drag on each of the cones and watch the object move only along that axis, as if it's on a track. The axis locks on the top toolbar work for the Move, Scale and Rotate tools, but each tool has its own memory for locks. Be sure to choose the tool first and then set the locks.

In addition to using these tools, you can make these basic transformations in the Coordinates Manager or in the Coordinates panel of the Attributes Manager. When animating, you will often change the value in the Attributes Manager Coordinates panel by typing in a value or dragging the tiny black arrows on the right of the input box to adjust the value.

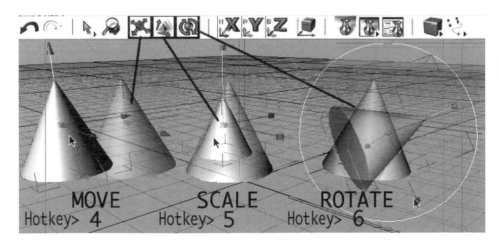

Figure 1.26 Move, Scale, Rotate Hotkeys

■ **Shortcut:** The Move, Scale, and Rotate tools can be accessed temporarily with shortcut keys. Hold down the 4 (Move), 5 (Scale), or 6 (Rotate) keys and drag the mouse in an open area of the editor window. Note that the icons on the toolbar do not change during this temporary access.

Spin the Galaxy!

Figure 1.27 Object Tool

Step 1   From the top menu, choose File>Revert to Saved and click Yes on the Dialog Box for Lose Changes. Select the *GALAXY* object in the Objects Manager.

Step 2   From the lefthand toolbar, choose the Object tool, which should always be active when animating.

Figure 1.28 Current Time 0

Step 3   Make sure the current time on the Animation toolbar is at 0 frames.

0 F	90 F

Step 4   In the Attributes Manager, click on the Coordinates panel. Command-click (Right-click) on any of the letters R (R.H, R.P, R.B; for Rotation Heading, Rotation Pitch, and Rotation Bank, respectively) in the right-hand column and drag to Animation>Add Keyframe. Hold down the mouse as you slide sideways, moving across one menu list to the next.

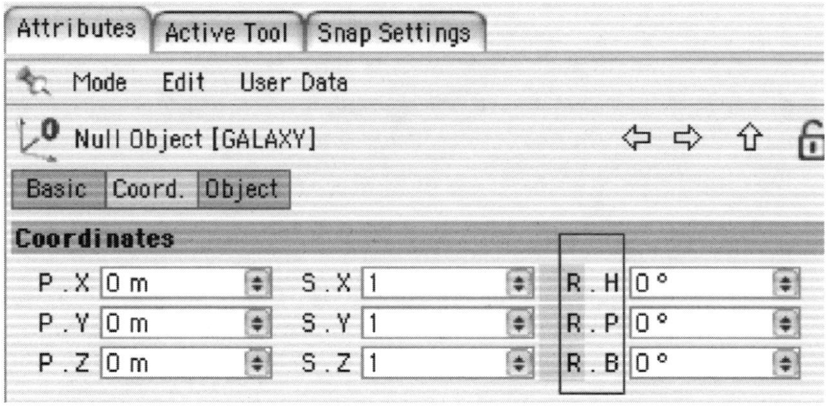

Figure 1.29 Letters R.H, R.P and R.B

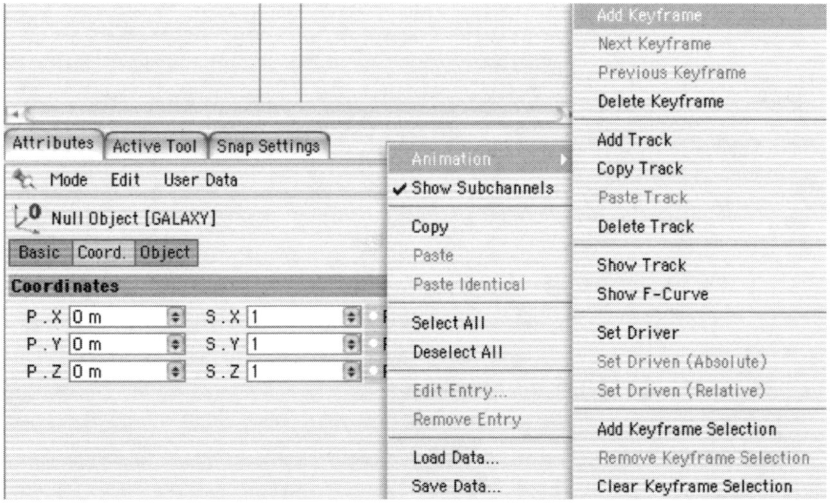

Figure 1.30 Sliding to Animation>Add Keyframe

Step 5   Click on Go to End of Animation on the Animation Toolbar.

Figure 1.31 End of Animation

Step 6   In the input box next to R.H (Rotation Heading) in the Coordinates panel of the Attributes Manager, enter 360 and press Return (Enter). Command-click on the letter H (in R.H) and drag to Animation>Add Keyframe.

Figure 1.32 360 degrees H (Heading)

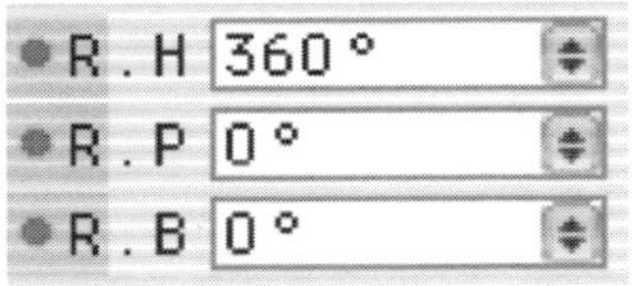

You only keyframed the H, or Heading Rotation value. Had you clicked any of the letters R and set a keyframe, all values (Heading, Pitch, and Bank) would have been keyframed at once.

Figure 1.33 Rotation Animation Enabled

- **Shortcuts:** Pressing the F9 key is a shortcut for keyframing selected values, but the specific kind of animation must be enabled in the Animation toolbar. The F8 key plays an animation. (Note: certain systems may have functions already assigned to these keys, so if these shortcuts don't work you'll have to decide priorities for your F-keys and reassign functions if desired.)

Step 7   Drag the current time slider to 20 frames and enter 20 in the input box next to R.P (Rotation Pitch). Press Return (Enter). Set a keyframe by Command-clicking on the P in R.P and sliding over to Animation>Add Keyframe. (If you have a multiple button mouse on a PC or Mac, clicking the right mousebutton is the equivalent of Command-clicking.) At frame 90 enter a value of 0 in the input box for R.P and set a keyframe.

Figure 1.34 20 Frames

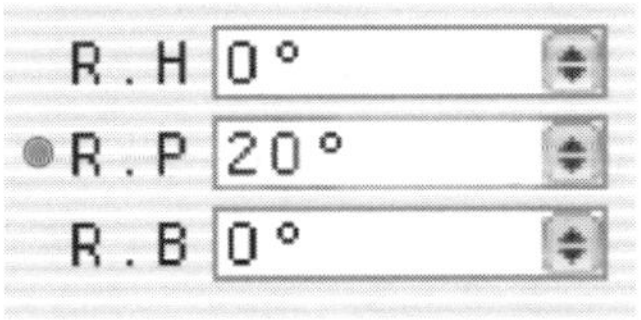

Step 8   Click the Play button on the Animation toolbar or use the shortcut, F8.

Figure 1.35 20 Degrees Pitch

Now you are an animator!

The Barometer Cone

Making the Model

Step 1   Choose File>New to open a new scene and select Display>Wireframe from the menu immediately over the editor window. Save the file as Barometer Cone in your Models folder (File>Save; Cmd+S/Ctrl+S).

Step 2   Choose Primitive>Add Cone Object. In the Attributes Manager click the Object panel to access Object Properties. Enter a value of 300 for Height and choose –Y in the Orientation pulldown menu.

Step 3   Control-drag a copy of the Cone in the Objects Manager, and rename the copy Mercury.

Step 4   With Mercury still selected, click the Attributes Manager Coordinates panel and enter a value of 0.7 in the input boxes next to S.X, S.Y, and S.Z to scale the Mercury to 70 percent. Press Return (Enter).

Figure 1.36 A Cone in a Cone

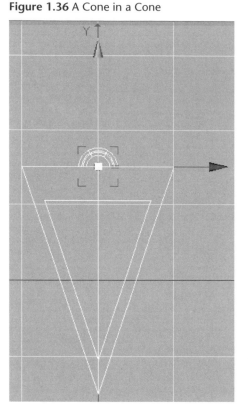

Figure 1.37 Barometer Cone

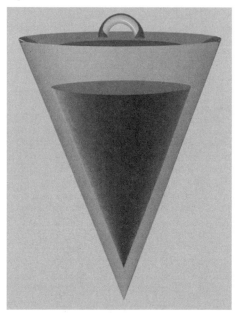

Step 5 Choose Primitive>Torus. (Now that you're experienced in choosing Primitives, we'll just say Torus and drop those extra words.) In the Attributes Manager Coordinates panel enter 0.1 into the input boxes next to S.X, S.Y, and S.Z. Click on the Slice panel, and check the Slice check box.

Step 6 Click the Object panel and choose –Z from the Orientation pulldown menu. Double-click the object Torus and rename it Hanger.

Step 7 With Hanger still selected, drag the green handle of the Move tool upward until the Hanger rests on top of the cone. (Make sure the Model tool is selected, since you are modeling.) A maneuver like this should be done in an orthographic view, like Front, so you can see precisely if the hanger is resting on top of the cone.

Step 8 Click in the open gray area of the Objects Manager, (a good habit to make sure that Manager is the active one), select all (Edit>Select All, Cmd+A/Ctrl+A) and press the G key to Group. Rename the group Null Object as Barometer Cone.

Materials for the Cone

Step 1 In the Materials Manager, choose File>BhodiNUT Volume>BhodiNUT Banji. Double-click the material thumbnail. In the SLA Editor, choose the Transparency parameter and reduce the Index of Refraction to 1.1. From the menu over the Objects Manager, choose Unfold All. Place the Banji material on the Cone and Hanger inside the Barometer Cone hierarchy.
8.5 Update Choose File>Shader>Banji. Double-click the material thumbnail. Edit Transparency in the Material Editor rather than the SLA Editor.

Step 2 In the Materials Manager, choose File>BhodiNUT Volume>BhodiNUT Cheen. In the SLA Editor, choose the Roughness parameter. Choose Cell Voronoi as the Bump Function. Place the Cheen material on the Mercury. Type Control-R for a test rendering of the Editor Window, then click the window to clear the rendering.
8.5 Update Choose File>Shader>Cheen. Double-click the material thumbnail. Edit Roughness in the Material Editor.

Color Drops

Creating the Model

Step 1 Choose File>Open and navigate to Chapter 01>C4D Files>Color Drops. c4d on the DVD. Choose File>Save As and save the file as Color Drops into your Models folder.

Step 2   Choose Primitive>Sphere. In the Attributes Manager under Object Properties, enter a Radius of 5 and Segments of 50.

Step 3   With the Sphere still selected, choose Functions>Duplicate from the Top menu. In the input box for Copies, enter 5 and leave the box for Generate Instances unchecked.

   Under the column for Move, enter a value of 200 for Y. (Don't press Return yet.) Under the column for Scale, enter 4 in the X, Y, and Z Boxes. Click OK or press Return.

Step 4   Rename the resulting Null Object as Color Drops. In the Objects Manager, drag the name Sphere and drop it onto the name Color Drops.

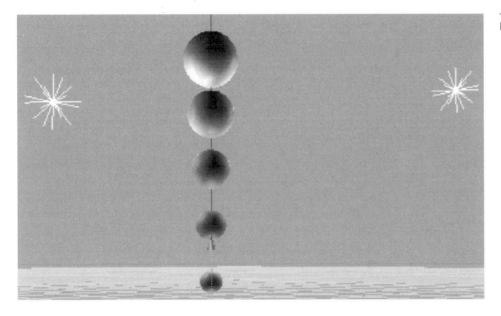

Figure 1.38 Color Drops

Placing the Materials

Place a different jewel color from the Materials Manager on each of the Spheres. You can also drag a material directly to the object in the Editor window.

Animating the Color Drops

Step 1   In the Objects Manager, make sure the hierarchy of Color Drops is open. (Click on the plus sign (+) to the left of the name if it isn't. If you see the minus sign (–), it is already open.)

Step 2   Select Sphere.4. Choose the Object tool and the Move tool.

Step 3   Make sure that the current time slider in the Animation Toolbar is on frame 0.

Figure 1.39 Position Enabled

Figure 1.40 Record Button

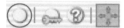

Figure 1.41 Sphere Position at Frame 10

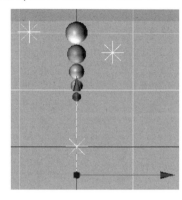

Figure 1.42 Height

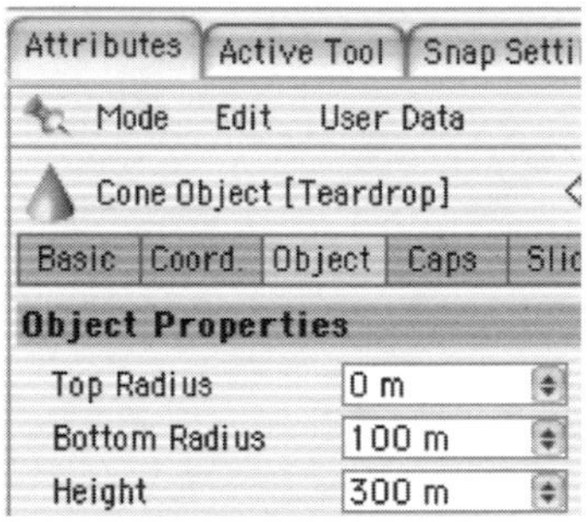

Figure 1.43 Caps

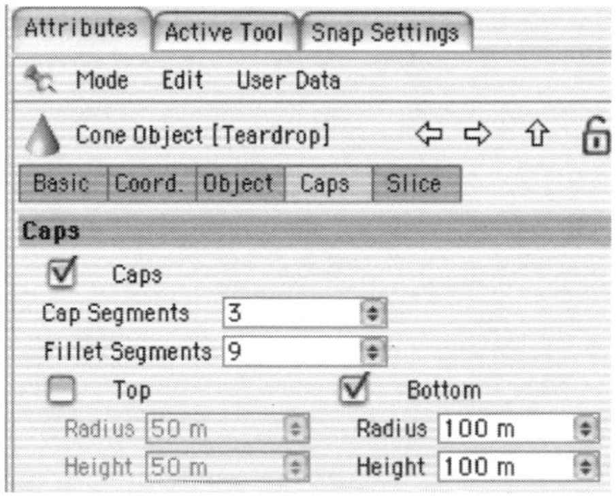

♦ *Tip:* To see whether the spheres are aligned correctly, work in the Front View.

Step 4 Drag the green handle of the Move tool upward until Sphere.4 touches the bottom of the top sphere. On the Animation Toolbar, turn on recording for Position (only) and click the Record button (or press the F9 key).

Step 5 Starting with Sphere.3 and working upward in the hierarchy, move each sphere (with the green handle) to touch the one above it and keyframe the position as you did in Step 4 until all the spheres are keyframed to be touching in Frame 0. Remember to click the Record button after moving each sphere.

Step 6 Move the current time slider to Frame 10. Select the smallest sphere at the bottom of the stack (Sphere), and in the Attributes Manager Coordinates panel, enter a P.Y value of –50 and press Return (Enter). (You may need to choose Edit>Frame Scene from the Menu over the View to be able to see the entire stack.) Press F9 to set a keyframe or click the Record button.

Step 7 To make the spheres drop one at a time, you'll need to keyframe the "dropped" position of Sphere.1 at 20 frames, Sphere.2 at 35 frames, Sphere.3 at 50 frames, and Sphere.4 at 65 frames. Starting with Sphere.1 (at frame 20) and working upward to Sphere.4, manually drop each sphere down to rest on the one below it, keyframing each position with the F9 key or Record button. See the example file and finished movie on the DVD.

Step 8 Choose File>Save (or Cmd+S/Ctrl+S) and File>Close.

The Bubbling Teardrop

Composing the Model

Step 1 Choose File>New to open a new scene and select Display>Wireframe from the menu immediately over the editor window. Save the file in your Models folder as Bubbling Teardrop by choosing File>Save or Cmd+S (Ctrl+S).

Step 2 Choose Primitive>Cone. Rename the Cone as Teardrop.

Step 3 In the Attributes Manager Object Properties (you may have to click the Object panel), enter a value of 300 for Height and press Return (Enter). Click the Caps panel. Click the check box next to Bottom, enter a value of 100 for both Radius and Height and press Return (Enter). In the input box for Fillet Segments, enter 9.

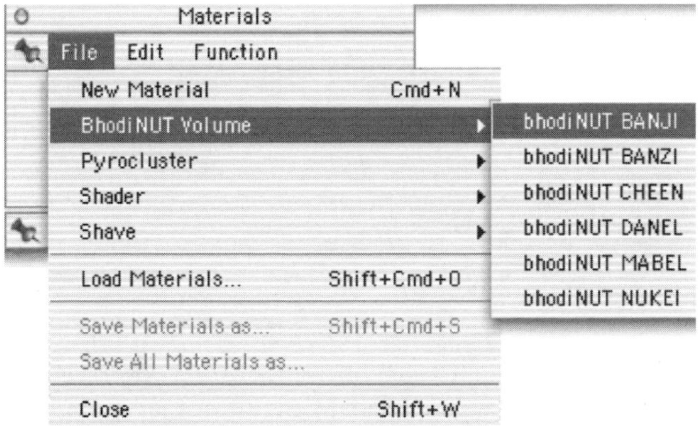

Figure 1.44 Banji

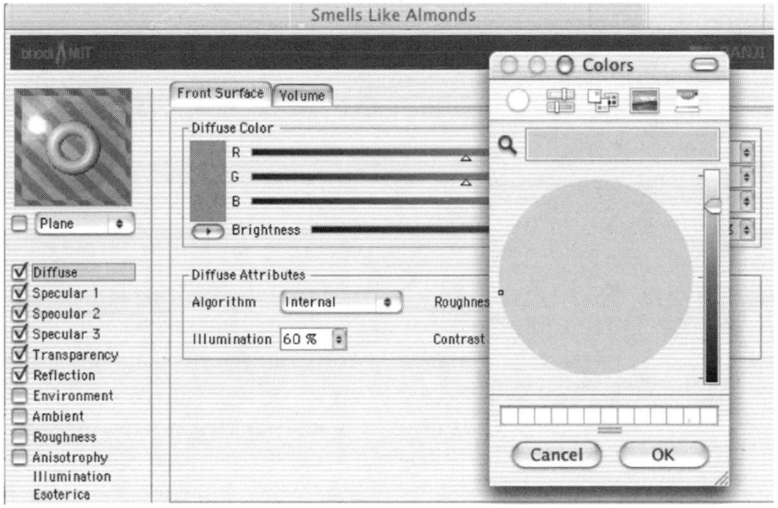

Figure 1.45 SLA Edit

Assigning a Material

Step 1   From the Materials Manager at the bottom left of the screen, choose File>BhodiNUT Volume, BhodiNUT Banji.
8.5 Update   Choose File>Shader>Banji.

Step 2   Double-click on the material thumbnail that appears in the Materials Manager and make sure a gray band appears over the word Diffuse in the Smells Like Almonds editor window. Double-click on the Diffuse Color box at the upper left of the page and choose a turquoise blue. You can use the RGB sliders to adjust the color if you prefer.
8.5 Update   Edit the Diffuse color by double-clicking the horizontal rectangle.

Step 3   At the top of the Diffuse page, click on the Volume tab and edit the color to be more like a royal blue.
8.5 Update   In the bottom panel of the Diffuse page, edit the horizontal tab for volume color.

Figure 1.46 Volume Tab

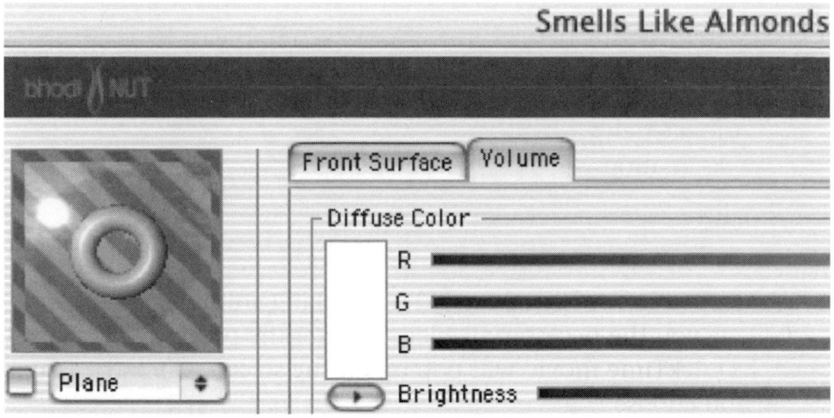

Figure 1.47 Roughness

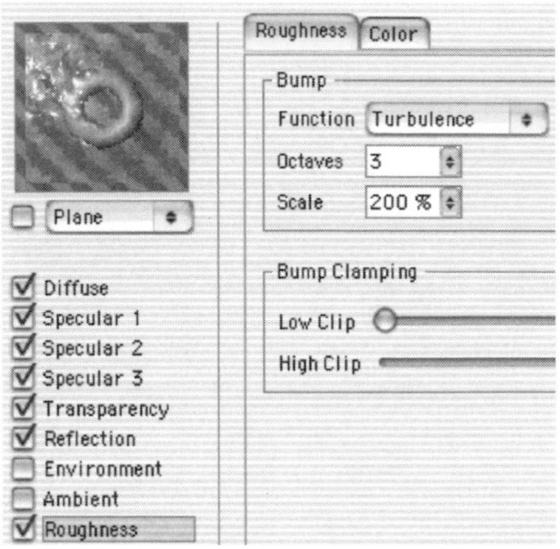

Figure 1.48 Bubbles

Step 4 On the left side of the Smells Like Almonds editor window, click the panel for Roughness. Next to Bump Function, choose Turbulence from the pulldown menu. Click OK to close the SLA Editor. Place the new material on the Teardrop.
8.5 Update Edit Roughness in the Material Editor. Bump Function is now Function.

Import Some Bubbles

Step 1 Choose File>Merge. Navigate to the Color Drops.c4d file you just finished and click Open in the dialog box. (It should be in your Models folder. You could also use the sample file in Chapter 1>EXAMPLES>Color Drops on the DVD.)

Step 2 In the Objects Manager, select Color Drops.

Step 3 In the Attributes Manager, click the Coordinates panel and enter a value of 180 in the box next to R.B (Rotation Bank). Press Return or click Apply.

Step 4 Still in the Coordinates panel, drag the small black arrows to the right of the box for P.Y until the largest sphere inside the Color Drops object is just inside the bottom of the Teardrop.

Step 5 Choose Primitive>Torus. In the Attributes Manager under Object Properties, enter 25m for Ring Radius, 5m for Pipe Radius and choose +Z from the Orientation pulldown menu. Rename the Torus as Ring. Place the material you created for the teardrop on the Ring.

Step 6 Choose the Model tool and Move tool. Drag the green handle of the Move tool in the editor window to move the Ring to the top of the Teardrop.

Step 7 Select Teardrop and Color Drops, and press the G key. Rename the Null Object as Teardrop. Drag the object Teardrop into the object Ring. With

Ring selected, press G again and name the resulting Null Object as Bubbling Teardrop.

Step 8   Press the F8 key or click the Play button to play the animation. Note that when you merged the Color Drops file into the current file, all the animation and materials came with the object.

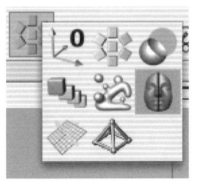

For a preview rendering of the animation with materials, choose Render>Make Preview from the top menu. In the panel for Preview Mode, choose Full Render. (If you were only interested in checking animation, choosing As Editor would give you the necessary feedback.) After the preview calculations are finished, a QuickTime movie will pop up on the screen. Click the Play button to play it, and choose File>Save to save it if you wish.

The DNA Spinner

Making the Model

Step 1   Choose File>New and save the file as DNA Spinner in your Models folder by choosing File>Save or Cmd+S (Ctrl+S).

Step 2   Choose Primitive>Cylinder. In Object Properties, enter a radius of 10. Set the Orientation to +X.

Step 3   Now choose Primitive>Sphere and enter a Radius of 25 and press Return.

Step 4   Choose a Symmetry object from the Array toolbar icon in the top toolbar and drop the object Sphere into the Symmetry object. Rename Symmetry as Spheres.

Step 5   Select Spheres, and in the Attributes Manager set the Mirror Plane as ZY. Select the Sphere (inside the object Spheres) and use the red handle of the Move tool to pull both spheres out to the opposite ends of the cylinder.

Figure 1.49 Play

Figure 1.50 Symmetry

Figure 1.51 Move Sphere

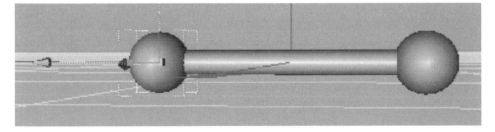

Step 6   In the Objects Manager, drag the object Spheres into the object Cylinder so Spheres will be a child of Cylinder.

Step 7   Select Cylinder and choose Functions>Duplicate from the top menu. In the Duplicate editor window, remember not to press Return until the

Figure 1.52
DNA Flipped

Figure 1.53
DNA Spinner

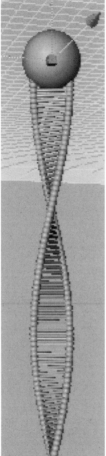

Figure 1.52
DNA Flipped

Figure 1.53
DNA Spinner

values are entered in all the boxes. Enter 100 for Copies and check the checkbox for Generate Instances.

In the Move column, enter 3000m for Y. All Scale values should be left as 1. Under Rotation, type a value of 360º in the H box and click OK or press Return. (Choose Edit>Frame Active Object from the menu over the editor window to see the elongated model.)

Step 8 Rename the Null Object as DNA. Drop Cylinder into the DNA object. Select DNA. In the Attributes Manager Coordinates panel, enter a Rotation B value of 180º and press Return (Enter). (Now the axis is at the top so we can animate a swinging action later.) Choose Edit>Frame Active Objects once again.

Step 9 Choose Primitive>Sphere and give it a Radius of 175m in Object Properties.

Select Sphere and DNA. Press the G key to group them and rename the Null as DNA Spinner.

What are Instances?

When you check the check box for Generate Instances in the Duplicate window, you give CINEMA 4D permission to display "ghosts" that refer to an original object. Not only does this save storage space, but also it saves time and work. Because the referenced duplicates are only additional displays from the data of an original object, any change made to the original will update in the instances.

Making the Material

Step 1 In the Materials Manager, choose File>New Material and double-click the material thumbnail. In the Material Editor, select the Color parameter. Click the small black triangle at the right of the Texture panel, and slide over to BhodiNUT Channel>BhodiNUT Gradient.
8.5 Update Click on the small black triangle (now at the left of the texture panel) and choose Gradient.

Step 2 In the Texture panel, click the Edit button. In the SLA editor window, double-click the lefthand color tab (currently black) at the bottom of the window, and edit the color to be a medium green. Click OK. Place the material on the DNA object.
8.5 Update To edit the Gradient shader, click the word Gradient in the long middle button.

Step 3 Click on the Browser tab to the right of the Objects Manager tab. Choose File>Import File from the Browser menu and navigate to the Chapter 01>EXAMPLES>Galaxy Ball.c4d file. Double-click the thumbnail to open the

Galaxy Ball file. In the Materials Manager, copy the Gold material with Cmd+C (Ctrl+C). Choose the DNA Spinner.c4d file from the Window menu. Click on the Materials Manager and paste the Gold material thumbnail Manager using Cmd-V (Ctrl-V).

Step 4 Click the Objects Manager tab, and place the Gold material on the sphere.

Step 5 Render the Editor Window with Ctrl-R.

The Browser, Your New Best Friend

In the Browser, you can open folders of materials (in their graphics formats) or .c4d files containing materials. Double-clicking a Browser thumbnail opens the file, and objects or resources can be cut and pasted between currently open files. Putting the concept of Browser libraries to work will keep you organized and save hours of repetitive work.

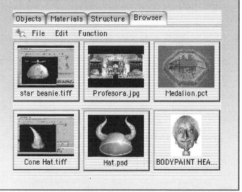

Figure 1.54 Browser Thumbnails

Spin the DNA

Animate the DNA Spinner to rotate H (heading) 360º in the same way that you animated the Galaxy Ball in the first project of this chapter.

The Starlight Lantern

Making the Model

Step 1 Choose File>Open and navigate to Chapter 01>C4d Files>Starlight Lantern on the DVD. Choose File>Save As and save the file as Starlight Lantern in your Models folder.

Step 2 Choose Primitive>Cylinder. Use the top, middle parametric handle to shorten the height to about 150m. (You can keep your eye on the value for Y size in the Coordinates Manager while you drag the parametric handle.)

◆ **Tip:** If the Parametric handles ever refuse to move or appear, check these "gotchas": the Model tool and the Move, Scale, or Rotate tool must be selected; the X, Y, Z lock for the attempted direction must be unlocked (an outline is apparent around the letter); and the object must have not already been made editable.

3D Famous Saying

"If only I could find that model I made last year." Take the time to create a filing system for storing models, materials, splines, and your other libraries. When you need an element in a hurry, opening a single folder in the browser will give you fast access.

Figure 1.55 Symmetry

Figure 1.56 Hanger

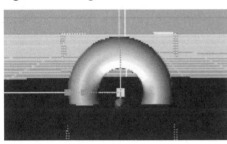

Step 3 In the Objects Manager, Control-drag a copy of the cylinder. Rename the copy as Band. In the Attributes Manager under Object Properties, enter a Height of 10m.

Step 4 From the top toolbar, choose a Symmetry object. Drop the object Band onto the object Symmetry in the Objects Manager.

Step 5 Select the Symmetry object, and in the Attributes Manager, choose XZ from the Mirror Plane under Object Properties.

Step 6 Choose the Move tool and select the Band. Slide the green handle upward until the bands are neatly capping the top and bottom of the cylinder.

Step 7 Choose Primitive>Torus. In the Attributes Manager, give the Torus a Ring Radius of 5m and a Pipe Radius of 2m. Choose +Z from the Orientation pulldown menu. Rename the Torus as Hanger.

Step 8 Choose the Move tool, and using the green handle, pull the Torus ring upward to form a hanging ring for the Lantern.

Step 9 In the Objects Manager, rename the Symmetry object as Bands. Hold down the Shift key and select Hanger, Bands, and Cylinder. Press the G key to create a group (Null Object) and rename the group as STARLIGHT LANTERN.

Step 10 Drag the object named Lamplight into the STARLIGHT LANTERN Group.

Materials with Punch

Step 1 In the Materials Manager, choose File>New Material.

Step 2 Double-click on the material thumbnail and in the Material Editor, select the Color parameter. In the Texture panel of the Color page, move the mouse to the small black triangle (to the right of the empty box) and drag over to Shader>Checkerboard.
8.5 Update From the black triangle (now on the left of the texture panel) choose Surfaces>Checkerboard. Note: this is where everything from the Shader list in former versions can now be found.

Step 3 In the Attributes Manager, enter 12 in the box for U frequency and 0 in the box for V frequency. Rename the new material as Stripes (Double-click on the red words Mat.1 at the bottom of the thumbnail) and drag the material thumbnail onto the name Band in the Objects Manager.
8.5 Update In the Material Editor, click the word Checkerboard in the elongated button to edit the UV frequencies. (Alternately, you can access all the Shader buttons in the Attributes Manager after selecting a channel.)

Step 4 In the Materials Manager, choose File>New Material.

Step 5 Double-click on the material thumbnail and in the Material Editor, select the Color parameter. Again in the Texture panel of the Color page, move the mouse to the small black triangle (to the right of the empty box) and drag over to Shader>Gradient.

8.5 Update Click on the small black arrow and drag to Gradient.

Step 6 In the Attributes Manager under Shader Properties, double-click the lefthand color tab and choose a red. Edit the righthand color tab to be purple. Click the bottom of the color band to add a new tab and in the Colors box edit its color to be white. Choose 2D-V from the Mode menu.

8.5 Update Click the word Gradient in the elongated button to edit as in Step 6.

Step 7 Back in the Material Editor, select the Alpha Channel and check its check box.

Step 8 Click the small black triangle and drag to Shader>Stars.

8.5 Update Drag to Surfaces>Stars.

Step 9 In the Attributes Manager under Shader Properties, enter 5 in the box for Streaks and 5 in the box for Density.

8.5 Update Click the word Stars to edit the shader as in Step 9 above. In the Material Editor, click the word Stars on the elongated button to edit the shader as in Step 9 above.

Step 10 Rename the new material Star Gradient, and drop it onto the STARLIGHT LANTERN object in the Objects Manager. Click on the Texture Tag that appears in the righthand column. In the Attributes Manager, enter 50% for Length X.

Step 11 Press Ctrl+R to render the editor window.

Twirl the Lantern

Animate the Lantern to rotate H (heading) 360° in the same way that you animated the Galaxy Ball in the first Project of this chapter.

The Cosmic Receiver

Creating the Model

Step 1 Choose File>New and save the file as Cosmic Receiver in your Models folder by choosing File>Save or Cmd+S (Ctrl+S).

Step 2 Choose Primitive>Torus.

Step 3 In the Attributes Manager under Object Properties, enter a value of 10 for Ring Radius and 1 for Pipe Radius.

Step 4 Choose Functions>Duplicate. Enter 9 in the box for Copies, leave Generate Instances unchecked, and enter 500 in the Y box in the Move column. In the Scale column enter 20 for X, 1 for Y and 20 for Z. Click OK. Choose Edit>Frame Scene to fill the working space with the object.

Figure 1.57 Starlight Lantern. The lights already placed in the file are volumetric lights and will take longer to render. Because the lights will honor the holes in the material's Alpha channel, the computer has more calculating to do.

Figure 1.58 Cosmic Receiver

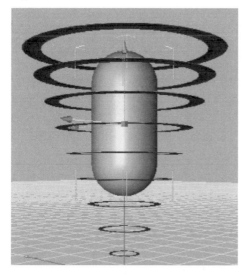

Figure 1.59 Visibility Off

Step 5 Rename the resulting Null Object as Cosmic Rings.

Step 6 Choose Primitive>Capsule. Use the parametric handles and the green handle of the Move tool to adjust the Capsule so it floats comfortably inside the rings.

Step 7 Select the Torus in the Objects Manager and in the column to the right of the name, click the top gray dot twice so that it turns red. Now the original Torus is not visible in the editor window. Also click the bottom gray dot twice to keep the Torus from rendering.

Step 8 Select the Torus, Capsule, and Cosmic Rings. Press the G key to group them and name the resulting Null Object as Cosmic Receiver.

Add Some Materials and a Light

Step 1 In the Materials Manager, choose File>BhodiNUT Volume>Danel.
8.5 Update Choose File>Shader>Danel.

Step 2 In the Smells Like Almonds editor window, change the Diffuse color to turquoise, Specular 2 to light blue, and Specular 3 to light green.
8.5 Update Double-click the Material thumbnail and edit the Diffuse and Specular colors in the Material Editor.

Step 3 In the Materials Manager, choose File>BhodiNUT Volume>Banji.
8.5 Update Choose File>Shader>Banji.

Step 4 Place the Danel material on the Cosmic Rings object and the Banji material on the Capsule.

Figure 1.60 Light Icon

Step 5 Now for something new—click on the Light toolbar symbol in the top toolbar.

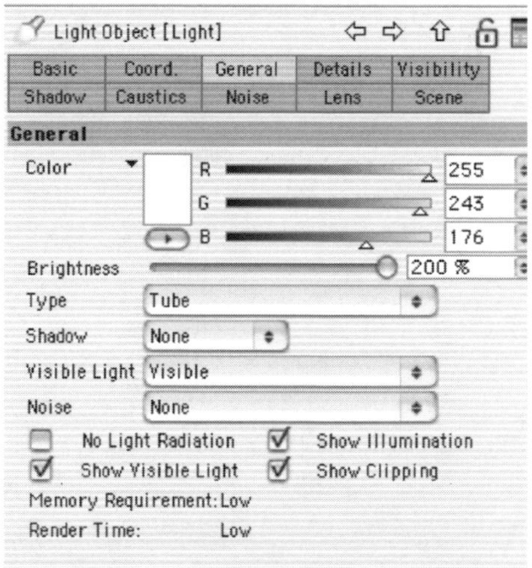

Step 6 In the Attributes Manager under the General panel, double-click the Color box and choose a pale creamy yellow for the light's color. Choose Tube from the Type pulldown menu.

Figure 1.61 Tube Light

Step 7 Select Volumetric from the Visible Light menu.

Step 8 Click the Attributes Manager Coordinates panel and enter 90º in the box for R.P (Pitch) and press Return (Enter).

Step 9 With the Light still selected, choose Functions>Transfer from the top menu.
Make sure only Position is checked and type the letters CA (for capsule) in the Search For box. Click OK. The light magically jumps to the position of the Capsule.

Step 10 With the Model and Move tools selected and Light still the active object, drag the orange handles at the outer circles defining the light until the Tube fits well inside the Capsule. Leave enough room around the Tube so that it can be seen clearly in the Capsule.

Animate the Rings

Step 1 Select Cosmic Rings in the Objects Manager.

Step 2 From the top menu, choose Functions>Randomize. In the Randomize box, enter 5º in the boxes for P and B, and press Return (Enter).

Step 3 In the Attributes Manager Coordinates panel, click the letter H and enter a value of 0 for Heading at frame 0. Set a keyframe. At 90 frames, set a keyframe with a R.H value of 360º. Choose Render>Make Preview with Full Render checked.

Figure 1.62 Randomize Box

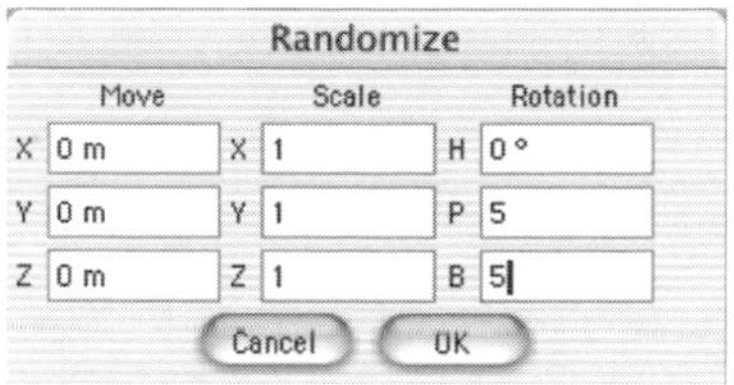

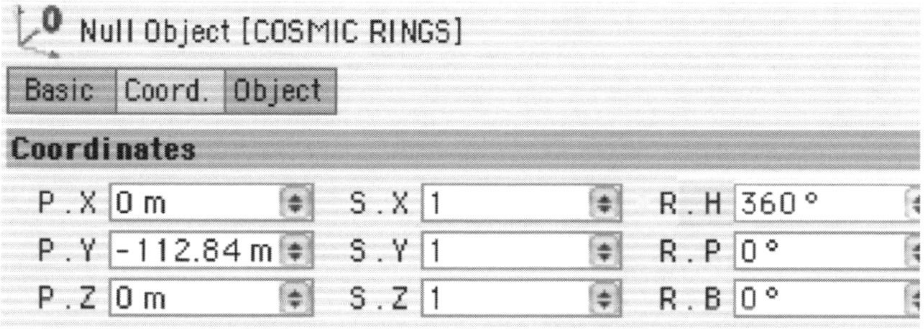

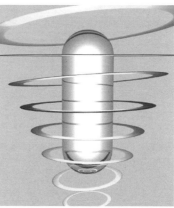

Figure 1.64 Cosmic Final

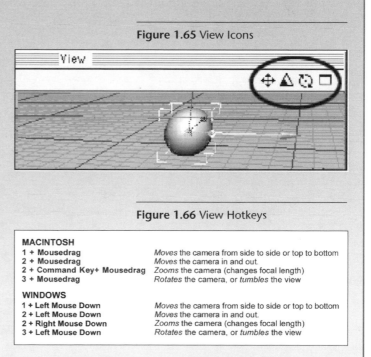

Figure 1.63 H Keyframe

Null Object [COSMIC RINGS]		
Basic	Coord.	Object

Coordinates

P.X	0 m	S.X	1	R.H	360°
P.Y	-112.84 m	S.Y	1	R.P	0°
P.Z	0 m	S.Z	1	R.B	0°

Navigating the 3D World

The icons on the top right of each view window allow you to navigate the editor camera in the 3D space. You'll probably prefer using these keyboard hotkeys. Mac Users: Hold down the appropriate key as you drag the mouse. The 1 key "tracks" or moves the view side to side or up and down. The 2 key moves the camera in and out. If you want to zoom the camera rather than move it (because zooming changes its focal length and distorts perspective), use Cmd+the 2 key (right-click). The 3 key rotates or tumbles the view. (Cmd+3 performs a Dutch tilt. Try it to see what it looks like!) Cmd-Shift-Z and Cmd-Shift-Y undo and redo views.

Windows Users: The 1 key + Left Mousebutton moves the view side to side or up and down. The 2 key + the left Mousebutton moves the camera in and out. The 2 key + Right Mousebutton Zooms the camera. The 3 key + the Left Mousebutton rotates or tumbles the view (add the Command key to that for a Dutch Tilt). (Ctrl-Shift-Z) and (Ctrl-Shift-Y) undo and redo views.

Figure 1.65 View Icons

Figure 1.66 View Hotkeys

MACINTOSH

1 + Mousedrag	Moves the camera from side to side or top to bottom
2 + Mousedrag	Moves the camera in and out.
2 + Command Key+ Mousedrag	Zooms the camera (changes focal length)
3 + Mousedrag	Rotates the camera, or tumbles the view

WINDOWS

1 + Left Mouse Down	Moves the camera from side to side or top to bottom
2 + Left Mouse Down	Moves the camera in and out.
2 + Right Mouse Down	Zooms the camera (changes focal length)
3 + Left Mouse Down	Rotates the camera, or tumbles the view

Pandora's Box

Making the Model

Figure 1.67 Symmetry

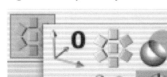

Step 1   Choose File>New and save the file as Pandora's Box in your Models folder by choosing File>Save or Cmd+S (Ctrl+S).

Step 2   Choose Primitive>Cube. In Object Properties, enter 150 for Size Y. Check the check box for Fillet, and enter 3 for both Fillet Radius and Subdivision.

Step 3   Choose the Front view by pressing the F4 key or choosing View>View 4. In the Objects Manager, Control-drag a copy of the original cube and rename it Band. In Object Properties, enter 40 for Size.Y.

Step 4   Choose a Symmetry object from the top toolbar, and set the Mirror Plane to be XZ. Drop the object Band onto the Symmetry object.

Step 5   Select the Band object. Use the green handle of the Move tool to position the mirrored Bands at the top and bottom of the original cube.

Figure 1.68 Box and Bands

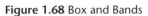

Step 6   Rename the Symmetry object as Bands. Choose File>Save or press Cmd+S (Ctrl+S).

Create a Decorative Lock

Step 1   Choose File>New. (Leave the Pandora's Box file open.)

Step 2   Choose Primitive>Torus. In Object Properties, give the Torus an orientation of –X. Click the Slice panel and check the check box for Slice.

Step 3   From the top toolbar, choose Functions>Duplicate. Enter 12 for Copies. In the Move column, enter 500 in the box for Y. (All Scale values should remain at 1, and all other values should be 0.) Under Rotation, type 180 for the B (bank) value. Press Return (Enter).

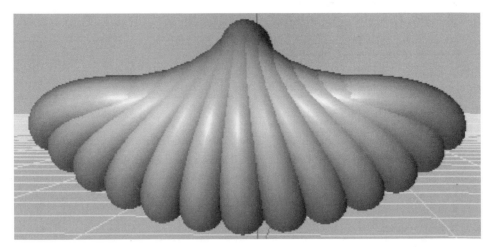

Figure 1.69 Lock Detail

Step 4 Rename the resulting Null Object as Lock Detail. Drag the original Torus into the Lock Detail. Select the Lock Detail object, then type Cmd+C (Ctrl+C) to copy it. Choose File>Close from the top menu to close the Lock Detail File. You may want to save it for future use in your models folder.

Step 5 In the Pandora's Box file, type Cmd+V (Ctrl+V) to paste the Lock Detail into the scene.

Step 6 Make sure the Model tool is selected in the left toolbar. Rotate the Lock Detail to the proper orientation by entering 180 for R.H and –90 for R.B in the Attributes Manager Coordinates panel. Working in All Views (F5), use the Move and Scale tools to manually size and position the lock on the box.

Choosing Materials

Step 1 Choose File>New Material from the Materials Manager menu. Double-click the new material thumbnail and in the Material Editor, select the Color parameter.

Step 2 In the Texture panel of the Color page, click the small black triangle and slide over to Shader>Checkerboard. In the Attributes Manager, enter 10 for U Frequency and 8 for V Frequency. Place the Checkerboard material on the Cube object.
8.5 Update Choose Surfaces>Checkerboard and click the word Checkerboard to edit the shader as in Step 2, above.

Step 3 Click the Browser tab (to the Right of the Objects Manager tab). Choose File>Import File and navigate to the Chapter 1>EXAMPLES>Galaxy Ball.c4d file. Double-click the Galaxy Ball thumbnail and Shift-click to select the Gold material and a purple material. Press Cmd+C (Ctrl+C) to copy the materials. Return to the Pandora's Box file via the Window menu list.

Step 4 Click the Materials Manager to assure that it is the active window, and paste the materials with Cmd+V (Ctrl+V). Click the Objects Manager tab. Place the Gold material on the Lock Detail, and the purple material on the Bands symmetry object.

Easy and Breezy

Choosing the Models

Step 1 Choose File>New and save the file as Easy and Breezy in your Models folder by choosing File>Save or pressing Cmd+S (Ctrl+S).

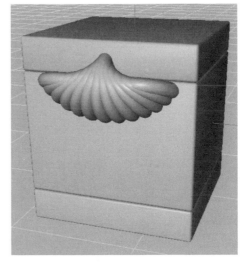

Figure 1.70 Lock on Box

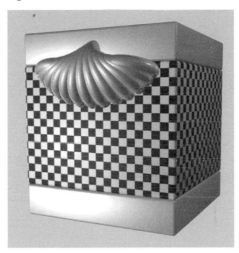

Figure 1.71 Pandora's Box

Figure 1.72 Atom Array

Figure 1.73 Easy

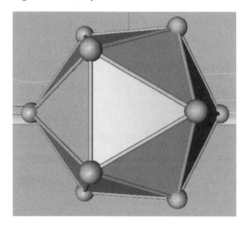

Step 2 Choose Primitive>Platonic. In the Attributes Manager Object Properties, choose Icosa from the Type pulldown menu. Rename the Platonic as Surface.

Step 3 Control-drag a copy of Surface and rename it Frame Icosa.

Step 4 Choose an Atom Array from the Top toolbar (under the Array toolbar icon.)

Step 5 Drop the object Frame Icosa onto the object Atom Array, and rename the Atom Array as Frame.

Step 6 Select Frame, and in the Attributes Manager enter 2m for Cylinder Radius, 10m for Sphere Radius, and 15 for Subdivisions.

Step 7 Select Frame and Surface. Press the G key and rename the resulting Null object as Easy and Breezy.

Time for Materials

Step 1 Open the Browser and choose File>Import File. Navigate to Chapter 01>EXAMPLES>Galaxy Ball.c4d.

Step 2 Double-click the thumbnail for Galaxy Ball.

Step 3 Copy the Gold and any color material that you wish using Cmd-C (Ctrl-C). Choose File>Close. Click No when asked to save changes.

Step 4 Return to the Easy and Breezy file, and paste the materials into the Materials Manager with Cmd+V (Ctrl+V).

Step 5 Place the Gold material on the Frame object.

Figure 1.74 Material Edit

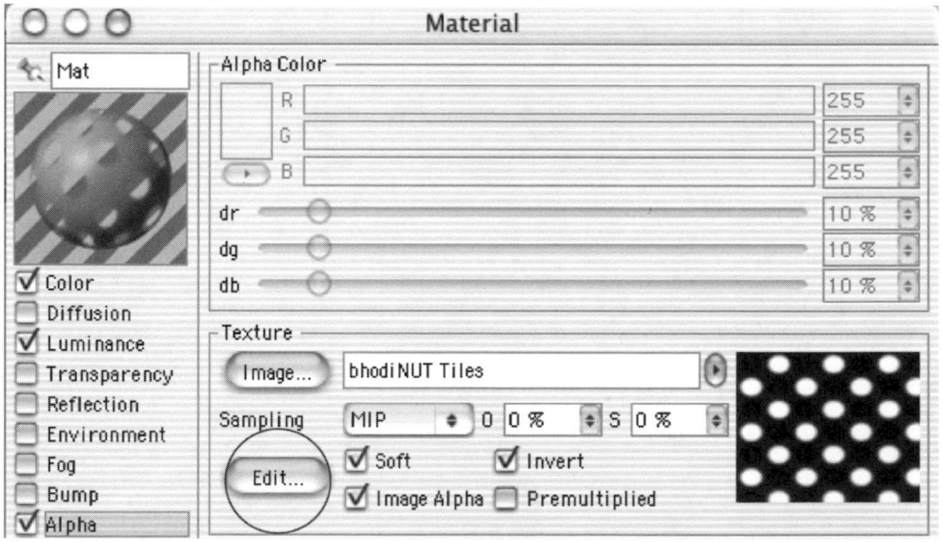

Step 6   In the Materials Manager, double-click the second material thumbnail. Choose the Alpha parameter and check its check box. In the Texture panel, click the small black triangle and slide down to BhodiNUT Channel>BhodiNUT Tiles.
8.5 Update Slide down to Surfaces>Tiles (rather than BhodiNUT Channel>BhodiNUT Tiles)

Step 7   In the Texture panel, click the Edit button. In the Smells Like Almonds editor window, drag on the pulldown menu in the lower left panel (Squares is the default) to select Circles 1.
8.5 Update In the Material Editor, click the word Tiles in the elongated button to edit the shader as in Steps 7 and 8.

Step 8   At the top of the SLA window, double-click Tile Color 1 and change it to black. Change Tile Color 2 to white. In the lower right panel, increase Global Scale to 150 percent and press Return (Enter). Name the material you just created Polka Dot and place it on the Surface Object. Render the Editor window with Ctrl-R.

Step 9   Double-click the Polka Dot material icon and click on the Alpha parameter pane. Check the checkbox next to Invert and render the Editor again.

Figure 1.75 Tile Edit

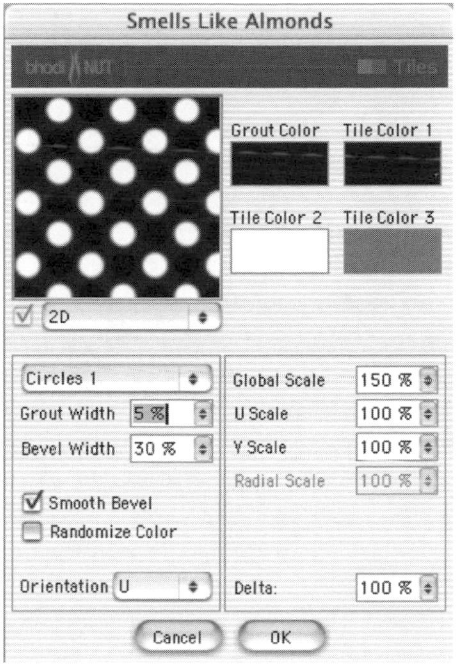

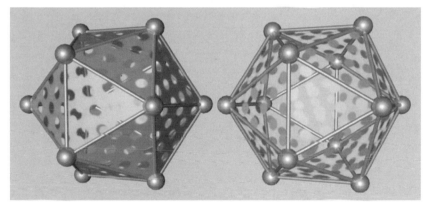

Figure 1.76 Inverted and Not Inverted

A Touch of Animation

Step 1   Set the current time to 0 frames.

Step 2   In the Objects Manager, select the Frame object. In the Attributes Manager Object Properties, Command-click (right-click if you have a two-button mouse) on the words Sphere Radius, and slide to Animation>Add Keyframe. A red dot will signal that a keyframe has been set.

Figure 1.77 Radius Keyframe

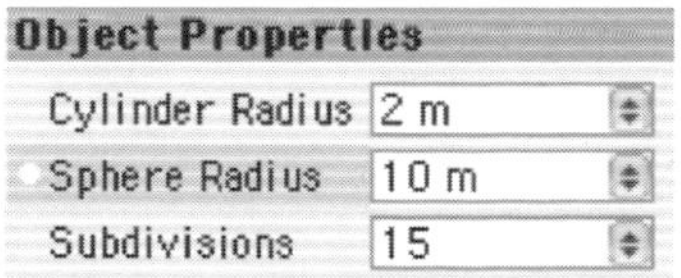

Object Properties

Cylinder Radius	2 m	
Sphere Radius	10 m	
Subdivisions	15	

Step 3   Forward the time slider to 60 frames.

Step 4   Enter 15 for Sphere Radius and press Return (Enter). Set a keyframe.

Step 5   At 90 frames, set a keyframe with the original Sphere Radius of 10.

Step 6   Click the Play button (or press F8) and watch the model "breathe."

The Gyro

Constructing the Gyro

Step 1   Choose File>New and save the file as Gyro in your Models folder by choosing File>Save or pressing Cmd+S (Ctrl+S).

Step 2   Choose Primitive>Torus. In Object Properties, enter 150m for Ring Radius and 10 for Pipe Radius. Set the Orientation to +X. Increase the Ring Segments to 50.

Step 3   Choose Functions>Duplicate. Enter 1 for Copies, 0 for all Move values, and 90º for B Rotation. Click OK. In the Objects Manager, type Cmd+A (Ctrl+A) to select all, then press the G key to group. Rename the resulting Null Object as Outer Frame.

Figure 1.78 Outer Frame   **Figure 1.79** Spinners

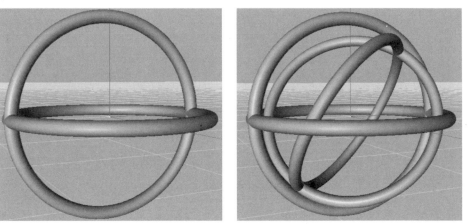

Step 4   With Outer Frame selected, choose Functions>Duplicate again. Under Rotation, enter 0 for H and 50 for both P and B. Rename the new Null Object as Inner Frame.

Step 5   In the Attributes Manager Coordinates panel, enter 0.89 in the S.X, S.Y, and S.Z boxes.

Step 6   Shift-click to select Outer Frame and Inner Frame, and type G. Name the Null Object as Spinners.

Step 7   Choose Primitive>Sphere and in Object Properties, increase the segments to 40. Control-drag a copy of the Sphere. Scale one Sphere to float just outside the Spinners and leave the other to be a smaller core sphere inside the Spinners. Title the Outer Sphere and Inner Sphere.

Step 8   Choose Primitive>Cylinder and Primitive>Torus. Using parametric handles and the Move, Rotate, and Scale tools, craft a hanger with these

Figure 1.80 Gyro Hanger

primitives. Group the Cylinder and Torus by pressing the G key, rename the group as Hanger, and place it at the top of the outer Sphere.

Step 9   In the Objects Manager, select the Spinners, Outer Spheres, and Inner Sphere and press the G key to Group. Rename the group Gyro.

Step 10   So the whole object will rotate from the Hanger, drop the name Gyro (as the child) onto the name Hanger (the parent). With Hanger selected, press the G key again and rename the new Null Object GYRO.

The Well Dressed Gyro

Step 1   In the Materials Manager, choose File>BhodiNUT Volume>Banji. Double-click the material thumbnail, and in the SLA editor window, select the Transparency page. Set the Refraction value to 1 and place the material on the Outer Sphere.
8.5 Update   Choose File>Shader>Banji, double-click the thumbnail and edit the Transparency in the Material Editor.

Step 2   Now choose File>BhodiNUT Volume>Nukei. Double-click the material name and rename it as Turquoise. Place the material on the Inner Sphere.
8.5 Update   Choose File>Shader>Nukei.

Step 3   In the Materials Manager, Control-drag a copy of the Turquoise material thumbnail. Rename the copy Silver Blue. Double-click the material thumbnail and in the SLA editor window, select the Diffuse page. Edit the color to be a light blue and click OK. Place the Silver Blue material on the Torus, Cylinder, and Spinners.

The Firefly Lantern

Building the Lantern Frame

Step 1   Choose File>New and save the file as Firefly Lantern in your Models folder by choosing File>Save or pressing Cmd+S (Ctrl+S).

Step 2   Choose Primitive>Cylinder. In Object Properties, enter 8 for Rotation Segments.

Step 3   Control-drag a copy of the Cylinder. Rename the original Cylinder as Frame and the copy as Paper.

Step 4   Choose an Atom Array from the Array toolbar icon in the top toolbar. Drop the object Frame onto the object Atom Array. Rename the Atom Array as Lantern Frame.

Step 5   In the Attributes Manager Object Properties, edit the Atom Array to have a Cylinder Radius and Sphere Radius of 1.

Figure 1.81 Refraction

Figure 1.82 Finished Gyro

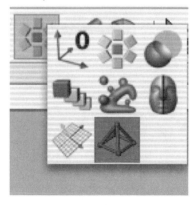

Figure 1.83 Atom Array

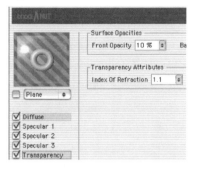

Figure 1.84 Atom Array Object Properties

Figure 1.85 Paper SLA Material

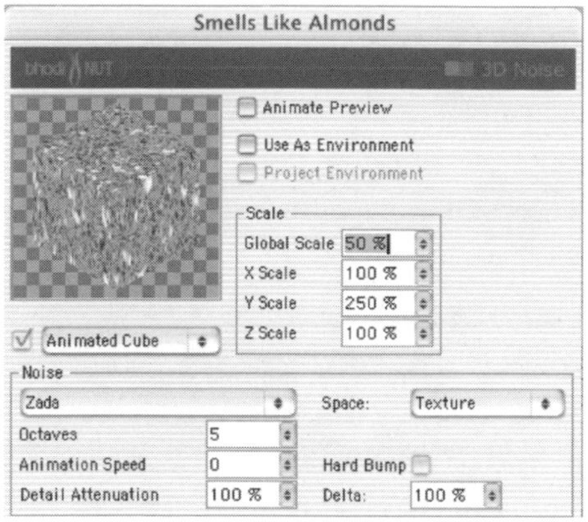

Figure 1.86 Light Position

Step 6   Click on the Objects Manager, Select all with Cmd+A/(Ctrl+A) and press the G key to group the Lantern Frame and Paper objects. Rename the resulting Null Object as FIREFLY LANTERN.

Add Materials and Lights

Step 1   In the Materials Manager, choose File>New Material. Select the Color parameter in the Material Editor. Edit the color to be Khaki, a medium tan.

Step 2   Select and check the Transparency parameter; click the small black triangle in the Texture panel and slide to Shader>BhodiNUT Channel> BhodiNUT 3D Noise. Click Edit. In the SLA editor window, choose Zada from the Noise menu. In the Scale panel, reduce the Global Scale to 50 percent but increase the Y scale to 250. Click OK. Name this material Paper and place it on the Paper object in the Objects Manager.
8.5 Update   After clicking the black triangle, slide to Noise rather than BhodiNUT Channel>BhodiNUT 3D Noise. Click the word Noise to edit the shader as in Step 2. There is no Scale panel, but you'll see Global Scale.

Step 3   In the Materials Manager, choose File>BhodiNUT Volume>BhodiNUT > Banzi. In the SLA editor window, change the left color tab on the Wood page so that it is medium tan. Place this material on the Lantern Frame.
8.5 Update   Choose File>Shader>Banzi. Double-click the thumbnail and edit the shader in the Material Editor as in Step 3.

Step 4   Click on the Lighting toolbar icon to create a default Omni light. Use the green handle of the Move tool to slide the light to the bottom of the lantern.

Step 5   With the Light still selected, click the General tab in the Attributes Manager. Set the Visible Light to Visible. Click the Visibility tab, set the Outer Distance to 20 and press Return. Rename the Light as Firefly 1.

Figure 1.87 Visibility Settings

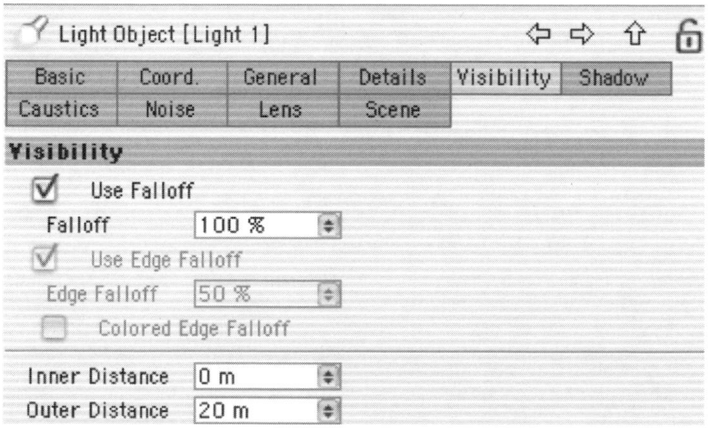

Step 6 Click the Light toolbar icon one more time to create a light to illuminate the outside of the lantern. Name the light Main and in Attributes manager Coordinates, give it Position values of 150 X, 50 Y, and –175 Z.

Animate the Fireflies Using F-Curves

Step 1 To make the animation longer, choose Edit>Project Settings from the top menu. Enter 200 in the box for Maximum, press Return (Enter) and close the window.

Step 2 Select Firefly 1 and click the Coordinates panel in the Attributes Manager. At frame 0, set a keyframe for the current Position Y on the floor of the lantern. At frame 100, drag the upper small arrow next to P.Y until Firefly reaches the top of the Lantern and set a keyframe. Go to the end of the Animation, move Firefly 1 back to the Lantern floor and set a final keyframe.

Step 3 In the Objects Manager, Control-drag two copies of Firefly 1. Rename them as Firefly 2 and Firefly 3. Shift-click to select all the Fireflies and drag them into the name Firefly Lantern.

Step 4 Working in the Top view, move the camera in for a close view (press the 2 key and drag the mouse left to right) and use the X and Z Move handles to position the Fireflies in a triangle on the floor of the Lantern. Return to the Perspective view.

Step 5 Choose the Animation Layout from the Layout icon at the top of the left toolbar.

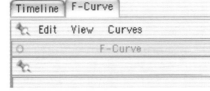

Figure 1.90 F-Curve Tab

Step 6 On the bottom left of the screen, click the F-Curve Tab.

Step 7 In the Objects Manager, Shift-click to select all the Fireflies. (Alternately, you can drag a selection rectangle over all the names.)

Step 8 In the F-Curve window, you now see all the Firefly names in red and a graph. Choose View>Frame All from the menu over the F-Curve window.

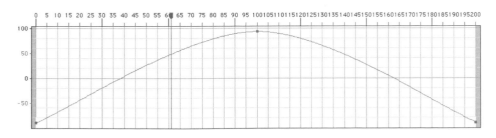

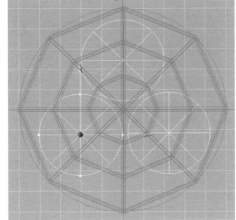

Figure 1.88 Fireflies from Top

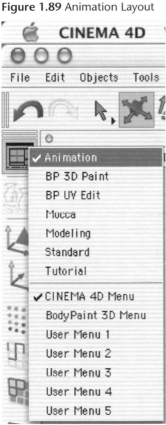

Figure 1.89 Animation Layout

Figure 1.91 All Graphs

You are looking at the graphs for all the fireflies at once, although they are aligned on top of each other and appear to be only one.

Step 9   In the F-Curve graph window, click on the green key on the top of the curve at frame 100. Move it left to frame 30 and lower it to a value of 40 on the graph. Choose the next green key (at frame 100), move it to Frame 130 and lower it to a value of 50. The value of 50 on the Y graph is how high the firefly is jumping. Leave the last high point keyframe at frame 100 where it was. Play the Animation by pressing the Play button on the Animation Timeline or press the F8 key.

Figure 1.92 All Graphs, Edited. Ah ha! By moving the keys on the graph, you can easily control how high and when the fireflies jump. Want to add more bounces? By Control-clicking on the graph line, new keys can be added and positioned at 0 on the Y graph. Later, you'll learn much more about using these powerful curves to control the nuances of motion.

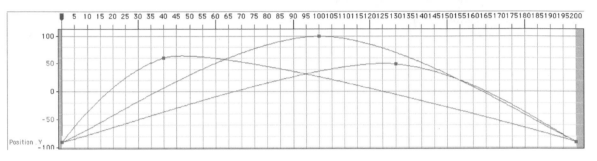

The Color Barrel

Constructing the Model

Step 1   Choose File>New and save the file as Color Barrel in your Models folder by choosing File>Save or pressing Cmd+S (Ctrl+S).

Step 2   Choose Primitive>Cylinder. In Object Properties, enter 20 for Height and +X for Orientation.

Step 3   With Cylinder still selected, choose Functions>Duplicate. Enter 8 for Copies, leave Generate Instances unchecked, and enter 170 for the X value (Y and Z should be 0) in the Move column. (All Scale values should be 1, and all other values 0.) Click OK. Rename the Null Object as Color Bands.

Step 4   With Color Bands selected, choose Functions>Randomize. In the Randomize window, enter 180º in the box for P Rotation. Click OK. Drop the original Cylinder into Color Bands.

Figure 1.93 P Randomized

Randomize		
Move	Scale	Rotation
X 0 m|	X 1	H 0 °
Y 0 m	Y 1	P 180 °
Z 0 m	Z 1	B 0 °
Cancel	OK	

Step 5   Click the (+) to the left of Color Bands to open the hierarchy. Shift-click to select Cylinder and Cylinder.8 (the two end cylinders). By selecting them together, a value can be edited for both at once.

In Object Properties, enter a Height of 3m. Choose the Scale tool and the Model tool, and drag in the gray area of the window from right to left so that the end cylinders move closer to the inner seven. With the two cap cylinders still selected, enter 50 for Radius.

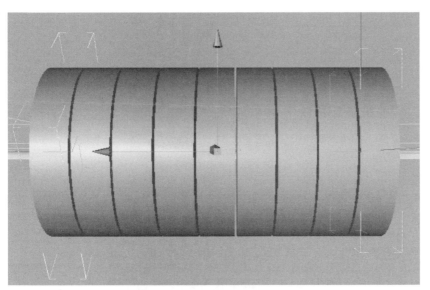

Figure 1.94 Cap Cylinders Shift Selected

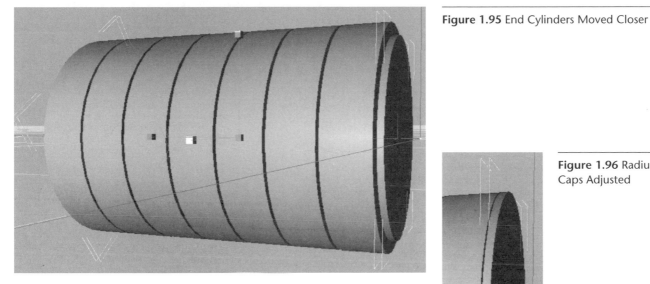

Figure 1.95 End Cylinders Moved Closer

Figure 1.96 Radius of Caps Adjusted

Step 6   Click the Browser tab, and choose File>Import File. Navigate to the Chapter 01>EXAMPLES>Gyro.c4d file, and double-click the thumbnail to open the file. Click the Objects Manager tab, and choose Unfold All from the Objects Manager menu.

Step 7   Shift-select Torus and Tube, and copy them with Cmd+C (Ctrl+C). Return to the Color Barrel file via the Window menu, click on the Objects Manager, and paste the objects with Cmd+V (Ctrl+V).

Step 8   With Torus and Tube still selected, press the G key and name the Null Object as Hanger. Make sure Hanger is selected. Choose Functions>Transfer from the top menu and type Cylinder.4 into the Search For box.

Figure 1.97 Hanger Position

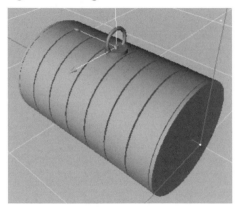

Figure 1.98 Texture Tags

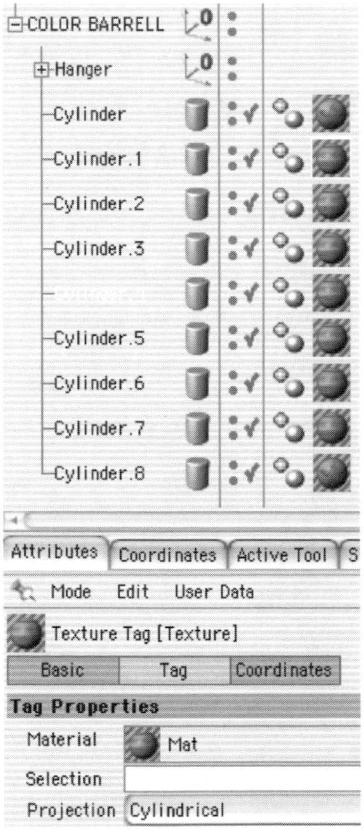

Step 9 Working in All Views (F5) and Isoparm Display, use the Scale tool to make the hanger small enough to fit inside the top of the middle color band, Cylinder.4. Using the Move tool, move the hanger into position at the top of the barrel. Make the Color Bands object a child of the Hanger.

Placing Materials

Step 1 In the Materials Manager, choose File>New Material and Control-drag a copy of the new material thumbnail.

Step 2 Double-click the name of the first Materials icon and rename it Color Swatches. Double-click the new material thumbnail and select the Color parameter. In the Texture panel, click the button for Image. Navigate to the GOODIES>MATERIALS>ImageMaps folder on the DVD and open the file Color Swatch1.psd.
8.5 Update The button to navigate to an image is now the tiny button with three small dots, on the far right.
 Click Yes in the box that appears asking if you want to create a copy of the Image. The name of the image file will appear in the Image box. Place the material on each of the seven inner color bands.

Step 3 Shift-click to select the Texture tags for all the Cylinders (.1 through .7). In the Attributes Manager Tag Properties, choose Cylindrical from the Projection pulldown menu.

Step 4 Select the Texture Tag for Cylinder.1. Enter 5 in the box for Tiles Y.

Step 5 Repeat Step 4 for each of the cylinders through Cylinder. 7, but vary the Tile Y value for each cylinder so there are interesting and random differences in the height of the stripes. Make sure the View Display is Gouraud. Drag the small black arrows next to Tiles Y so you can see the stripes change in real time.

Step 6 Double-click the name of the second material thumbnail and rename it Glitter Star. Double-click the new material thumbnail and select the Color parameter. In the Texture panel, click the button for Image.

Figure 1.99 Random Y Tiles

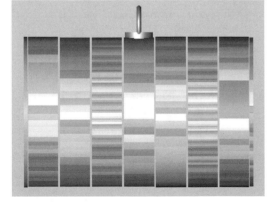

Navigate to the GOODIES>MATERIALS>ImageMaps folder on the DVD and open the file Glitter Star.jpg. Click Yes to the Search Path box.

Click the Bump parameter and check its checkbox. On the Bump page, click the Image button and navigate to the GOODIES>MATERIALS>ImageMaps folder again to open the Glitter Star Bump.jpg file. Close the Material Editor and place the material on both end cylinders.

Figure 1.100 Glitter Star

Step 7 Choose File>Save Project so that the image files will be saved in a folder with the .c4d file. Title the file Color Barrel and save it into your Models folder.

Animate Some Random Twists

Step 1 Shift-select all the cylinders inside the Color bands object. At frames 0 and 90, set keyframes for the current Pitch rotation values (R.P). (Remember, you randomized all the cylinder rotations, so they will all be different.)

Step 2 Select Cylinder.1. At frame 45, add +360 to the right of the current R.P value, and press Return (Enter). Set a keyframe.

Step 3 On the remaining Color Bands (except Cylinder.4 which will be stationary for the hanger), repeat step 1 but vary the rotation on each cylinder. For example, with Cylinder.2 type –180 after the current value at 30 frames. The idea is to spin the cylinders back and forth at different times speeds and directions so the colors are randomly twisting back and forth. Naturally, more degrees between keyframes will cause a faster motion. Play with it.

Figure 1.101 + 360

R . H	0 °
• R . P	12.5+360
R . B	0 °

A Line and a Pole

Making the Model

All these creations need something to hang from. A jazzed-up fishing pole will be just right.

Step 1 Choose File>New and save the file as Line and Pole in your Models folder by choosing File>Save or pressing Cmd+S (Ctrl+S).

Step 2 Choose Primitive>Cylinder. In Object Properties, enter 3 for Radius and 600 for Height. Rename the Cylinder as Pole.

Step 3 Choose Primitive>Sphere. In Object Properties enter 5 for Radius. Use the green handle of the Move tool to pull the Sphere up to the top end of the pole.

Step 4 Working in the Front view, Control-drag a copy of the Pole in the Objects Manager. Rename the copy as Line.

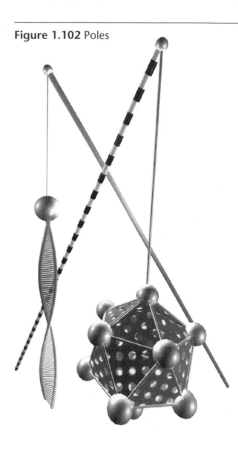

Figure 1.102 Poles

Step 5 With Line selected, in the Attributes Manager Coordinates panel enter 0.2 in the S.X, S.Y, and S.Z boxes. Enter a value of –35 in the R.B box.

Step 6 Use the green and red Move handles to position the Line so that it is coming out of the center of the Sphere.

Step 7 Make the Line a child of the Sphere, and the Sphere a child of the Pole.

Step 8 Select the Pole and drag the tiny black arrows to the right of the R.B box until the Line is hanging vertically.

Adding the Pole to a Model

Step 1 Open one of the Dynamic Dozen model files. Open the LineAndPole.c4d file.

Select the Pole and press Cmd+C (Ctrl+C) to copy it. Return to the model file and paste the Pole into the file using Cmd+V (Ctrl+V).

Step 2 With the model (or its hanger if it has one) selected, choose Functions> Transfer and type Line in the Search For box.

Step 3 If you need to, scale the model.

Step 4 Use the green handle of the Move tool to slide the model vertically into position on the line.

Step 5 Make the model a child of the Line by dropping the model's name onto the word Line. (Move the Pole to test it out.) If a line is too short for a model, you can always open the Pole hierarchy to lengthen and reposition the line.

Material Matters

After merging a pole into a model file, make materials that enhance that particular model and assign them to the Line, Sphere, and Pole. They might repeat some of the colors in the model or maybe show off the model by being complimentary in color (opposite the main color of the model on the color wheel). The pole might be patterned for interesting reflections into a plain glass model material. Check out the color wheel on the last page of the color section, and the finished "Dynamic Dozen" in Chapter 01>MOVIES/STILLS.

In this first incarnation, the Dynamic Dozen are hanging from poles, to be ceremoniously (or not) carried by characters you will make later. However, one of the most fun things about virtual 3D worlds is the total disregard for scale. Take the Gyro, for instance. It could be a mammoth manmade planet careening through space. In other scenes it might end up perched on top of a bedpost, functioning as the base of a sword, or swinging as a decorative light fixture. In yet another life, it could become a tiny charm on a chain around a character's neck. Keep your models predictably filed and they can see many lives.

On the DVD: Ready for a more challenging model? Try the advanced project, "Hypno TV," in the Chapter 01>EXTRA!EXTRA!>InDepth folder on the DVD.

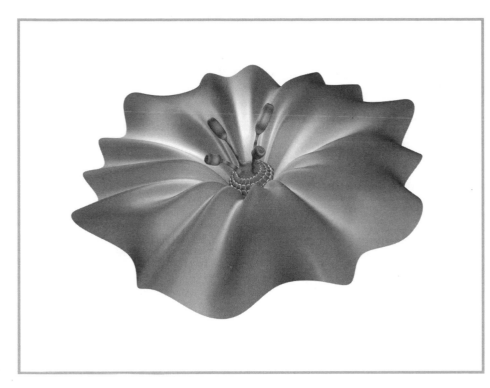

2

Under the Hood

Figure 2.1

Mechanics 101

If your goal is to become an unlimited 3D artist with the power to make anything, don't even think about skipping this chapter. Here, you'll build the skill set to supercharge your artistic vision. While this behind-the-scenes work isn't the most stimulating part of your 3D workflow, the ability to create, edit, and repair the fundamental elements in CINEMA 4D is critical. The time you spend becoming proficient at these tasks will yield a big payoff. So roll up your sleeves and let's get to work!

Making Primitives Editable

A parametric primitive may be easily converted into a polygonal surface for more complex or organic restructuring. The polygonal surface is made up of interconnected polygons that are quadrilateral or triangular planes defined by points or vertices. Adjoining polygons share an edge. The surface, or mesh, may be pushed and pulled into virtually any form by manipulating the polygons themselves, the edges connecting them, or the defining points. CINEMA 4D has a wealth of tools which will give you the power to transform the surface far beyond its primitive beginnings.

Figure 2.2 Make Editable

■ ***Shortcut: Make Editable*** To make a primitive editable, click the Make Editable icon on the left toolbar or press the C key. Multiple objects may be selected by Shift-clicking and made editable at once.

Tools for Editing Surfaces

Figure 2.3 Points, Edges and Polygons

On the left toolbar, three tools give you access to the elements on the polygonal surface. When you want to push and pull points, choose the Points tool. For working with edges, click the Edge tool, and if it's polygons you want to manipulate, select the Polygons tool. Although you have a sophisticated set of selection tools for selecting all these elements, you can also select single or multiple points, edges, and polygons using the Move, Scale, and Rotate tools. The points, edges, or *polys* of an editable surface may be transformed singly or in groups selected by Shift-clicking with the same Move, Scale, and Rotate tools you used with primitive objects in Chapter 1. You need to click on the element first to select it before attempting to Move, Scale, or Rotate.

A Petunia

Step 1 Navigate to the folder Chapter 02>C4D Files and open Petunia.c4d. Choose File>Save As and save it in your Models folder.

Step 2 Choose Primitive>Disc. Press the C key to make the Disc editable.

Figure 2.4 Hyper NURBS

Step 3 Click the HyperNURBS icon on the top toolbar. In the Objects Manager, drop the object Disc onto the object HyperNURBS. Rename the HyperNURBS as Petunia and select Disc.

The HyperNURBS object is a generator and will be continually rounding off and softening the more blocky form of the polygonal mesh. The HyperNURBS functions interactively as you continue to work with the points, edges and polygons of the cage around it.

Step 4 Select the Move tool and the Edge tool. Randomly select edges by Shift-clicking similar to the pattern in Figure 2.5. Use the green handle of the Move tool to raise the Disc's ridges up into a ruffle.

Step 5 Select the Points tool. Click the point in the exact center of the Disc. Use the green Move handle to pull it downward to a Y value of –40m, using the Coordinates Manager as a guide.

Step 6 Working in the top view and Wireframe display, Shift-click to select random points all around the edge. Choose the Scale tool and drag the

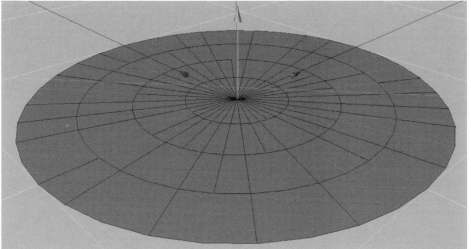

Figure 2.5 Petunia Edge Selection

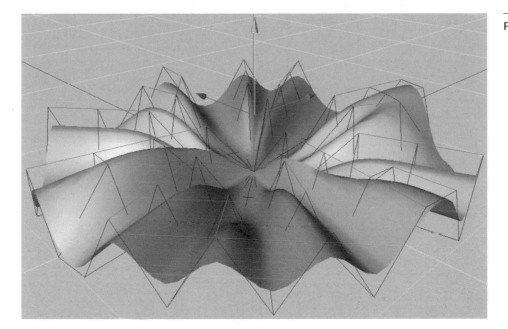

Figure 2.6 Raised Ridges

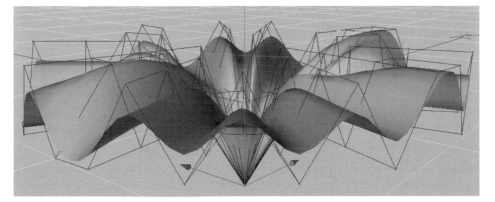

Figure 2.7 Center Point

mouse right to left in the editor window to scale the points as a group
to create a ruffled edge.

Figure 2.8 Random Edge Points

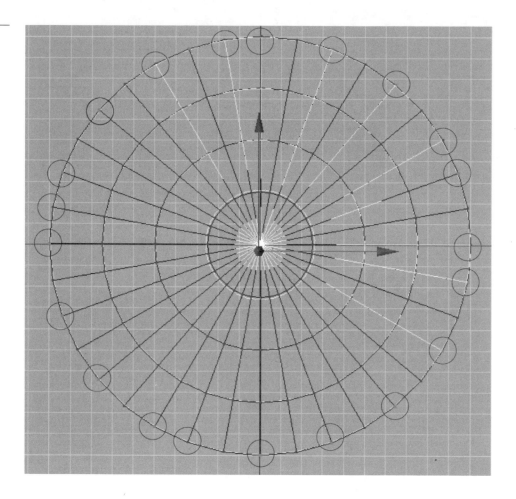

Step 7   Place the material Pink on the Petunia. In the Attributes Manager under Tag Properties, choose Spherical for projection.

Creating A Center

This cartoon center for the Petunia will let you try out some classic tools for selecting and manipulating polygons.

Step 1   Choose File>New. Save the new file as Cartoon Flower Center (File>Save
or Cmd+S/Ctrl+S).

Step 2   Working in the Front view, choose Primitive>Sphere. Press the C key
to make it editable. Select the Polygons tool from the left toolbar.

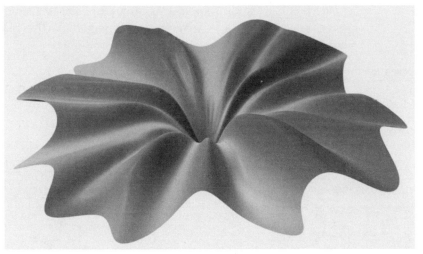

Figure 2.9 Petunia

Step 3   Choose a HyperNURBS object from the top toolbar and drop the Sphere into it. Rename the HyperNURBS as Center. Select the Sphere inside the HyperNURBS object.

Step 4   Select the Rectangle Selection tool from the top toolbar. Click the Active Tool tab (next to the Attributes Manager) and uncheck Only Select Visible Elements. Level with the second band of polygons above the X Axis, drag the rectangle from the outside left all the way across the sphere. Release the mouse on the outside right. Type the Delete key to remove the selected polygons.

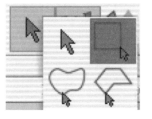

Figure 2.10 Rectangle Selection Tool

Figure 2.11 Rectangular Selection

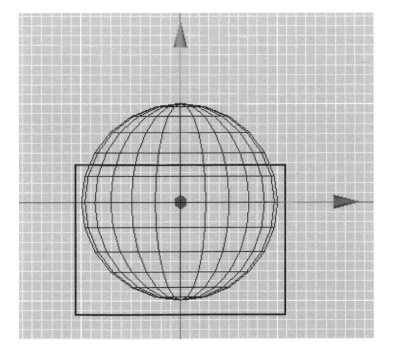

With any selection tool, unchecking Only Select Visible Elements enables selection all the way through an object. Make these kinds of selections in orthographic views (Front, Top, or Side).

Step 5   Select the Live Selection tool from the top toolbar.

Switch to the top view and paint all the polys shown in Figure 2.13. If you miss some, you can hold down the Shift key to add more to the selection. If you want to remove some, hold down the Control key and paint the polys you want to remove.

Figure 2.12 Live Selection Tool

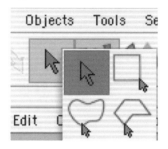

Figure 2.13 "Painted" Live Selection

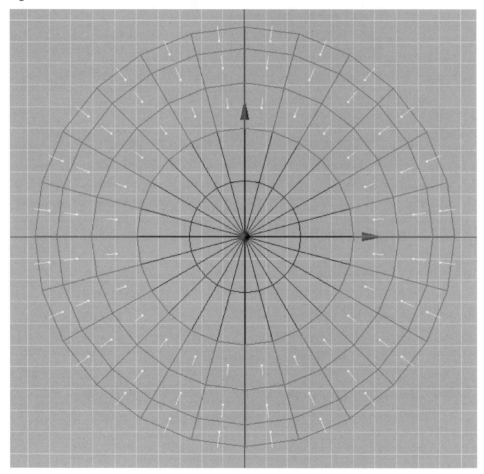

Figure 2.14 Active Tool Tab

Attributes	Active Tool	Snap Setting

🐾 Extrude

Maximum Angle	89 °	
Offset	15 m	
Variance	50 %	
Edge Bevel	0 m	
Edge Angle	0 °	
☑ Snap Angle	15 °	
☐ Preserve Groups	Apply	

Step 6   Return to Perspective view. From the top menu, choose Structure> Extrude.

In the Active Tool Manager, make sure Preserve Groups is unchecked. Enter 15m for Offset and 50 percent for variance. (You could also drag the mouse in the editor window to interactively control the distance of the extrusion.)

■ ***Shortcut: Extruding*** Press the D key to access the Extrude tool.

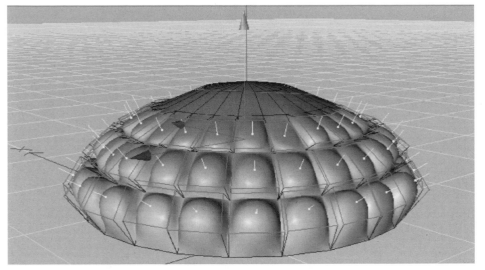

Figure 2.15 Outside Polys

Step 7 With the polygons still selected, choose Selection>Set Selection from the top menu. You will be needing these polygons later. Double-click the Polygon Selection tag that appears in the Objects Manager, and in the Attributes Manager click the Basic panel. Enter "Outside Polys" in the box. Click anywhere in the open gray area of the Objects Manager to deactivate the Selection tag, and press Cmd+Shift+A (Ctrl+Shift+A) to deselect the polygons.

Step 8 Press the 3 key and drag the mouse to tilt the view so you can easily access the top of the model. Reselect the sphere object. Using the Move tool, click four equidistant polygons on top as seen in Figure 2.16.

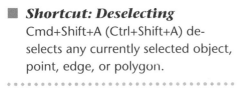

■ ***Shortcut: Deselecting***
Cmd+Shift+A (Ctrl+Shift+A) deselects any currently selected object, point, edge, or polygon.

Figure 2.16 4 Top Polys

Figure 2.17 Matrix Extrude

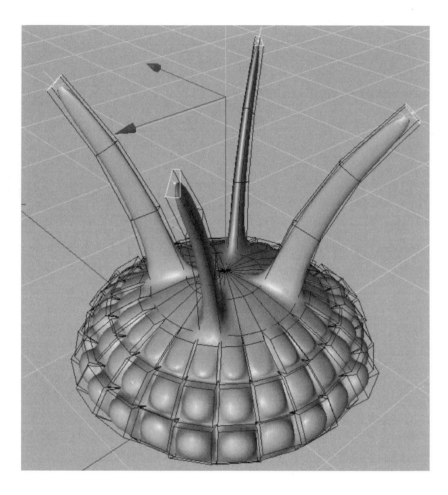

Figure 2.18 Extrude Inner/Outward

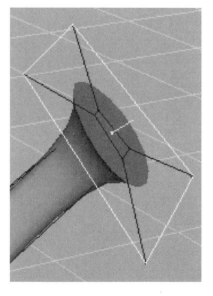

Step 9 From the top menu, choose Structure>Edit Surface>Matrix Extrude. In the Matrix Extrude Box, enter 3 for Steps. Press Return (Enter).

Step 10 With the end polys still selected, choose Structure>Extrude Inner from the top menu.

In the Active Tool tab, enter –20 for the Offset value. (You could also drag the mouse to the right for interactive extrusion of the polygon.)

■ **Shortcut: Extrude Inner** Press the I key to access the Extrude Inner tool. Dragging the mouse to the right slides the new polygon away from the center of the original polygon but keeps it moving along the same plane. Dragging to the left slides the new polygon toward the center of the original polygon.

Step 11 Press the D key and drag the mouse from left to right in the editor window to make the slightly elongated form in Figure 2.19. Press the I key again, but this time drag the mouse right to left to slide the new poly toward the center of the original one.

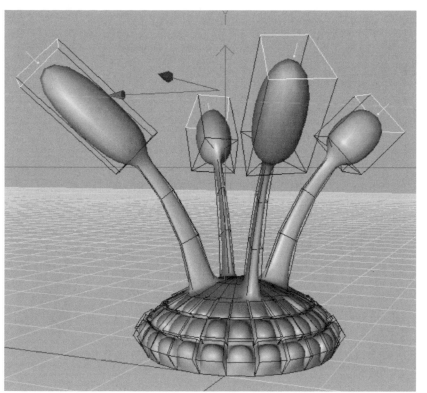

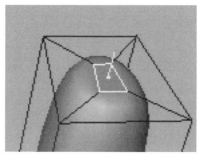

Figure 2.19 Extrude Again

Figure 2.20 Extrude Inner/Inward

Figure 2.21 Center Close-Up

Step 12 Press the D key one more time, and barely drag the mouse from right to left in the window to make a slight depression in the form. Select Center and press Cmd+C (Ctrl+C) to copy it. Save the file (File>Save or Cmd+S/Ctrl+S)

Step 13 Open the Petunia.c4d file in your Models folder (or choose it from the Window menu if you didn't close it) and use Cmd+V (Ctrl+V) to paste the flower center into it. Choose the Model tool. Scale and move the center to fit inside the flower.

Using Set Selection

Step 1 Choose Unfold All from the Objects Manager menu, and drop the Pink material on the object Sphere inside the Center.

Step 2 In the Materials Manager, select File>New Material. Double-click the New Material icon, and in the color property of the Material Editor, choose a medium green. Drop the green Material icon onto the name Sphere inside the Center.

Step 3 In the Attributes Manager, click the Tag panel and type the name of the Selection, Outside Polys, in the box next to Selection. Press Return

(Enter). The spelling and spacing must be exact for the selection to be recognized. Render the Editor window, and save the file.

Repositioning an Object Axis

After an object has been made editable, you can also move its axis to any position.

Step 1   Open Barometer Cone.c4d file in Chapter 01>EXAMPLES. Choose File> Save As and save the file in your Models folder as Barometer Rising.

Step 2   Choose Unfold All from the Objects Manager menu. Select Mercury. Click the Object panel in the Attributes Manager. Drag up and down on the small black arrows next to Height and watch the behavior of the Mercury cone. Not good—what's happening is that the height is changing in relation to the object's centered axis.

Step 3   From the top menu, choose File>Revert to Saved. Click Yes in the Are you sure? box.

Figure 2.22 Centered Axes

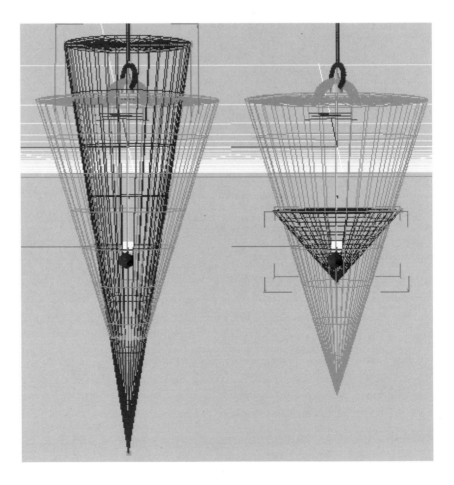

Step 4 Working in the Front view, select the Mercury object again. Using the 1 and 2 keys while dragging the mouse in the editor window, negotiate the view so you have a close-up look at the cone.

Step 5 Press the C key to make the Mercury object editable.

Step 6 From the left toolbar, choose the Object Axis tool.

Step 7 Use the green Move handle to move the object's axis to the very bottom tip of the Mercury cone.

Figure 2.23 Object Axis Tool

Figure 2.24 Axis Moved

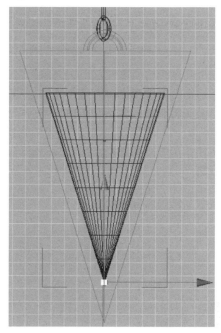

Step 8 From the left toolbar, choose the Object tool.

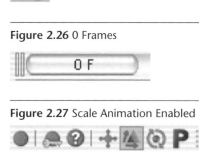

Figure 2.25 Object Tool

Step 9 With the current time slider at 0 frames, click the icon to enable animation of Scale. Choose the Scale tool, making sure all the X,Y, and Z locks are free. Drag the mouse in the editor window from right to left until the Mercury is barely visible. Press the F9 key or click the Record button to set a keyframe.

Figure 2.26 0 Frames

Figure 2.27 Scale Animation Enabled

Step 10 Go to the end of the animation. Drag the mouse from left to right, until the mercury level rises. See Figure 2.28. Set a keyframe. Press F8 or click Play to preview the animation.

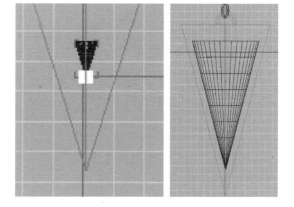

Figure 2.28 Low Level Close-up/High Level

◆ **Tip:** Use this same process to make the Line holding one of your models swing correctly from the top of the Pole. Just move the Line's axis up to the Sphere at the top of the Pole and animate the Line in a gentle rotation.

On the DVD: For more practice with adjusting Object Axes, see Chapter 02>EXTRA!EXTRA!>InDepth>ROBOT Extra Project.

Creating and Repairing Polygonal Surfaces

You can make a single polygon by choosing Primitive>Polygon. In this section, you'll learn how to "stitch" two separate surfaces together, how to use the bridge tool to connect meshes in useful ways and how to make a continuous polygonal surface. Note that these constructions are exercises designed to point out techniques, and they are not how you would actually build these objects.

Stitching Meshes Together

Step 1 Choose File>Open and navigate to Chapter 02>C4D Files>Plastic Curtain.c4d. Choose Save As and save the file to your Models Folder.

Step 2 From the top toolbar, choose Primitive>Plane. Give the Plane 20 Width segments, 4 Height segments, and an Orientation of +Z. Press Return (Enter).

Step 3 Working in the Front view, Control-drag a copy of the Plane in the Objects Manager. In the Editor window, use the red handle of the Move tool (be sure you are in the Model tool) to move the copy to the immediate right of the original. Shift-click both Planes to select them and press the C key to make them editable.

Figure 2.29 Plane

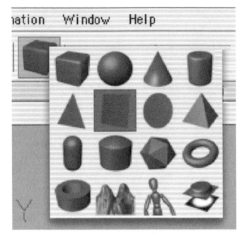

Figure 2.30 Side by Side Copies

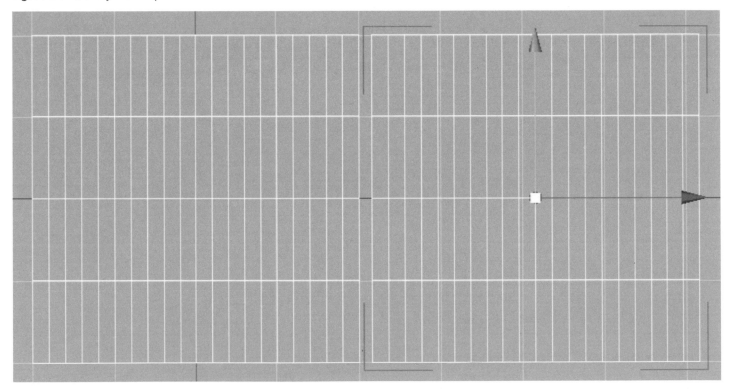

Step 4 Choose the Points tool from the left toolbar and notice that you are seeing points for only one plane, the one currently selected.

Step 5 Shift-click to select both Planes. From the top menu, choose Functions> Connect. Delete both Plane objects and rename the Plane 1 object as Connected. With Connected selected, notice that now you can see all the points.

Step 6 Make sure the Move tool is selected. Shift-click to select the two points at the top of the gap between the two parts. From the top menu, choose Structure>Edit Surface>Weld. The two points become one.

Step 7 Work your way down, two side-by-side points at a time. Shift-click to select two points, and again choose Structure>Edit Surface>Weld. Be sure to deselect the previously welded point before you Shift-click to select the next pair down.

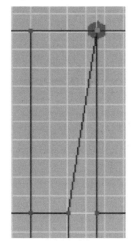

Figure 2.31 Weld

How Many Polygons?

As you begin to make more complex models, you'll become interested in the number of polygons in models and scenes. The most efficient model looks as good as it needs to with the fewest polygons. A distant camera may not require a model with a smooth edge (and higher poly count). An animated model won't be sticking around long enough to be scrutinized, so fewer polys may do the job and can be more easily animated. Unnecessary polygons just take up storage space and processor power. To find out the polygon count of an object, choose Objects>Object Information from the menu over the Objects Manager. For a count on the total scene, choose Scene Information.

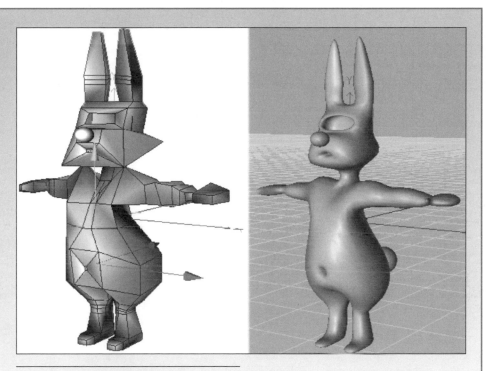

Figure 2.32 A Low Poly Model, Low Poly Model in HyperNURBS Object

Making Models That Can Move

There are many ways of going about making any one model, and there is usually a best way. In addition to thinking out a construction method that will be most efficient in polys, it's important to think ahead on how you want the model to be able to move.

The number and orientation of polygons directly affect how well a model can be deformed and animated later. Some old-fashioned sketching with pencil and paper can help you visualize how you want the model to move and the best approach for building it.

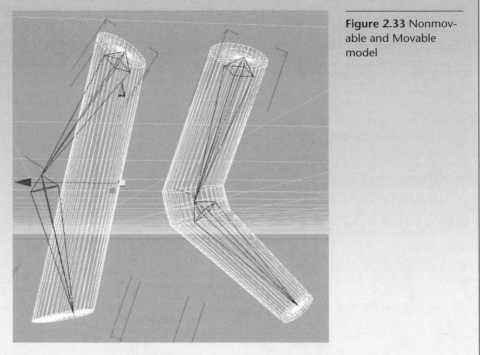

Figure 2.33 Nonmovable and Movable model

Using the Knife Tool

■ *Shortcut: Knifing* Press the K key to access the Knife tool.

Step 1 With the Points tool still selected, choose Structure>Knife from the top menu.

Step 2 Hold down the Shift key. Click the mouse outside the top left of the plane (just under the top edge) and drag all the way across to the outside right. Make one more horizontal "cut" under the first one. Now knife vertically down through the gap left from where you welded points. See Figure 2.34

Figure 2.34 Subdivisions Made with the Knife Tool

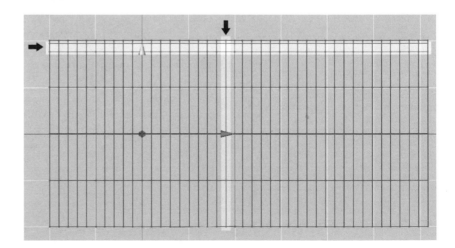

Step 3 Switch to the Polygon tool and the Move tool. Starting on the right side, skip a polygon and then Shift-click to select every other polygon in the second row from the top. Press the Delete key to remove the selected polygons. (The Display should be Gouraud, so you can see the result.)

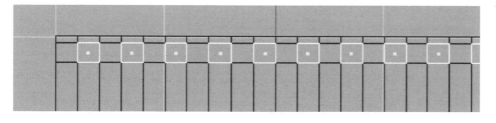

Figure 2.35 Holes

Subdividing vs Knifing

An entire surface of polygons may be subdivided by choosing Structure>Subdivide from the top menu. Use a light touch when entering values in the Subdivision box, because a value of only 1 creates four polys where once there was one. Do the math and you'll see how high values could bring a computer down. Subdividing occurs at the center of each poly in both directions. A surface must be made editable to be subdivided.

   Another way to add more detail to a surface is to use the Knife tool. Knifing doesn't cut the mesh but rather divides polygons. Unlike subdividing, which halves all polys in an overall manner, using the Knife tool lets you add divisions one at a time to specific locations on the mesh. This is more economical for your polygon count because divisions are only made where you really need them. Unless you choose Restrict to Selection in the Active Tool tab to limit the knifing to a specific polygon (or set of polygons) the knife tool goes all the way through the object by default. Use the orthographic views of Front, Side, or Top for a straight shot at the object. To constrain a cut to horizontal, vertical, or 45º, hold down the Shift key.

The Push and Pull Trick

Step 1 Select the Points tool. Choose the Rectangle selection tool and Shift-select about half of the vertical rows of points. Choose all the points from top to bottom in each row. Every other vertical row would be too perfect. Try a more random pattern of single and double vertical lines.

Step 2 Switch to the Perspective view (View 1). Press the 3 key and drag the mouse to turn the view so you are facing the plane. Using the Move tool, hold down the Cmd key and drag the mouse in the editor window until the Z value is around 30 in the Coordinates Manager.

Figure 2.36 Random Rows of Points Selected

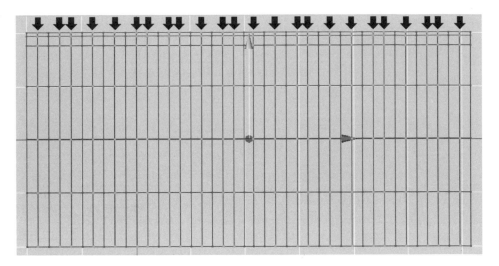

Holding down the Cmd key (or holding down the Right mouse-button) while dragging the Move tool lets you move selected elements perpendicular to the screen (not necessarily the Z axis). A mouse drag to the right moves elements toward you, and dragging the mouse to the left moves elements away from you. This works on objects, points, edges, or polygons.

Step 3 Place the material Red Polka Dot on Connected, choosing Flat Projection in the Attributes Manager Tag Properties.

Step 4 Create a HyperNURBs and rename it Curtain. In the Attributes Manager, give the HyperNURBS a value of 3 for Editor and Renderer.

Figure 2.37 Finished Curtain

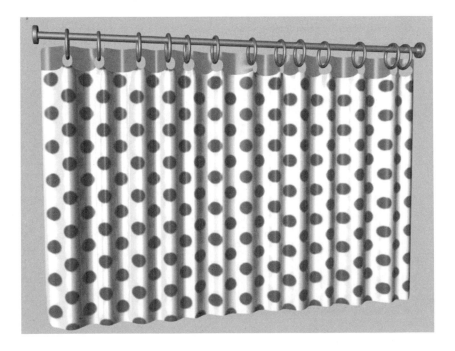

Step 5   Drop the Connected object into the HyperNURBS object and type Ctrl+R to admire your curtain.

The Magnet Tool and Point Level Animation

Step 1   Chose File>Open and navigate to Chapter 02>C4D Files>Moving Curtain.c4d. Save a copy of the file into your Models folder (File>Save As). Use the Perspective view.

Step 2   Choose Selection>Deselect All to assure there are no selected points.

Step 3   Choose Structure>Magnet tool. Make sure all X,Y, and Z locks are free.

Step 4   In the Active Tool Manager, enter a Radius of 300m.

Step 5   In the Animation toolbar, make sure only the PLA icon is enabled for animation.

Step 6   At frames 0 and 90, click the Record button to record keyframes for "neutral" positions of the curtain before any Magnet tool is applied.

Step 7   At frame 45, mouse with the Magnet tool to billow the bottom edge of the curtain out slightly. Set a keyframe.

Step 9   Press F8 or click Play to preview the animation.

Figure 2.38 X,Y and Z Locks in Unlocked State

Figure 2.39 PLA Enabled

Figure 2.40 Moving Curtain

P Is for Pipe

For more practice with mesh construction, let's make the letter *P* in an unorthodox way.

Step 1 Chose File>Open and navigate to Chapter 02>C4D Files>P for PIPE.c4d. Choose File>Save As and save the file to your Models Folder. Render the existing model to see what you will be making, then select the Pipe and delete it.

■ *Shortcut: The Bridge Tool*
Press the B key to access the Bridge tool, which lets you quickly build a continuous mesh on points you have drawn. When you reach the end of any section you are bridging, you must deselect the points before moving to another section.

Step 2 Working in the Front view, choose the Points tool. From the top menu, choose Objects>Polygon Object. Using the Move tool, hold down the Ctrl key and click points in the configuration shown in Figure 2.41.

Step 3 From the top menu, choose Structure>Bridge. Click on the upper left point and drag across to the upper right point. Both points will turn red. Now drop down to the next row. Click the left point and drag to the one to its right. Continue this maneuver, moving downward, until you reach the bottom.

Figure 2.41 Points for P

Figure 2.42 First Row

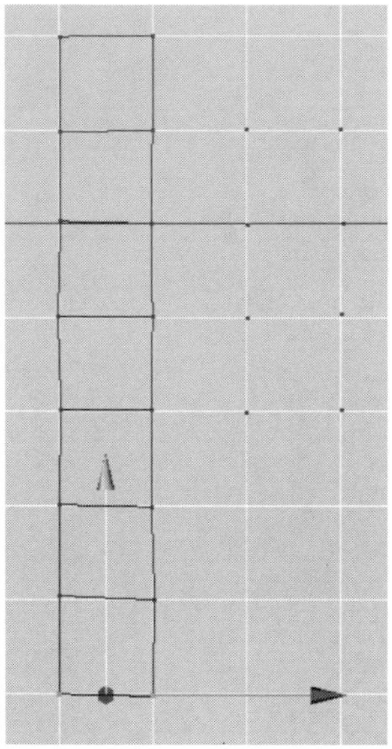

Figure 2.43 Second Row

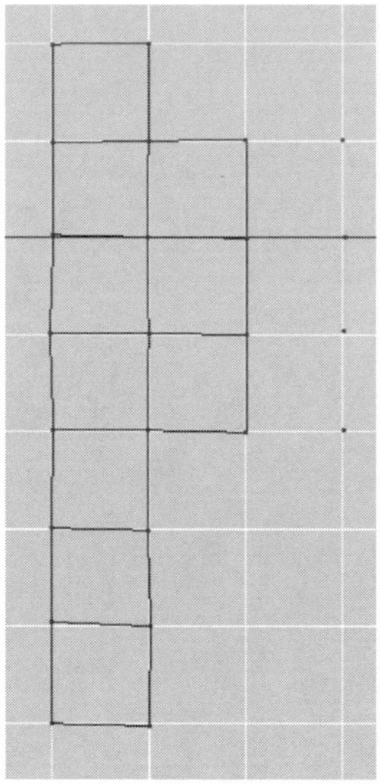

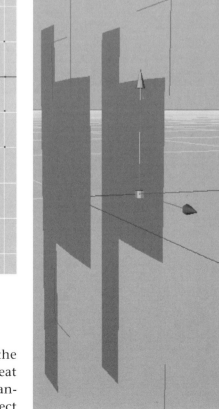
Figure 2.44 A Copy of the Polygon Moved Behind

Step 4 Press Cmd+Shift+A (Ctrl-Shift-A) to deselect.

Step 5 Start again at the top of the point structure and repeat the left-to-right drags in another vertical row. Deselect

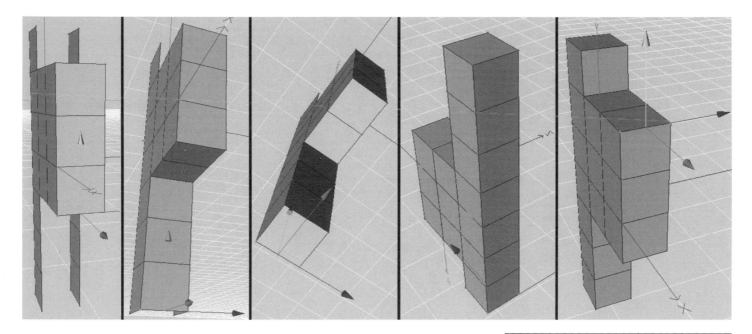

Figure 2.45 Tumbling the View

at the bottom of the row and finish the last section of points with the same bridging motion.

Step 6 Switch to Perspective view. Choose the Model tool. In the Objects Manager, Control-drag a copy of the Polygon. In the Attributes Manager Coordinates panel, enter a value of 100m for P.Z.

Step 7 Press Cmd+A (Ctrl-A) to select all, and choose Functions>Connect from the top menu. Delete both Polygon objects and select Polygon 1.

Step 8 You'll be giving the 3 key a real workout in this maneuver. Select the Points tool and press the B key to access the Bridge tool. Starting with any two sets of points, drag a point on the edge of the front of the *P* to the corresponding point on the back. Bridge horizontal sets of points until you work all the way around the edge of the letter. To make this happen, you'll have to keep tumbling the world around sides of the letter P, pressing the 3 key while dragging the mouse to tumble the view and the 1 key to reposition the model as the view changes.

Step 9 Now while you're still in the Perspective view, choose the Polygons tool and the Move tool. Select and delete the polygon in the middle of the large square section of the model. Use the 3 key again to position the view so you can see all 4 corners of the polygon directly behind the open square. Delete the center polygon in the back also.

Step 10 Select the Points tool and the Bridge tool. Starting at the top left corner of the hole you are looking through, bridge front corner point to back corner point. Work your way around the square until the hole has sides

Figure 2.46 Deleting Center Polys

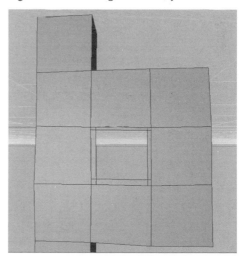

Figure 2.47 Bridging Though

Figure 2.48 Top and Bottom Polys

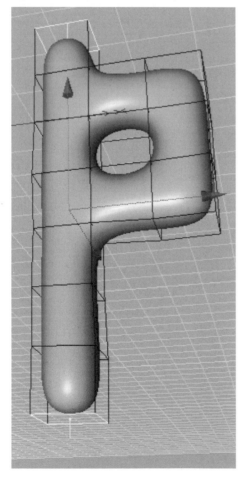

all around. At times, you may have to use the 3 key to tilt the view slightly so you can see both target points.

Step 11 Create a HyperNURBS, and drop the Polygon.1 object into it. Assign a Phong tag to Polygon.1 and check the Angle Limit box. Set a value of 3 for HyperNURBS Editor and Renderer. Rename the HyperNURBS as Pipe.

Finishing Touches for the Pipe

Step 1 Choose the Polygons tool. Working on the Polygon.1 object inside the HyperNURBS, Shift-click to select the top and bottom polys on the long, vertical part of the letter *P*. Press the I key and in the Active Tool Manager, enter an offset value of –50m. Remember to click Apply or press Return (Enter) after entering values in the Active Tool Manager.

Step 2 Press the D key. Enter a value of 50 for Offset in the Active Tool Manager.

Step 3 Press the I key again, and set the Offset value to 60.

Step 4 Press the D key one last time, and enter –300 for Offset.

Figure 2.49 Polys Extrude Inner

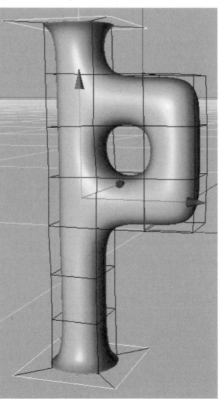

Figure 2.50 Extrude Pipe

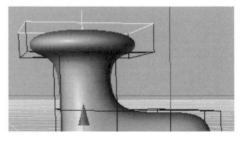

Figure 2.51 Top Extrude Inner

Figure 2.52 Extrude Down Into

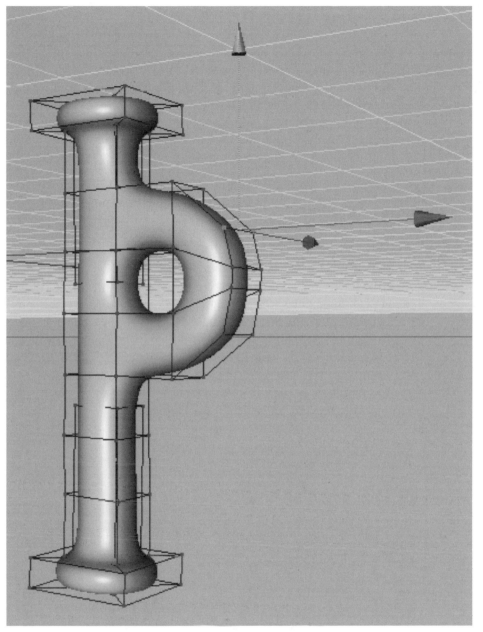

Figure 2.53 Rounding Off the Letter

Figure 2.54 P for Pipe

Step 5 Working in the Front view, use the Rectangle selection tool to select all the points on the right edge of the model. Make sure Only Select Visible Elements is unchecked in the Active Tool manager so you get the points on the front and back.

Step 6 Choose the Scale tool and drag down on the green handle to round off the letter. You can push and pull individual points with the Move tool to adjust the form further.

Step 7 Place the material Grungy on the pipe with UVW Projection.

Splines, Your Invisible Friend

Now you'll learn how to create splines, major players in the world of 3D. It may seem that you have nothing to show for all your work, as splines are invisible in the renderer. But by saving these basic practice splines into a file, you'll create a library of useful spline elements that will be ready to go in future projects. Splines and Tangents and Beziers, oh my! Working with splines can be one of the most challenging aspects of 3D modeling. For more information about types of splines and advanced spline editing, see the Splines in Depth.pdf on the DVD and in the CINEMA 4D manual.

A Cloud-shaped Spline

Step 1   Create a new file and save it as MySplineLibrary.c4d in your Models folder (File>Save As).

Step 2   From the top menu, choose Object>Spline Object. Select the Points tool from the left toolbar and the Move tool. Working in the Front view, press the 2 key and drag the mouse to adjust the view so the smaller grid sections are about one-inch square on your screen. Control-click the mouse at 0,0 where the Y and X axes intersect, then Control-click again four grid squares up on the Y axis. Control-click two squares over to the left.

You just created two splines with Hard Interpolation. Between each set of points, the lines or segments are straight.

◆ *Tip:* Always draw splines in the an *orthographic* view: Front, Side, or Top.

Figure 2.55 Hard Splines

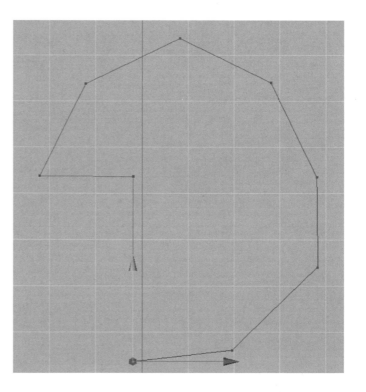

Step 3   Use the 1 and 2 keys with the mouse to adjust the view so you can continue to Control-click points in the configuration seen in Figure 2.55. Make the last click on the point you started on. This creates a closed spline.

Step 4   Skipping over the first three points you drew, shift-click to select all the other points on the spline. From the top menu, choose Structure>Edit Spline>Soft Interpolation. Deselect the points by typing Cmd+Shift+A (Ctrl+Shift+A), then click on just one of them.

Figure 2.56 Tangent Handles

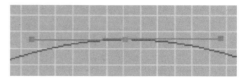

Converting these points to Soft Interpolation causes the splines to curve out of the points. The magenta tangent handles control the direction and expansion of the curve. Drag a tangent handle out from its point to see how it flattens the curve. Then, move the handle up and down in a seesaw motion. Notice how the opposite ends of the curve move in a connected way. Click the Move tool on a point, and then drag the Move handles to change the location slightly. Double-click on a point. A box appears with numerical values for the point and its tangents. Holding down the Shift key and independently dragging a handle allows you to break the rigid tangent and send the opposite ends of the tangent in different directions. Use Cmd+Z (Ctrl+Z) to undo these experiments!

Step 5   Shift-click to select the fourth point you made. Continue to hold the Shift key and drag the tangent handles independently. To make a cloud

Figure 2.57 Cloud Spline

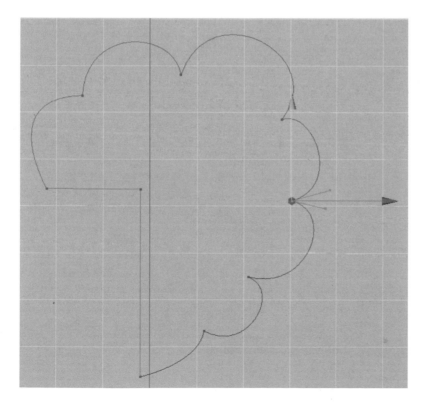

outline, move the tangent handles closer together so they dip inward. Leave the first three points you drew as they are, but edit all the others to create the outline of a puffy cloud. Use the Move tool to move points if necessary.

Step 6   When you are satisfied with your cloud shape, rename the spline as Cloud and click the top gray button in the second column of the Objects Manager to turn off its visibility.

A Lightbulb Spline

You made the cloud spline by creating an empty spline object and Control-clicking points to go inside it. This time, you'll use an interactive spline tool to create a Bezier Spline on the fly. The cool thing about splines is that they can always be edited later, even when they are a working component of a finished model.

Step 1   Work in the Front view. From the top toolbar, choose Spline>Bezier Spline Tool.

Figure 2.58 Bezier Spline Tool

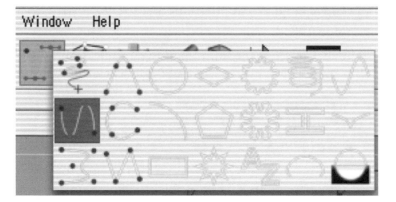

Beginning on the Y axis, click a point. Release the mouse. Then, drop slightly down and to the right, but this time click and drag over slightly to the right as you click to create tangent handles for the point.

Any time you click and drag a point, it is "born" with Soft Interpolation and has tangent handles.

Figure 2.59 Light-bulb Start

Step 2   Position the next point as shown in Figure 2.60 and drag the tangent handle down and to the left, stretching it out to round out the curve. Click (but don't drag) the next point one grid unit directly below the last. Click (but don't drag) a last point horizontally to the left and back on the Y axis.

Step 3   Rename the Spline as Bulb 1. Control-drag a copy of it. Turn off editor visibility for the original, and name the copy Bulb 2.

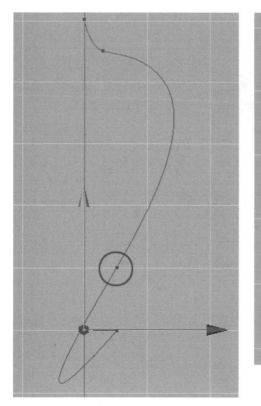

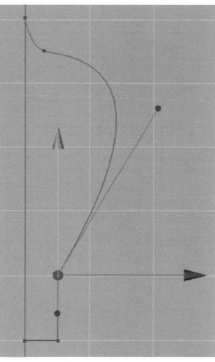

Figure 2.60 Funny Loop

Figure 2.61 Loop Fixed
Oops! What's that funny loop? Go back and click on the offending point (circled in Figure 2.60) to access the tangent handles. Holding down the Shift key, shorten and straighten the lower handle so that the curve coming out of the point becomes a straight line. If you want to avoid those funny loops in the future, you can use the Shift key to independently drag the tangent handle immediately after you have clicked a point but before you let up on the mouse.

Adding Points to a Spline: Lightbulb 2

Step 1 Control-click on the halfway point of first segment (the top one) to add a new point.

Step 2 Hold the Shift key and drag the bottom tangent handle out horizontally to create a rounded curve.

Step 3 Turn off the editor visibility for Bulb 2.

Spline Primitives

The Spline palette also contains powerful ready-made splines which you can use as-is or edit to create legions of different shapes.

Step 1 From the top toolbar, choose Spline>Star. Experiment with changing the values in all the Object Properties boxes. For example, a Points value of 5 would yield a classic 5-pointed star.

Figure 2.62 Spline Bump. Control-clicking on a spline adds a new point, which can be edited for added detail to the spline.

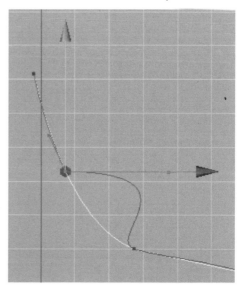

Figure 2.63 Star Possibilities

Now enter 100 for Points, 185 for Inner Radius, and 85 percent for Twist. Whoa! A saw blade.

Step 2   Press the C key to make the Star Spline editable. Switch to the Perspective view. Use the Move tool to select points on the primitive and move them anywhere in the 3D space. Remember, you can also Control-click on these splines to add points and detail. If you want to delete an existing point, just select the point and press the Delete (Backspace) key.

Creating Complex Splines with Create Outline

Step 1   In the Front View, choose Spline>Flower Spline.

Figure 2.64 Flower Spline

Step 2   Press the C key to make the spline editable.

Step 3   From the top menu, choose Structure>Edit Spline>Create Outline.

Step 4   Drag on the flower spline with the tool. After dragging one outline, go back and drag on one or two others. (The separate outlines will remain as one spline object.)

Step 5   Rename Flower as Complex Spline and turn off its visibility for now.

Figure 2.65 A More Complex Spline

Figure 2.66 A Spline Library

On the DVD: All the splines in Chapter 02>C4D Files>Spline Library.c4d on the DVD may be made with the skills you just learned. Turn on their visibility one at a time and practice making them. Save this Library and add your own splines to it for future use.

Importing Splines

CINEMA 4D can import splines from any vector program or custom shapes from Adobe Photoshop. In Chapter 17, you'll learn how. Also, the Internet has a wealth of custom shape libraries and type outlines that slide right into CINEMA 4D and make themselves at home!

On the DVD: For more "Under the Hood" skills, see Chapter 02>EXTRA!EXTRA!>InDepth>More About Splines.

Figure 3.1

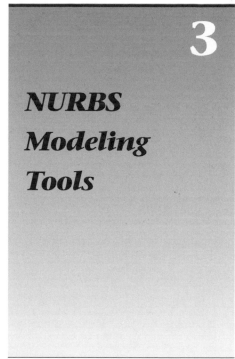

3

NURBS Modeling Tools

I t's time to explore CINEMA 4D's powerful NURBS (Nonuniform Rational B-splines) modeling tools. All but one of these tools generate a new geometry by making a spline or splines a child of the NURBS modeling object. The splines inside this generator define certain profiles of the object and may be changed at any time, giving you serious editing capabilities. In this chapter, you'll be using the NURBS tools to create different parts of an animated box with lots of widgets, lights, and sounds.

The Peephole Box: Extrude NURBS

Step 1 Choose File>New and Save the file as Peephole Box Front in your Models folder (File>Save or Cmd+S /Ctrl+S). Working in the Front view, choose Spline> Rectangle Spline from the top menu. In the Attributes Manager Object Properties, change the Width to 300. Rename the Rectangle as Box Shape.

Step 2 Control-drag a copy of Box Shape in the Objects Manager, and change the Width to 150m and the Height to 75m. Position the new rectangle slightly above the vertical center of the first one, and re-name it Stage Shape.

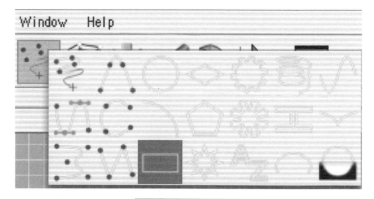

Figure 3.2 Rectangle Spline

Figure 3.3 Stage and Bottom Circle Outlines

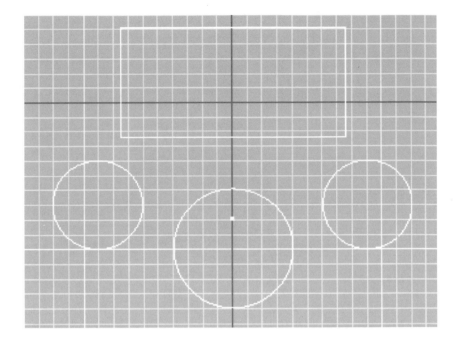

Step 3　Now choose Spline>Circle. Give the Circle a Radius of 40 and center it below the small rectangle. Control-drag two copies of the Circle. Shift-click to select them and enter a Radius of 30m. Position them slightly above and to each side of the first Circle. Use Figure 3.3 and the editor grid lines as a guide for positioning. Name the circles Circle 1, Circle 2, and Circle 3.

Step 4　Shift-click to select all three circles, and press G to Group them. Rename the Group as Bottom Circles. Control-drag a copy of Bottom Circles, and rename the copy as Top Circles. Click the (+) next to Top Circles, and rename the circles inside Circle 4, Circle 5, and Circle 6. Select Top Circles, and use the green handle of the Move tool to position that group of circles above the Stage Shape in the Editor window.

Step 5　With Top Circles still selected, click the Coordinates panel in the Attributes Manager and enter a value of 180º for R.B (Bank) to flip the circles.

Step 6　From the menu above the Objects Manager, choose Objects>Unfold All. Shift-click to select Circles 1 though 6, Stage Shape, and Box Shape. Press the C key to make all objects in the multiple selection editable. Select Box Shape and choose the Points tool. Using the Scale tool, Shift-click to select the bottom two points on the Box Shape spline. Drag the mouse right to left until the bottom of the shape is slightly tapered. Refer to Figure 3.4.

Step 7　Shift-click to select Circles 1 though 6, Stage Shape, and Box Shape again. Choose Functions>Connect. Rename the new spline object Circle as Box Face Template.

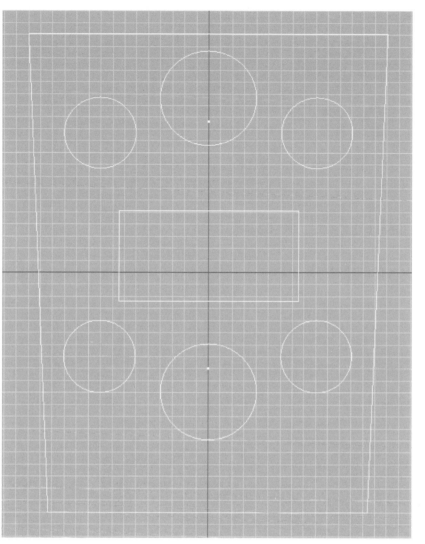

Figure 3.4 Box Face Template

Figure 3.6 Peephole Box Front

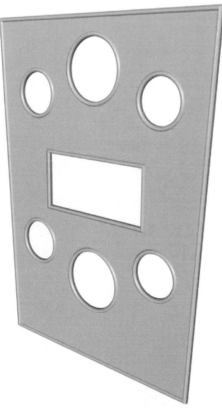

Step 8 Move the mouse to the NURBS tool icon in the top palette, and drag to choose an Extrude NURBS object. Drop the Box Face Template onto the object Extrude NURBS. Rename Extrude NURBS as Box Front.

Figure 3.5 Extrude NURBS

Step 9 With Box Front selected, click the Object panel in the Attributes Manager. Enter 3m in the Movement box on the far right side (the Z value).

Step 10 Click the panel for Caps. In the Start pulldown menu, choose Fillet Cap. Enter 3 for Steps and 5m for Radius. In the Fillet Type pulldown menu, choose Half Circle. Save the File (File>Save or Cmd+S/Ctrl+S).

NURBS Tools at a Glance

NURBS (Nonuniform Rational B-splines) have no polygons of their own but are algorithmically calculated surfaces. Most NURBS generate objects from elements or objects placed inside them.

Figure 3.7 The NURBS Tools

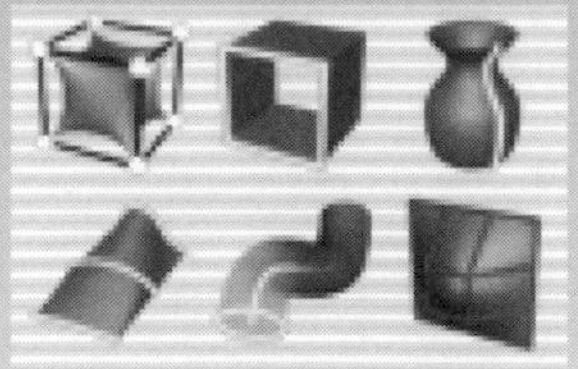

- The HyperNURBS rounds off an object placed inside it into a more curvilinear, organic version of the more geometric original.
- The Extrude NURBS extends a shape as an extrusion, using a 2D object to create a 3D object.

- The Lathe NURBS revolves a profile spline in a rotation around the Y axis to create surfaces. Think thrown pottery or wood turning.
- The Loft NURBS stretches a surface over profile splines or ribs. A single spline will create a flat object, while any number of multiple ribs will create 3D surfaces that change according to their profiles. Loft NURBS may be created from open or closed splines.
- The Sweep NURBS moves a profile spline along the path of another spline. The profile may be scaled as it moves along the path, and the path may be animated to grow.
- The Bezier NURBS is simply a surface defined by X and Y Bezier curves with control points. This is the only NURBS tool that requires no child objects.

Peepholes: Splines inside Splines

CINEMA 4D interprets a spline or multiple splines inside a spline as a hole in the shape. All the splines must first be made editable. Selecting all the splines and choosing Functions>Connect will combine all the splines into a single spline object.

Box Top Decoration: Loft NURBS

Step 1   Choose File>Open and navigate to Chapter 02>C4D Files>Spline Library on the DVD. Copy the Profile for Loft spline using Cmd+C (Ctrl+C). Close the file (File>Close).

Step 2   Choose File>New and working in the Front view, paste the spline with Cmd+V (Ctrl+V). Choose Edit>Frame Scene. Use the green handle of the Move tool to raise the spline so it sits on the X axis, and rotate the spline 90º H (Heading). Choose File>Save or Cmd+S (Ctrl+S) and save the file as Box Top Detail to your Models folder.

Step 3   Control-drag nine copies of the spline. Rename the Splines Profile 1, Profile 2 through Profile 10.

Step 4   Make sure you are in the Model tool. Using the blue Move handle, drag Profile 1 four grid large units to the left. In the Coordinates panel, enter a Rotation P value of –90. Refer to the lefthand spline in Figure 3.8.

Step 5   Select the Profile 2 and drag it to the right side of the first profile. Continue dragging the remaining splines, in numerical order, until they are lined up 1/2 large grid units apart.

Step 6   Select Profile 2 and use the Rotate tool to lean it toward the left side –45º. Shift-click to select Profiles 3, 5, 7, and 9. Select the Scale tool and drag the green Scale handle down until the splines are about half the height of Profile 2.

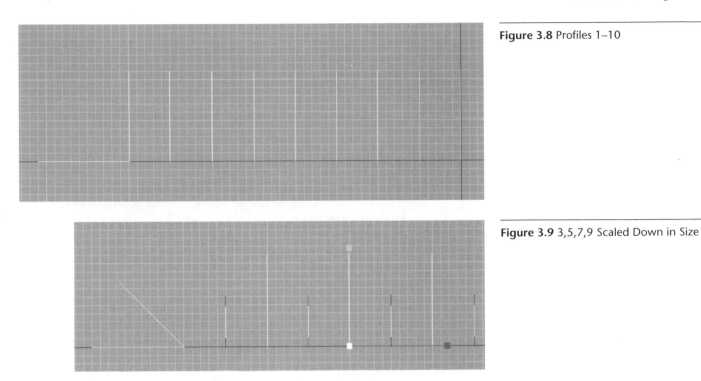

Figure 3.8 Profiles 1–10

Figure 3.9 3,5,7,9 Scaled Down in Size

Step 7 Select Profile 4 and scale it to about one and a half times its original height. Scale Profile 6 to double its original height, Profile 8 to two and a half times the original size and Profile 10 to triple the original size. See Figure 3.10.

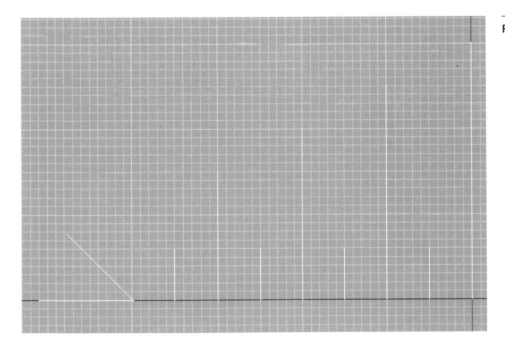

Figure 3.10 Profiles 4,6,8,10 Scaled Up in Size

Figure 3.11 Loft NURBS

Step 8   From the NURBS tool palette, choose a Loft NURBS object. Rename it as Box Top Detail.

Step 9   Starting with Profile 1 and continuing in order, drop the objects Profiles 1 though 10 onto the Loft NURBS. Choose Display>Wireframe.

Step 10   From the Window menu, choose New View Panel. Enlarge the window, choose Gouraud shading and navigate so you have a good view of the model surface. While looking at the model in the new view, work in the wireframe view. Use the blue handle of the Move tool and the Rotate tool to move and rotate the splines so you design the decoration to your liking. This Loft object will be half of the finished decoration, so you may want to rotate the splines all to the left. See Figure 3.12. Save using File> Save or Cmd+S (Ctrl+S).

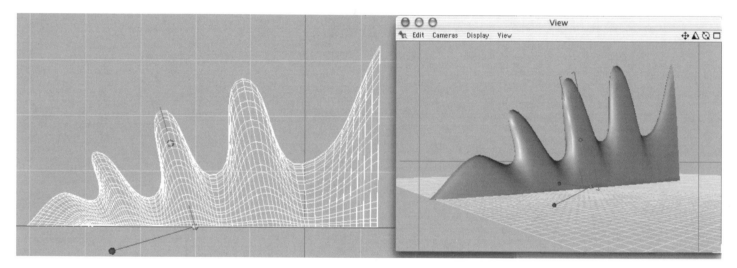

Figure 3.12 The Loft Object in Two Windows. Once a spline has been rotated, its axes are tilted. To move the spline only along the X axis, choose the World Coordinate System icon from the top toolbar. Then choose the Move tool and make sure the X lock on the top toolbar is the only one unlocked.

Figure 3.13 World Coordinates

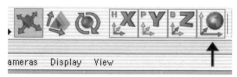

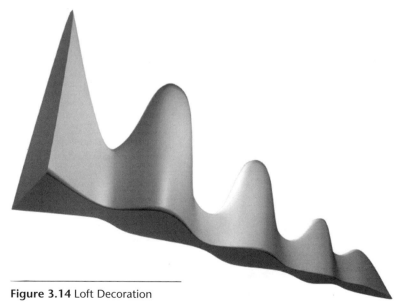

Figure 3.14 Loft Decoration

Curly Glass Tubes: The Sweep NURBS

Step 1   Choose File>New and Save the file as Curly Glass Tube in your Models folder (File>Save or Cmd+S/Ctrl+S).

Step 2   In the Front view, choose Spline>Helix from the top toolbar. In the Attributes Manager Coordinates panel, enter–90º in the R.H box and press return to rotate the Helix on the Heading. In Object Properties, enter a Start and End Radius of 100, an End Angle of 1450, a Height of 500m, a Height Bias of 25 percent and Subdivisions of 20.

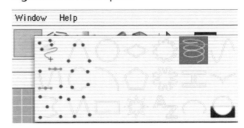

Figure 3.15 Helix Spline

◆ *Tip:* Want a quick way to figure out what all these Helix settings do? Make a helix, then drag the small black arrows next to each of the values while watching the effects realtime in the Perspective view.

Figure 3.16 Helix Settings

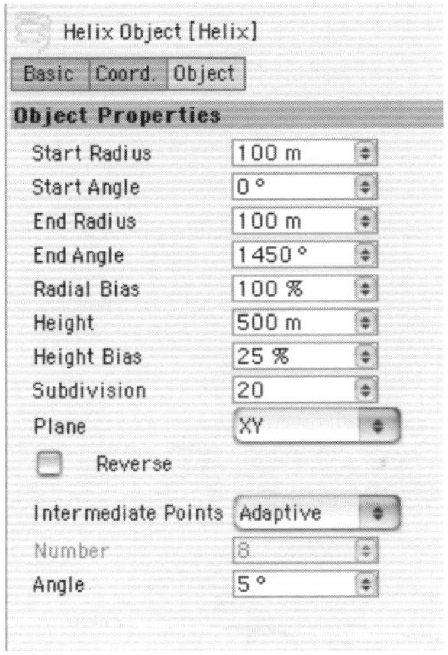

Step 3   With the Helix selected, press the C key to make it editable. Choose the Points tool and the Move tool. Hold down the Ctrl key and click a new point on the left side of the Helix, three grid units down and three grid units to the left. Move the second point more to the left and use the tangent handles to round out the curve.

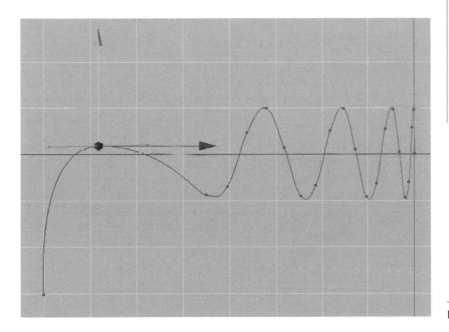

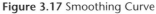

Figure 3.17 Smoothing Curve

Step 4   Click the Editor window to make it active, and press Cmd+A (Ctrl+A) to select all the points on the Helix. Choose Structure>Mirror. Click the point on the far right end of the Helix. (If your mirroring flips on a different axis and does not end up looking like Figure 3.18, use the Undo command and try again until you click on just the right spot. For future reference, notice that in the Active Tool tab you can set the mirroring to occur on any axis or coordinate system.)

Figure 3.18 Mirrored Points

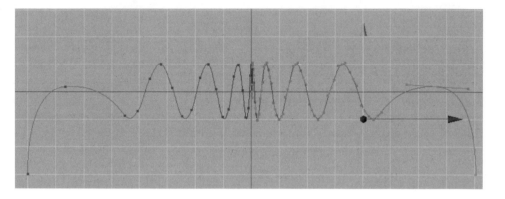

Step 5   Choose Spline>Circle and give the Circle a Radius of 15. You can make the tube any thickness you want at any time by scaling the circle.

Figure 3.19 Sweep NURBS

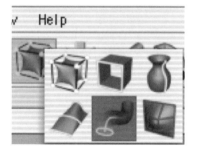

Step 6   Choose NURBS>Sweep NURBS. Drop the path spline in first (the Helix) and then drop the cross section profile (the Circle).

Step 7   Rename the Sweep NURBS as Coil One. Control-drag a copy of it and name the copy Coil Two. Choose the Model tool and the Move tool. In the Top view, move Coil Two in front of Coil One.

Step 8   Choose Display>Isoparm. With the Points tool chosen, select the Helix inside each coil and use the Move tool to carefully edit the point positions and tangents so that the coils look smooth in top view. Note that deleting some points may help you structure a smoother coil.

Step 9   Still in Points, edit Coil Two to look slightly different from Coil One. Remove some points, move some others, and then switch to the Model tool and scale the whole tube to be about 85 percent smaller than Coil One. Save the file (File>Save or Cmd+S/Ctrl+S), then choose File>Save As and save a copy as Animated Tube. Leave the animated Tube file open for the next exercise.

Figure 3.20 Coil Differences Front View

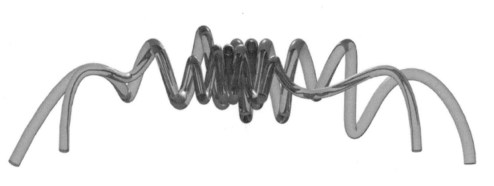

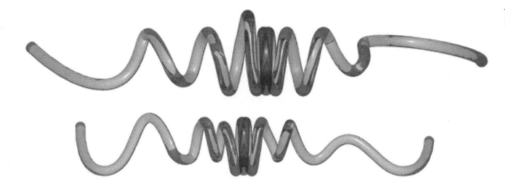

Figure 3.21 Coil Differences Top View

Time for a Sideshow: Animating Sweep NURBS

Step 1   Working in the file Animated Tube, delete the Coil Two object, and select Coil One.

Step 2   Make sure the current time is at 0 frames.

Step 3   In the Attributes Manager Object Properties, enter 0 percent in the box for Growth. Command-click on the word Growth and slide to Animation>Add Keyframe.

Step 4   Move the current time to the end of the animation.

Step 5   Enter 100 percent in the Growth box and set a keyframe. Play the Animation.

Remember that this spline was originally mirrored, which accounts for the interesting growth from one end and then the other. When the growth of a non-mirrored spline is animated, the Sweep NURBS simply grows from the beginning of the path spline to the end. If you want the spline to grow from the opposite end, select the path spline and choose Structure>Edit Spline>Reverse Sequence.

> **3D Famous Saying**
>
> "Ten percent of your time will be spent making something, and 90 percent of your time will be spent making it look dirty, full of dinks and dents and otherwise like it's an inhabitant of real life." In other words, you have to work hard to keep 3D models from looking "too perfect." Coil Two is a good example. It needs some aberrations and differences to keep it from being just a stale copy of Coil One. See what you can do.

Antique Lightbulbs: Lathe NURBS

Step 1   Choose File>Open and navigate to Chapter 02>C4D Files>Spline Library on the DVD. Click the (+) next to Lightbulbs and select Bulb 2. Press Cmd+C (Ctrl+C) to copy the spline. Leave the file open.

Step 2   Choose File>New and working in the Front view, paste the spline with Cmd+V (Ctrl+V). Save the new file as Antique Bulbs to your Models folder (File>Save As). Choose Edit>Frame Scene.

Notice how the spline is positioned in relation to the Y Axis, and that the Bulb's object axis is on the Y axis. A Lathe NURBS will always

Figure 3.22 Lathe NURBS

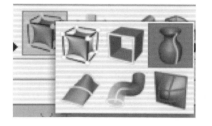

Figure 3.23 Rendered Bulb. Ouch! That point on the top of the bulb is too sharp. The most awesome thing about NURBS tools is that splines used by the the NURBS generator may always be edited later, so you can rethink shapes at any time.

Figure 3.24 Editing Bulb Top

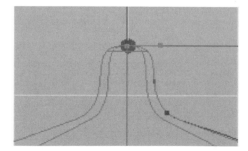

be created by spinning a profile around the Y, so any spline intended as a lathe profile must be positioned properly in regard to the Y center of rotation.

Step 3 Choose NURBS>Lathe NURBS. Drop the name Bulb 2 onto the name Lathe NURBS. Rename Lathe NURBS as Bulb Glass.

Step 4 Click the (+) next to the name Bulb Glass and select Bulb 2. Choose the Points tool, and click the top point on the spline. From the top menu, choose Structure>Edit Spline>Soft Interpolation. Drag the right tangent handle out to the right horizontally to make a more friendly topknot for this bulb.

Step 5 If you left the Spline Library file open, select it from the list at the bottom of the Window menu. (If not, open it again as in Step 1.) Select the spline Bulb Base Spline Narrow from the Lightbulbs object and press Cmd+C (Ctrl+C) to copy it.

Step 6 Return to the Antique Bulb file via the list in the Window Menu. Paste the spline (Cmd+V/Ctrl+V), and make sure the Model tool is chosen since you want to manipulate the spline as a whole. Use the Move and Scale tools to position the Bulb Base spline at the bottom of the Bulb Glass. You may want to scale the base on just one axis to make it fit this bulb.

Step 7 Create a new Lathe NURBS and drop the Bulb Base spline into it. Rename the new Lathe NURBS as Bulb Base.

Step 8 The bulb needs some inner workings. For now, (Leaving the Antique Bulb file open) choose File>Open and navigate to Chapter 03>C4D Files>Filaments. Choose a Filament and copy it with Cmd-C (Ctrl-C). Choose File>Close and press Cmd-V (Ctrl-V) to paste the Filament of your choice into the Antique Bulb file. Scale and position the Filament inside the bulb.

Select the chosen Filament, Bulb Glass, and Bulb Base and press the G key to group them. Rename the Group as Antique Bulb 1.

Step 9 Control-drag a copy of Antique Bulb 1 and rename the copy Antique Bulb 2. Turn off editor visibility for the first bulb. Open the hierarchy of Antique Bulb 2, and (using the points tool) edit the profile of the Bulb 2 spline so that the bulb is a totally different shape. Control-click on the spline to add points or move and adjust the tangent handles of existing points. Lengthen the base to differentiate it from the first base.

Step 10 Use the Model tool and Move tool to move the new bulb to the side of the first one, and turn visibility back on for Antique Bulb 1 so you can compare the bulbs and edit them further. Save with File>Save or Cmd+S (Ctrl+S).

Figure 3.25 New Bulb Top

Figure 3.26 Bulb Base

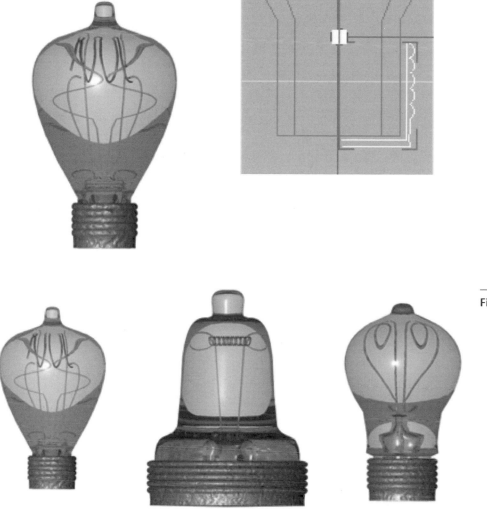

Figure 3.27 Antique Bulbs

● *Springboard!* You will need a variety of Antique bulbs for the Peephole Box. Make them all in the Antique Bulbs file, using visibility to isolate individual bulbs as you work on them. Make some of your own sets of Inner Parts using Bezier Splines, Helix splines, and other basic modeling you have already mastered. Invent a bulb with spinning parts. (You could reuse the Galaxy Ball from Chapter 1.) There are some more bulb and base splines in the Spline Library for your use, and you can create more of your own. Research antique light bulbs on the web for ideas.

On the DVD: See the Library of finished bulbs in Chapter 03>EXAMPLE>Antique Bulbs.

The Stage Curtain: The Bezier NURBS

Figure 3.28 Bezier NURBS

Step 1 Choose File>New and save the file as Stage Curtains into your Models folder (File>Save or Cmd+S/Ctrl+S). Work in the Front view.

Step 2 From the top toolbar, choose NURBS>Bezier NURBS.

Step 3 In the Attributes Manager Object Properties, enter 15 for Subdivision X.

Step 4 Click the Coordinates panel. With the current time at 0 frames, enter a value of 1.25 for S.X and Command-drag (or right-click) to Animation>Add Keyframe. Go to the end of the animation, change the S.X value to 0.25 and set a keyframe.

    Play the animation. By animating the scale of the Bezier NURBS on the X axis, you created the basic motion for opening the curtains.

Step 5 Press the C key. Select the Object Axis tool and the Move tool. Move the axis for the Bezier NURBS to the far left side of the object.

Step 6 With the current time at 0, choose the Points tool. Use the Rectangle selection tool and, skipping the first column (starting from either side), drag a rectangular selection over every other vertical column of points while holding down the Shift key.

Figure 3.29 Rectangular Point Selections

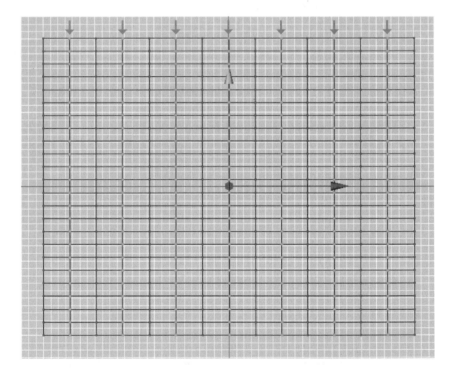

Step 7 Switch to the Perspective view, but angle the view so you are facing the curtain. Choose the Move tool and hold down the Cmd key (Right

Mousebutton). Move the mouse from left to right until the Z value is about 50.

Step 8 Choose NURBS>HyperNURBS and drop the Bezier NURBS into it. Rename the HyperNURBS as Curtain.

Step 9 Choose a Symmetry object from the Array tool palette. Give the Symmetry object a mirror plane of ZY. Drop Curtain into it. Rename the Symmetry object Curtains. Select the Curtain inside Curtains.

Step 10 Make sure the current time is at 0 frames. Using the Model tool and the red handle of the Move tool, position the Bezier NURBS (inside the Curtain object) so that its axis is on the outside of the Curtains, and the curtains meet in the middle.

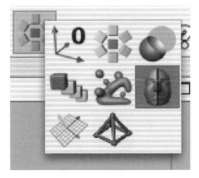

Figure 3.30 Symmetry Object

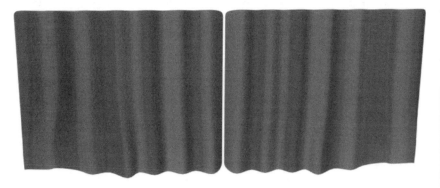

Play the animation again by pressing the Play button or the F8 key. The motion of the curtains looks stiff and mechanical. Later you can use the Magnet tool, deformers or some F-Curve magic magic to naturalize them a bit!

Figure 3.31 Stage Curtains

Figure 3.32 Cube for Sides

Putting It All Together:
The Peephole Box

Step 1 Choose File>Open and open the file Peephole Box Front.c4d from your Models folder. Choose File>Save As and save a new copy of the file as Peephole Box.

Step 2 Choose Objects>Unfold All from the menu over the Objects Manager. Control-drag a copy of Box Shape. Choose NURBS>Extrude NURBS and drop the copy of Box Shape into the new Extrude NURBS at the top of the list. Rename the new Extrude NURBS as Box Back. Use the blue Move handle to pull the Box Back to about 50 on the Z. (The depth will need to accommodate the bulbs you have created.)

Step 3 Choose Primitive>Cube. Adjust the orange parametric handles so that the cube fits just inside the Box Front and is the correct depth to lie between the Box Front and Back.

Figure 3.33 Peephole Box

Step 4   With the Cube still selected, press the C key. Choose the Polygons tool and click on the front polygon of the cube. Press Delete (Backspace).

Step 5   Place the Antique Bulbs you made inside and behind Circles 1–6. Position the Curly Glass Tubes above and below the Stage, and insert the Curtains behind the Stage opening. (Choose File>Recent Files to easily locate these files you were just working on.)

Step 6   Open the Box Top Detail.c4d file. Copy and paste the Box Top Detail into Peephole Box file. Create a Symmetry object with an ZY mirror plane and rename the Symmetry object Top Decoration. Drop the Box Top Detail into the Top Decoration Symmetry Object and place the decoration on the top of the Cube, down behind the Box Front.

Step 7   Create your own materials for the box and its associated parts., or open the file Materials>Peephole Materials on the DVD in the Browser and use those. After you learn BodyPaint in Chapter 16, the front of this box would make a great canvas.

Step 8   Save using File>Save or Cmd+S (Ctrl+S). We will be using this box in other chapters.

● ***Springboard!*** Time to go off on your own. Using the modeling and construction skills you've learned, create your own personal touches for this basic box. See the examples on the DVD. Wacky dials and gauges, cranks, audio speakers, or a smokestack for spewing glitter. Go for it!

On the DVD: See Chapter 03>EXAMPLES for Peephole Box examples.

The Amphibber: The Power of HyperNURBS

What is an Amphibber? This cartoon car is an amphibious vehicle that spews incincere fibs out of the front horn. The ugly truth sputters out of the back horn as it rolls past.

Forming a Cartoon Car Body

Step 1   Choose File>New and save the file as Amphibber into your Models folder (File>Save or Cmd+S/Ctrl+S). Perspective view is fine for now.

Step 2   Choose Primitive>Cube. In Object Properties, enter 200 for Size.X, 100 for Size.Y, and 500 for Size.Z. Give the Cube three Segments on X, three Segments on Y, and seven Segments on Z. Press Return (Enter). Choose

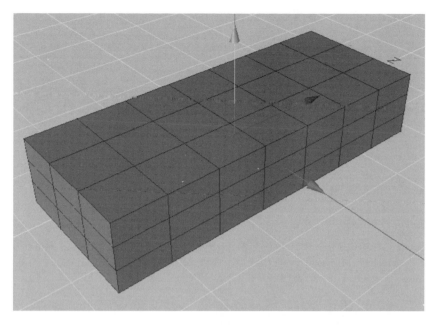

Figure 3.34 The "Starting Block"

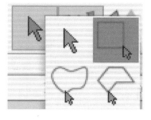

Figure 3.35 Rectangle Selection Tool

NURBS>HyperNURBS and drop the Cube inside. Name the HyperNURBS object Body. Select the Cube inside the Body object.

Step 3 Press the C key to make the Cube editable and choose the Polygons tool.

Step 4 Switch to the Top view. Choose the Rectangle selection tool, and in the Active Tool Manager, make sure Only Select Visible Objects is unchecked. Choose the Points tool. Select the top five rows of points. In the Coordinates Manager, enter 190 in the box for Size Z and press Return. See Figure 3.36.

Step 5 Now select the second and third row of points from the bottom. Enter 125m in the Size Z box and press Return

Figure 3.37 Polys Proportioned

Figure 3.36 Top Polys Condensed

(Enter). In the Z Position box, enter –125. Use Figure 3.37 as a guide for the proportion of the polygons.

◆*Tips:* Is "Press Return (Enter)" getting to be a habit now? Let's save some page space by making that an assumed part of entering values.

Heads Up! It's easy to enter values in the wrong Coordinates column. Always double check before entering values that you are in the correct column. A Size value in a Position box, or vice versa, will wreck havoc on the basic shape.

Step 6   With the Cube still selected, switch to the Perspective view. Choose the Polygons tool and the Move tool. Shift-click to select the polys shown in Figure 3.38. Enter a Size X of 30.

Figure 3.38 Center Hood Polys Scaled

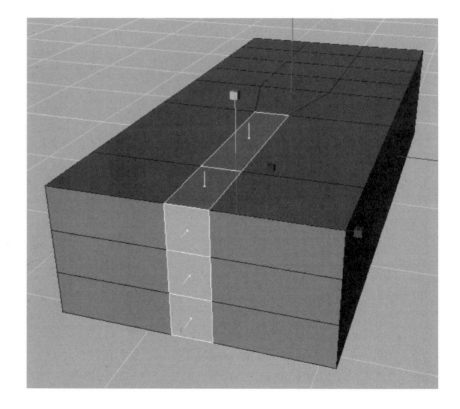

Step 7   Now select the polys shown in Figure 3.39. Press the D Key and enter a value of 15m for Offset in the Active Tool Manager.

◆*Tip:* Be sure to press Cmd+S (Ctrl+S) to save the file frequently.

Step 8   Press I for Extrude Inner, enter an Offset value of 25m, and make sure Preserve Groups is checked. In the Coordinates Manager, enter a Position Y value of 85.

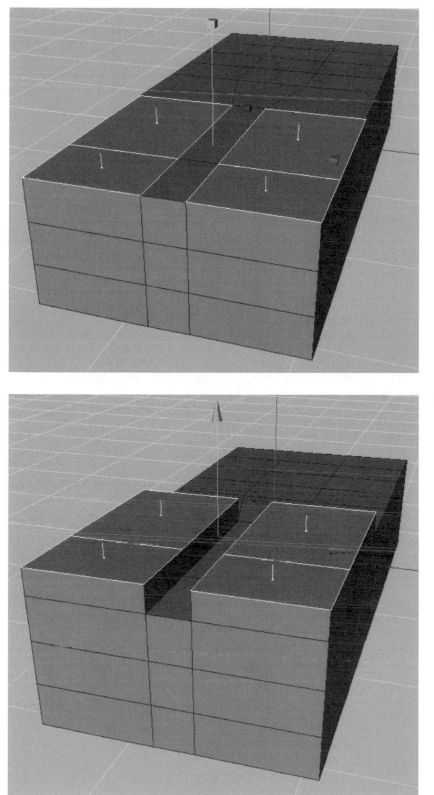

Figure 3.39 Front Hood Polys

Figure 3.40 Front Hood Polys Extruded

Step 9 Select the polys shown in Figure 3.41. Press I for Extrude Inner and in the Active Tool Manager, enter an Offset of 10. With the same polys still selected, press the D key and enter an Offset value of –50.

Figure 3.41 Seat Polys

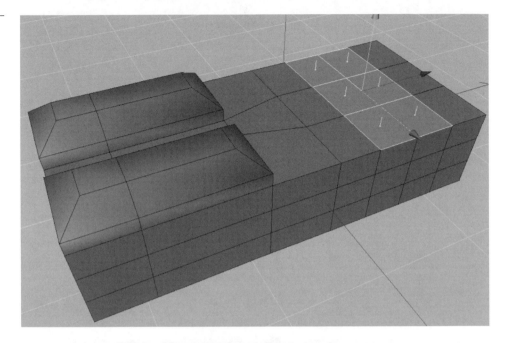

Figure 3.42 Seat Polys Down

Figure 3.43 HyperNURBS Off

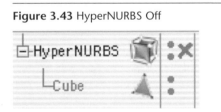

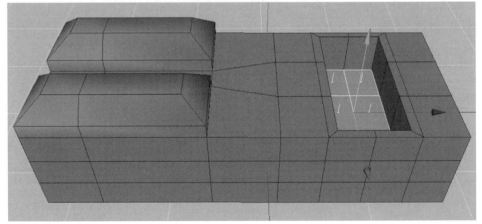

Figure 3.44 Starting Polys for Windshield

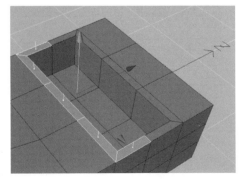

Use the green check mark to the right of the HyperNURBS name in the Object manager to turn the HyperNURBS off when you need to see the polygons clearly.

Step 10 Select the polys shown in Figure 3.44. Press D and drag the mouse left to right to raise the windshield. Round out the windshield by moving the polys shown in Figure 3.45 toward the front of the car. Use the red handle of the Rotate tool to lay the windshield back about –15º. Use the red handle of the Rotate tool to pitch the end polys shown in Figure 3.46 over toward the front of the car, and move them slightly forward.

Figure 3.45 Front and Center Polys Moved Forward

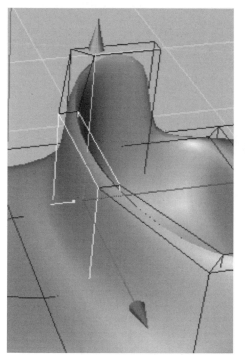

Figure 3.46 Windshield Sides Tilted Forward

Figure 3.47 Hood Polys Selected

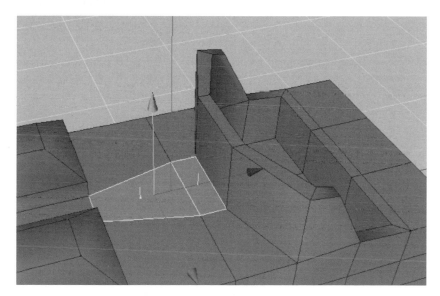

Figure 3.48 Center of Windshield Raised

Step 11 Select the polys shown in Figure 3.47. Enter a *Y Position* value of *75*.

Step 12 Select the top front poly of the windshield shown in Figure 3.48. Use the green handle of the Move tool to raise it up so the contour of the windshield is more rounded. Save by choosing File>Save or pressing Cmd+S (Ctrl+S).

Finishing the Front End

Step 1   Select the polys shown in Figure 3.49. Enter a Size Y value of 50.

Figure 3.49 Front Polys Selection 1

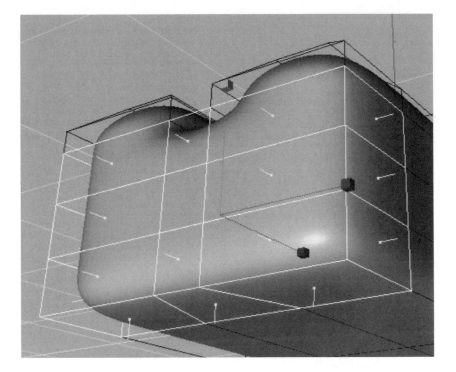

Step 2   Select the polys shown in Figure 3.50. Enter a SizeX value of 150.

Figure 3.50 Front Polys Selection 2

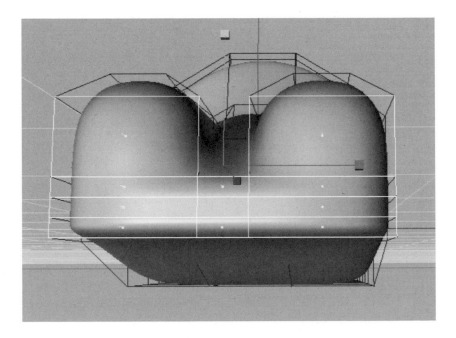

Step 3 Select the large poly on the right front (Figure 3.51 and enter a value of 50 for X Position. Then select the poly in the same place on the left and give it a value of –50 for X Position.

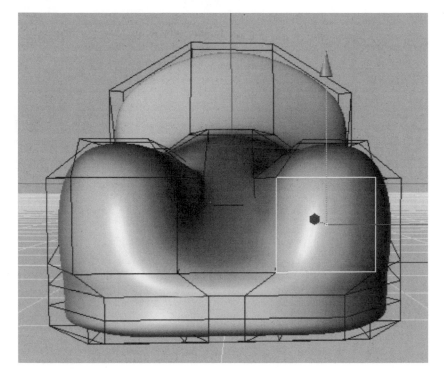

Figure 3.51 Move Right Poly

Step 4 Continue to Shift-click to select points and polys to shape the front end as you like. Arrange three polys on the front into a grille shape as in Figure 3.52.

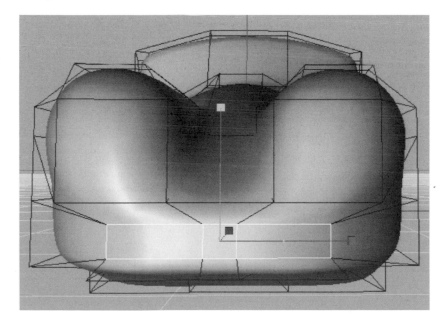

Figure 3.52 Grille Shape

◆*Tip:* To round off boxy corners, face the corner in Perspective view. Holding down the Cmd key (Right Mousebutton), move the mouse gently right to left to push the points in and soften the corner. This also works with polys and edges.

Figure 3.53 Facing Corner Points

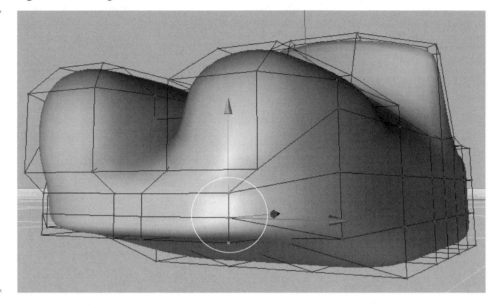

●*Springboard!* Save the copy of the basic Amphibber you have so far (File>Save or Cmd+S/Ctrl+S), then choose File>Save As to save some copies for practicing the pushing, pulling, scaling, and rotating of points, edges, and polys on the mesh inside the Body HyperNURBS object. The fine-tuning of the Amphibber design is up to you. Remember that any single point, edge, or poly (or selected sets of these elements) may be moved, scaled, or rotated to sculpt the surface.

Overriding HyperNURBS Influence

At times in the design process, you'll want to soften or even eliminate the rounding power of the HyperNURBS on the surface. Hold down the period (.) key as you drag on a point, edge, or polygon. The drag distance determines how much the element will ignore the HyperNURBS rounding. Use this technique when you want sharp points and edges to emerge from an otherwise rounded surface.

Figure 3.54 Controlling HN Influence

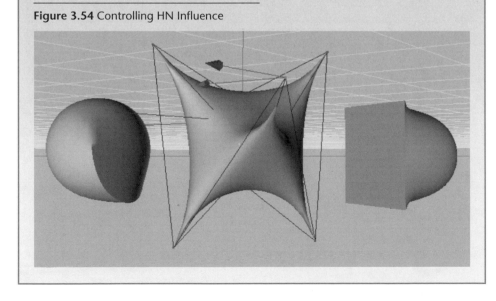

Bringing Up the Rear

Step 1 Working in the Side View, choose the Rectangle selection tool and make sure Only Select Visible Elements is unchecked. Choose the Points tool.

Step 2 Drag the rectangle over the three columns of points on the right, and use the blue Move handle to lengthen the seat. Then select only the far right column of points and move them back further as in Figure 3.56.

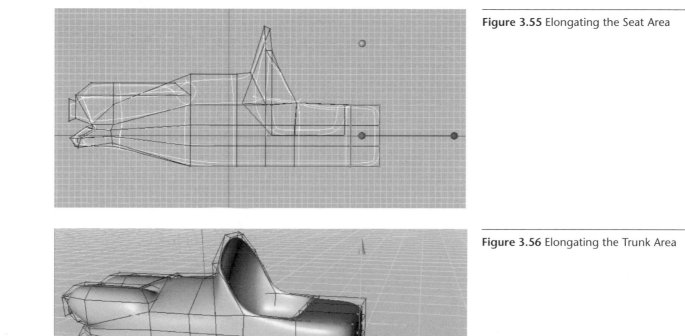

Figure 3.55 Elongating the Seat Area

Figure 3.56 Elongating the Trunk Area

Step 3 With the end points still selected, scale the set of points to taper the back of the car. Select the middle poly. Move it out slightly on the Z axis and lift it to round the back contour.

Step 4 Select the polygon on the top of the back section and pull it up with the Move tool to round the top.

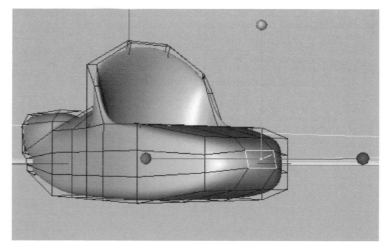

Figure 3.57 Back Rounded

Step 5   In the Top view, select the Points shown in Figure 3.58. Scale them closer together so that the outer polygons become more rectangular. Switch back to Perspective view and the Polygon tool.

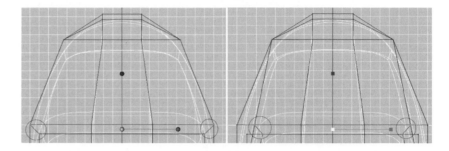

Figure 3.58 Points Selected/Points Scaled

Step 6   Select the outer Polygons on the top of the rear section. Press I to Extrude Inner, using an Offset value of 15m. Shift-click to select the new outer polys and press D to Extrude them up into tail fins.

With both tail fin polys still selected, scale them on the X axis to pull them together. Use the Move, Scale, and Rotate tools to adjust their shape and angle.

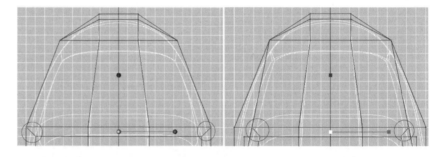

Figure 3.59 Outer Polys

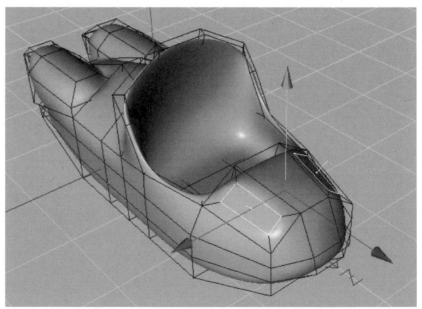

Figure 3.60 Tail Fins Bases

All in the Details

Step 1 Select the polys shown in Figure 3.61 and extrude them down inside the car (but not beyond the bottom). Select the polys shown in Figure 3.63 and 3.64. Delete them, since they will not be seen.

Figure 3.61 Footrest Selected

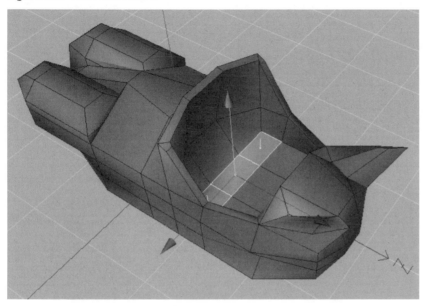

Figure 3.63 Inside Windshield Selected

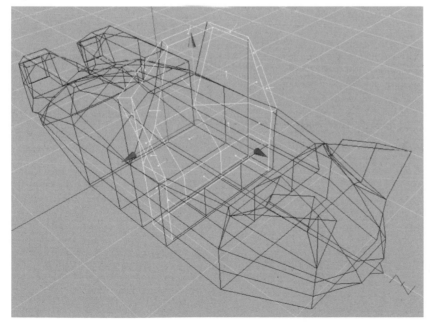

Figure 3.62 Footrest Dropped

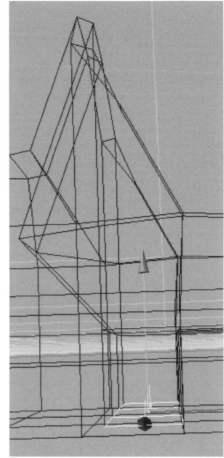

Figure 3.64 Inside Polys, Isolated View

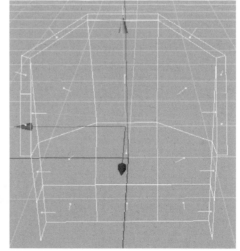

Figure 3.65 Outer Rim

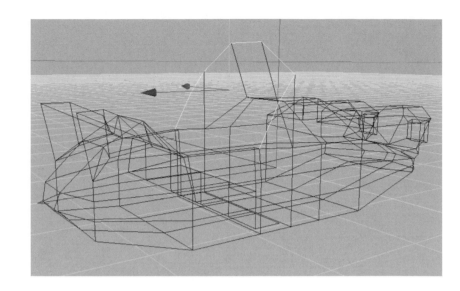

Step 2 Choose the Edge tool and the Move tool. Shift-click to select the outer rim of the windshield.

Choose Structure>Edge Selection to Spline. Choose Spline>Circle and give the circle a Radius of 2. Choose NURBS>Sweep NURBS. Drop

Figure 3.66 Matching the Corner

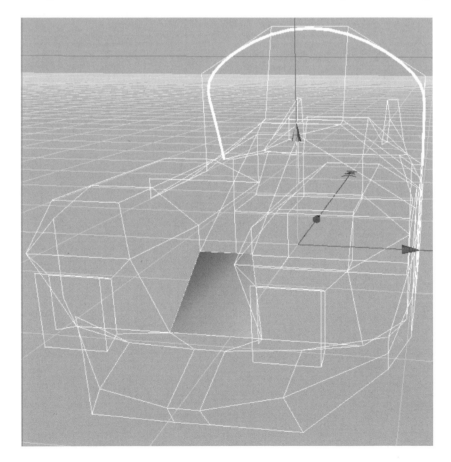

Figure 3.67 Poly for the Horn

the object named Cube Spline first into the Sweep NURBS, then the Circle. If necessary, adjust points on the Cube. Spline or use the period (.) key to adjust the HyperNURBS mesh to meet the trim. See Overriding HyperNURBS Influence (Figure 3.54).

Step 3   Rename the Sweep NURBS as Windshield Trim. In the Objects Manager, drop the name windshield Trim onto the name Cube inside the Body object hierarchy.

Step 4   Select the Cube object inside Body. Using the Move tool and Polygon tool, select the poly shown in Figure 3.67.

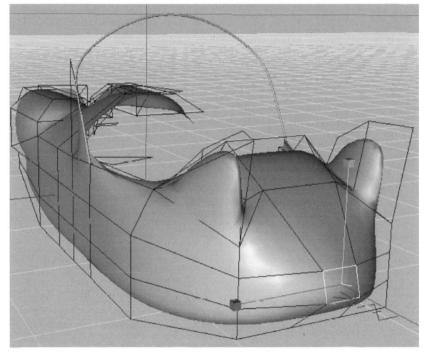

Figure 3.68 Backface Culling

Bogging Down?

As your model becomes more complex, you'll notice that the screen redraw begins to drag. These tricks will help will speed things up.

- Wireframe or Isoparm display will redraw faster than Gouraud.
- In the Display menu, uncheck Disable Backface Culling. This prevents the editor from drawing elements on the back of objects. Also in the Display menu, the Level of Detail may be lowered.

- Again, the HyperNURBS generator can be completely off while working the Polygons.
- In the Object Properties of a selected HyperNURBS object, you can enter subdivision settings for the Editor and the Renderer. The higher the number, the more smooth the surface, but the smoothness has a price: high memory usage and slower screen redraw and rendering. If the display begins to drag, keep Editor subdivision low (1 or 2) and ignore the blocky contours in favor of speed.

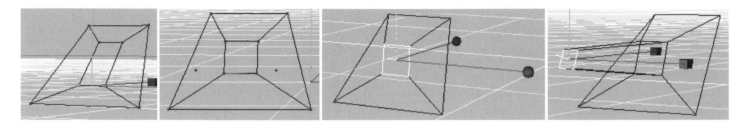

Figure 3.69 Steps for Horn

Step 5 Perform an Extrude Inner and edit the points of the new inner poly so that it is square. Rotate the square poly on the pitch so it faces forward. Extrude it out, then scale it down.

Figure 3.71 Horn, Back Poly

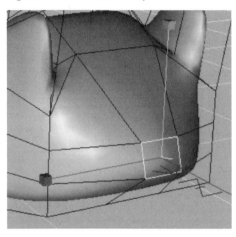

Figure 3.70 Horn Finished

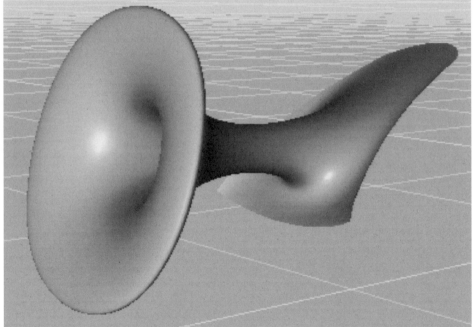

Figure 3.72 Back Horn Finished

Step 6 Now press I for Extrude Inner again, but move the mouse left to right to create a horn shape. Use the Move tool to pull the horn out slightly on the Z axis. Press I again, but this time drag right to left. Press D to Extrude the horn opening back into the base of the horn. Use the Move tool to raise the poly so it falls within the walls of the horn stem. If the face of the Horn shape is too faceted around the edge for a close-up view, choose Structure>Subdivide (checking the HyperNURBS Subdivide box) before proceeding to make the inner opening of the horn.

Step 7 Repeat Steps 5 and 6 to make a smaller horn on the back of the Amphibber. Select the poly shown in Figure 3.70 to begin.

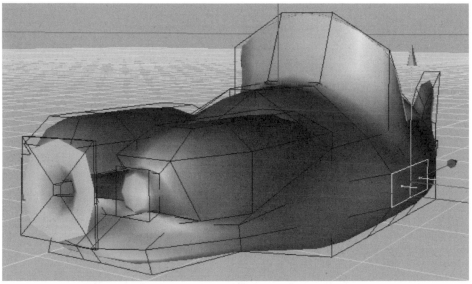

Figure 3.73 Widening the Body

Step 8 Add some shape to the vehicle by pulling out some of the polys on each side.

Step 9 Select Primitive>Torus and Primitive>Sphere to create a headlight and a rim. Make both objects editable (by pressing the C key), and use the blue Scale tool to flatten them. Position the Torus around the Sphere and Group them, renaming the Group as Headlight. Make a copy of the Headlight and position both headlights on the front of the Amphibber. You may want to make a more detailed headlight and rim later.

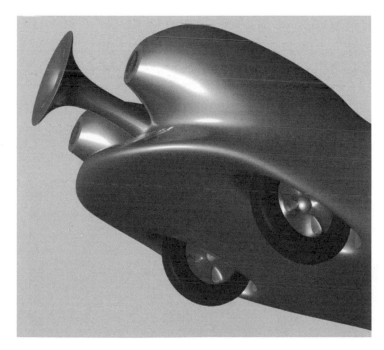

Figure 3.74 Headlight and Rim

Figure 3.75 Optional Wheels

Converting NURBS Objects Back to Polygonal Meshes

Occasionally, you may want to convert an object made with any of the NURBS tools back into a polygonal mesh. Press the C key to change the object itself back to a mesh, or choose Functions>Current State to Object to create a copy of the NURBS object that is a polygonal mesh. This will come in handy later to freeze copies of animated or deformed objects in a particular state. The icons to the right of objects in the Objects Manager identify their state.

Figure 3.76 HyperNURBS and Polys Made with Functions>Current State to Object

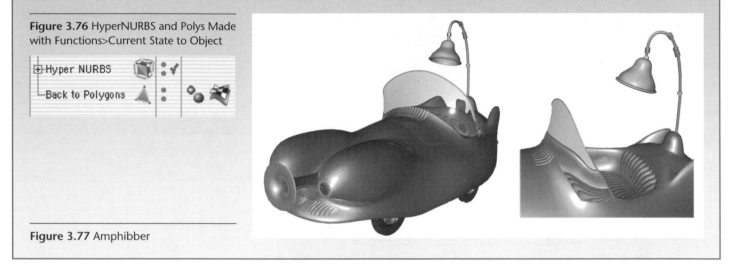

Figure 3.77 Amphibber

● *Springboard!* Use the modeling skills learned in Chapters 1 and 2 to create lathed rims for the headlights, a grille for the car front, tufted seats, rearview mirrors, trim for the side, wheels, steering wheel and dashboard, or other details as you design your personal Amphibber. Even though the interior details and wheels are not necessary if the car will only be seen from the outside, you may want to make a more detailed version as a learning experience.

On the DVD: In Chapter 03>C4D Files>Amphibber, you'll find example models of Amphibbers and Accessories.

In MATERIALS>Amphibber you'll find some useful materials. There are also materials in the Example folders that you can copy or check their Edit boxes for help in making your own materials.

The Mesh Surgery plug-in offers major enhancements to the modeling process. See the URL for the Demo download in Chapter 03>EXTRA!EXTRA!>Resources.

● *Springboard!* Now that you have some basic modeling and construction skills, try some complex models like the Locomotive Engine in Figure 3.78.

Figure 3.78 Union Pacific 4-8-8-4 "Bigboy" by Darrin Woods

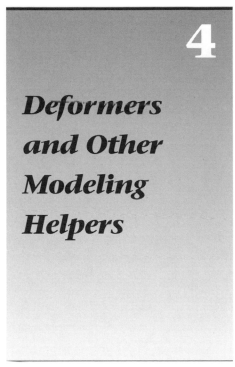

Figure 4.1

Deformers and Other Modeling Helpers

4

Figure 4.3 Pyramid Twisted

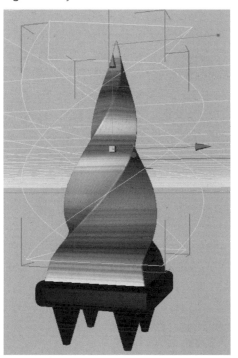

T he plot thickens—in this chapter you'll add modeling helpers to your toolbox and enliven your creative repertoire.

Lively Props: Bend and Twist Deformers

Step 1 Choose File>Open and navigate to Chapter 04>C4D Files>Pyramid Prop>PyramidProp.c4d. Choose File>Save As and save the file as Pyramid Prop in your Models folder.

Step 2 From the top toolbar, choose Deformers>Twist Deformation. Drop the object Twist onto the object Pyramid, so the deformer is a child of the mesh. With Twist selected in the Objects Manager, enter 415m in the middle Size column (Y) under Object Properties. Leave the Mode as Limited. Drag the small black arrows next to angle up and

Figure 4.2 Twist Deformer

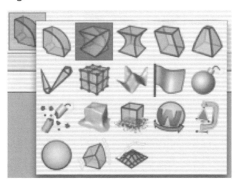

95

Figure 4.4 Bend Deformer

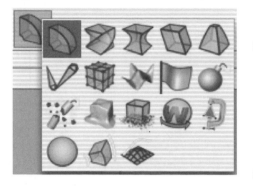

Figure 4.5 Deformer Hierarchy

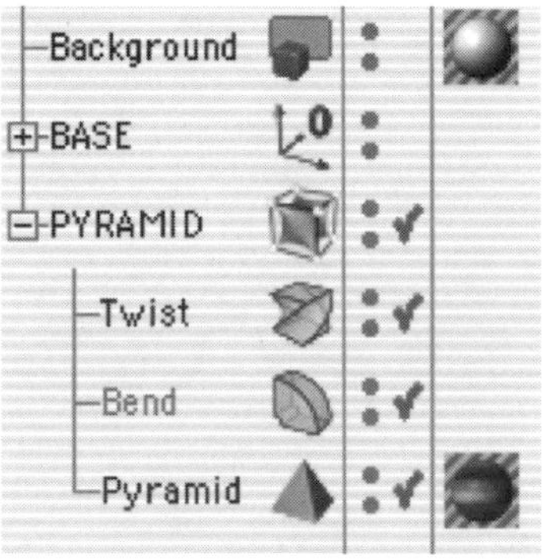

Figure 4.6 Pyramid Bent and Twisted

down and see how the twist is affected. You could alternately drag the orange interactive handle to control the twist. Now type 300 in the box for Angle in Object Properties.

Step 3 Now choose the Model tool and the Move tool. Make sure all X, Y, and Z locks are free. Move the mouse in the Editor window and see how the position of the deformer affects the pyramid. Now choose the Rotate tool and rotate the red and blue handles. The pyramid could be easily made to dance back and forth just by keyframing the position or rotation of the deformer. Press Cmd+Z (Ctrl+Z) to undo the moves and rotations, but leave the Twist at 300º.

Step 4 Choose Deformer>Bend Deformation and drop the object Bend on the object Pyramid. In the Hierarchy, pick up Bend and reposition it under Twist. It will behave better in this order.

Step 5 Locate the orange interactive handle for the Bend deformer in the editor window. You may need to choose Isoparm display to see it clearly.

Step 6 Choose File>Save As and save several copies to experiment with animation. On your first try, select the word Twist. At frame 0, Command-click the word Angle, enter 0 for the value and drag over to Animation>Add Keyframe. Forward the timeline to 50 frames, change the Angle to 300, and set a keyframe. Play the animation. Now select the Bend, and keyframe positive and negative Strength values at different points in time. Go back to frame 0 and choose the Model and Move tools. At 25 and 50 frames, move the Twist Deformer cage so the pyramid sways from side to side and set keyframes by Cmd-clicking (Right-clicking) on the P.X values in the Attributes Manager Coordinates Panel.

As you combine the keyframing of different deformer attributes, position, rotation, and scale you'll find this stiff pyramid is capable of infinite organic moves. Note two adjustments made to the original Pyramid that are enhancing smooth deformation: 1) Segments for the Pyramid were increased in Object Properties, and 2) A Phong Tag was assigned to smooth the appearance of the surface. For smooth motion, you may want to make the animation longer and avoid drastic changes that are too close together in time.

On the DVD: See Chapter 04>MOVIES/STILLS>Deformers for example movies with deformers in action. Also see Chapter 04>EXTRA!EXTRA! for more examples of Deformers.

A Lump in the Pipe: Bulge Deformer

Step 1 Choose File>Open and navigate to Chapter 02>C4DFiles>PforPipe on the DVD. Choose File>Save As and save the file as PforPipeBulge in your Models folder.

The Basics of Deformers

- Deformers are made a child of the object you want to deform.
- For successful deformation, the target object needs a sufficient number of subdivisions.
- Deformers work on Primitives, Polygonal Meshes, Groups—even Splines.
- To interactively edit a Deformer object, make sure you have the Deformer selected so you see its blue cage. (The Move, Scale, or Rotate tool and the Model or Object tool must be chosen for interactive editing with the orange handle.)
- Deformers usually have to be rotated, scaled, and positioned to get the desired effect. Use the Move, Scale, and Rotate tools to transform them like any other object. These basic transformations can also be keyframed for animated effects.
- More than one deformer can be placed on an object, and varying the order of deformations in the Hierarchy will yield different results.
- If you want to temporarily disable a deformer, click the green check mark to the right of its name in the Objects Manager.
- To freeze a deformed position as a polygonal mesh, choose Current State to Object from the Functions menu.

Changing Animation: Replacing Keyframes or Starting All Over

If there is a red dot next to an attribute, there is an existing keyframe already in place for that value. If you want to change the value at that time, enter the new value and choose Add Keyframe again to replace the former keyframe. (In other words, you can't just change the value.)

Sometimes, especially when you're learning, animation just doesn't work out and starting over is the best course of action! Here's how to delete animation:

- Choose the Animation Layout. Click the Timeline tab. If the lock in the upper right corner of the Timeline is unlocked, type Cmd-A (Ctrl-A) and Delete to delete all animation. If the lock is locked, choose Show All Animated before selecting all and deleting.
- If you want to remove animation on only one object or attribute, find its name in the Timeline list. Click the track to the right of the name and press Delete.

Now you can go back and start animating the object again without the former keyframes getting in the way.

Step 2   Choose Deformer>Bulge and drop the object Bulge onto Polygons inside the Pipe HyperNURBS object. Select Bulge. In Object Properties, enter 156m for all Size values. Change the mode to Within Box. In the

Figure 4.7 Bulge Deformer

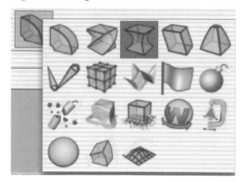

editor window, position the deformer at the bottom of the pipe and check the side view to make sure it is centered around the pipe.

Step 3 At frame 0, click the Coordinates panel and set a P.Y keyframe. Go to the End of the Animation. Use the green handle of the Move tool to position the deformer cage at the top of the pipe, just under the lip and set another P.Y keyframe.

Step 4 Go back to frame 0. Click the Object panel in the Attributes Manager, and keyframe a value of 0 for Strength. At frame 5, keyframe a Strength value of 100 and at frame 13 keyframe the value at 150. Continue to scrub through the animation, setting keyframes for the Strength values only when needed to adjust the bulge. You may also need to add more Strength keyframes (reducing the deformer strength and height) at points where the inner surface of the pipe is exposed. After setting initial keyframes, you can always scrub back though the animation and adjust the deformation to make the surface behave. At the end of the animation, give the Pipe a little squeeze by setting a keyframe of –25 for Strength. Save the file (File>Save or Cmd+S/Ctrl+S).

Figure 4.8 "Lump" Rising

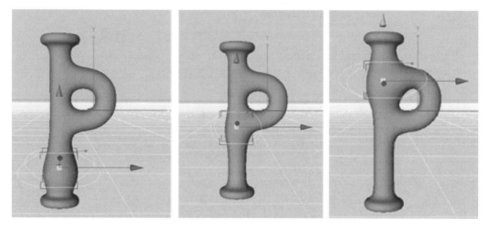

On the DVD: See Chapter 04>MOVIES/STILLS>Deformers>Pipe.mov.

Boom! Explosion Deformation

Figure 4.9 Explosion Deformer

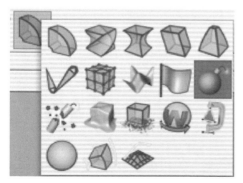

Step 1 Choose File>New and save the file as Simple Explosion in your Models folder using File>Save or Cmd+S (Ctrl+S).

Step 2 Choose Primitive>Sphere and enter 100 for Segments.

Step 3 Choose Deformer>Explosion and drop the Explosion deformer onto the Sphere in the Objects Manager.

Step 4 Select Explosion. At frame 0, Command-click the word Strength in Object Properties and set a keyframe for a value of 0. At frame 70, change the Strength value to 100 percent and set a keyframe. Save the file.

Preview this animation with Render>Make Preview set on Full Render, then try some variations. Experiment with increasing the Speed, Angle Speed, and End Size and preview the results.

Step 5   Choose File>Revert to Saved.

Step 6   Select Explosion. Let's reverse the keyframes and make an implosion. At frame 0, enter a new Strength value of 100 percent and set a keyframe. At frame 70, enter 0 percent and set a keyframe. Preview the animation.

Step 7   Create a colorful material (a Gradient or Spectral shader would work) to place on the Sphere so the explosion particles have color.

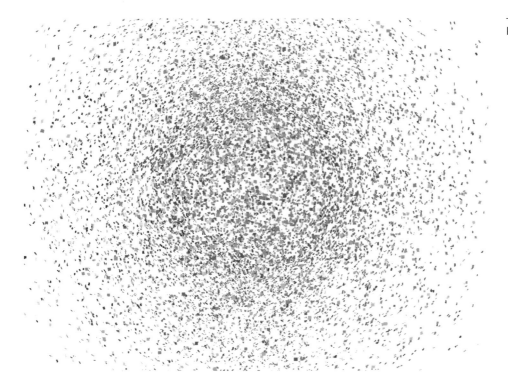

Figure 4.10 Sphere Exploding

On the DVD: See examples in Chapter 04>MOVIES/STILLS>MOVIES. In the Chapter 04>EXTRA!EXTRA!>InDepth folder, you'll find example files for a different explosion deformer, ExplosionFX. Study the settings for these examples to see how this deformer offers a wide range of control over explosions.

Broken Glass: The Shatter Deformer

Step 1   Choose File>Open and navigate to Chapter 04>C4DFiles>Van De Graaff on the DVD. Choose File>Save As and save the file as Shattered Generator. Work in the Front view.

Figure 4.11 Shatter Deformer

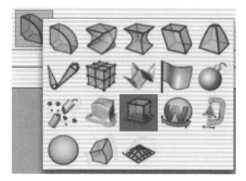

Step 2 Choose Deformer>Shatter Deformation and make the Shatter a child of Outer Glass Sphere.

Step 3 Make sure the current time is at 0 frames and set a Strength keyframe of 0 percent.

Step 4 At 20 frames, keyframe the Strength value as 80 percent.

Step 5 At 80 frames, keyframe 100 percent Strength. Switch to Perspective view and play the animation.

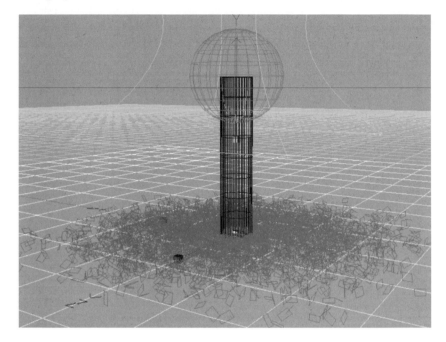

Figure 4.12 Shatter with Bulge

Figure 4.13 Wind Deformer

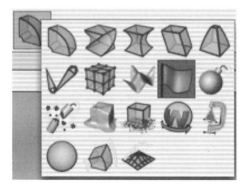

On the DVD: See Chapter 04>MOVIES/STILLS>MOVIES>Van De Graaff.mov. In the example movie, a bulge deformer was added to the Outer Sphere Glass and animated to coax the falling glass pieces into a more natural shape. Try it.

Flag on the Play: Wind and Shear Deformers

Step 1 Choose File>Open and navigate to Chapter 04>C4DFiles>FLAG>Flag on the DVD. Choose File>Save As and save the file as Flag in your Models folder. Choose Deformer>Wind and drop the object Wind on the Plane object in the Objects Manager.

Figure 4.14 Object Axis Tool

Step 2 With Wind selected, choose the Object Axis tool and the Move tool. Use the red Move handle to position the deformer's axis on the left side of the plane at the flagpole. In Object Properties, check the check box for Flag.

The Flag option holds the Y axis stationary, enabling the left edge of the flag to appear fixed to the flagpole.

Step 3   In Object Properties, start with settings of 40m for Amplitude, 5 for Frequency, and 2 in fx and then experiment with changing the settings one at a time. Attributes may be keyframed to change over time, but keyframing is not necessary for the deformer to set the flag in motion. Play the animation.

Step 4   Choose Deformer>Shear and place the object Shear on the Plane object also. Rotate the deformer 90º on the B (Bank) and position the cage over the flag in the editor window. Leave the Mode on Limited. Use the orange interactive handle of the Shear deformer to droop the right end of the flag down. Keyframe some various Strength values at different times if you want your flag to rise up and down.

Roll The Dice! Boolean Operations

This Hierarchy will be your most complex so far. It will be important to pay attention to capital and lowercase letters in the renaming process.

Step 1   Choose File>New and save the file as Dice into your Models folder (File> Save or Cmd+S/Ctrl+S). Work in the Front view and Wireframe Display.

Step 2   Choose Primitive>Cube. In Object Properties, click the Fillet box and enter 20 for Fillet Radius.

Step 3   Choose Primitive>Sphere. Give the sphere a radius of 24. Choose the Model and Move tools. Use the red Move handle to move the sphere to the right, positioning so that its Y axis lines up on the far right edge of the cube. Rename the sphere as ONE.

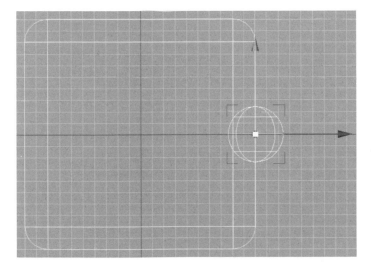

Figure 4.15 Shear Deformer

Figure 4.16 Flag Flying

Figure 4.17 First Sphere

Step 4 In the Objects Manager, Control-drag three copies of ONE. Rename the copies as Three 1, Three 2, and Three 3. Use the green Move handle to move all three up so that their horizontal midline rests on the top edge of the dic. Then use the red Move handle to position them equidistantly, as in Figure 4.18. Select all three and press the G key to group them, naming the group THREE.

Step 5 Now Control-drag a copy of THREE, renaming the copy FOUR. Use the green Move handle and move the FOUR group down so the midlines rest on the bottom edge of the cube. Click the (+) next to Four, and select Three 3. Control-drag a copy of Three 3 and make sure it remains in the FOUR Group. Rename all the children in FOUR group as Four 1, Four 2, Four 3, and Four 4.

Step 6 Select THREE group. In the Objects Manager, Control-drag a copy and rename the copy as Six. With Six selected, type 90 in the box for Bank Rotation in the Coordinates Manager and click Apply. Making sure the Model and Move tools are selected, use the green Move handle to move the copy over and center the sphere axes on the left edge of the die. Then use the red handle to center the copy vertically on the left edge.

Figure 4.18 Hierarchy and View

Figure 4.19 SIX Symmetry

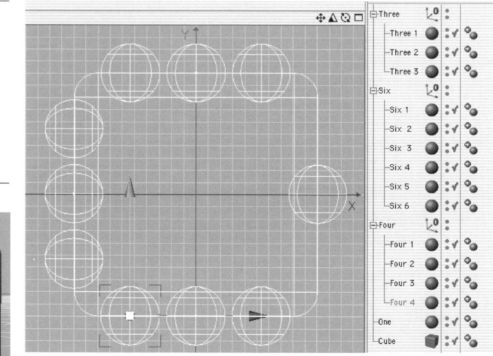

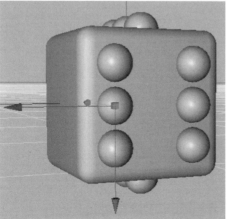

Step 7 Switch to the Side View (View 3). Choose a Symmetry Object from the top menu, and drop Six into it. In Object Properties, set the Mirror Plane for the Symmetry Object as XY. Select Six inside the Symmetry Object

Figure 4.21 Two Moved Up

Figure 4.20 Threes Moved

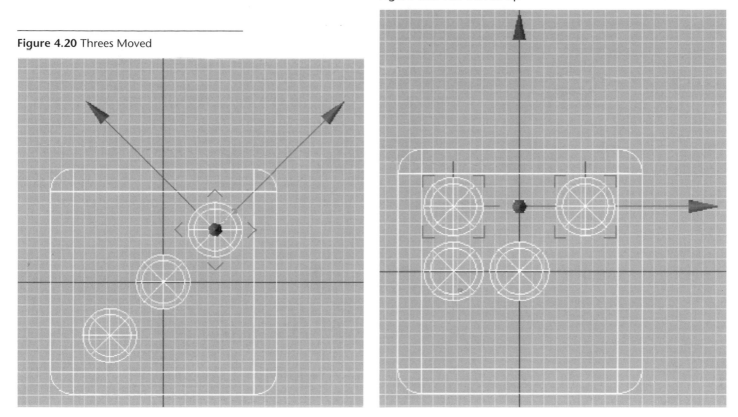

and use the blue Move handle to spread the spheres to the opposite edges of the cube. Rename Symmetry as SIX.

Step 8   Switch to the Top view, (View 2) and select the THREE Group. In the Coordinates Manager, enter 45° for H (Heading) Rotation. Using the red Move tool handle, nudge both outer Three spheres a little further into their respective corners.

◆ ***Tip:*** In Figure 4.20, the other Groups (One, Four, and Six) had their top gray visibility dots clicked to Red so you could see the THREE group more clearly. You may want to do the same thing as you work on specific groups.

Step 9   Still in the Top view, click the visibility dots so only the FOUR Group and the Cube are visible. Now select the FOUR Group. Select two of its spheres (a left and right sphere) and use the blue Move handle to move them to the top of the cube in the editor window. Use the blue and red Move handles to position the other two spheres so the FOUR group has a child sphere in each corner.

Step 10 Select FOUR again. Control-drag a copy and rename the copy FIVE. Open the FIVE Hierarchy. Make sure FIVE is deselected. Select any one of the spheres inside FIVE, and Control-drag a copy. Position the copy in the center of the four spheres. Rename the FIVE children as Five 1, Five 2, Five 3, Five 4, and Five 5.

Figure 4.22 FIVE Sphere Centered

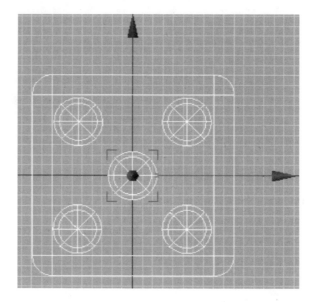

Step 11 Switch to the Side view (View 3). Select the FIVE Group. In the Coordinates Manager, Enter a P (Pitch) Rotation of 90º. Use the blue and green handles to position the FIVE Group on the left edge of the cube, centered vertically.

Figure 4.23 FIVE Moved to Left

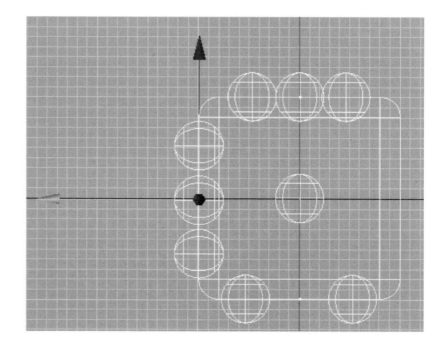

Step 12 Select the FOUR Group and make sure its visibility dot is gray. In the Objects Manager, Control-drag a copy of FOUR and rotate the copy 90º on the Pitch. Rename the Copy as TWO. Use the green and blue move handles to position and vertically center the TWO Group on the right edge of the cube.

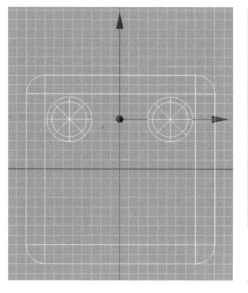

Figure 4.24 TWO Axis Centered

Figure 4.25 Checking Sphere Positions

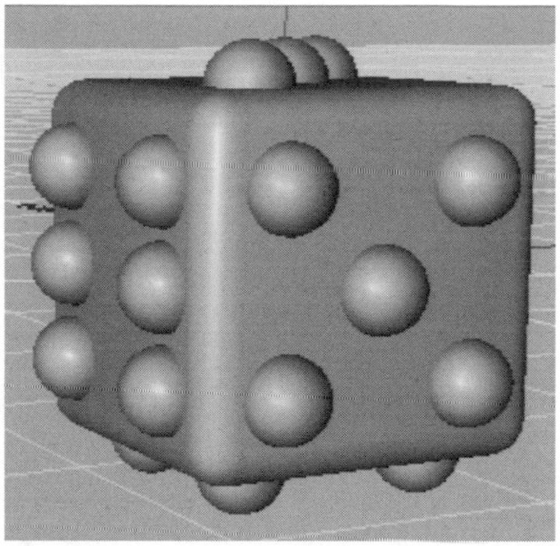

Step 13 Choose the Front View and make only the TWO Group and the Cube visible. Select the bottom two spheres (as they appear in the editor window) and delete them. Rename the remaining spheres as Two 1 and Two 2. Select the TWO object. Using the Object Axis tool and the Move tool, move the axis back up so it is centered between the two spheres.

Step 14 Choose the Model tool and use the blue Move handle to lower the spheres to the vertical midpoint of the die. Choose the Rotate tool and drag the green rotation axis axis handle until the P value in the Co-ordinates Manager is 45º. Use the red Move handle to slide Two 1 and Two 2 further into their respective corners.

Figure 4.26 Boolean Object Icon

Step 15 In the Hierarchy, place Groups ONE through SIX in numerical order just for good housekeeping, then select them all. Be sure to leave Cube unselected. Press the G key to group all the spheres, and rename the new group CUTTERS. Rename Cube as CUTTEE.

Step 16 In the Materials Manager, choose File>New Material. Control-drag a copy of the material thumbnail. Edit the first material to have a color of red and a Transparency of 25 percent. For the second material, just slide the brightness slider of the default gray to 100 percent for a pure white. Place the red material on the CUTTEE and the white Material on the CUTTERS.

Figure 4.27 Finished Dice

Step 17 From the menu over the Objects Manager, choose Objects>Unfold All. Make sure all visibility dots in the entire Hierarchy are returned to gray. In Perspective view, check the sphere positions.

Step 18 From the top toolbar, choose a Boolean Object from the Array palette. Rename the Boolean object as DIE. Drop the object CUTTERS on the object DIE first, then drop the object CUTTEE onto DIE.

Step 19 Make a copy of DIE so you have a set of dice.

● **Springboard!** Who knew simple objects like dice would take so many steps to make? But the good news is that if you do your archiving homework and keep your library in good shape you'll never have to make dice again. Research all the material "flavors" dice come in by going to Google>Image and typing Dice in the search box. Copy this die and try different materials on the copies. You may also want to edit the Fillet on some of the cubes, since some dice have more rounded edges than others. Save all your Dice.c4d files in a folder named Dice Library and place it in in your Models folder.

Boolean Operations

There are four basic boolean operations. The number of subdivisions in objects placed in booleans will affect the smoothness of cut edges. Not only can groups of objects be used in booleans (as in the DICE project), but animated objects can be used inside booleans to create changing forms. If the surface of your boolean object exhibits some strangeness, take these measures. In version 8.2, choose Plugin>Boole>Boole Replacer. In version 8.5, click the High Quality checkbox in Object Properties for the Boole.

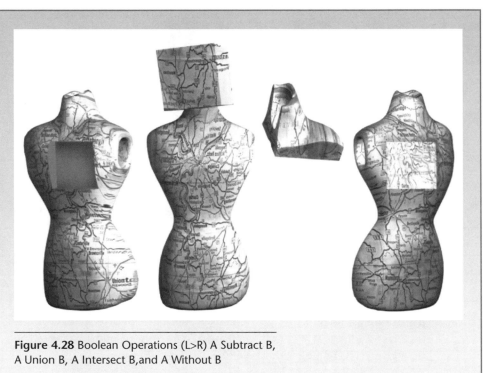

Figure 4.28 Boolean Operations (L>R) A Subtract B, A Union B, A Intersect B, and A Without B

On the DVD: See Chapter 04>MOVIES/STILLS>MOVIES>Animated Boolean.mov. To see how the animation was set up, see Chapter 04>EXAMPLES>BOOLEANS> Animated Boolean.C4D.

A String Of Dice: The Arrange Function

Step 1 Choose File>Open and navigate to Chapter 04>C4D Files>Bakelite Die. Choose File>Save As and save the working copy to your Models folder.

Step 2 Select DIE, and choose Functions>Duplicate. Leave Copies with a value of 8 and check Generate Instances. The value for X, Y, and Z Move should be 0. Click OK.

Step 3   Rename the Null Object as DICE and select it. From the top menu, choose Functions>Arrange. In the Search For box, press the letters Sp and click OK.

Any number of like or different objects can be arranged on a spline using this function. The uppermost objects in a Group Hierarchy will occur at the beginning of the spline.

Figure 4.29 String of Dice

Step 4   With DICE still selected, choose Functions>Randomize. Enter 10 for X Move, and 35 for H, P, and B Rotation. Click OK.
Click the (+) next to DICE. Note that if you wanted to, you could still select each DIE and animate their rotation individually.

Great Green Gobs: The Metaball Object

In this tutorial, you'll use the Metaball object to make great green gobs of grody, grimy grease to plop out when the lump reaches the top of the pipe.

Step 1   Choose File>Open and navigate to Chapter 04>C4D Files>PforPipeBulge .c4d. Choose File>Save As and save a new working copy of the file in your Models folder. In the top menu, choose Edit>Project Settings. Enter 200 in the box for Maximum, press Return (Enter) and close the box.

■ **Shortcut:** Ctrl+D is the keyboard shortcut for Project Settings.

Step 2   Command-click (or right-click) on Pipe. Drag to New Tag>Display Tag. In the Attributes Manager under Object Properties, click the check box next to Use Display Mode and drag down to Isoparms.

Step 3   In the top menu, choose a Metaball Object from the Array Palette.

Step 4   In Object Properties, enter 3 percent for Hull Value. Click the Coordinates panel, and enter 0.1 for S.X, S.Y, and S.Z.

Step 5   From the top menu, choose Objects>Polygon Object. In the Objects Manager, drop the object Polygon into the MetaBall. Select the Polygon object.

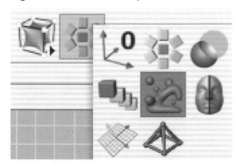

Figure 4.30 Metaball Object Icon

Step 6 Working in the Front view, choose Points and the Move tool. Starting at the top of the pipe, Control-click a dozen points downward (until even with the top of the hole in the P). Check the side view to be sure the Metaball object is centered in the pipe.

Figure 4.31 Starting Points for Metaball

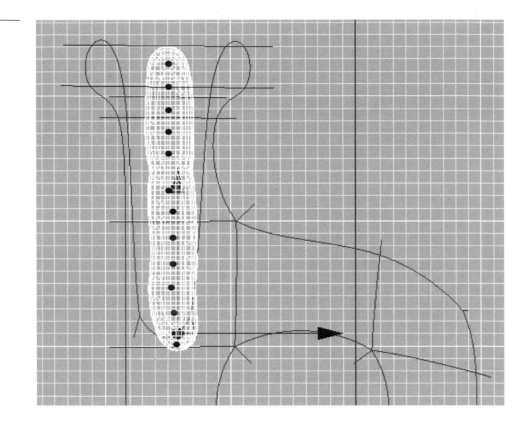

Step 7 Go ahead and drop the Greasy Green Material onto the "gob" so you can preview render it occasionally with Ctrl+R.

Decreasing the Hull value gives the Metaballs object more "stretchiness." With a high value, an element moved against the Metaball skin will quickly pop out into its own separate skin. With a low value, the skin stretches to accommodate the movement. Spheres, splines, and points may be placed inside a Metaball object for sculpting the surface from the inside. You can also place polygonal objects inside a metaball, but the points of the mesh will be understood as spheres.

In this animation, the lump in the pipe should be reaching the top at frame 90. At that point, you'll be animating the points inside the metaballs object to "squish" out of the pipe, slide out and down the side.

Step 8 Make sure the Polygon object is selected in the Objects Manager. Choose Points and the Move tool.

Step 9 In the Animation Toolbar, enable only Point Level Animation. At frame 88, press the record keyframe button or press F9 to set a keyframe for the current position for the points.

Step 10 Drag the current time to frame 91. Press F5 to work in All Views so you can keep the Metaball within the edges of the pipe as you sculpt the surface. In order to see the points inside the Metaball hull, use the 2 key with the mouse to move in close. Using the Move tool, select and move points upward to reshape the gob so that it is widening and coming up out of the pipe. Set a keyframe.

Step 11 Drag the current time forward four or five frames at a time, stopping each time to move points up and out. Don't forget to keyframe the change in state each time you move points. Test render with Ctrl+R once in a while to make sure things are looking good.

●***Springboard!*** This kind of animation takes patience. You may have to practice this a few times to get a smooth creepy-crawly motion. While you can Shift-click to select groups of points to move larger sections of the form, and speed up the process, the "too much, too fast" approach may be counterproductive. In the long run, the more points that are moved independently over small distances and the closer the frames are together, the more organic your grease will be. Try making some other Metaball forms using spheres, splines, and polygonal objects as children.

On the DVD: See Chapter 04>MOVIES/STILLS>STILLS/Great Green Gobs.mov.

Figure 4.32 Metaball Creeping

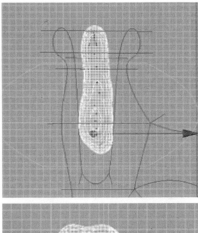

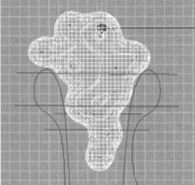

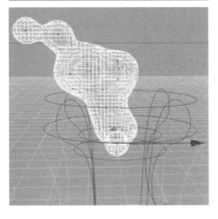

Figure 5.1

Materials in Depth

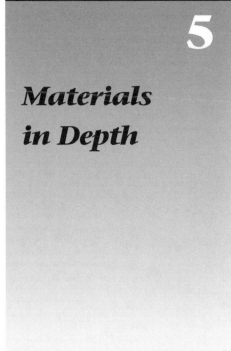

Y ou've already been working with the Materials Manager and Material Editor, and have some idea of the process which visually describes surfaces in 3D. In the broader 3D world, these are often referred to as Textures, but CINEMA 4D uses the term Material. A single Material, represented by a thumbnail in the Materials Manager, is an integrated "stack" of instructions or parameters. Each type of instruction resides in a single channel and can be edited on a separate page, but visually the attributes combine to create a unique look for a surface. Picture a cylindrical primitive, then see it as a bubbly glass bead, a grungy gray pipe, a decorative box, or a column of wood. The Material is critical in forming the identity of the 3D object.

The vast combinations of material properties possible in CINEMA 4D could fill many volumes. In the process of producing the diverse materials in these projects,

Figure 5.2 Cylinders

Editing Material Parameters

Double-click on a thumbnail in the Materials Manager to edit parameters in the Material Editor. In the Material Editor, select the parameter you want to work with (the gray band denotes selection) and edit the values and sliders on its page. You can also single-click the thumbnail to edit parameters in the Attributes Manager. Click the Parameter Page you want to edit at the top of the Attributes Manager.

Figure 5.3 Material Thumbnails

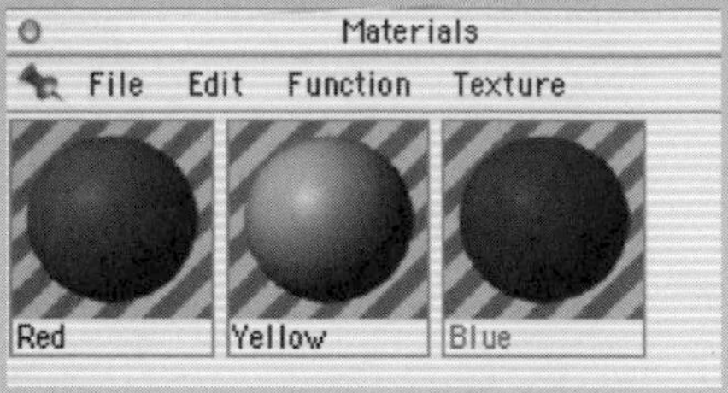

Figure 5.4 Material Editor

Figure 5.5 Attributes Manager

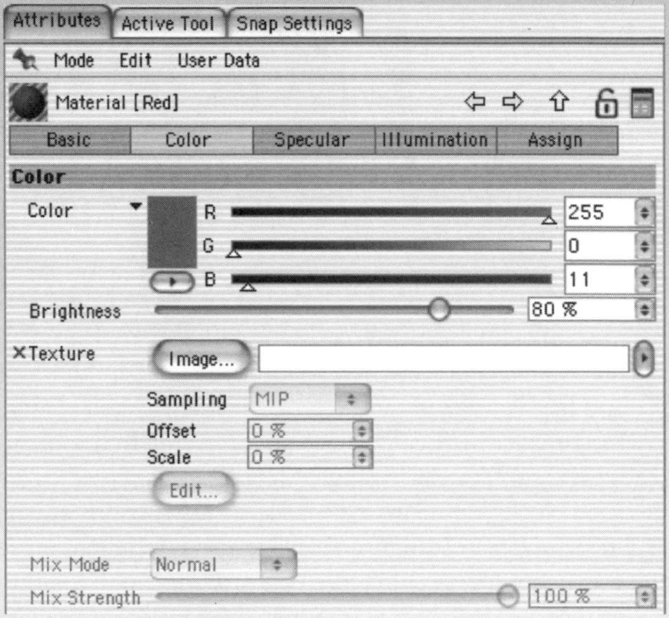

you'll gain understanding of the different types of materials available in CINEMA 4D and the general process of how they can be crafted. Exploring all the infinite combinations will take a lifetime.

Alternately, procedural textures called Shaders can be used to visually define a channel. Shaders are mathematically calculated textures, and because they are not based on pixels, they appear the same at any proximity. 2D Shaders remain on the object surface, but 3D Shaders apply to the object volumetrically.

The most sophisticated Shaders, the BhodiNUT Smells Like Almonds, are complex and powerful shading engines that offer intense editability. These thinking shaders calculate the look of the material based on other factors in the scene. The serious 3D artist will avoid the temptation to use these inherently beautiful shaders with clip art ease but rather will want to spend hours exploring the power of these engines for unique looks.

Image Maps vs. Shaders

What materials look like or where and to what degree they are active on a surface may be defined by images. These flat images (raster or vector) are placed into the channel of a parameter. For example, photographs, illustrations, hand-drawn textures, or movies placed into the color channel function as the actual image of the surface. But a image placed in other channels, like Bump or Reflection, uses value differences to define where the particular characteristic is fully active and where it isn't. Image maps are highly effective in capturing photographic detail; however, the resolution of pixels becomes critical when a camera moves close to the image.

Figure 5.6 Image Maps

Figure 5.7 Image Map (L) and Procedural Shader (R)

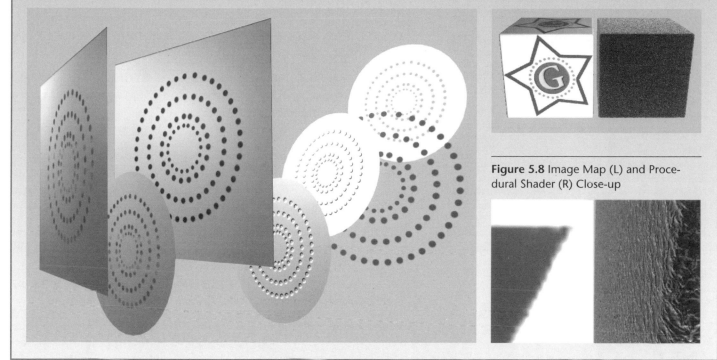

Figure 5.8 Image Map (L) and Procedural Shader (R) Close-up

Figure 5.9 BhodiNUT Volume

◆***Tip:*** Be sure to look at the color version of Figure 5.9 on the DVD.

Figure 5.10 Texture Tag and Attributes

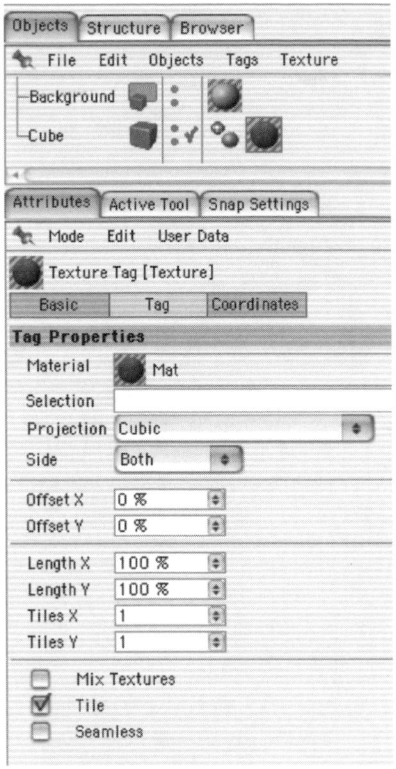

Figure 5.11 Stapled Wood

A Texture Totem: Exploring Materials

These Material creations will be placed on simple geometrics. Later, you can stack them on a Texture Totem of your own design. Choose File>Open and navigate to Chapter 05>EXAMPLES to see a sample of a finished Totem. These projects were chosen for their surface variety and potential for showing off some interesting parameters and shaders. You can add more objects of your own, or use models from previous projects to construct your personal Totem.

A Dark and Grungy Wood

Step 1   Choose File>New. Choose File>Save As and save the file as Grungy Wood in your Models folder.

Step 2   From the top toolbar, choose Primitive>Cube. In the Objects Manager, enter 625m in Size.X, 1000m in Sixe.Y, and 250m in Size.Z. Click the Fillet check box and enter a Fillet Radius of 30m.
Choose Edit>Frame Scene.

Step 3   In the Materials Manager, choose File>New Material. Double-click the thumbnail, and in the Material Editor Color page, click the Image button. Navigate to GOODIES>MATERIALS>ImageMaps>Stapled Wood.jpg. Click Yes in the Image Search Path box.

Step 4   Check the Bump check box and click the Image button in the Texture panel. Navigate to MATERIALS>ImageMaps>StapledWoodBump.jpg. Click Yes in the Image Search Path box. (From now on, let's assume you know to do that.) At the top of the Material Editor, drag the Bump Strength slider to 15 percent. Uncheck the check box for Specular.

Step 5   Place the Wood material on the Cube by dragging the thumbnail onto the object Cube in the Objects Manager. The texture tag that appears in the Objects Manager to the right of the object name can always be selected and edited in the Attributes Manager. Under Tag Properties, change the Projection to Cubic.

Step 6   From the Objects Manager menu, choose Texture>Fit to Object. Press Ctrl+R to render an editor preview.

Light Wood and a Decal

Step 1   Choose File>New. Choose File>Save As and save the file as Woodand-Decal in your Models folder.

Step 2   From the top toolbar, choose Primitive>Cube. In the Objects Manager, enter 100m in the Size.Z box, check the Fillet check box and enter a Fillet Radius of 5m.

Step 3 In the Materials Manager, choose File>New Material. Double click the thumbnail, and in the Material Editor Color pane, click the Image button. Navigate to GOODIES>MATERIALS>ImageMaps>Wood.jpg.

Step 4 Check the Bump check box and click the Image button in the Texture panel. Navigate to GOODIES>MATERIALS>ImageMaps>WoodBump. jpg. At the top of the Material Editor, drag the Bump Strength slider to 40 percent. Uncheck the check box for Specular. Double-click the name of the Material to rename it as Wood.

The Specular highlight is a shininess that occurs where lights hit the object and create a highlight. Unless wood has a layer of varnish or shellac, it will need little or no specularity. These woods are rough and natural, so we are turning the Specular channel off.

Step 5 In the Materials Manager, Control-drag a copy of the Wood material thumbnail. On the Color pane, click the small black arrow to the right of the Image button and drag to Copy Channel. Click the small black arrow once again and drag to BhodiNUT Channel/Bhodinut Fusion. Click the Edit button in the Texture Panel.
8.5 Update Instead of choosing BhodiNUT Channel>BhodiNUT Fusion, just click the small black triangle and choose Fusion. Click the word Fusion to edit the shader as in Steps 6 through 8.

The BhodiNUT Fusion shader is an energetic workhorse for blending materials. Its blending modes (yes, like Photoshop) and masking let you choose how and in what areas the materials mix. This shader can also be used to mask off a particular area of any other shader.

Step 6 In the Smells Like Almonds editor window, locate the Base Channel at the bottom of the pane. Click the small black arrow at the right of the empty Image box and choose Paste Channel.

Step 7 At the top of the SLA box, click the Image button in the Blend Channel pane. Navigate to GOODIES>MATERIALS>ImageMaps>Star Decal.jpg.

Step 8 Now at the bottom of the left pane of the SLA window, click the check box for Use Mask. Then, in the Mask Channel pane to the middle right, click the Image button and navigate to GOODIES>MATERIALS>Image Maps>StarDecal Alpha.jpg. Experiment with the Blend slider in the left pane to get the level of "fadedness" you want the decal to have.

Step 9 Name the second Material as Decal.

You may be wondering why you created two materials. Because we only want the decal on one side, we will use a selection to limit the Material with the Decal only to the front of the cube. Notice the cracks in the decal, and study the Star Decal Alpha file. They were created in Photoshop by incorporating a photo of

Avoiding the Dreaded Texture Error

When you import any outside images to be used in a Material by clicking the Image button, a box appears asking, "Do you want to create a copy at the document location?" Clicking Yes places a copy of the file, which CINEMA 4D must have access to in order to render, at the same hierarchal level as the C4D file. For housekeeping purposes, you can make a folder titled "Tex" ahead of time and place it in the same directory (folder) with the CINEMA file. CINEMA 4D also knows to look there for associated textures. (Actually, for the projects in this chapter, you could just move a copy of the MATERIALS>Tex folder into your Models folder so the textures will be in place when you render.) Alternately, any time you save a project with associated outside images, you can choose File>Save Project (as opposed to File>Save or Save As) and the Tex folder with the images will be created and saved with the file. By making sure associated images are in the place where C4D expects to find them, you'll avoid a texture error when rendering.

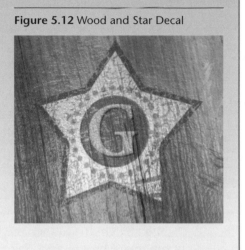

Figure 5.12 Wood and Star Decal

cracked paint in the Alpha mask. All the files for these projects are created for you, but if you aim for materials success, mastery of Photoshop or another raster image editing program will be a critical part of your 3D skill set.

On the DVD: See Chapter 17>EXTRA!EXTRA!>Photoshop for a minilesson on creating Image Maps in Photoshop Skills.

Step 10 Choose the Cube object and press the C key. Choose the Polygons tool. Select the front polygon. Choose Selection>Set Selection and in the Basic Properties panel, name the selection FRONT.

Step 11 Place the Wood material on the Cube. In the Tag panel, change the Projection to Cubic.

Step 12 Now place the Decal material on the object Cube. Select the Texture tag for the Decal material in the Objects Manager. Make sure the Tag panel is showing. Change the Projection to Cubic. In the box for Selection, enter FRONT. Render the editor window with Control-R.

Step 13 Choose File>Save Project and save it to your Models folder.

Net Worth

Step 1 Choose File>Open and navigate to Chapter 05>C4D Files>Clown Collar.c4d. Choose File>Save As and save the file as Clown Collar in your Models folder.

Step 2 In the Materials Manager, choose File>New Material. Double-click the thumbnail, and in the Material Editor Color page create a red as the base color. Activate the Alpha parameter. Click on the small black arrow next to the Image button, and drag down to BhodiNUT Channel>BhodiNUT Tiles.

8.5 Update After clicking the small black arrow on the left, choose Surfaces>Tiles instead of BhodiNUT Channel>BhodiNUT Tiles.

Step 3 Click the Edit button, and in the SLA window change Tile Color 1 and Tile Color 2 to white. Change the Global Scale to 10 percent and enter 0.5 for Grout Width. Back in the Material Editor, check the check box for Invert in the Texture panel. Name the material Net.

8.5 Update Click the word Tiles to edit in the Material Editor as in Step 3.

Step 4 Create a new material thumbnail. On the Color page create a light purple. Check on the Reflection parameter, click the black arrow next to Image, and choose BhodiNUT Channel>BhodiNUT Tiles.

8.5 Update Choose Surfaces>Tiles instead of BhodiNUT Channel> BhodiNUT Tiles.

Step 5 Click Edit and in the SLA editor, choose Circles 1. Edit Tile Color 1 to be black and Tile Color 2 to be white. Change Global Scale to 80 percent.

8.5 Update Click the word Tiles to edit in the Material Editor as in Step 3.

Step 6 Back in the Material Editor, click the small black arrow again and drag to Copy Channel. Activate the Alpha parameter page. Click the black arrow again and drag to choose Paste Channel.

Step 7 Activate Specular Color. Edit the color to be a bright pink. Name the material Mylar Dot.

Step 8 Place Both Materials on the Clown Collar, Net first and then Mylar Dot.

Figure 5.13 Clown Collar

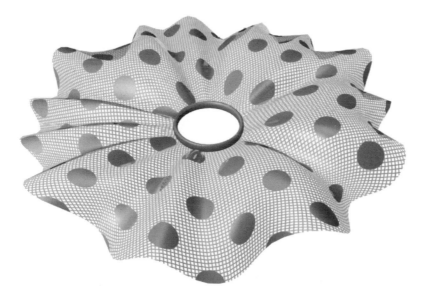

Figure 5.14 Other Alpha Examples

This technique is useful for all kinds of materials with open detail like lace, screens, or metal with decorative openwork. The global scale of the pattern (as in the Square pattern used to make the net) may need to be adjusted as the camera is closer or farther away. The Alpha channel determines in what areas the surface is 100 percent there, visible with some percentage of fade, or not there at all. Use materials whenever you can to save modeling cutout detail.

Fake Façades

Complex organic surfaces can be faked by placing the right image maps on flat geometry. The theater-set mentality of creating "flats" to give the illusion of three-dimensional structures translates well to digital worlds. Sometimes it's only the front that counts.

Step 1   Choose File>Open and navigate to Chapter 05>C4D Files>Fake Facade.c4d. Choose File>Save As and save the file as Fake Column in your Models folder.

Take a minute to look at this 3D Model. Choose Objects>Object Information. Whoa—how's that for a low poly count?

Figure 5.15 Fake Facade

Step 2   In the Materials Manager, choose File>New Material. Double-click the thumbnail. On the Color pane click the Image button and navigate to GOODIES>MATERIALS>ImageMaps>Column.jpg.

Step 3   Check on the Bump channel and import the ColumnBump.jpg from the same location.

Step 4   Activate the Alpha channel, and import ColumnAlpha.jpg.

Step 5   Place the Material on the name Polygon in the Objects Manager.

Render a preview of the Editor with Ctrl+R. All that richness is communicated by one little polygon mapped with a well-lit photograph. The lesson here is to use illusion whenever you can to economize on polygons and save modeling time.

Decorative Glass

This glass is made with channel shaders and is edited to have interesting color qualities. After you've made this version, copy the file and experiment with your own changes to the parameter pages.

Step 1 Choose File>Open and navigate to Chapter 05>C4D Files>GlassPalladian .c4d. Choose File>Save As and save the file as Glass Palladian in your Models folder.

Step 2 In the Materials Manager, choose File>New Material. Double-click the thumbnail, and in the Material Editor Color page choose a light warm green as the base color. (R 215, G215, B65, and 85 percent Brightness will work.)

Step 3 Activate the Transparency parameter. Edit the Color rectangle to be a bright yellow (255, 255, 0) and set the Brightness to 85 percent. In the top right corner, set the Refraction value as 1.1. Check the check box for Fresnel. Choose Shader>Turbulence from the Shader list.
8.5 Update The Refraction menu has been moved slightly down and to the left. Instead of Shader>Turbulence, choose Surfaces>Simple Turbulence.

Step 4 Turn on the Reflection channel.

Step 5 In the Bump channel, click the black arrow and choose Shader>Turbulence.
8.5 Update Instead, choose Surfaces>Simple Turbulence.

Step 6 In the Specular channel, enter 50 percent for Width and 20 percent for Height.

Step 7 Activate Specular Color and edit the color box to be shocking pink. (255, 0, 246 with a Brightness of 150 percent.) Place the material on the Palladian and render the editor with Control-R.

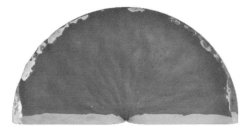

Figure 5.16 Glass Palladian

Photo Face

Photos or illustrations can be wrapped around models. The Photoshop tutorial on the DVD will show you how to prepare Image Maps for Spherical or Cylindrical projection.

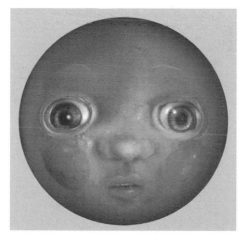

Figure 5.17 Littlehead

Step 1 Choose File>New and save the file as Littlehead.c4d. into your Models folder (File>Save or Cmd+S/Ctrl+S).

Step 2 Choose Primitive>Sphere.

Step 3 In the Materials Manager, choose File>New Material. Double-click the thumbnail, and in the Material Editor Color pane click the Image button. Navigate to GOODIES>MATERIALS>ImageMaps>Littleface.c4D.

Step 4 Activate the Bump channel and navigate to MATERIALS>ImageMaps> Littleface Bump.c4D to import the image map for the Bump.

Step 5 Place the material on the sphere.

Placing and Adjusting Materials

Materials can be mapped with different types of projection onto the 3D model. Figure 5.18 illustrates how, in general, the projection style is similar in form to the object itself. The manual and the Help PDF (available from the top menu if it was included in your C4D installation) that come with CINEMA 4D have excellent diagrams illustrating different types of mapping.

Attributes about a material's placement may be edited numerically in the Attributes Manager. Offset moves the texture side to side or vertically, The X and Y Lengths determine how far the texture is stretched in a direction; Tiling determines how many times the texture is repeated in each direction. In addition, materials can be interactively adjusted by using the Texture and Texture Axis tools in conjunction with the Move, Scale, and Rotate tools. Cages appear that give you an idea of how the material is positioned in relation to the object. With project types other than UVW, a texture can be coaxed to fit an object by choosing Texture>Fit to Object from the Objects Manager menu.

Notice that the Texture tag is independent from the material itself. Once mapping is defined in a tag, it can be copied to many objects and a different material thumbnail dropped into the Search For Box.

You may remember from earlier projects that you can apply a material to specific selection on the surface of an object. The name of the selection can be entered into the Selection box in Tag Properties. You can also limit materials to Caps and Rounding areas by entering C1 or C2 (Start and End Caps) and R1 or R2 (Start and End Rounding) in the Selection box, an option especially useful for custom 3D Type.

The default projection type, UVW, "sticks" the material to UVW coordinates that are inherent in Primitives and NURBS objects. UVW projection has certain advantages and disadvantages. A great advantage is that a UVW material sticks to an object's surface as it is animated or deformed. The downside is that adjusting UVW materials on complex objects and characters is a fairly complex venture. Because UV coordinates stretch in unhappy ways when the polygons on a mesh are uneven in size, extensive adjustment is often required to make the mesh and the UV texture coexist in believable ways. There are some excellent in-depth books on advanced character texturing recommended in Chapter 05>EXTRA!EXTRA!>References on the DVD.

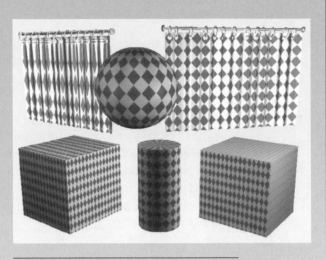

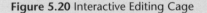

Figure 5.18 Common Types of Projection: Bottom row, L>R, Cubic, Cylindrical and Flat. Top Row, L>R, UW with distortion from uneven polygons, Spherical, and Flat

Figure 5.19 Texture and Texture Axis Tools

Figure 5.20 Interactive Editing Cage

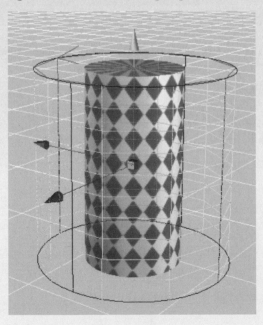

Glitter and Sequin Star

These challenging materials make use of image maps to isolate small points of sparkle.

Step 1 Choose File>Open and navigate to Chapter 05>C4D Files>Glitter-Star.c4d. Choose File>Save As and save the file as GlitterStar in your Models folder.

Step 2 In the Materials Manager, choose File>New Material. On the Material Editor Color pane click the black arrow next to Image and drag to Bhodi NUT Channel>BhodiNUT Fusion. Click Edit. In the Blend channel, navigate to GOODIES>MATERIALS>ImageMaps>AFewSequins.jpg. In the left panel of the SLA window, click Use Mask. In the Mask channel, import A FewSequinsAlpha.jpg from the same location. In the Base channel, place Glitter.jpg from the same folder. Click OK.
8.5 Update Click the small black arrow on the left and choose Fusion instead of BhodiNUT Channel>BhodiNUT Fusion. Click on Fusion to edit the shader as in Step 2, but working in the Material Editor.

Step 3 Activate Reflection and import AFewSequinsReflect.jpg from the same location.

Step 4 Turn on Bump and import the GlitterBump.jpg from the same folder.

Step 5 Edit the Specular channel to have a Width of 25 percent and a Height of 60 percent.

Step 6 Place the Material on the Star with Cubic projection. In the Objects Manager, choose Texture>Fit to Object. Click Yes when asked to include sub-objects. Use the Texture tool and the Move and Scale tools to adjust the texture so that none of the sequins slide off the edge of the star.

Figure 5.21 Glitter and Sequin Star

Pushing the Limits: Grunge and Sparkle

The ability of 3D applications to create mechanically perfect objects can be your worst enemy as an artist. On one end, perfection, you'll be spending many hours making surfaces look like they live in the real world. The diffusion channel is the main workhorse for dirtying, scratching, and otherwise grunging surfaces so they look like they have been through the vigors of life. The new Dirt shader in version 8.5 goes beyond the ability to selectively darken a material. It actually goes down in the cracks and crevices like the real thing.

On the other end of boringly normal, you may also be working hard to enhance surfaces toward supercharged or surreal color and high levels of sparkle, glitz, and "bling, bling." Selectively mapped points of reflection and the highlights and glows you'll explore later in the Advanced Rendering Chapter will help you push the limits.

Embossed Gold

So many nuances on a metal surface! Image maps thoughtfully placed emulate the real thing.

Step 1   Choose File>Open and navigate to Chapter 05>C4D Files>Metal-Crown.c4d. Choose File>Save As and save the file as Metal Crown in your Models folder.

Step 2   In the Materials Manager, choose File>New Material. On the Material Editor Color pane choose a light warm gold as the base color. (R 255, G 248, B 123, and 100 percent Brightness will work.)

Step 3   Activate the Diffusion channel, click the small black arrow and choose Shader>Turbulence. Click the Edit button. In the Attributes Manager, leave U Frequency to 1 and change the V Frequency to 2. Reduce the Diffusion mix to 75 percent.
8.5 Update Instead of Shader>TurbulAnce, choose Surfaces>Simple TurbulAnce.

Step 4   Click on the Reflection parameter. Turn on the Bump channel, and click the Image button. Navigate to MATERIALS>ImageMaps>CrownInvertedMap.jpg. From the Shader manu, choose Copy Channel.
8.5 Update Copy channel is now accessed from the small black arrow on the left.

Step 5   Edit the Specular page to have 40 percent width, 80 percent Height, and Falloff 5 percent. Turn on the Specular Color pane and edit the color to be a light green. Name the material Gold 1.

Step 6   Create a second material. On the Color pane, choose a light gold with 125 percent Brightness.

Step 7   Activate the Bump and Alpha channels, and choose Paste Channel to place Crown Inverted Map.jpg into both. In the Alpha pane, check the check box for Soft. Name this material Gold 2.

Step 8   Place both materials on the crown, making sure Gold 2 is on the far right. Shift-click to select both material tags, and in the Attributes Manager, drag the Offset X value to align the tallest part of the embossed design with the tallest part of the crown (–25 Offset X).

Step 9   In the Materials Manager, Control-drag a copy of Gold 1 and rename it Plain Gold. Delete the image map from the Reflection pane, and uncheck the Bump channel. Place Plain Gold on the Bottom and Top Rims of the crown.

Punched Paper

Step 1   Choose File>Open and navigate to Chapter 05>C4D Files>PaperCrowns.c4d. Choose File>Save As and save the file as Paper Crowns in your Models folder.

Figure 5.22 Embossed Crown

Step 2   In the Materials Manager, choose File>New Material. On the Material Editor Color pane create a medium red. Place this material on the Inner Crown and the Rim.

Step 3   Create another material and edit the color to be a medium purple.

Step 4   Turn on the Bump channel and place the shader of your choice in the Image box to add some embossed texture to the paper.

Step 5   Give the Specular channel a Width and Height of 50 percent. Turn on the Specular Color channel. Activate the Alpha channel, and navigate to GOODIES>MATERIALS>ImageMaps>Harlequin Map.jpg. Place this material on the Outer Crown. Choose Cylindrical mapping.

Step 7   From the menu over the Objects Manager, choose Texture>Fit to Object. In the Attributes Manager Tag Properties, enter 2 in the Tiles X box.

Step 8   Choose the Texture tool and the Move tool. Drag the Move tool to adjust the position of the harlequin holes. The holes should be as high as possible without cutting into the top edge of the crown.

Multicolor Magic

Choose File>Open and navigate to Chapter 05>EXAMPLES>MulticolorMagic. c4d. Investigate this Library of multicolor embellishments by browsing through the material parameters. Study the placement styles by clicking the Texture tags. Some of these materials use unorthodox texture placement to get totally different

Figure 5.23 Paper Crowns

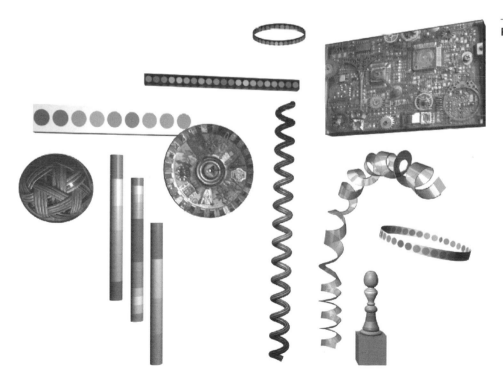

Figure 5.24 Multicolor Magic

results from the usual placements. For example, the Color Dots material is behaving quite differently on the Helix because of the UW projection. Add some of your own multiolor creations to this Library. Color details like these will add pizazz to your Totem.

Editing Volume Shaders: BhodiNUT Charm

While materials produced with the BhodiNUT volume shading engines can be predictable, they can be incredible tools for the 3D artist. Their powerful and infinitely editable calculations can deliver amazing realism or intense drama. Their ease of use comes in handy when generic materials, quickly made, are truly all that is called for. Just remember, everyone has these shading engines so it's up to you to explore them creatively so your materials are unique.

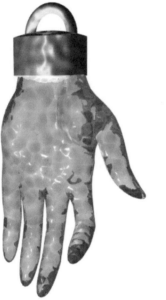

Figure 5.25 Hand Charm

Step 1   Choose File>Open and navigate to Chapter 02>C4DFiles>HAND CHARM .c4d on the DVD. Choose File>Save As and save the file as Hand Charm in your Models folder.

Step 2   In the Materials Manager, choose File>BhodiNUT Volume>BhodiNUT Danel. Change the Diffuse color to a light yellow green. Leave Specular 1 at white, change Specular 2 to light blue, and change Specular 3 to bright turquoise green. Turn on Roughness and choose Turbulence as Bump Function. Check the check box for Anisotrophy. Place the material on the Hanging Fixture object.

Step 3   Now choose File>BhodiNUT Volume>BhodiNUT Banji. On the Diffuse page, change Front Surface and Volume color to a deep turquoise. Change the color of Specular 2 and Specular 3 to a lavender blue. Check Roughness, and choose Voronoi 1 as the Bump Function. Place the material on the HAND object.

8.5 Update   The former BhodiNUT shading engines are now accessed by choosing File>Shader in the Materials Manager.

On the DVD: See GOODIES>MATERIALS>BhodiNut Presets for an awesome collection of Smells Like Almonds classics.

Using a Movie as a Material

Step 1   Choose File>Open and navigate to Chapter 05>C4DFiles>Hypno TV on the DVD. Choose File>Save As and save the file as Galaxy TV in your Models folder.

Step 2   In the Materials Manager, Choose File>New and click the Image button on the Color Pane. Navigate to Chapter 01>MOVIES/STILLS>Galaxy-Ball.mov.

Batch Rendering

CINEMA 4D will work while you snooze. Long renders (which you may certainly run into when the BhodiNUT engines start calculating) can be placed in the Batch Render queue. For any given file, set up all your render settings ahead of time. Save the file with Save Project. Then, with any C4D file open, choose Render>Batch. Click the Job button, and navigate to each file you want to render. You can set up as many as ten files to render overnight, but be certain you set up all the render settings and enter different titles for the files.

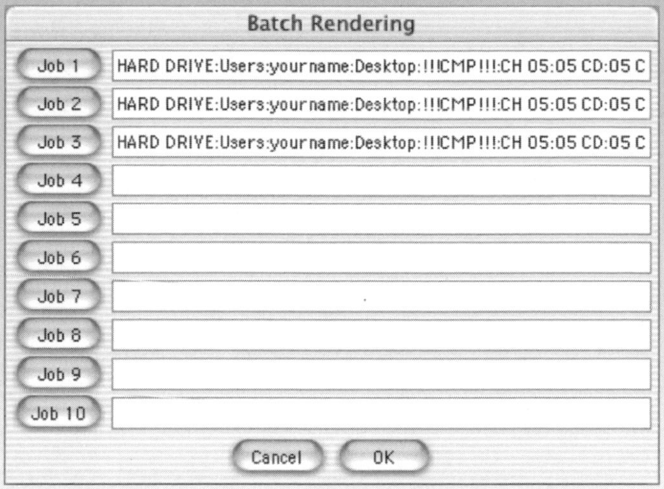

Figure 5.26 Batch Rendering

Step 3   Click the Edit button, and in the Movie Data box enter 90 in the To box. Click OK.
8.5 Update Click on the words GALAXY BALL.mov, and click the Animation panel to edit as in Step 3.

Step 4   Choose Objects>Unfold All from the Objects Manager menu. Drop the Galaxy Ball movie Material on the Disc object.

Figure 5.27
Hypno TV

When you render the Hypno TV animation, the Galaxy movie will play on the TV screen.

Animating Materials

In this project, you'll learn how to animate colors to change over time and copy animation tracks from one object to another.

Step 1   Choose File>Open and navigate to Chapter 05>C4DFiles>StringOfHands on the DVD. Choose File>Save As and save the file as String of Hands in your Models folder. Materials have already been placed on each hand.

Step 2   Open the Animation Layout from the left palette.

Step 3   Open the hierarchy for Hand 1 in the Objects Manager and drag the red texture tag to the right of the Cube object across the editor window and into the empty left area of the Timeline Window.

Step 4   Command-click (or right-click) on the name Tag:Texture in the Timeline window, and drag to New Track>Parameter>Material. On the new

Figure 5.28
Choosing the Animation Layout

track that appears in the Timeline window, Control-click on the track at 0 frames to create a keyframe. Note that the Attributes Manager (Key Properties) now shows information on the single key and the color currently in the Material box is Red.

Figure 5.29 Timeline Track and Key

Timeline
F-Curve
File Edit View Filter Objects Sequences Layer
5 10 15 20 25
Tag: Texture
Material

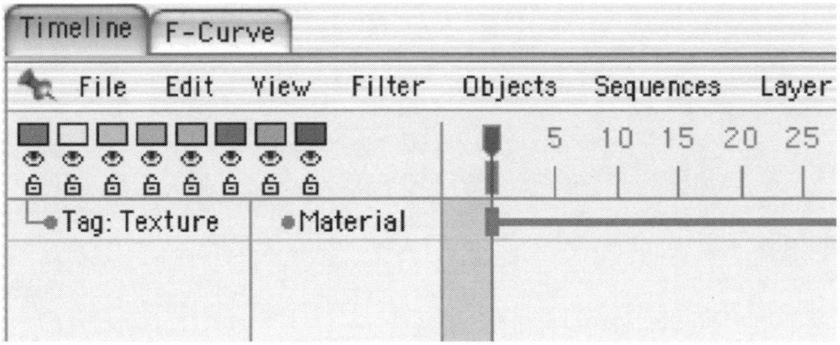

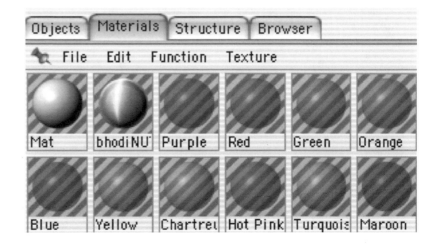

Step 5 Go to 25 frames and Control-click a new key on the track. Click the Materials tab next to the Objects Manager Tab to open the Materials Manager. Drag the thumbnail for Blue into the Material box under Key Properties (down in the Attributes Manager).

Step 6 Control-click new keys every 25 frames across the Timeline, dropping a different color from the Materials manager into the Attributes Manager Material box for each key. If you need to check or adjust the order of colors, just click back on each key and see what color name is in the Material box.

Figure 5.30 Key Properties

Key Properties
Name
Material
Time
25 F
Material
Blue

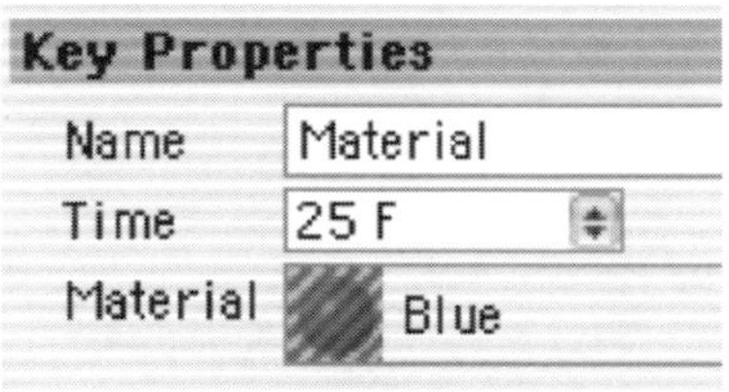

Play the animation by pressing the Play Button or the F8 key and watch Hand 1. The colors appear to be changing suddenly from one to the next every 25 frames. Actually, that's not so. The editor preview doesn't show what's really going on. If you were to render a movie, you'd see that the color is interpolating from one keyframe color to the next. For example, frame 0 is red and frame 25 is Blue, so frame 12 should be about halfway in between, or Violet.

Figure 5.31 Materials Manager

Objects
Materials
Structure
Browser
File Edit Function Texture
Mat
bhodiNU
Purple
Red
Green
Orange
Blue
Yellow
Chartreu
Hot Pink
Turquois
Maroon

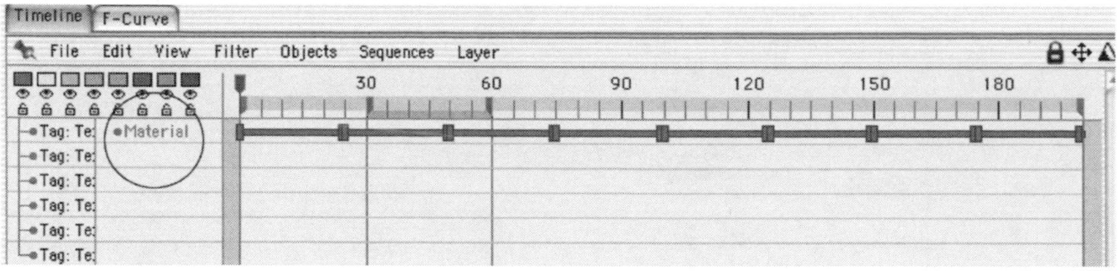

Figure 5.32 Material Selected

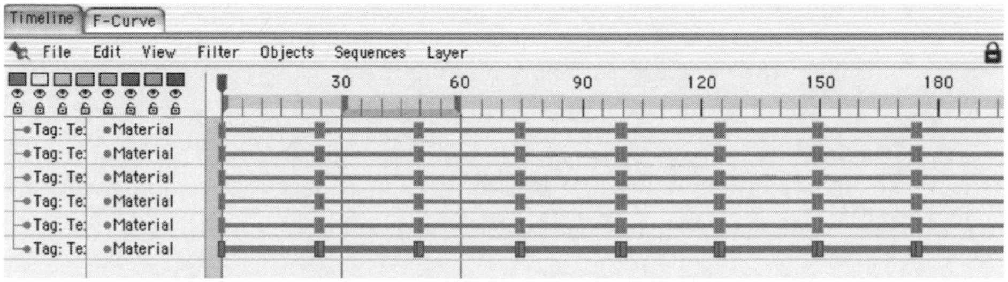

Figure 5.33 Copied Tracks and Keys

Sometimes you want this effect, but what if you want the color to change suddenly from one to the next? You can Control-drag a copy of the red key at 0 and place it at frame 24, so there is a sudden jump to blue. You can do this later if you want, as a last step in setting up this animation.

Step 7   In the Objects Manager, close the Hand 1 Hierarchy. Open the hierarchy so you can see all the remaining Hands. The plan is to drag the Texture tag of the Cube object inside each Hand to the Timeline window. You can Shift-click to select them all at once, and drag them to the Timeline in a group. If you touch the bottom of the Objects Window with the mouse, it will scroll and allow you to keep adding objects to the selection.

Step 8   Select the word Material next to the top tag in the Timeline window. Then hold down the Control key and drag a copy of the track and its keys down to each texture tag below.

Play the animation again by pressing the Play button or the F8 Key. Synchronization looks better in swimming. The vertical columns of keyframes represent identical colors beginning at the same times. For varied colors to change at different times, what needs to happen? The keyframes need to be randomly jumbled up across and down through the tracks. Later, you'll learn how to use Expressions to randomize this type of thing. For now, get in there and play leapfrog with those keyframes. Be careful that you don't select tracks, but carefully pick up keys and move them to different positions on the other tracks.

Step 9   Make sure no tracks are selected. Starting with the left vertical column, move keys to other locations on their respective tracks. Things happening at the same time produce a mechanical effect and is the animation

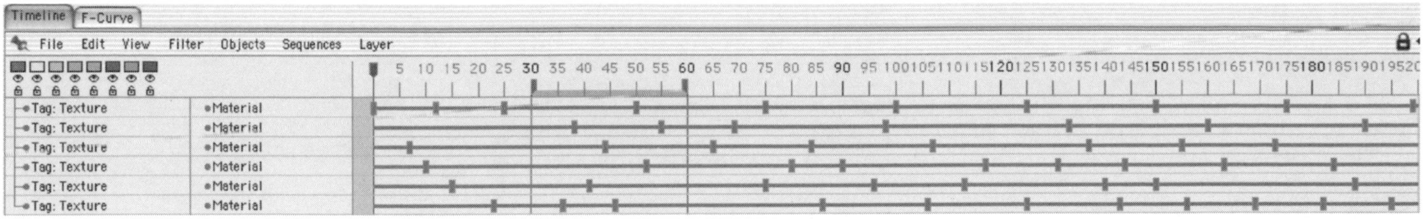

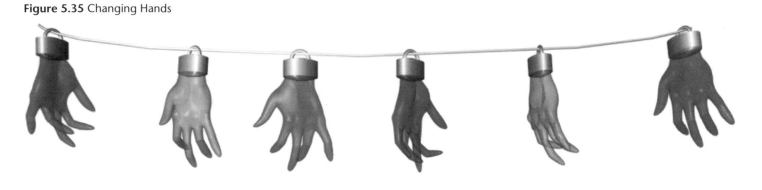

Figure 5.34 Randomized Keys

equivalent of a model that is too clean and perfect. Vertical columns of keys are a red flag that too many things are changing at the same time so start shifting keys sideways, varying the spacing between them.

Preview occasionally to see if you are starting to get the fidgety random look as in the example movie on the DVD. Figure 5.34 shows a nice random set of keys. When you satisfied with the spread of keys, render a movie.

On the DVD: See Chapter 05>MOVIES/STILLS>CHANGING HANDS.mov.

Figure 5.35 Changing Hands

● ***Springboard!*** Now that you know how to animate materials, try another one. Open GOOD-IES>MATERIALS>Materials Library 1 and save a copy of the file to your Models folder. Then choose five or six very different materials like wood, marble, and glass. Place one of the materials on a sphere, then use the steps above to animate these to change suddenly. By positioning a copy of a key immediately before the next different one, you'll hold the current value and prevent it from interpolating.

● ***Springboard!*** After you finish the next chapter on lighting, reopen String of Hands.c4d and place some randomly blinking lights inside the hands. These will look fabulous hanging in the spooky art museum you'll create in Chapter 15, Environment, Mood and Magic.

On the DVD: See Chapter 05>MOVIES/STILLS>PRESTO CHANGO.mov. And see Chapter 05>EXTRA!EXTRA! for web resources and other ideas for materials.

8.5 Update Beyond the changes you have seen reflected in these exercises are many exciting new ways of working with materials in Version 8.5. See the 8.5 Update for information on using exciting new shaders like the Layer shader, the Dirt shader and others. The new methods for building Materials allow infinite stacking of shaders, bringing a new level of rich imagery to your work.

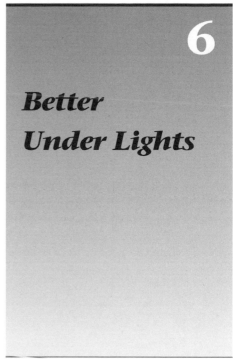

6

Better Under Lights

Figure 6.1

CINEMA 4D includes a default light every time you open a new scene, and if just illuminating a scene were the only function of lighting, you would never need to create or edit a light. Artistically, however, light can be used to invoke mood and drama, enhance modeling and spatial depth, paint the scene with color, influence textures, focus attention, invent magic, and so much more. After an introduction to basic lighting setup, this chapter will concentrate on some creative possibilities of lighting. Time spent studying different types of lights and their settings in the C4D manual and investigating resources about photographic or theatrical lighting will pay big dividends in the look of your work.

On the DVD: See Chapter 06>EXTRA!EXTRA!>Resources>Lighting.

The Virtual Studio: Three Point Lighting

The classic three point lighting system borrowed from the world of traditional photography provides a great starting place for dependable lighting setups. As your knowledge of lighting grows, you'll have fun adding many creative twists to the basics.

Step 1 Choose File>Open and navigate to Chapter 06>C4D Files>Photographic Lighting.c4d. Choose File>Save As and save the file as Photographic Lighting in your Models folder.

Figure 6.2 Lighting Icon

Step 2 Click on the Lighting icon located on the top palette.

The light that appears is a default Omni light. This kind of light shines out in all directions at once. Press Ctrl+R to preview how the light looks in general, noting how the surfaces of the objects are either light or quite dark. Using the Model and Move tools, take the light for a test drive around the space. Lights can be moved manually using the Move tool, or you can enter numerical coordinates for the light.

Step 3   Rename the Light as MAIN. In the Attributes Manager, click the Coordinates panel. Enter –70 for P.X, 50 for P.Y, and –70 for P.Z. Click the General panel, and drag the Brightness slider to 90 percent.

A typical position for a Main light (sometimes called Key light), is above the subject and 45º to one side.

Step 4   Control-drag a copy of MAIN and rename the copy FILL. In the Attributes Manager, click the Coordinates panel. Enter 120 for P.X, 12 for P.Y, and –60 for P.Z.

The FILL light is usually placed on the opposite side of the MAIN, and below the MAIN light. The relationship or ratio of the brightness of the MAIN light to the FILL light is variable. Typically, you want the side of the subject not illuminated by the MAIN to be illuminated enough so you can see detail on the surface yet dark enough so the two sides are appreciably different in value. It is this difference that creates the sense that the object is a 3D solid. However, the FILL light can be increased in brightness for softer contrast and a lighter look overall.

Figure 6.3 Main to Fill Ratios (L) Low Ratio, (R) High Ratio

A low MAIN to FILL ratio has softer contrast and more overall brightness. Notice how the front and side planes of the cube are close in value. A high MAIN to FILL ratio is more harsh and dramatic, with more dark and less detailed shadow areas.

Step 5   Click the General Panel and drag the Brightness slider for the Fill light to 40 percent. Test render with Ctrl+R.

Step 6:   Notice the hotspot on the back wall. Disturbing! Shift-click both the MAIN and FILL lights and click the Scene panel. Drag the object ROOM from the Objects Manager list into the XObjects box. Test render again with Ctrl+R.

This ability to Exclude or Include scene objects is a great feature, and can be used to tell a light NOT to shine on any object.

Step 7   On the other hand, we don't want the back wall to be black. Click the Light palette again to create another Omni light. Working in All Views, place it close behind the cube right above the floor. Assign the light a

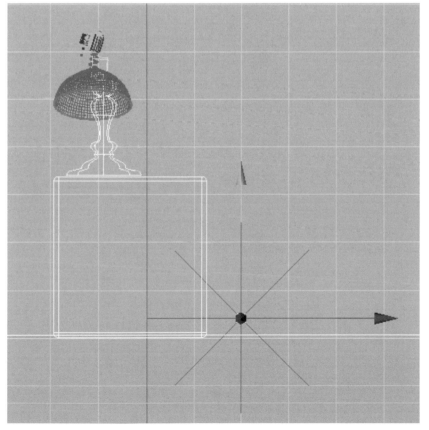

Figure 6.4 Background Light Position

Brightness of 40 percent and name it Background as we are using it to softly illuminate the backdrop.

None of these Attributes are set in stone. When using multiple lights in a 3D space, the Brightness of all lights that are radiating light will need to be turned down and balanced so that the overall illumination isn't overexposed. If a surface has a solid white area with no detail (a photographer would call this "blown out") it's time to turn down the Brightness of your lights. In addition, the form of a model may require you to move the lights to different positions so the shadows are nicely shaped. Use your eyes and adjust the lights so that the subject looks good through the camera. At the moment, the camera is the default editor camera. Later you will learn how to create scene cameras and your lights should be set up in relation to the camera you are using.

Changing The Type Of Light

Let's change the MAIN light from an Omni to a round Spotlight that points in a specific direction.

Step 1   Make sure the MAIN light is selected, and in the General panel, choose Spot (Round) from the Type pull-down menu.

Spotlights have to be aimed. You could use the Move and Rotate tools to aim the light at the subject. Let's try an easier method, and use a Target Expression to point the light at a specific object.

Step 2   Command-click (right-click) on the MAIN light, and drag to New Expression>Target Expression in the contextual menu. Choose Objects>Unfold All from the Objects Manager menu.
　　　　　　Making sure the Target Expression tag is selected, drag the BEANIE (much further down inside the BEANIE CAM object) into the Target Object box.
　　　　　　If you want to edit the width of the light cone, you can use the orange interactive handles in the Editor window or change the values in the Attributes manager Details panel. Reduce the brightness if necessary.

Step 3   Render the scene (Ctrl+R). Notice anything weird? A light that strong just has to have a shadow. C4D needs to be told that. With MAIN selected, choose Hard from the Shadow pulldown menu in the General panel. Test render. Then try the other two types of shadows, noticing that Area Shadows have more subtle shading but take a lot longer to render.

Step 4   At the moment, you see the effects of the light falling on objects, but you don't really see the light beam itself. In the General panel, choose Visible from the Visible Light pulldown menu.
　　　　　　You may want to set the shadow back to Soft for faster rendering.

Step 5   Click the Color box and give the MAIN light a slightly warm tone. (255 R, 249 G, 201 B). Select the FILL light, and in the General tab, give the color a touch of pale lavender blue (199 R, 189 G, 255 B).

Figure 6.5 Main and Fill (Area Shadow)

Choosing Appropriate Lighting

The best 3D scenes communicate clearly, have cohesive design, and are spatially believable. Understanding the specific qualities of light and learning how to manipulate light behavior in the 3D world is crucial to the unity of a scene. It's important to make conscious decisions about emotion and design ahead of time, so lighting is chosen and edited to enhance the overall goals for the scene. By having a clear idea of what you want the viewer to get from the scene, you can use the many qualities of light toward that end. Here's a partial checklist.

- What is the mood of the scene and what overall brightness is appropriate? Which type of light will best fit the scene's sense of time and place?

- How do individual lights in a multiple light arrangement relate to each other in brightness and contrast? How will this ratio affect modeling and shadows?

- Should the light come from one source for a hard edged, dramatic look or have multiple points of origin for a softer, more diffused feel?

- How rapidly will the intensity of the light fall off?

- Will light travel in one direction and stop or bounce from surface to surface?

- What color is the light? Should the color convey a specific mood? Can the warmth or coolness of lights be used to articulate space or establish time of day?

- What kind of shadows are appropriate for the mood of the scene?

- Will the light be animated to move, flicker, surge, or change in brightness or color over time? Will the light have shadow patterns moving through it?

- Is the light visible? Does it honor the mass of objects in its path? Is it clean or is it filled with dust?

General Tips for Lighting in C4D

- Name lights by the function they are performing in the scene. Names like 70 percent Main, 40 percent Fill, Backlight, or Right Blue Puff say so much more than Light 1 and Light 2.

- Set up lighting in regard to the camera the scene will be viewed through.

- Shift-click to select multiple lights for simultaneous editing.

- Use Gouraud shading for feedback on how the lights are affecting the scene.

- Use the gray visibility switches to turn lights on one at a time to see the effect each light is having on the model.

- Model for lighting. Sharp corners have no surface to catch light. Create fillets, roundings, and bevels on your models to show off the highlights.

- If the scene calls for multiple lights, turn off radiation on most of them so the dominant light still comes from one direction. Not only will too many radiating lights quickly overexpose the scene, but light from too many directions can be visually chaotic. Set up a strong basic structure of light and shadow, then add puffs of visible color that add interest but contribute no illumination to the scene. Think of it as painting with light.

- Turn off textures temporarily to see lighting effects more accurately.

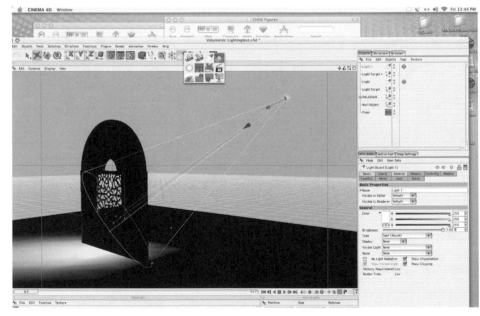

Figure 6.6 Target Light

Turn Up the Volume

Volumetric lights are visible light beams that honor the volume of objects in their path and shadow the light beam accordingly. Long rendering times are the price, but the payoff can be spectacular.

Step 1 Choose File>Open and navigate to Chapter 06>C4D Files> Volumetric Lighting.c4d. Choose File>Save As and save the file as Volumetric Lighting in your Models folder.

Step 2 Click on the Lighting palette and drag to the Target light on the far right of the top row.

Step 3 With the Light still selected, click the Attributes manager Coordinates panel and enter 100m for P.X, 1000 for P.Y, and 900 for P.Z.

Step 4   Click the Target tag to the right of the Light. Drag the Null Object from the Objects Manager into the Target Object box in the Attributes Manager.

Figure 6.7 Target Tag

◆ ***Tip:*** Null Objects come in handy when you need something invisible to use as a target for a light or camera.

Step 5   With Light selected, click the General panel. Choose Spot (Round) for Type, choose Soft from the Shadow pulldown menu and Volumetric from the Visible Light pulldown menu.

Step 6   With the Light still selected, click the Visibility panel in the Attributes Manager. Adjust the Outer Distance of the light beam so that it it long enough to extend through the floor. You could use the orange interactive handle in the center of the light cone to do the same thing. In the editor window, drag the orange interactive handles on the circle to widen the cone so it covers the object.

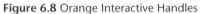

Figure 6.8 Orange Interactive Handles

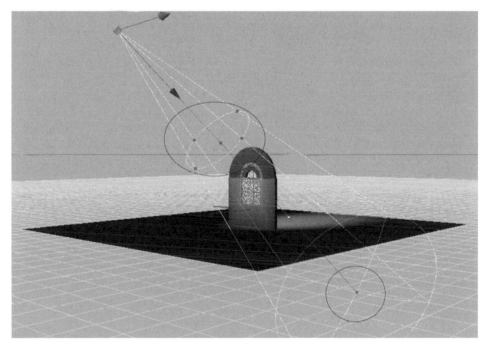

● ***Springboard!*** Try moving the light behind the object so the light patterns spill out in front.

On the DVD: See Chapter 06>EXTRA!EXTRA!>Lighting Examples to see setups for other types of lights.

Figure 6.9 Volumetric Light

Figure 6.10 Cone Position

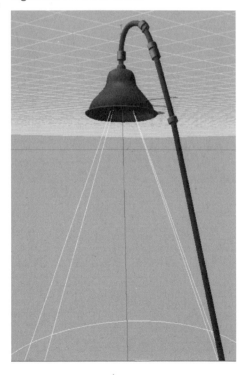

Throwing Shadows with Gobos

In the theater set world, *gobos* or cookies are patterned gels placed in front of a light to fake the appearance of shadows. For example, a leaf pattern placed over a light could create the illusion of the sun shining through a tree and cast the shadow on a floor or wall. In C4D, still images or movies can be placed on lights to create all kinds of illusions. In this project, the gobo will cause the light streaming down out of the lightcaster to have more visible rays.

Step 1 Choose File>Open and navigate to Chapter 06>C4D Files>Lightcaster> Lightcaster.c4d. Choose File>Save As and save the file as Lightcaster in your Models folder.

Step 2 Click on the Lighting palette. Rename the new light Blue Spotlight.

Step 3 In the Attributes Manager General panel, change the Type to Spot (Round), the Shadow to Soft, the Visible Light to Volumetric, and the Noise to Visibility.

Step 4 Working in All Views, use the Move and Rotate tools to position the cone of light inside the Lamp Head object, and point the light beam downward. Make sure the light is low enough in the lamp head, so that the geometry of the lamp head doesn't block the light. Use the orange interactive handles to adjust the width and length of the light beam.

Step 5   With Blue Spotlight still selected, click the Attributes Manager Visibility panel. Make sure Use Falloff is checked and enter 60 percent as the value. Check Edge Falloff and enter 10 percent. Check Colored Edge Falloff. Check the check box for Custom Colors. Edit the Inner Color to be a light sky blue, and the Outer Color to be a pale green.

Step 6   Click the Attributes Manager Noise panel. With Soft Turbulence as the Type, enter 8 for Octaves. Enter 50 percent for Velocity and 125 percent for Contrast. Enter 10m for Wind and 5m for Wind Velocity.

Step 7   In the Materials Manager, click the SHADOW MAP Material thumbnail. This Material will be the Gobo, so inspect the Material Editor Parameters to see how it's set up. The Gobo pattern always goes in the Transparency channel. Place the material SHADOW MAP on the Blue Spotlight object in the Objects Manager.

Step 8   Now, inspect the material thumbnail BEAM MAP. Drag and drop the material thumbnail onto theShadow Map texture tag (already on the light) to replace it.Test render (Ctrl+R). Experiment with editing the BhodiNUT tile shader in the BEAM MAP Material to get different thicknesses of Beams, or try different Tile values in the texture tag properties.

Step 9   If you want to, animate the Spotlight to rotate and the LAMP HEAD to swing gently back and forth. The Noise in the Spotlight is already set up to move though the light.

Blinking Puffs of Light

Step 1   Choose File>Open and navigate to Chapter 06>C4D Files>AntiqueBulb .c4d. Choose Save As and save the file as Antique Bulb in your Models folder.

Step 2   Click the Lighting palette and use the green Move handle to move the Light upward into the widest part of the bulb. Make the Light a child of the Antique Bulb object. Rename Light as Bulb Light.

Step 3   In the Attributes Manager General panel, choose Visible for Visible Light. Edit the color to be a warm gold (255 R, 236 G, 175 B). Check the check box for No Light Radiation to prevent too much distracting change in the base color during animation.

Step 4   Edit the size of the Visibility to your liking by using the orange interactive handles in the editor window, or changing the Outer Distance settings in the Visibility panel.

Step 5   Command-click (right-click) on the name Bulb Light and drag to New Tag>Display Tag. In the Attributes Manager, check the checkbox for Use Visibility.

Figure 6.11 Lightcaster

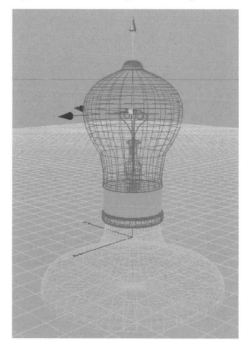

Figure 6.12 Positioning the Bulb Light

◆ **Tip:** Remember that unless you double up on the keyframes, CINEMA 4D will interpolate between 0 and 100 so that the light fades in and out. If that's what you want, try it, but for sudden blinks you need the hold key right before the changed key.

Step 6 At 10 frames, keyframe a value of 100 percent by Command-clicking (right-clicking) on the word Visibility and dragging to Add Keyframe. Then at frame 11, keyframe a Visibility value of 0 percent. At frame 13, keyframe 0 percent again, and then at frame 16, keyframe 100 percent.

Step 7 Open the Animation Layout and drag the Display Tag from the right of Bulb Light in the Objects Manager and drop it into the Timeline window.

Step 8 In the Timeline window, drag a selection rectangle over the four keys so that only they, and not the track, are selected. Control-drag copies of the keys across the Timeline. Render a preview or movie, and then go back and play with the timing of the blinks by dragging the keys to different times. If you want shorter blinks, just move the 0 percent keys closer together.

Figure 6.13 Copied and Moved Keyframes

Timeline	F-Curve

File Edit View Filter Objects Sequences Layer

0   5   10   15   20   25   30   35   40   45   50   55   60   65   70   75   80   85

Tag: Display ⊞•Visibility

Figure 6.14 Antique Bulb

Use this basic technique to illuminate the bulbs in your Peephole Box. Have fun experimenting with different timing for all the bulbs so they randomly flicker on and off. Need some stars in a night sky? Use this same technique, but edit the nonradiating lights to have the tiniest puffs of Visibility Outer Distance.

On the DVD: See Chapter 06>EXAMPLES>Finished Peephole Box.

Editing Multiple Lights

Step 1 Choose File>Open and navigate to Chapter 06>C4D Files>Light Mine .c4d. Choose File>Save As and save the file as Light Mine in your Models folder.

Step 2 Click the Light palette icon. In the Attributes Manager General panel, choose a very light blue for the Color and choose Visible from the Visible Light pulldown menu. In the Visibility panel, change the Outer Distance to 100m. Make the Light a child of LittleSphere.

Step 3 In the top menu, click the Array Object. Drop the object LittleSphere into the object Array.

Step 4 Make sure the Array is selected, and in the Attributes Manager enter a Radius of 200m.

Step 5 Select the Light inside the LittleSphere. In the Attributes Manager General panel, change the Brightness to 50 percent. Change the Type to Spot (Round).

If you now wanted to edit each light independently (for instance, making each one a separate color) you still can.

Step 6   Select the Array object and press the C key. Now each LittleSphere and the light inside it can be edited individually. Drag the Purple material from the Materials Manager onto every other LittleSphere in the Editor window.

Step 7   If you wanted to edit another attribute on all the lights at once, that's still possible. In the Objects Manager, Shift-click to select all the lights inside LittleSpheres. Click the Visibility panel and change the Outer Distance to 500. All lights are edited together. If you wanted to, you could animate the Visibility Distance to surge in and out over time (you can Command-click the Outer Distance and keyframe away). That animation would apply to all selected lights.

Step 8   Now, Shift-click to select Array, Rims, and Bigsphere, press G to group them and rename the group Light Mine. Animate the Light Mine to rotate 360º. Sit back and watch the light show.

◆ ***Tip:*** The multiple lights inside the array are instances, so if you edit the original light all the instances will change in the same way. These lights at 100 percent would be too bright, so you can edit the original to "take down" all the lights at once.

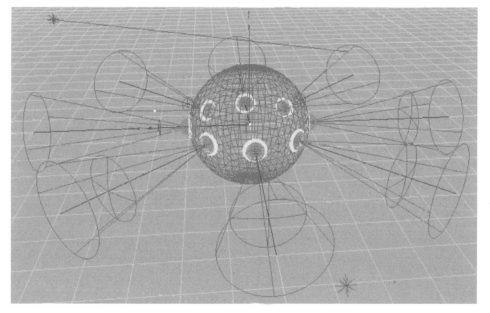

Figure 6.15 LightMine

Animating Light Position

Step 1   Choose File>Open and navigate to Chapter 06>C4D Files>LightSpiral. c4d. Choose File>Save As and save the file as Light Spiral in your Models folder.

Step 2   Click the Lighting palette. Rename Light as Purple.

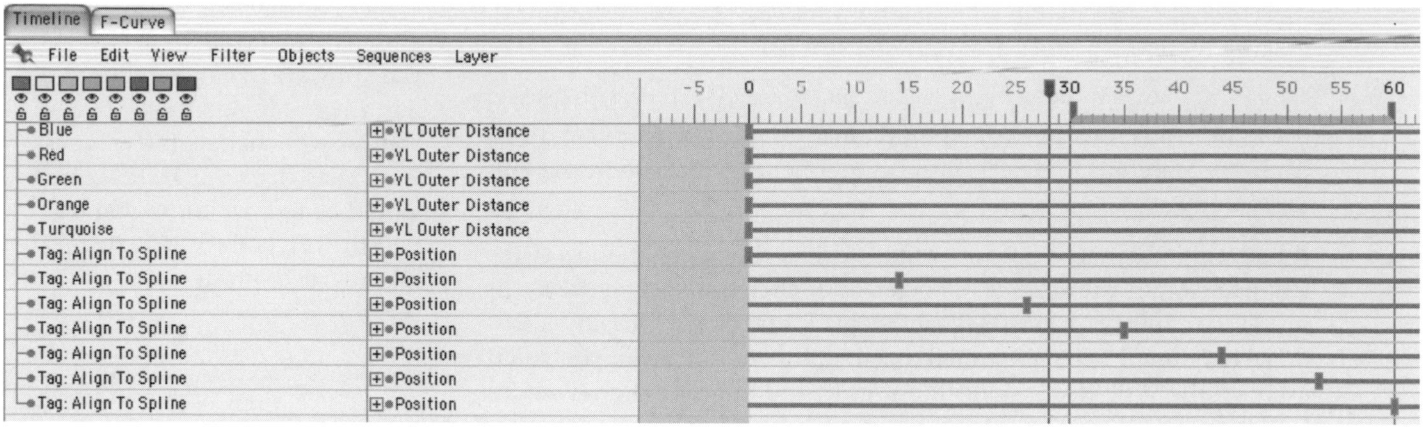

Timeline | F-Curve

File   Edit   View   Filter   Objects   Sequences   Layer

		-5	0	5	10	15	20	25	▌30	35	40	45	50	55	60
Blue	⊞•VL Outer Distance														
Red	⊞•VL Outer Distance														
Green	⊞•VL Outer Distance														
Orange	⊞•VL Outer Distance														
Turquoise	⊞•VL Outer Distance														
Tag: Align To Spline	⊞•Position														
Tag: Align To Spline	⊞•Position														
Tag: Align To Spline	⊞•Position														
Tag: Align To Spline	⊞•Position														
Tag: Align To Spline	⊞•Position														
Tag: Align To Spline	⊞•Position														
Tag: Align To Spline	⊞•Position														

Figure 6.16 Align to Spline Keys

Figure 6.17 Light Spiral

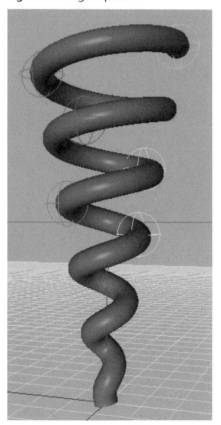

Step 3   In the Attributes Manager General panel, choose Visible for Visible Light. Edit the color to be purple. Check the check box for No Light Radiation.

Step 4   Click the Visibility panel and change the Outer Distance to 100m. Keyframe that value at 0 frames. Change the current time to 90 frames and keyframe an Outer Distance of 30m.

Step 5   Select the Purple object. Command-click (right-click) and drag to New Expression>Align to Spline.

Step 6   Make sure the Align to Spline tag is selected in the Objects Manager. In the Attributes Manager, drag the object Helix from within the Sweep NURBS into the Spline Path box under Tag Properties.

Step 7   Place the current time slider at 0 frames. Command-click (Right-click) on the word Position and set a keyframe of 0 percent (completion along the path) at 0 frames. Change the current time to 90 frames, enter 100 percent next to Position, press Return (Enter), and set a keyframe.

Step 8   Control-drag seven copies of Purple in the Objects Manager. Change the color of each copy to a different color of the rainbow and rename the lights accordingly.

Step 9   Open the Animation Layout. Shift-click (or drag a rectangular marquis over) all the Align to Spline Tags in the Objects Manager and drag them all into the Timeline window.

Step 10   Skip the top Align to Spline Position track, but starting with the next track down, drag the first key for each color (originally at 0 frames) so that the trip down the helix begins later and later. The last tag should be at 60 frames. Check Figure 6.16 for an example of key positions. Render a movie. (Information about rendering an animation into a movie is in Chapter 12, the Art of Rendering, or in the Appendix.)

Painting with Light

Step 1 Choose File>Open and navigate to Chapter 06>C4D Files>PaintingWith Light.c4d. Choose File>Save As and save the file as Painting with Light in your Models folder.

Step 2 Select all the colored lights in the Objects Manager, and in the General panel choose Visible under the Visible Light menu and Visibility from the Noise menu. Check the checkbox for No Light Radiation. In the Visibility panel, set the Visibility Outer Distance to 500. Render with Ctrl+R.

Step 3 Now try making two custom colors for each light in the Visibility panel. Limit your choices to soft colors.

Step 4 With all the lights selected, animate a subtle Heading rotation so the camera will see the lights from slowly changing angles.

On the DVD: Investigate Chapter 06>MOVIES/STILLS for some examples of light paintings. See Chapter 06>EXTRA!EXTRA!>InDepth! for the Light Saber extra project and for other example files demonstrating creative light power.

● ***Springboard!*** Experiment with different Falloff values in the Visibility tab. If you want to animate the lights changing in color, click the color name in the Timeline and choose File>New Track>Parameter>Color>R, G, or B to change the color over time.

● ***Springboard!*** Think of ways to combine lights with all you have learned so far. Use the Arrange, Duplicate, and Randomize functions to create all kinds of Light Sets. Reopen String of Hands.c4d and place some lights inside the hands.

Figure 6.18 Top Spotlight with Hard Shadow, (Tree courtesy of OnyxTREE)

Animation ABCs

7

Figure 7.1

Animation is so much more than just moving things from here to there, up and down, and round and round. You've already been working with motion and other changes over time and have had a chance to see how almost any attribute in CINEMA 4D can be easily animated. You also already know that keyframes contain information about the current state of a specific attribute of an object at any single point in time. Technically speaking, animation occurs when the hardware/software team in your computer interpolates or calculates the gradual changes between those keyframes. In this chapter we will spend more time getting to know the Timeline and F-Curve manager, intuitive working environments for setting up what will happen to all the objects in your scene over time. Using these powerful tools to tweak movement and change will make the difference between mechanical motion and models that spring to life.

After all the homework of setting up the animation is done, the rendering process produces a sequence of still picture frames which will be displayed rapidly at a speed determined by your chosen media (TV is 29.9 frames and film is 24). The illusion of motion, or a movie, is born.

Hence the technical description of animation, but it's the aesthetic or artistic side of the word that makes audiences believe a totally invented character is thinking, feeling, and moving of his or her own volition. The one-word definition of *animation* is liveliness, and as an animation artist you'll be aiming for creative motion, believability and expression. Craft and digital technology are expanding in quantum leaps, providing exciting tools for the artist and exciting new aesthetics in the field of animation.

On the DVD: See Chapter 07>EXTRA!EXTRA!>References

A is for Airplane Hat:
Working Out Timing

In this simple flying animation, you'll be working with the Timeline and F-Curves to master timing and lifelike motion.

Step 1   Choose File>Open and navigate to Chapter 07>C4D Files>Airplane Hat.c4d. Choose File>Save As and save the file as Airplane Hat in your Models folder.

Step 2   Work in the Front view and use the 2 key to close in on the hat for a good view. Select the Airplane Hat object, and using the Object Axis tool and the green handle of the Move tool, move the axis to the floor. Select the Model tool when you are finished.

Figure 7.2 Axis to Floor

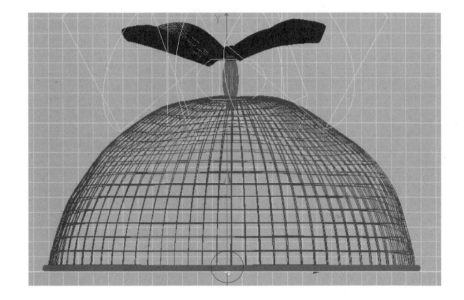

Step 3   With Airplane Hat selected, click the Attributes Manager Coordinates panel. Click any of the letters P, and set a starting keyframe at frame 0 for all three current position values. (Command-click or right-click and drag to Animation>Add Keyframe.) Choose the Animation Layout.

Step 4   In the Timeline, select all three keys (not the tracks) and Control-drag a copy of them to frame 120 (at which point the hat will take off into the air).

At the beginning of the animation, we want the hat to sit and think about taking off and even struggle a little to make it happen. Frames 0–120 provide time for some preliminary action to occur, using the animation principle of anticipation. By copying the keys, we are making the hat stay in that position for

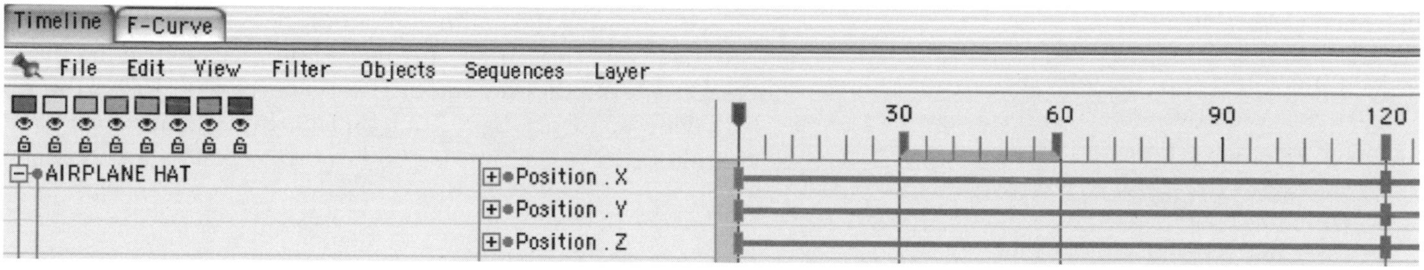

Figure 7.3 Copied Keys

a while. We could have created that keyframe with other methods as you already know, but in this project most of the work will be done in the Timeline and F-Curve manager.

Step 5 From the Timeline menu, choose View>Frame All. Control-drag another copy of those keys to frame 700. Select a key at frame 700. Notice how all three keys are selecting together. That's because Vector Selection is activated. In the Timeline menu, click the Edit menu and uncheck Vector Selection.

Step 6 With the current time to Frame 700, switch to Perspective view. Select only the Position.X key at frame 700 in the Timeline. In Attributes Manager Key Properties, drag the small black arrows next to the P.X value and watch the editor window. Then enter 2000 in the box and press Return (Enter).

Figure 7.4 Uncheck Vector Selection

You have animated the broad motion of the hat from "here to there."

Step 7 Now click the F-Curve tab. Choose View>Frame All from the F-Curve menu. So that you can work only on the vertical motion of the hat, click Position.Y.

Note that you are totally bypassing use of the Object tool/Move tool and the Attributes Manager Coordinates keyframing. Everything can be animated in these powerful windows by Control-clicking new keys or copying keys and tweaking their values in the Timeline or F-Curve.

Step 8 At frame 165, Control-click a new key on the Position.Y curve and in the Attributes Manager Key Properties, enter a value of 1000. Choose View>Frame All if you need to see the whole graph. If you wanted a lot of rollercoaster action, you could click as many keys as you wanted and drag them up and down on the curve, interactively controlling the height of the hat in the Editor window.

- If it is difficult to see the exact time on the time ruler, feedback for the precise time and value appears at the lower left of the Timeline.
- You can Control-click a key on a track in the general vicinity and then enter the exact value in the Time box in Key Properties.
- Note that the blue current time tab in the Timeline or F-Curve manager gives more specific control when working in zoomed views than the Current time slider in the Animation Timeline.

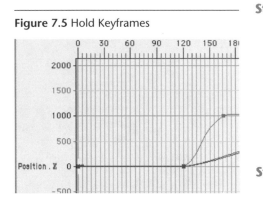

Figure 7.5 Hold Keyframes

Figure 7.6 Ease Ins at Frame 700

Step 9 Now we want to swing the hat in and out of the Z space. Click on Position.Z. At frame 240, create a key and drag it upward to 400 on the graph. At frame 330, add another key and drag the value to –400. Check the top view for a better sense of what's going on with the animation path and play the animation. (Click the Play button on the Animation Timeline or press F8.)

Working with Custom Tangents

When you previewed the animation, you saw the hat dipping below the floor at the beginning. (That occurred because the sudden rise of the hat at Frame 165 affected the whole curve.) Click the Position.Y graph and you'll see the dip on the graph between frames 0 and 60. Also, the hat is traveling along the path at the same monotonous speed.

Step 1 First let's fix that dip. In the left panel of the F-Curve window, click on Position.X, Position.Y and Position.Z so they are all red (selected). Drag a rectangular selection rectangle over the keys (stacked on top of each other) at Frame 0. Command-click (right-click) on the keys at frame 0. From the contextual menu, choose Hold. Now the original vertical position is maintained until it changes at the next keyframe.

Step 2 Now we'll customize tangents for more natural timing by creating some Ease-ins on the keys at frame 700. Make sure Position.X, Position.Y, and Position.Z are selected (red) and choose View>Frame All so you can see all the graphs. Drag a selection rectangle over all the keys at frame 700. Command-click (right-click) any one of the keys, and choose Curves> Custom Tangents>Soft Interpolation to make tangent handles appear. Then (from the same contextual menu) choose Curves>Custom Tangents>Flat. Drag the tangent handles for each curve back to the frame 500 mark on the graph.

Step 3 With Airplane Hat still selected, set the current time to frame 120. In the Attributes Manager Coordinates panel, click any of the letters R and set starting keyframes. Move the current time to 700 frames. Then click on just the H in R.H, and keyframe a value of 360 degrees. The hat will spin in a full 360 degree rotation from frame 120 to frame 700.

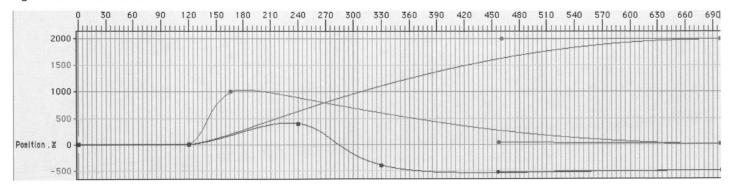

Take It Easy: Ease Outs, Ease Ins, and Easy Ease

A classic principle of animation is that most motion does not happen and end suddenly, but eases into and out of the action. On a graph, a straight diagonal line between two keys means that the change is beginning immediately and happening at a constant rate.

Ease Ins: In Step 2 you created Ease Ins on the final X, Y, and Z Position keys. By flattening these curves, you caused the values of the selected keys to be effective sooner and longer. The effect is that the hat will slow down and float to the floor.

A Typical Ease Out Example: By placing an Ease Out on a 0 value key at Frame 0 of a Position.Y track, the object does not rise immediately but sits still a moment, then starts to rise slowly, and then picks up speed. (The flat part of the curve keeps the motion at its starting value longer, as the more drastic part of the curve shows a more accelerated progression toward the new value.)

Easy Ease: Choosing Easy Ease from the contextual menu places an Ease In on the incoming tangent and an Ease Out on the outgoing tangent of a selected key.

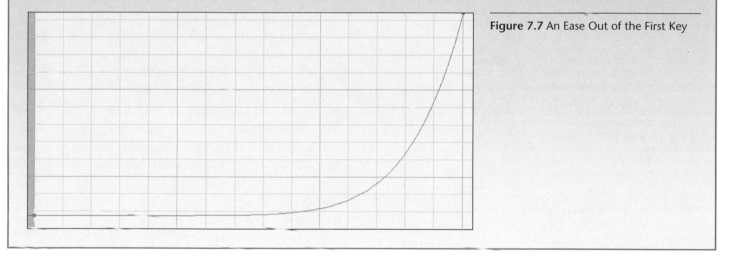

Figure 7.7 An Ease Out of the First Key

Step 4 Working in the F-Curve window, select the words Rotation.P. Choose View>Frame All.

Scrub through the timeline and when you feel the time is right, Control-click a few new "pitch" keys on the curves. Make sure the current time is on the selected key you are currently adjusting so you see the effects correctly in the editor, and drag the small black handles to the right of the Value box in Key Properties, or simply drag the key up or down on the graph. For now, make only a few gentle tilts to give the idea that the hat is blowing in the wind. (Once you get the basics down, you can copy this file and flip the hat all over the place.)

Step 5 Select Rotation.B and give the hat a few gentle bank tilts as well.

Step 6 At frame 700, Pitch and Bank values will need to be "zero'd out" (returned to 0 value) so the hat will sit flat on the floor.

On the DVD: See Chapter 07>EXAMPLES>Airplane Hat.c4d.

◆ *Tips:*
- When fine-tuning animation, work in Wireframe or Isoparm view in the Editor.
- Rendering as Editor (on the first page of the Render Settings) will tell you what you need to know about the movement without long render times.

◆ *Tips:*

- A picture is worth a thousand words! To clearly understand this complex motion, study the F-Curves of the Example C4D file. (Chapter 07>EXAMPLES> Airplane Hat.) As you work to fine tune each element, check out the corresponding graph in the finished animation.

- Less is more. It's tempting to add lots of keys, isn't it? You animation will be more elegant if you use fewer keys and use the tangent handles to adjust the curves for smooth motion. Look at the example C4D file to see how few keys are on the F-Curves.

- Control-click on the Timeline ruler to create markers for important points in the animation. Double-click the marker to enter identifying text.

- To temporarily turn off Vector Selection (so you can select individual keys), hold down the Opt (Alt) key.

Animating the Propeller

Step 1 In the Objects Manager, open the Hierarchy and select the Propeller on Stem object. In the Attributes Manager Coordinates panel, keyframe a R.H value of 0 at frame 0.

Step 2 Drag the name Propeller on Stem and drop it into left window of the F-Curve manager. Choose View>Frame All. Control-drag a copy of the frame 0 key to frame 700, and give the new key a value of 5000.

Step 3 Between frames 0 and 120, we want the propeller to sputter tentatively. At frame 20, keyframe a value of 600, and at frame 25 set a keyframe of 0. (Again, the easiest way to do this is to Control-click a new point on the track and drag it to the correct time while watching the feedback line. Then, enter the Rotation value in the Key Properties value box.)

Step 4 Choose View>Frame all. Drag a rectangular selection over all three keys. Control-click on any one of the selected keys and drag two copies of them to the right on the track. Center the first copy of three keys on frame 50 and the second copy at frame 90. The very last key of the keys that you just copied (a 0 value key) should be around frame 100.

Step 5 Now go back and experiment with raising the values of the keys at frame 50 and 85, and adjust the spacing between the keys to get the effect you want. The propeller can gradually gain strength or begin in a sudden spurt as it tries to start up. Try setting Frame 50 at 1500 and frame 90 at 5000. This value you are currently working with is how many degrees the propeller is spinning.

By now you have noticed that the curves are dipping down below 0 between some of the keys. Actually that could be a good thing in this case. It's creating a "recoil" effect and displaying one of the classic animation principles. (See "Some Animation Principles at Work.") This tiny bit of action communicates the idea that the hat is alive and trying oh so hard to get up steam so it can take off. If you did not want that dip, just place a Hold on the third key of each set.

Step 6 Use the Move and Scale tools at the top right of the F-Curve window (you have to drag on the tool icons) to position the graph so you can see frames 90 though 700. Shift-click to select the keys at frame 100 and 700 and choose Curves>Custom Tangents>Soft Interpolation, and then Curves>Custom Tangents>Flat. (Those can be chosen from the Timeline Menu Curves menu, or by Command-clicking (right-clicking) on one of the selected points to access the contextual menu.)

Step 7 You can use the tangent handles of the keys at frames 100 and 700 to control the slope of the curve and fine tune the rotation of the hat as it takes off and lands.

On the DVD: For more about Animation Principles, See Chapter 07>EXTRA! EXTRA!>References.

Some Animation Principles at Work

- **Anticipation.** Preliminary action that sets the stage for the major action. The bouncing of the airplane hat creates a build-up before take-off.

- **Exaggeration.** The overdone vertical scaling of the Airplane Hat as it stretches upward after a bounce is an exaggerated motion that adds drama and helps the viewer grasp what's going on.

- **Self-Driven Characters.** The short sputters of the Airplane Hat propeller create the illusion that the hat itself is struggling to fly, and not being manipulated by some outside force.

- **Arcs.** The hat moves on an elegant path of arcs, rather than straight lines here to there.

- **Asymmetry.** Jumbled keys (Batty Box) and the Vibrate Expression (Crown of Stars) are typical randomizations that prevent motion from looking too planned and mechanical.

Anticipatory Hops

Step 1   In the F-Curve window you should still see the Rotation.H curve for the Propeller on Stem.

Drag the object Airplane Hat to the F-Curve window also. Click on only Rotation.H (for Propeller on Stem) and Position.Y (for Airplane Hat). Drag a rectangular selection over the keys from frame 0 through 130 and choose View>Frame Selection.

Step 2   Working on the Position.Y track, Control-click new keys and position them to lift the hat in response to the propeller. (When the propeller stops, return the hat to its original vertical position. These little hops will add to the anticipation and build up toward the actual liftoff of the hat.

Step 3   Command-click on these points and choose Tangents>Soft Interpolation. You can then hold down the Shift key and adjust the tangent handles independently. By dragging the tangent handles slightly upward, you can *influence* the curve to rise in the areas where the hat should lift into the air.

In other words, you don't have to place *keys* at the high points of the hops but can use the tangent handles to raise the curve. Fewer keys and more work with curves will make for smoother motion and a much less cluttered graph! It's the position of the *curve* at any point in time determines "how high" the hat is positioned. These little hops will add to the *anticipation* and buildup toward the actual lift off of the hat. Now that you've been introduced to the power of working with Tangent handles, you could go back and delete the keys on the Rotation.H curve at Frames 20, 50, and 90 (which are currently defining the highest degrees of rotation) and use tangent handles to shape those curves.

Step 4   The hat is sitting still for a few frames between hops. To insure that the 0 value is maintained between two "0" keys on the Position.Y curve, Command-click on the first one of the pair and and choose Hold from the contextual menu.

Figure 7.8 Anticipatory Hops, Rotation.H (Propeller on Stem) and Position Y (Airplane Hat) Curves

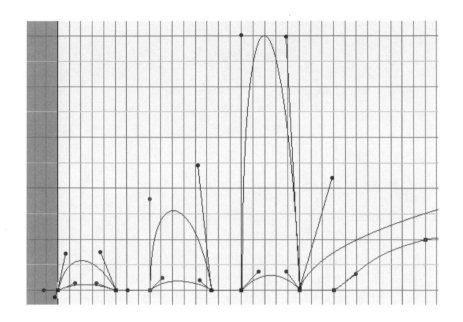

On the DVD: See Chapter 07>EXAMPLES>Airplane Hat for the C4D file and Chapter 07>MOVIES/STILLS>Airplane Hat for a finished movie.

Squash and Stretch

Step 1   Select the Airplane Hat object in the Objects Manager, and click the Coordinates tab in the Attributes Manager.

Step 2   At frame 0, click the Y in S.Y and set a starting keyframe. Drag the object Airplane Hat into the F-Curve window again and click only Scale.Y.

Step 3   Scrub though the timeline. Set keyframes for the Y Scale that make the hat appear to squash down every time it hits the floor. You won't want the value to interpolate between the scale of 1 (the unsquashed state) and the lower scale value, causing the hat to squash before it hits the ground. To prevent this, use a Hold key or copy an unsquashed state key to the frame right before the hat hits the ground. Every time the hat leaves the floor, you could increase the Y Scale slightly to give the illusion that the hat is springing and stretching up toward its destination. (This is the animation principle of exaggeration hard at work.) Scrub through the example C4D file in a close-up Front Editor view and zoom in on the keys in the F-Curve manager to study the setup.

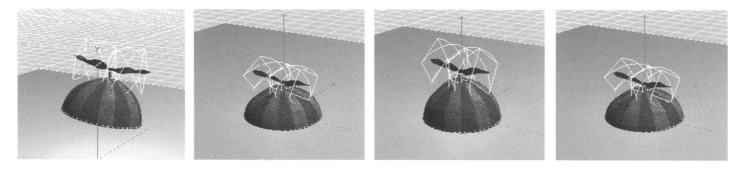

Figure 7.9 Squash and Stretch

Step 4 For even more realism, go back and keyframe the X and Z scale values to work along with the Y squashes you just keyframed. In order to maintain its volume, an object squashed on the Y axis would stretch (increase in scale) slightly on the X and Z at the same time.

Adjusting The Working Views

When working on fine-tuning like the hops and squashes above, it is critical that you adjust your views so you can see what you're doing. For example, use a close-up Front view so you can clearly see the relationship of the object to the floor. For a close view of keys in the Timeline and F-Curve windows, you can use the Move and Scale icons on the top right of the windows, or better yet, make the habit of using the 1 and 2 keys (just like you use them in the Editor window to move and scale).

In the View menu for the Timeline and F-Curves, choose Frame All when you need to see the overall picture. In the fine-tuning stage, however, that view is nothing but mass confusion. Drag a selection rectangle only over the keys in the area you are working on. The fewer keys, the better. Choose View>Frame Selection. Then, click on only the tracks necessary for comparing events in time and you'll have a clear picture of the keys and tangents. If you need to move on to the next section, use the 1 key to slide over as you work.

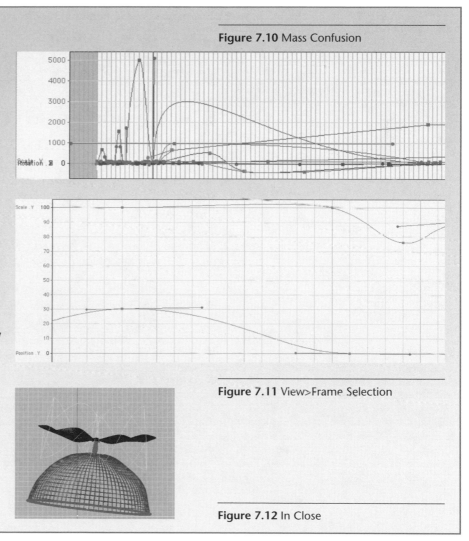

Figure 7.10 Mass Confusion

Figure 7.11 View>Frame Selection

Figure 7.12 In Close

Make further adjustments to the animation as you work toward smooth and believable motion. Command-click (right-click) on keys and choose commands like Hold and Custom Tangents>Soft Interpolation from the contextual menu to make the object behave like you want it to. Add some flips, as if the hat were suddenly hit by a gust of wind, by adding Rotation keys. Study the example movie to see the tangent handles and other adustments. Save several copies of this file so you can practice all kinds of maneuvers.

● ***Springboard!*** In Chapter Five, you learned how to copy animation when you copied the tracks of Materials in the Timeline. In that case, you copied tracks with keys to objects that had no previous animation. In this case, when you copy the Airplane Hat in the Objects Manager, all its animation comes along with it and everything happens identically for the two objects. (If you played the animation you would only see one hat, because they would occupying the same space.) However, by tweaking keys, you can quickly send the copy on an individual path and its propeller spinning to the beat of a different drum. Try it. Copy Airplane Hat, drag the name of the copy into the F-Curve window and start tweaking keys.

B Is for Batty Box: Combining Time Curves and PLA

This project will show you how to use Time Curves to make fidgety motions that are natural and random and how to add interacting Point Level Animation for a more organic feeling.

Figure 7.13 Bat Wing Hierarchy

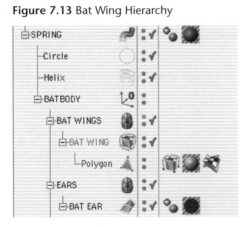

Step 1   Choose File>Open and navigate to Chapter 07>C4D Files>Batty Box> Batty Box.c4d. Choose File>Save As and save the file as Batty Box in your Models folder.

Step 2   Open the hierarchy and select the Bat Wing object (inside BAT WINGS). The wings are in a good starting position, so in the Attributes Manager Coordinates panel, Control-click (right-click) the H in R.H and set a starting key for the current rotation at frame 0.

Step 3   At frame 90, enter –45ºs in the Rotation.H box and set a keyframe.

Step 4   Choose the Animation Layout. Drag the object Bat Wing into the Timeline window. Look at the Timeline and you see that there are only two keys, one for an "open" state of the wings and one for when the wings are drawn back. How's that for boring animation?

Step 5   In the Timeline, select the word Bat Wing. From the Timeline menu, choose File>New Track>Time.

Step 6   Click on the Bat Wing Rotation.H track. Notice that the Sequence Properties for that track sequence appear in the Attributes Manager and that there is an empty box labeled Time Track.

Step 7   Now you will apply the Time Track to a specific sequence, the Rotation.H of the Bat Wing. In one motion, click and drag the word Time next to the Time Track across the Timeline Window and drop it into the Time Track box in the Attributes Manager. (In other words, don't click the word Time first, and then try to drag it.)

The Time Track you just created is a graph that shows what percentage of the animation is completed at a given point in time. The first gray line above the line labeled 0 represents 100 percent. Study the graph and you'll see that at frame 0 the animation is 0 percent complete and at frame 90, the end, it is 100 percent complete. That's pretty much a no brainer. This turns out to be much cooler than it appears on first glance. By Control-clicking (right-clicking) keys along the timeline you can cause the Rotation.H state of the wings to be at any position between the two states you set. And the ability to copy keys allows you to set up many up and down, and somewhere in between positions very rapidly. This comes in really handy any time you need fidgety, randomly flappity motion.

Step 8   Starting at Frame 5 on the ruler, Control-click seven keys. Drag them up and down to slightly random positions, alternating the high and low values. See Figure 7.14.

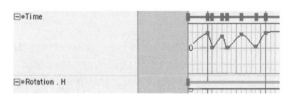

Figure 7.14 First Bat Wing Keys

Step 9   Drag a rectangular selection tool over the existing keys, and Control-drag (right-click) a copy. Continue to copy keys across until you have keys every 3–5 frames. Want to make some of the flaps faster? Just select a section of frames and drag the red handles on the top of the ruler closer together.

Step 10   Now do a little hand work. Move some of the keys, further randomizing the values between 0 and 100 percent, and also make the horizontal spacing between the keys more uneven. See Figure 7.15.

If you render a movie at this point, you'll see some fine flapping. However, the wings themselves are stiff and don't seem to be responding to the motion or

Figure 7.15 All Bat Wing Keys

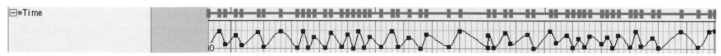

resisting air. By creating some Point Level keyframes that contain the position of all the points one key, you can create some different states of the mesh to interact with the wing rotations.

Figure 7.16 PLA Enabled

Step 11 In the Timeline, select the first key on the Polygon>PLA track. (These keys were created ahead of time as examples.) Control-drag copies of it to frames 10, 15, and 20. Make sure the Enable PLA button is the only one depressed on the Animation Timeline.

Step 12 Select the Polygon object inside BATBODY in the Objects Manager, and then select the key at frame 10. Choose the Points Tool, then choose Structure>Magnet. Gently tug the wing into a different shape. When you are satisfied with the new shape, click the Record button. The information for all the points will be housed in that one key at frame 10, so you can copy it anywhere on the Timeline to invoke that shape, which will interact with any other animation at that time.

Step 13 Create different wing shapes for the keys at frame 15 and 20, and Control-drag copies the different wing shapes across the Timeline so they coincide advantageously with the wing rotations.

◆ *Tips:*
- To move more of the mesh at one time, give the Magnet tool a larger radius in the Active Tool Manager.
- Turn the view sideways and use the Magnet tool to create some changes on the Z axis too.
- Remember that once you place the PLA keys you create using the Magnet tool, there will still be interpolation between one state and another.
- Be sure to line up the current time marker with the key you are editing for an accurate picture of what the wing will look like at that time.
- Drastic stretching of the mesh will blur UVW textures.
- If the Magnet tool refuses to work, points may be selected. Press Cmd+Shift+A (Ctrl+Shift+A) to deselect all points.

Figure 7.17 Bend Deformer Hierarchy

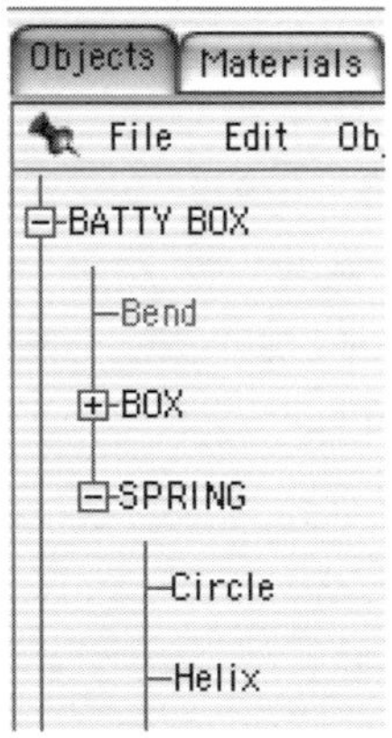

```
Objects  Materials
  File  Edit  Ob
□-BATTY BOX
  ─Bend
  ⊞-BOX
  □-SPRING
    ─Circle
    ─Helix
```

Bend the Spring

Place a Bend deformer on the Batty Box Object. In the editor window, scale it down to fit over the Spring. Choose Limited for the Mode, and animate the strength and angle values so the bat sways back and forth on the Spring during the animation.

Adding Sound

In the Timeline, select Bat Wing. From the menu, choose File>New Track>Sound. Control-click a key at the beginning of the track. Click on the track, and in the

Figure 7.18 Bend Deformer

Attributes Manager Sound Properties panel click the small (unlabeled) button to the right of the empty Sound box. Navigate to LIBRARIES>MUSIC AND SOUND EFFECTS>Squeaking.wav on the DVD.

CINEMA does not render the sound out with the movie, but since most people prefer to put sequences of animation together with sound in a compositing application that's not generally problematic. If you don't have a compositing program you can use the inexpensive QuickTime Pro or free iMovie to add final sound.

The sound previews on insertion, but to play it every time with the animation you have to turn on the Play Sound During Animation button in the Animation Timeline.

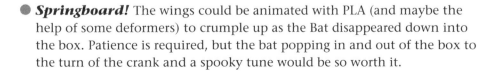

Figure 7.19 Play Sound

● ***Springboard!*** The wings could be animated with PLA (and maybe the help of some deformers) to crumple up as the Bat disappeared down into the box. Patience is required, but the bat popping in and out of the box to the turn of the crank and a spooky tune would be so worth it.

C Is for Crown

A crown of flying stars is the classic sign of a knocked-out cartoon character. Make your own 3D version in this project.

Step 1   Choose File>Open and navigate to Chapter 07>C4D Files>Crown of Stars.c4d. Choose File>Save As and save the file as Crown of Stars in your Models folder.

Step 2   Command-click (right-click) on the Glowing Star object and choose New Expression>Align to Spline.
    Click the Align to Spline tag and in the Attributes Manager, click the Tag panel. Drag the word Circle from the Objects manager into the box for Spline Path.

Step 3   Set the current time to 0, and keyframe a 0 percent Position value in the Attributes Manager Tag Properties. At 90 frames, enter a value of 100 percent and set a keyframe.

Step 4   Command-click (right-click) on the Glowing Star object, and drag to New Expression>Vibrate Expression. Check the check boxes for Enable Scale and Enable Rotation, giving Rotation an H Amplitude (only the first box) of 180º. Enter a value of 10 percent for Seed.

Step 5   Select Glowing Star and Circle. Press the G key to group them and re-name the Null Object as Glowing Star 1.

Step 6   Make three copies of Glowing Star 1 and rename the copies as Glowing Star 2, Glowing Star 3, and Glowing Star 4.

Step 7   Open Glowing Star 2, and select the Circle inside. From the top menu, choose Structure>Edit Spline>Move Down Sequence.

Step 8   Repeat Step 7 with Glowing Star 3 but choose Move Down Sequence two times, and with Glowing Star 4 choose Move Down Sequence three times.
    By changing the position of the first point on each Circle with Move Down Sequence, the trip along the Circles will start at a different point for each Glowing Star.

Step 9   Select Glowing Stars 1 though 4 and press G to group them, naming the group Star Track 1. Make two copies of Star Track 1, naming the copies Star Track 2 and Star Track 3.

Step 10 Switch to the top view. Use the Object Axis tool and the Move tool to center the axes of Star Track 1, Star Track 2, and Star Track 3. Choose the Model tool and the Rotate tool and use the green Rotate handle to rotate Star Track 2 and Star Track 3 as pictured in Figure 7.20. Give Star Track 2 a 25º Pitch rotation, and Star Track 3 a –25º Pitch rotation.

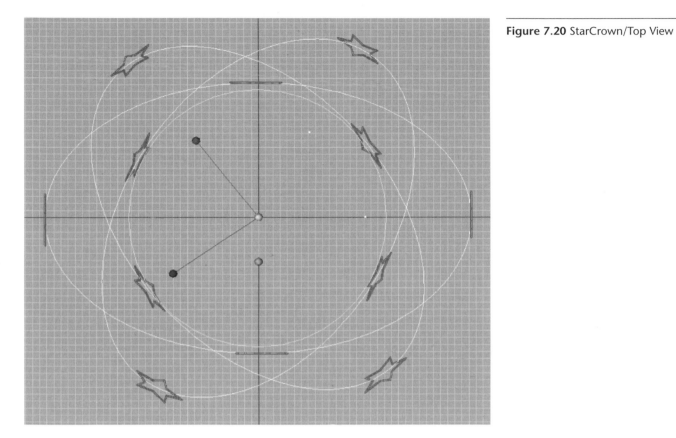

Figure 7.20 StarCrown/Top View

● ***Springboard!*** Experiment with animating color changes on the glow, copy the material and place slightly different color versions on each Star Track, or animate the Visibility of individual Stars for a more twinkling effect. You can also seesaw the tangent handles of all the circles for roller-coaster-style tracks.

On the DVD: Study the Animations in Chapter 07>EXTRA!EXTRA!>InDepth. For more information on the Timeline and F-Curve Manager see Chapter 07> EXTRA!EXTRA!>In Depth>More About the Timeline and F-curves.

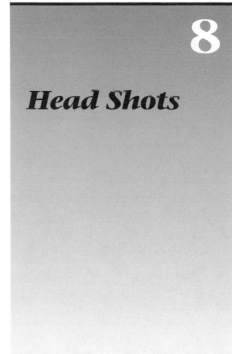

Figure 6.1

T here are infinite methods for building heads, human and otherwise. This tutorial employs one simple method for building a head with generic features.

On the DVD: See Chapter 08>EXTRA!EXTRA! for more head-building methods,
example files, instructional movies, and pointers to other tutorials for building
heads and facial features of various complexity levels.

The Symmetry Method

In this tried and true head-building process, only one side of the head is sculpted
inside a Symmetry object and later rejoined into a single mesh.

The Basic Head Shape

Step 1 In a new .c4d file (File>New), start with a Cube primitive and work in
Wireframe display. Enter 150 for Size.X, 175 for Size.Y, and 160 for Size.Z
in Object Properties. Press the C key to make it editable. Save the file as
Symmetry Head in your Models folder (File>Save As).

Step 2 From the top menu, choose Structure>Subdivide. Enter 2 in the Subdivision input box and check the check box for HyperNURBS Subdivide. Choose the Front view and choose Edit>Frame Active Object so
the head fills the window.

Figure 8.2 Rectangle Selection Tool

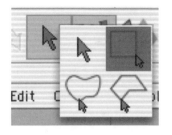

Figure 8.3 Head, Subdivided with the Knife Tool and Halved

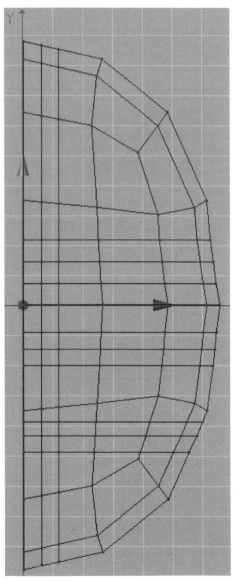

Step 3   Choose the Points tool, and press the letter K to access the Knife tool. You'll be using the Knife tool to add three new polygonal divisions in the first row of polys above the X axis. Click outside the form on the left and Shift-drag three lines all the way across the form. Release the mouse outside the form on the right each time you drag a line. Refer to Figure 8.3.

Step 4   Add three cuts in the row of polys below the X axis, and three more in the next row down, being careful not to intersect these last lines with the curved edges of polys above and below them. Then drag the Knife tool twice vertically in the first row of polys to the right of the Y axis, as shown in Figure 8.3.

Step 5   Choose the Rectangle selection tool, and in the Active tool uncheck Only Select Visible Objects. Drag a selection over the left half of the head, up to but not including the vertical midline, and press the Delete key to remove the points and polys. Don't forget to save every few steps (File>Save or Cmd+S/Ctrl+S).

Step 6   Still using the Rectangular selection tool, select all the points on the open left edge of the head. From the top menu, choose Selection>Set Selection. In the Attributes Manager, click the Basic panel and type EDGE in the Xname box. Click in the Objects Manager to deselect the Selection tag.

As you begin to model, these points may stray off of their current 0 position on the X axis. This selection may be quickly accessed to send the points to back to the center.

Step 7   Choose a Symmetry object, and place the Cube into it. Then create a HyperNURBS object and place the Symmetry object as its child. At any point in the modeling process, you can turn either of these off temporarily by clicking their green check mark so it turns to a red cross mark.

Creating a Nose

Step 1   Make sure the Cube is selected and switch to the Polygons tool and the Move tool. Shift-click to select the polygons, two across and three down, immediately under the X axis and on the left edge.

Step 2   Press the D key to access the Extrude tool. In the Active tool tab, enter 10 for offset and press Return (Enter). Then enter 5, and press Return (Enter) again.

Step 3   Switch to the Perspective view and use the 3 key to turn the view as in Figure 8.5. With the end polys still selected, scale them down on the X and Y axes. Select and Delete the new polys (on the inside edge of the half head) that were created when the nose was extruded. If you need

Figure 8.4 Nose Polys

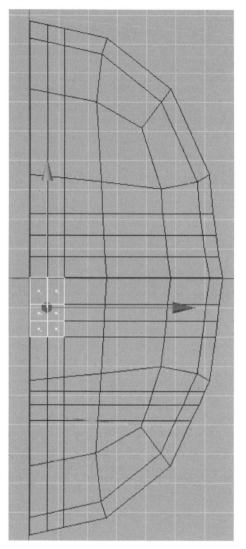

Figure 8.5 Tip Scaled, Inner Polys Deleted

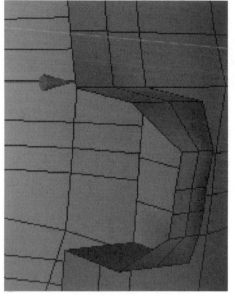

Figure 8.6 Upper Nose Polys

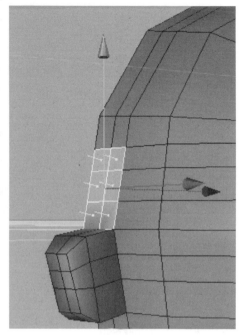

Figure 8.7 Upper Nose Polys Adjusted

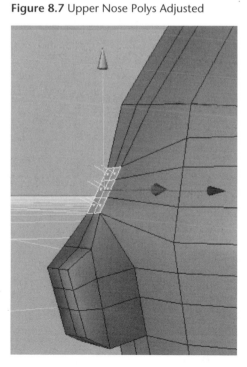

to, turn off the Symmetry object temporarily so you can see the polys more clearly.

Step 4 Now choose the Scale tool and select the two rows of three polys immediately above the extruded nose form. Scale these polys together to about half of their former size, and then use the Move and Rotate tools to adjust their position as in Figure 8.7.

Step 5 Use the 3 key to tilt the head so you can see the underside of the nose. Select the right-hand poly on the bottom of the nose and scale it on the X axis only to become wider and more square.

Figure 8.8 Nostril Poly

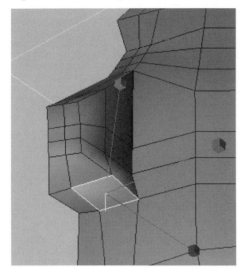

Figure 8.9 Nostril Extrude Inner

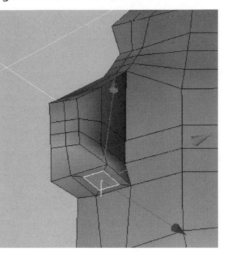

Figure 8.10 Nostril Base

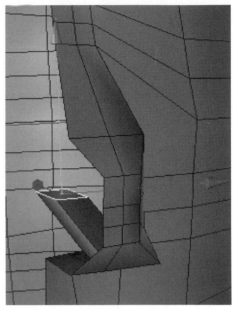

Figure 8.11 Widening Nose

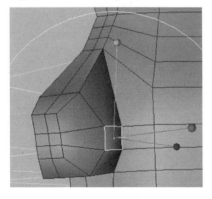

Figure 8.12 Shaping a Basic Nose

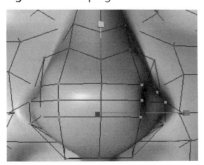

Press the I key for Extrude Inner, and drag right to left to pull the new poly inward. The size of this new poly will determine how big the nostril holes are. Press the D key and enter an offset of –10. Use the blue and red Move handles to position the base of the nostril back and toward the center as in Figure 8.10. While the poly is still selected, choose Selection>Set Selection to save the poly for later repositioning. Name the selection Nostril Base.

Step 6   Select the poly shown in Figure 8.11 and pull it out on the X axis to widen the base of the nose. Rotate its back edge slightly to the left, creating more shape at the back of the nose.

The basic form of a nose is now in place. At this point it is a rather chunky nose, but you can push and pull points to refine the nose shape. Press Cmd+S (Ctrl+S) to save.

Figure 8.13 Refining the Nose Shape

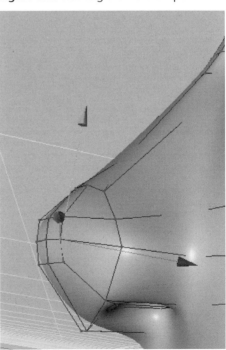

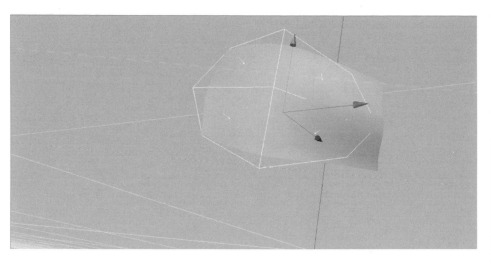

Figure 8.14 Starting Eye Shape Isolated

Figure 8.15 Starting Eye Shape

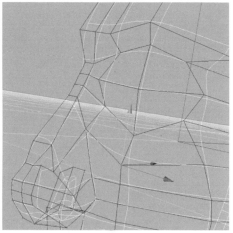

The Eye Shape

The secret to nicely contoured eyes is to prepare a good beginning shape. Depending on the style of eye you want to end up with, you can start with circles or rectangles or the octagonlike shape used here. Move some points into a good starting position like those shown in Figures 8.14 and 8.15.

Step 1 Choose the Polygon tool and select the four polys of the basic eye shape shown in Figures 8.14 and 8.15.

Step 2 Press I for Extrude Inner and drag the mouse from right to left three or four times (depending on how much detail and polygon count you have in mind) to create skinny polys aound the eye shape.

◆ **Tips:** Take care that you don't Extrude Inner so far that any of the points cross over each other.

Before you start moving the eye points around too much, you may want to take time to make some set selections of points to use later when you animate expressions.

Step 3 Push and pull points to create the eye shape you want. If you choose to use sphere primitives for eyeballs, insert a sphere now so you can push the surface of the eye to wrap around it correctly.

Step 4 If you want a raised rim around the eye opening, adjust the points of the polys created with the last Extrude Inner to be even slimmer and perform a slight Extrude to raise the rim.

Figure 8.16 Eye Rim Points

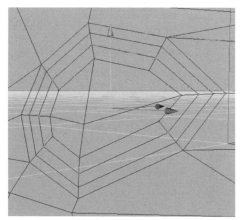

Step 5 Reposition some points around the inner corner of the eye to make a tiny square polygon. Inner Extrude and Extrude this polygon to create a tear duct, and then move all the corner points further toward the Y axis so the corner is offset from the eyeball. Select the four innermost polys in the eye area and move them back on the Z axis to create an eye cavity. You don't need all those polys on the inside, so you can delete any that won't be seen.

Figure 8.17 Rim Scaled/Extruded

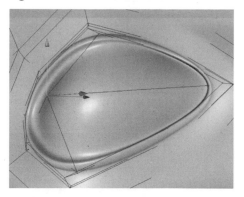

Step 6 Either apply the eyeball material in GOODIES>MATERIALS>CharacterMaterials> to a sphere, or use the Eyeball model in Chapter 08>EXAMPLES. (For cartoon-style heads, you could also move the four center eye polys back slightly and pull the center point forward to create an eye surface that remains part of the mesh.)

Figure 8.18 Inner Eye Corner

Those Elusive Points

When you modeling your first heads, it seems like points are forever dipping beneath the surface, tangling around each other and careening off into space. You can save a lot of frustration by setting up views so you can see exactly what you're doing. Set your display to Isoparm, and then go to Window>New View Panel and set its display to Gouraud. Use the 2 key and drag the mouse to place yourself close to the surface. You can work in either view, and when you can't see points beneath the surface, just click on a neighboring point you can see and then check the Isoparm view to trace the connecting line back to the hidden point.

When facing a point, edge, or poly, using the Cmd key and the Move tool to drag the element away from or toward the screen can be an intuitive way to work. Dragging the mouse with the righthand button depressed does the same thing and is much more natural, so a two or three-button mouse is a must-have accessory for Mac users who plan to spend a lot of time modeling. However, it can be tricky to judge the amount of movement when pushing points toward and away from you. Nudging the green, red, and blue Move handles of the point is often more accurate and you can easily comprehend a point's direction from almost any angle. By using the 3 key to keep the view tumbling, you can quickly tweak surface points and keep a critical eye how the point pushes are affecting the mesh.

Figure 8.19 Two Windows

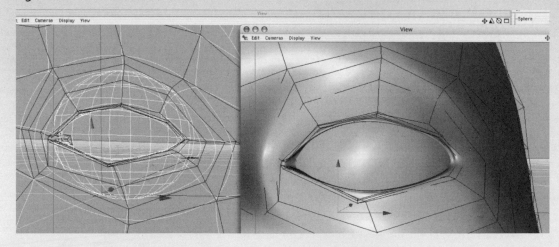

What's in the Road . . . Ahead? The Bad News and The Good News

Once the basic polygonal structure of facial features are set up, it can still be a long, long way to an elegantly hand-modeled head. The patient pushing and pulling of points, edges, and polys is the way to get there, and the journey can take some time. The good news is that every head you make will be born faster and better looking. And once you have made some decent ones, they can be copied and tweaked into a thousand other personalities. Review your welding skills from Chapter 2 as they will come in handy now. For example, select the mouth polys,

disconnect some copies, and create different mouths to weld in later. The head in Figure 8.20 was copied, and the mouth polys were replaced to create the different version in Figure 8.21. By using the Edit Structure>Disconnect and Split and saving extra copies, whole libraries of different features can be created for a basic head and welded back in later.

Figure 8.20 Alien

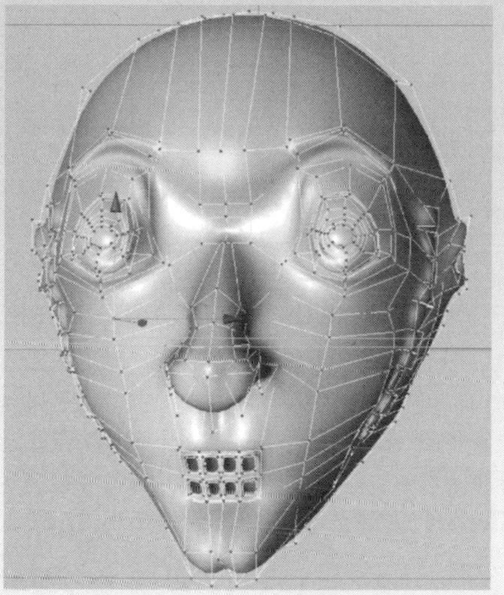

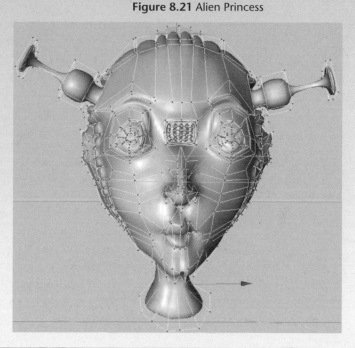

Figure 8.21 Alien Princess

Making An Ear

We'll make a simple ear for now.

Step 1 Before starting the ear, face the side profile of the head and select the Points tool. Use the Magnet tool to shape the back of the head (Radius 150) and the jaw (Radius 60).

Step 2 Move points to create a starting shape shown in Figure 8.22.

Step 3 Select the base ear polys, and press the I key to Extrude Inner once or twice. (The more detail you want, the more extrusions you need to add at every stage of making the ear form.) Type D to extrude. In the Active Tool tab, enter an offset value of 5 and click Apply. Choose the Scale tool

Figure 8.22 Adjusted Head and Ear Shape

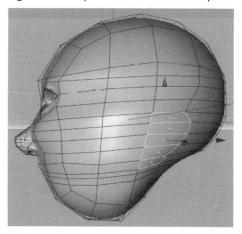

Figure 8.23 Ear Polys Extruded Inner

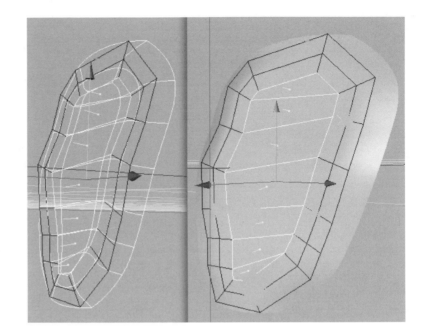

Figure 8.24 Ear Flared

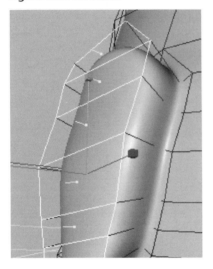

and drag the mouse from left to right, so that the ear flares out. Don't worry about the size of the ear for now, you can adjust it later. Press the I key for Extrude Inner, enter an offset value of 3, and click Apply two times.

Step 4 Choose the points shown in Figure 8.25, and pull them up, more toward the back of the head and back into the head. Select the polygon shown in Figure 8.26, and rotate its right hand edge back slightly. Press the D key to extrude the poly back into the head.

Figure 8.25 Points for Ear Canal

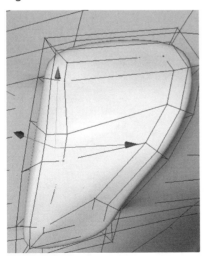

Figure 8.26 Poly for Ear Canal

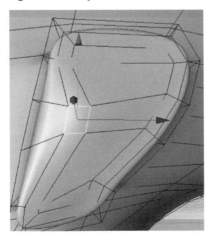

Figure 8.27 Ear Canal Formed

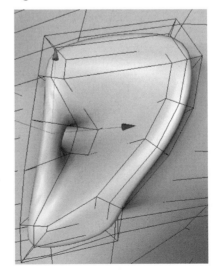

Figure 8.28 Poly for Ear Detail

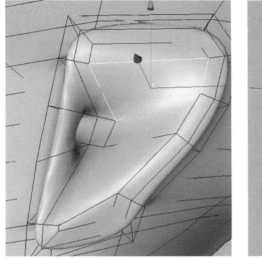

Figure 8.29 Ear

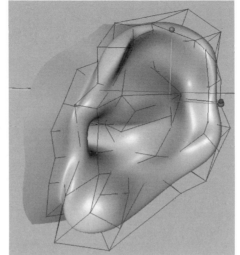

Step 5   Select a polygon like the one in Figure 8.28, and Extrude Inner to create some more points for detail of the bony structures inside the earlobe. Proceed to push and pull points and polys, shaping the ear. Study some reference photos, real ears, and the example files for help with the unusual and endlessly individual surfaces of the inner ear lobe. When you are finished, select all the polygons within that original ear shape you began with and choose Structure>Edit Surface>Disconnect. Save a copy of the file for your Library (File>Save As). Also, save a Selection of all the Ear points for size adjustment later.

◆ **Tip:** **Isolate** Select the polys of a single feature, and choose Select> Hide Unselected to clear away all those other things you are not currently working on. Choose Selection>Unhide All to bring everything back.

Shaping The Head

While still working on a symmetry object, you can go ahead and shape up the head a bit.

Step 1   Use the Magnet tool to round up the top of the head and sculpt the jaw. Be careful to use the correct magnet radius to keep from pulling already finished contours out of place.

Step 2   Pay some attention to the contours of the face from the profile view. You can select polygons in the cheek to pull them forward.

Step 3   For more forehead shape, face the side of the head and make an additional knife cut above the eyes. Then pull the front polys out for a more pronounced forehead.

Step 4   Now work with points to soften any ridges that may have popped up. Try to adjust the points so that the edges follow the muscle contours of the face as naturally as possible.

Figure 8.30 Cheek Poly Pulled Out

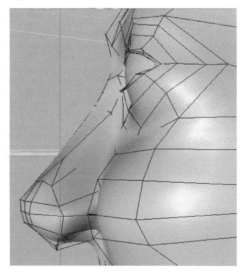

Figure 8.31 Added Knife Cut

Figure 8.32 Forehead Polys

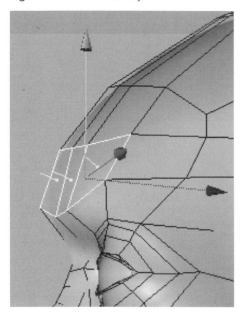

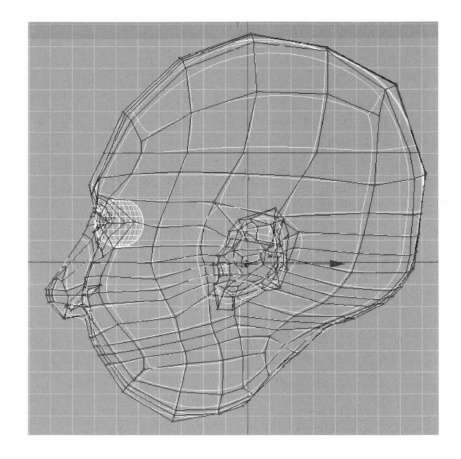

Figure 8.33 Half Head Finished

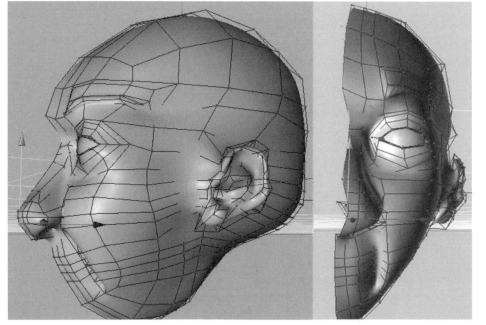

Step 5 You can always extrude inner anywhere you want more detail. In Figure 8.33, an eyebrow shape and a more detail around the mouth area were added. After an Extrude Inner, the extruded polygons are often scaled on one axis (in this case only the Y) or moved to create the needed contours.

At this point, don't worry about the edge of the half head or refinement of the nose shape, the mouth, or the chin. Those will be easier to work with after the Symmetry object is converted to one mesh. Let's do that now.

Step 6   Double-click on the Selection Tag titled EDGE to activate the points around the inner opening of the half head. Temporarily turn off the Symmetry object by clicking the green check mark in the column to its right in the Objects Manager. You can delete those stray points that are no longer being used. Because the modeling process has created new points on the edge, the selection is now incomplete. Hold down the Shift key and click to select the new points (around the nose and where you knifed the forehead), adding them to the selection. Be sure to choose Set Selection again to incorporate the new points in that selection tag. Choose Structure>Edit Surface>Set Value, change X to Set, and enter a value of 0.

Turn the Symmetry Object back on, and check the seam where the two halves join. You may need to adjust the position of the Cube object to realign the Cube object exactly on the Y axis. (Select the Cube with the Model tool and make sure the value is 0 on the X axis.) If the seam is standing up in a ridge, just select the offending points and use the blue Z handle to nudge them back on the Z azis until the seam disappears. It is sometimes helpful to increase the Tolerance of the Symmetry object slightly.

Step 7   When the seam looks smooth, choose the Symmetry object and choose Functions>Current State to Object. Delete the Symmetry object (the one with the Symmetry icon to its right) from the Objects Manager.

Now the two halves of the head are joined into one mesh, so you can drag the Cube directly into the HyperNURBS object and delete the Symmetry object. No more splitting seam worries. But, remember that you are no longer editing both sides simultaneously. It's fairly easy to Shift-click to select points or polys as you continue to edit the surface though, and in some cases you actually want asymmetry. For example, the easiest way to refine the nose shape is to Shift-click to select opposing points on the nose and scale them closer together (or farther apart) and move them on the Y and Z axes.

Making the Mouth and Chin

Before you start on the mouth, save yourself some grief by doing a little preliminary homework. By repositioning some points into some nice regular geometries that are fairly level on the Z axis, you'll have an easier time when you form the mouth and chin. Double-click on a point in the middle of the mouth area to determine its Z value, and then select all the points that define a general mouth area and choose Structure>Edit Surface>Set Value to set all those points to the same Z level. (In this case, we are using four polys across and three down, but it can vary depending on the style of mouth and the required detail.) Then use the Move and Rotate tools to establish a good starting plane for the mouth polys. This simple step will prevent some ugly things happening when you extrude the mouth.

◆ *Tip:* Save some extra copies of your head at this point (File>Save As). You may want to go back and make different mouths for this basic head.

Figure 8.34 Chin Polys

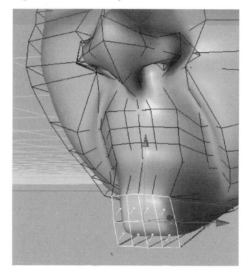

Figure 8.35 Mouth Polys

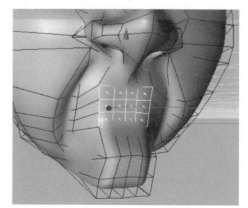

Figure 8.36 Mouth Extrude Inner

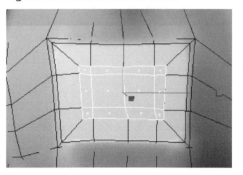

Figure 8.37 Inner Polys Scaled on the Y Axis

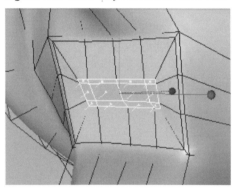

Figure 8.38 Mouth Area Isolated

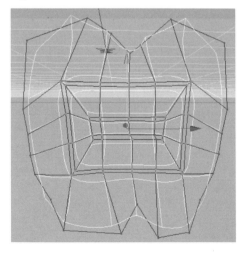

Figure 8.39 Tongue

Step 1 Select the Chin polys and use the Move and Rotate tools to set the basic position. For now, just concentrate on the overall form. Later you can push points to round the chin off and add detail.

Step 2 Now select the 12 beginning mouth polys shown in Figure 8.35. Extrude Inner two times as in Figure 8.36, and then scale the innermost polys only on the Y axis as in Figure 8.37.

Step 3 Select the mouth area shown in Figure 8.38, and choose Selection>Hide Unselected. Save some selections now for animation later. All Mouth Points, Top Lip, Bottom Lip, and Mouth Corners will all come in handy later. Also, make a selection of the two points immediately under the center of the nose. You'll push them back later to create that little dip above the upper lip. An Edge selection of the mouth opening will facilitate closing the mouth completely.

Step 4 Select the inner mouth polygons and press D, dragging the mouse right to left to extrude a mouth cavity. With the polys still selected, scale them to make the base of the mouth larger. Extrude Inner to create the base of a tongue, and extrude the tongue back toward the front of the face. You can add more detail to the tongue later if you want to.

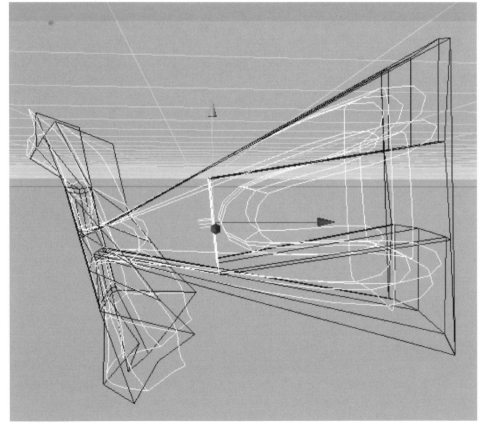

Figure 8.40 Mouth Polys Moved Forward

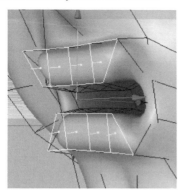

Figure 8.41 Mouth Polys Rotated

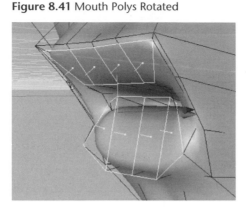

Figure 8.42 Pushing Mouth Points

Step 5   Begin forming the mouth by establishing the planes of the lips. Pull the selection in Figure 8.40 out on the Z axis, the rotate the top lip over so it faces downward more. Select the middle polys of the bottom lip as in Figure 8.41, and scale them on the Y axis to make the bottom lip fuller. Then move the polys down slightly and rotate them so the lip faces more upward.

Figure 8.43 Neck Polys

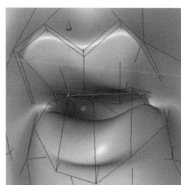

Step 6   Choose the Points tool, and start to push points to form the mouth. Push the corners away from you, and style the shape of the mouth to your liking. By choosing opposing pairs of points, scaling them to move them closer or farther apart, and moving them back in the Z axis, you can quickly create a very organic mouth. Make this mouth very generic and expressionless. You can create more expressions later with the selection sets you saved.

The mouth in Figure 8.44 is proportionally small. By clicking on the WHOLE MOUTH Selection Tag, you can scale the mouth points to change the mouth's size.

Figure 8.44 Head

Forming a Neck

Step 1   In the same way you prepared polygons for the mouth and chin (Figure 8.34), organize a set of polys on the bottom of the head.

Step 2   Extrude the polys down from the head, and adjust the points to smooth the neck form. Make a knife cut halfway down the neck and scale the new points down slightly to give the neck more shape.

Eye Targets

Figure 8.45 Eyes Looking at Target

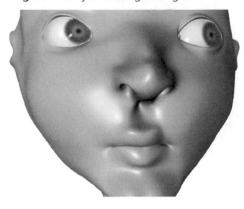

Step 1 Choose Objects>Null Object and place the Null out in front of the head.

Step 2 Command-click (Control-click) on Right Eyeball, and drag to New Expression>Target Expression. Click on the Target Expression tag and in the Attributes Manager Tag Properties, drop the Null Object into the Target Object box.

Step 3 Control-drag a copy of the Expression tag to Left Eyeball.

Drag the Null around and watch the eyes follow. Animate movement of the eyes by setting keyframes for the position of the Null.

Teeth

Step 1 Choose a Cube primitive. Give it three segments on each axis and a Size.Z of 50. Place the Cube into a HyperNURBS object and push points to make a front tooth.

Step 2 Copy the front tooth, and position the two copies as shown in Figure 8.46. Rotate the second and third teeth slightly and move them back slightly so the group of teeth forms an arc as in Figure 8.47. Depending on how unique you need the teeth to be, you can create the teeth on only one side and put them into a Symmetry object, or make them all individually.

Figure 8.47 Teeth From Top

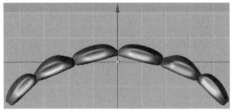

Figure 8. 46 Simple Top Teeth

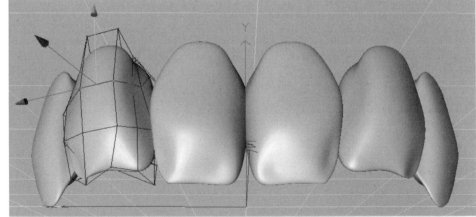

On the DVD: See Chapter 08>EXTRA!EXTRA! for extra projects and references for Heads and related items like eyeglasses.

Animating Facial Expressions

Here are two ways to animate expressions. Make copies of the file Chapter 08> C4D Files>CartoonHead from the DVD and use them to practice facial animation. Then, if your computer is up to it, practice animating expressions on copies of the more detailed head you just made.

Animating with PLA

Step 1 Select the cube inside the HyperNURBS.

Step 2 Enable PLA animation in the Animation Timeline and choose the Points tool.

Step 3 At Frame 0, click the Record button to set a keyframe for the expressionless state of the head.

Step 4 At Frame 15, use the Move tool to move points or use the Magnet tool to move larger sections of the face. Remember that you can also double-click on selection sets (such as MOUTH CORNERS or TOP LIP) and move them into different expressions. You may use a selection to begin crafting an expression and then push more points to customize the look. When you have a new expression, click the Record button.

Step 5 At Frame 30, copy the key at Frame 0 and start a new expression. (Drag the Cube object into the Animation Timeline to work with the keys.)

Step 6 Control-click the top of the Timeline ruler to set Markers and title your expressions. They can then be copied anywhere on the Timeline. Once you have some key expressions recorded, experiment with their relative positions on the Timeline to control how one interpolates into another.

◆ *Tips:*
- Remember that you can also scale and rotate sets of points to create variety in expressions.
- To edit an existing set of point states, select the key in the Timeline. Make sure the current time tab is aligned with the key so you are looking at the current state of the points. After making changes in the state of any points on the mesh, click the Record button again. If you want to freeze part of the face for a while and change another part, just copy the key and move it forward. Then edit the points you want to change and click the Record button.
- A change in one feature is often mirrored in other features. When a mouth opens in surprise, the eyes widen and the nostrils flare to complete the expression.
- If you want to avoid clicking the Record button every time you change points, turn on the Auto Keyframing option.

- If you are interested in matching facial states to speech, take digital photos of yourself enunciating vowels and consonants to use as modeling references. Save the state for each sound as a key in the Timeline labeled with markers.

Animating with Posemixer

If you have the Posemixer Plugin (Check the Plugins Menu for MOCCA>Pose-Mixer), try this method. Animating expressions with Posemixer is a little more complex and makes a larger file, but it lets you combine changed features in infinite mixes. Make another copy of the file Chapter 08>C4D Files>CartoonHead.

Step 1   Make five copies of the cube primitive inside the HyperNURBS. Leave the original as Cube. Rename the first copy as Base Pose, the second copy as Big Eyes, the third as Squinted Eyes, the Fourth as Flat Mouth, and the Fifth as Round Mouth. Make sure all these renamed cubes stay on the same hierarchal level as children of the HyperNURBS object.

Step 2   Select Big Eyes, and turn off visibility for everything else. Drag Big Eyes upward in the list so it is the first item under the HyperNURBS object. Double-click the selection tag for ALL RIGHT EYE POINTS. Scale and move the points so the eyes larger and rounder. If necessary, adjust the mesh so there are no creases at the edges of the eyes. Double-click ALL LEFT EYE POINTS and edit those points in the same way.

Step 3   Select Squinted Eyes, and move it as the first item under the HyperNURBS. Turn off visibility for everything else. Choose the selection tags for both eyes and flatten the eyes into flattened shapes.

Step 4   Edit the Flat Mouth and Round Mouth objects to reflect their titles, temporarily moving them as the first object under the HyperNURBS if you want them to be smoothed as you work.

Step 5   Move the Cube to the top of the list and turn its visibility on. Turn off visibility for all the renamed cubes.

Step 6   Choose Plugins>MOCCA>Posemixer. In the Objects Manager, make the Posemixer object a child of the Cube.

Step 7   In the Attributes Manager, click the Lock symbol at the top of the Attributes Manager and drag the object Base Pose from the Objects Manager into the Default Pose box.

Step 8   Drag Big Eyes into the empty box next to the L. Click the Add Pose button three times, and drag the remaining expression objects into the empty boxes.

Step 9   Drag the sliders one at a time to see the features morphing individually.

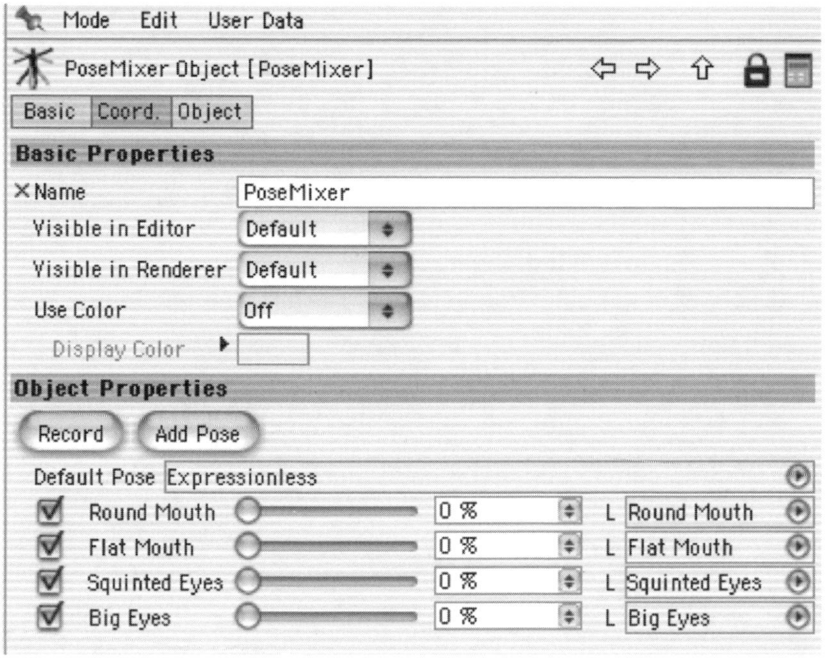

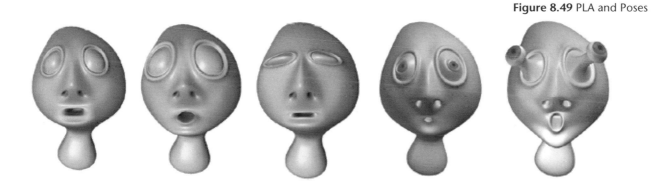

Figure 8.48 Posemixer Settings

Then play with combining the sliders in different ways to create different faces. Whenever you want to keyframe the mix, click the Record button at different points in time. If you want to edit one of the Posemixer keys, select the key and edit the sliders. Click the Record button again.

Figure 8.49 PLA and Poses

On the DVD: Scrub through the Cartoon Head PLA.c4d example file and watch the point-level animation. See Chapter 08>MOVIES/STILLS>MOVIES for more expression animations.

Color Plate 1.1 Frédéric Berli, "Something"

Masters of
CINEMA 4D

Color Plate 1.2 Anders Kjellberg, "Flintlock Gun"

Color Plate 2.1 Gerald Double, "Farm House"

Color Plate 2.2 Gerald Double, "Pocket Watch"

Color Plate 2.3 Anders Kjellberg, "The Pilot"

Color Plate 2.4 Anders Kjellberg, "Old Camera"

Color Plate 2.5 Gerald Double, "Film Editing"

Color Plate 3.1 Robert Drozd, "Stoned Kingdom"

Masters of
CINEMA 4D

Color Plate 3.2
Frédéric BERTI,
"Grand Rue"

Color Plate 4.1 Philip
Gray, "Neon"

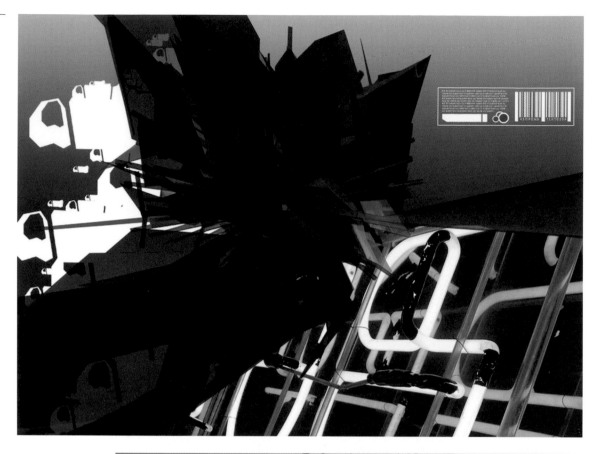

Masters of
CINEMA 4D

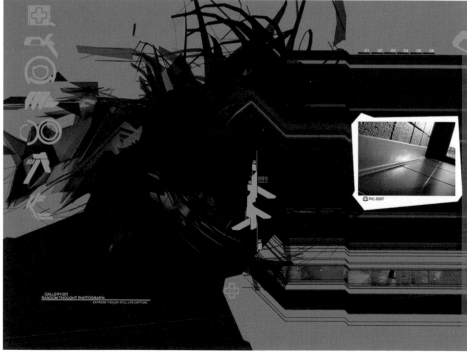

Color Plate
4.2 Philip Gray,
"Blue"

Color Plate 5.1 Doug Chezem, "Fast & Furious City"

Color Plate 5.2 Gerald Double, "Organica"

Color Plate 6.1
Eni Oken, "Little
Village Far, Far
Away"

*3D Guest
Gallery*

Color Plate 6.2
Eni Oken,
"Resident Alien"

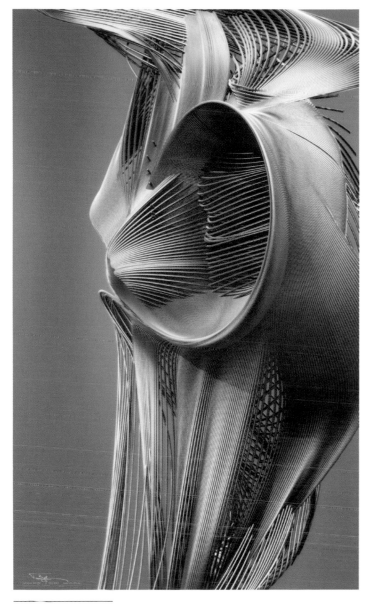

Color Plate 7.1
Tim Borgmann

Color Plate 7.2
Michael Young
WeWorkForThem,
YouWorkForThem,
"Emeric SA0001_
012"

Color Plate 7.3 Michael Young, WeWork-
ForThem, YouWorkForThem, "Design-
graphik, Serving Five"

Color Plate 8.1 CH16, BodyPaint Painted Prop

Color Plate 8.2 CH07, Airplane Hat Animation

Projects

Color Plate 8.5 CH03, Peephole Box

Color Plate 8.3 CH16, BodyPaint Sign

Color Plate 8.4 CH07, Batty Box Animation

Color Plate 8.6 Charm Library, DVD

Color Plate 9.1 CH13, Jenna Plugin, Allie

Color Plate 9.2 CH15, Eyefly Environment Entrance

Color Plate 9.3 CH03, Whirlygig Box, Extra Project

Color Plate 9.4 Dice and Cards Libraries, DVD

Color Plate 9.5 CH05, Texture Totem

Color Plate 10.1
CH 03, Anne Powers, "Peeping Bird Box"

Color Plate 11.1
CH 06, Animated Light Puffs

Color Plate 11.4
CH 06, Lightcaster

Color Plate 11.2 CH 08, Symmetry Redhead

Color Plate 11.3 CH 17, Illustrator Text Paths

Color Plate 11.5 CH 19, Planet Eternal Motion Graphic

Color Plate 11.6
CH 15, Alcove Door

Color Plate 11.7 CH 15, Hardware Library

Graphic Design/Type

Color Plate 12.1
CH 17, Anne
Powers,
Extruded
X-Form

Color Plate 12.2
CH 17, Phillip Gray,
"HWM"

Color Plate 12.3 Chris Cousins, "E"

Color Plate 12.4 Anne Powers, "Fractured Art"

Color Plate 12.5 Michael Young, WeWorkForThem,
YouWorkForThem "EmericSA0001_018"

Color Plate 16.1
CH 20, Red Doll Dress

Color Plate 16.2 CH 20, Sculpture 1

Color Plate 16.3 CH 20, Red Dress Model

Color Plate 16.4
CH 20, Touchable Texture

Color Plate 16.5 CH 20, Color Wheel

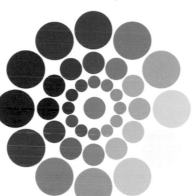

Color Plate 16.6 CH 20, Scrapbooking

Color Plate 16.7
CH 20, Sculpture 2

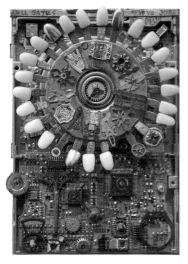

Color Plate 16.9
CH 20, Non-digital
Media

Color Plate 16.8 CH 20, Digital Collectibles

Inspiration

Outside

the Box

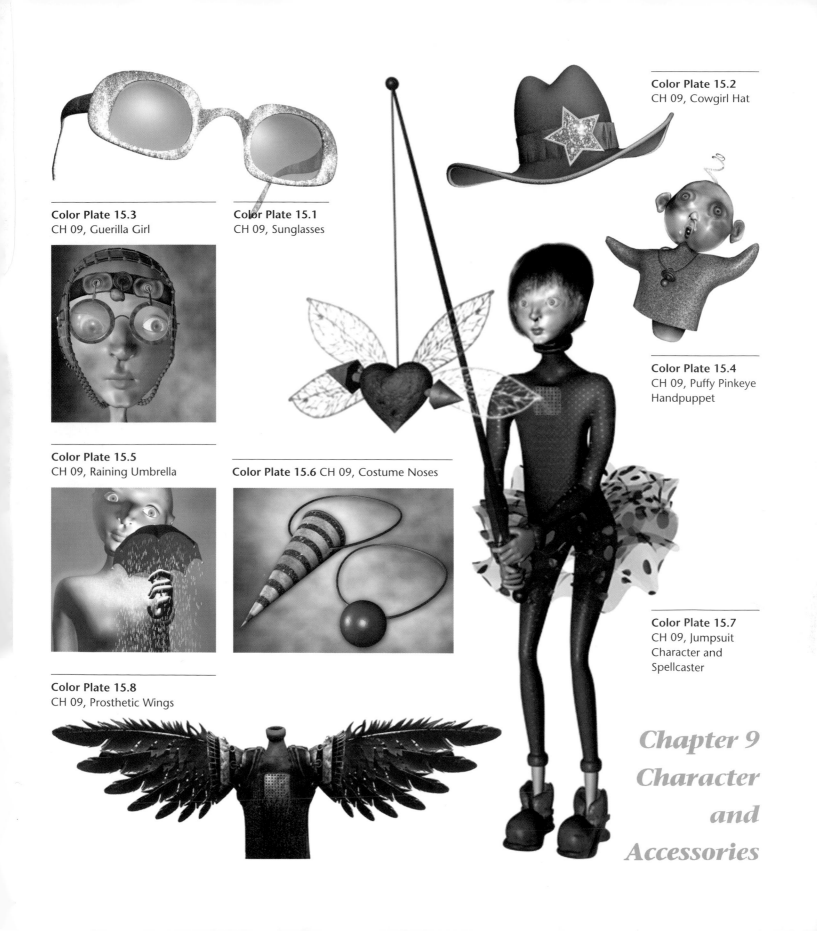

Color Plate 15.3
CH 09, Guerilla Girl

Color Plate 15.1
CH 09, Sunglasses

Color Plate 15.2
CH 09, Cowgirl Hat

Color Plate 15.4
CH 09, Puffy Pinkeye
Handpuppet

Color Plate 15.5
CH 09, Raining Umbrella

Color Plate 15.6 CH 09, Costume Noses

Color Plate 15.7
CH 09, Jumpsuit
Character and
Spellcaster

Color Plate 15.8
CH 09, Prosthetic Wings

Chapter 9
Character
and
Accessories

Masters of CINEMA 4D

Color Plate 14.1
CH 09, Chris
Cousins, "Chef"

Color Plate 14.2 CH 09, Mattieu Roussel, "Dog"

Color Plate 14.3
CH 09, Mattieu
Roussel, "Faune"

Color Plate 14.4 CH 09, Mattieu Roussel, "Monster"

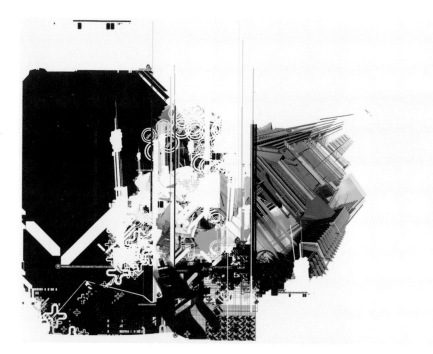

Color Plate 13.2 Chris Cousins, "Q"

Color Plate 13.1
Michael Young,
WeWorkForThem,
YouWorkForThem,
"User"

Color Plate 13.3 Chris Cousins, "S"

Color Plate 13.4
Michael Young,
WeWorkForThem,
YouWorkForThem,
Emeric SA0001_019

Color Plate 13.5 Anne Powers,
"Five Fragments"

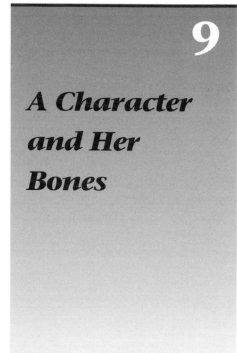

9

A Character
and Her
Bones

Figure 9.1

Character Animation (CA) is a gargantuan topic. By the time you bring to life a perfect character (one that glides well-timed across the screen without her skin stretching into bizarre distortions), you will probably have read several books specializing in CA, stepped through numerous tutorials, and birthed many frustrating, jerky-limbed characters. That's just the way it is, and even the most accomplished character animators had to go through this intense learning process and pay their dues. There is space available in this book for only the tip of the iceberg—an introductory look at how CA can be accomplished in CINEMA 4D. Because of the lengthy steps involved in setting up rigs, the text will cover basic explanation of MOCCA tools with the whole character PDF and example files on the DVD. In this chapter we'll look at the mesh and mechanism of a character that will be animated.

On the DVD: See Chapter 09>EXTRA!EXTRA!>InDepth>Character for a more complete character PDF, other character building methods, example files, instructional movies, and pointers to other tutorials for building characters of various complexity levels. In the Chapter 09>EXTRA!EXTRA!>References folder you'll find pointers to animation helpers and lists of specialized books for advanced study of CA.

Building a Character

A character can have one single and continuous skin, or mesh, which moves under the influence of bones placed inside it. Alternately, a figure can be constructed

Figure 9.2 Different Character Forms

Figure 9.3 Character Mesh with Separate Hands

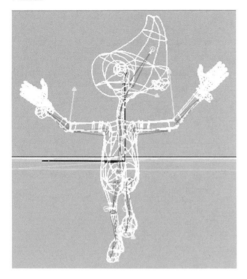

with separate models which are affected by bones as a group. Some characters may not even have bones, like a puppet made of animated primitives or a meta-ball alien blob animated with moving points. Whatever kind of form your character takes, the simpler, the better. An economical polygonal structure, or cage object, placed inside a HyperNURBS object will be smoother and easier to control in the animation process. Successful animation is critically dependent on a model created with animation in mind.

Modeling a Character Designed for Movement

Figure 9.4 Bend with (L) No Edgeloops Added and (R) Two Edgeloops Added

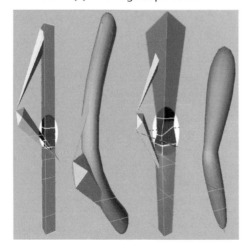

Having said simplicity is a good thing, there will be certain places in the mesh that will have to be more complex, or have more point density. Areas that you know will have to bend (such as shoulder joints, elbows, knees, and ankles) or have more intricate motion (such as facial expressions) will require more subdivisions. Rather than starting with a form that is highly subdivided all over, you might begin with the simplest of polygonal forms then and use modeling tools to add mesh detail in specific places. Some prefer to add the extra polyonal detail on the fly, adding, scaling and rotating subdivisions as the projections of the model are extruded. Others start with a simple, blocky form and then go back to add subdivisions and move or rotate sections of points into a starting position. A truly swift and elegant method for this kind of modeling is to use the Mesh Surgery Plugin described in Chapter 13. On the DVD, there are several movies that show these different methods in action (Chapter 09>EXTRA!EXTRA!>InDepth>Some Modeling Methods).

Characters are usually not modeled in a natural position but in a more splayed position so that it will be easy to place the bones inside. The bones will do their work later to coax the figure into natural positions.

While you could position bones in limbs folded into a complex position, it would require more work. An exception to this are knees and elbows. Slight bends in their starting positions can help prevent rotation problems with the bones later.

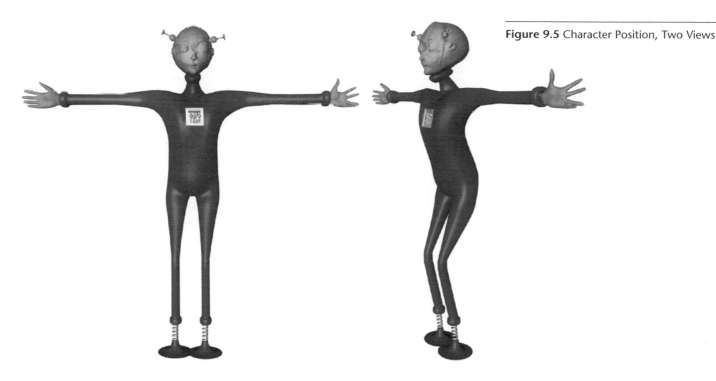

Figure 9.5 Character Position, Two Views

Forward Kinematics and Inverse Kinematics

FK (Forward Kinematics) and IK (Inverse Kinematics) are the two basic methods for animating skeletons (and other hierarchies of objects). Both methods have distinct advantages and disadvantages.

In the FK animation process, the rotations of bones are keyframed. FK is a more immediate process, but it requires the tedious, manual setting of many keyframes. However, it can be the best way to animate upper extremities that don't have to end up at a specific place. Note that FK is not practical when, for example, an arm has to move and end up with its fingertip resting on an elevator button. Manually adjusting every rotation in the shoulder, elbow, wrist, and fingers so that the fingertip ends up in the right place can get nightmarish. The walking character that must plant his feet on the floor is not the best candidate for FK.

IK, on the other hand, is quite easily animated, once the rig is properly set up (those being the operative words). In essence, when you create an IK setup, you are building a user interface that allows easier animation of the character. By interactively dragging control objects and keyframing their positions (and sometimes rotations), the figure is easily puppeted and animated. In the elevator example above, a control object attached to the finger would simply be placed on the button, and all the rotations of the arm would automatically adjust themselves (or solve the relationship between all the arm bones) to allow the movement. Setting up the rig is a complex process, even using CINEMA 4D's MOCCA module, which has helpful CA tools.

A Simple IK Example

This simple example of IK in action uses the standard tools in CINEMA 4D and will introduce you to the feel of IK (without using MOCCA).

Step 1   Navigate to Chapter 09>C4D Files> Bubblegum.c4d. Save a working copy to your Models folder (File>Save As).

Step 2   Study the hierarchy and notice that Sphere 3 has an Anchor Tag that will prevent it and those below it from moving. Select the Effector object.

Step 3   Choose the IK tool from the left palette.

Step 4   With the Effector selected, drag the mouse around the screen. The rotation of all the pieces of Bubblegum is being decided by the position of the Effector. Remove the Anchor Tag on Sphere 3 and see how the behavior changes.

Now we will add an interesting twist by creating a Goal object for the Effector to reach toward. This is a classic example of IK, as the position of the Goal or target will decide the position and rotation of the Bubblegum objects.

Had FK been used, each sphere would have been painstakingly rotated and the destination of the top sphere would have been difficult to control. With the computer solving the rotations, there comes an inherent loose control. MOCCA's Soft IK tools provide more bells and whistles for firmer management of the IK chain.

Step 5   Control-drag a copy of the Effector and move the copy to the top of the list, outside of the original hierarchy. Name the copy Goal.

Step 6   Cmd-click (right-click) on the Effector object in the Objects Manager, and choose New Expression>IK Expression. Drag the name Goal from the Objects Manager and drop it into the Target Object box in the Attributes Manager Tag Properties.

Step 7   Using the Model and Move tools, drag the Goal around the screen. Move the Goal side to side so the Bubblegum moves in a snakelike path, then pull it out away from the Bubblegum and notice how the objects appear to stretch toward the Goal.

Creating Bones

In this exercise, we will create some bones using the standard version of CINEMA 4D (without the MOCCA Module).

Step 1   On the DVD, navigate to Chapter 09>C4D Files>Arm For Bones.c4d. Save a working copy titled Arm with Bones to your Models folder (File>Save As).

Step 2   Select the ARM object. Work in the Front view and Isoparms Display. Choose Edit>Frame Active Objects.

Figure 9.6 IK Tool

Step 3 From the Deformer palette, choose the Add Bone Deformation icon. The bone is born pointing its small end away from you, so you need to go to the Coordinates Manager, enter a Rotation P value of –90 and press Return (Enter). Now the bone should have its small end downward.

Step 4 With the Model and Move tools selected, use the blue Move handle to raise the top of the bone to the top of the arm.

Step 5 With the bone still selected, move the mouse on the upper black arrow next to Length (under Object Properties) until the orange dot at the tip of the bone is at elbow position.

Step 6 With the bone still selected and the Model and Move tool chosen, make sure only the Z lock icon has a line around it so that the bone is unable to flip around on the X or Y axes. Control-click on the orange dot and drag a new bone out of the first one, stopping at the top of the Left Hand Wrist bone.

Step 7 Save the file as Arm with Bones (File>Save or Cmd+S/Ctrl+S).

Influencing the Mesh with Bones

Step 1 Rename the top Bone as Left Upper Arm Bone, and the lower one (a child of the first one) as Left Lower Arm Bone.

Step 2 Make the Left Upper Arm Bone a child of the ARM object.

Step 3 Drag the uppermost bone of the hand, Left Hand Wrist, as a child of the Left Lower Arm Bone. (Don't worry about any temporary weirdness of the mesh position.)

Step 4 Select Left Upper Arm Bone, and from the Objects Manager Objects menu, choose Fix Bones. Click Yes to the Subobjects message.

Fix Bones sets the beginning position of the bones, something you always want to do before starting to animate the bones. Reset Bones returns bones that

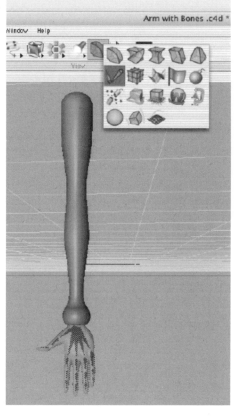

Figure 9.7 Bones Palette Icon

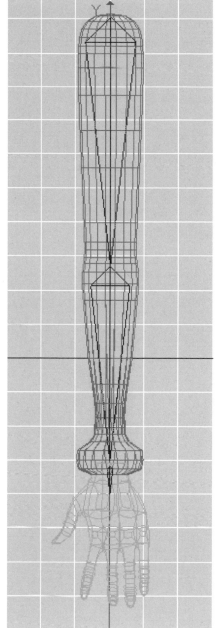

Figure 9.8 Position of Bones

■ **Shortcut:** The Objects Menu can be accessed as a contextual menu by Cmd-clicking (right-clicking) on the object name.

have been moved to the original Fixed position, and releases the binding of the bones to the mesh. By clicking Yes to the Subobjects message, the lower arm bone was also fixed along with its parent.

Step 5 Save the file. Choose the Object tool and the Rotate tool, and select the Left Lower Arm Bone. Move the mouse on the green Rotate handle to bend the arm. You'll notice the elbow might be a little rumpled. Select the Left Upper Arm Bone and experiment with the Function values in Object Properties. One further down the list will help out the elbow.

There are two methods in the standard CINEMA 4D application to control the strength of a bone on the mesh. Figure 9.9 (and the RangeLimitsAnimated.c4d file in Chapter 09>EXAMPLES on the DVD) shows the Range Limit method, useful for animating minimum and maximum strengths of a bone. There is a PDF on the DVD for using the other method, Vertex Weights and Restriction Tags. In most cases, MOCCA's Claude Bonet weighting does the best (and easiest) job of this.

Figure 9.9 Minimum and Maximum Range Limits Influencing the Strength of a Bone on a Mesh

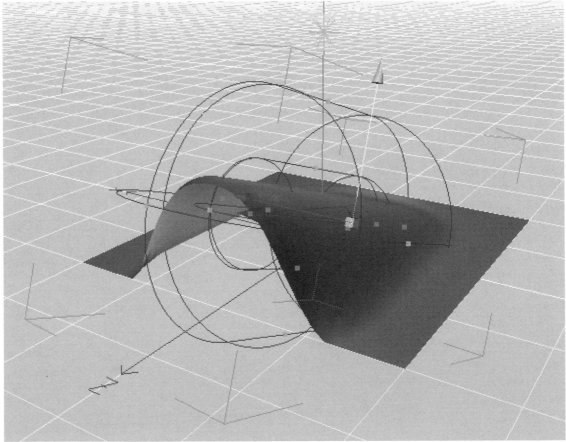

Introducing MOCCA

If you have the XL Bundle of CINEMA 4D or have purchased the MOCCA module, use these MOCCA tools to do the job.

Making Bones in MOCCA

Step 1   On the DVD, again navigate to Chapter 09>C4D Files>Arm For Bones .c4d. Save a working copy titled MOCCA FK to your Models folder (File>Save As). Click the Layout icon and MOCCA.

Step 2   Select the ARM object from the Objects Manager. Choose the Bone Tool from the MOCCA palette. Click on the Active Tool tab, and click the Add Bone button. Using the Coordinates panel in the Attributes Manager, drag the small upper black arrow next to P.Y to position the bone at the top of the arm. In the box next to R.P enter –90 and press Return.

Step 3   Double-click the name Bone, and rename it Left Upper Arm Bone. In the Attributes Manager, click the Object panel and drag the upper small black arrow next to Length until the tip of the bone is centered in the elbow subdivisions. Alternately, use the yellow interactive handles created by the Bone Tool in the Editor window to lengthen and rotate the bone.

Step 4   Make sure the Left Upper Arm Bone is still selected. Control-click at the wrist (at the top of the Left Hand Wrist bone) to make a new child bone. Rename this bone Left Lower Arm Bone.

Figure 9.10 MOCCA Layout

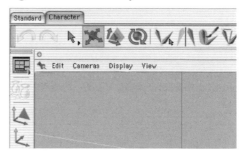

Figure 9.11 Position of the Left Upper Arm Bone Tip

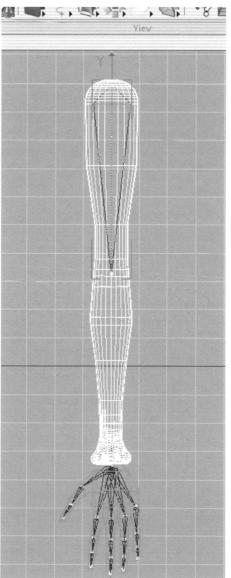

Figure 9.12 Left Lower Arm Bone Added>

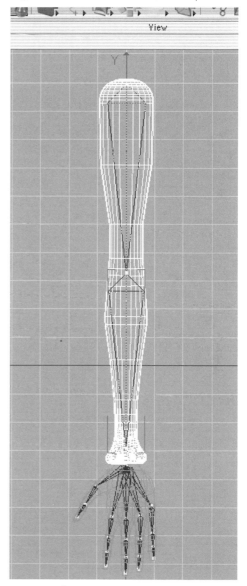

Step 5 Select the Left Upper Arm Bone, and in the Active Tool tab, click Add/Update Null Bone.

This creates a Null Bone, sometimes referred to as a Root Bone, which won't affect the geometry but can be used to control the rotation of its children. Rename the new Bone object at the top of the hierarchy Left Arm Null Bone. The Null Bone will take on the rotation of the Left Upper Arm Bone and will zero out the rotational coordinates of the Left Upper Arm Bone.

Step 6 Make the Left Arm Null Bone (and its children tagging along behind) a child of the ARM.

Step 7 Open the HAND hierarchy, and drag the Left Hand Wrist object and drop it as a child of the Left Lower Arm Bone.

Step 8 Select the Left Arm Null Bone, and choose Fix Bones before exiting the Bone tool. Click the Yes button in the Subobjects input box.

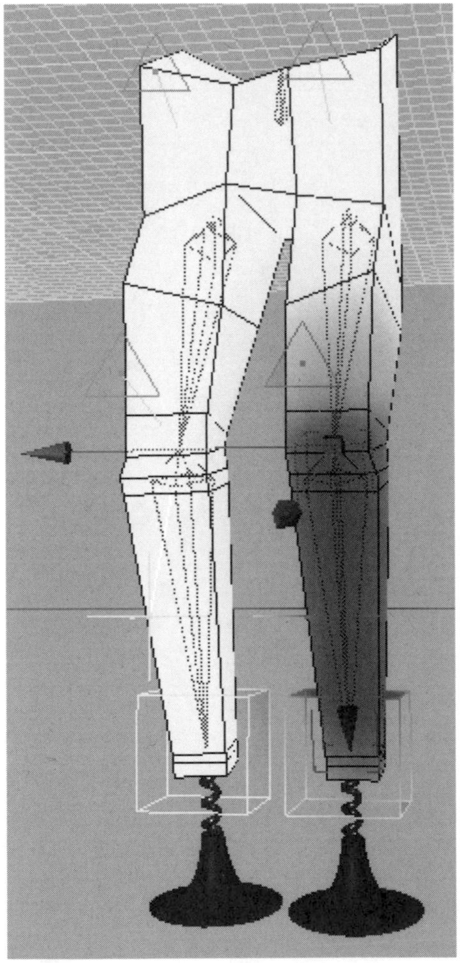

The word Bone is included in the titles for these first looks at character setups, and all the words are spelled out. It's easy to see which objects are bones by the icon to the right of the name. Later, you'll want to abbreviate words like Left, so a title of a bone might be only "L_Thigh." Remember though, it is very important that every object have a distinct title.

Claude Bonet

If you tried out Vertex Weights and Restriction tags (Chapter 09>EXTRA!EX-TRA!InDepth>VERTEXWEIGHTS.pdf on the DVD) you saw how each bone can be weighted, or told which parts of the mesh to influence and how much. Claude Bonet creates weighting too; it just does it in a more intuitive way.

Step 1 Work in the Perspective view. Select the Left Upper Arm Bone. From the MOCCA palette, choose the Claude Bonet tool. In the Active Tool tab, uncheck Only Modify Visible Elements and set the Strength to 30 percent. Paint the entire Arm and Hand, turning the object around and making sure you get in all the crevices.

Step 2 Now select the Left Lower Arm Bone, but this time paint only from slightly above the elbow down to the fingertips. If you need tighter painting control, reduce the radius of the brush in the Active Tool tab.

Step 3 Select the Left Hand Wrist Bone, and paint only from the wrist down to the fingertips.

Step 4 Choose the Rotate tool and rotate the Left Lower Arm Bone and then the Wrist Bone.

If the skins distorts, the painting of the mesh needs adjustment. Painting in the distorted state can show you exactly where the problem is, and as you paint the

Figure 9.13 Bone Tool

Figure 9.14 Claude Bonet Tool

Figure 9.15 Claude Bonet Map

mesh will correct itself. You can go back, select each bone, and repaint with the Claude Bonet tool. The coverage of the Claude Bonet painting may be extended (just select the bone again and paint more) or removed (hold down the Ctrl key and paint), or the sliders in the Active Tool tab can be used to adjust the strength. Red X marks next to your bones mean that they are not affecting the mesh. Choose Fix Bones again and they will become functional. The Character project on the DVD has more in-depth information about using Claude Bonet.

Step 5   Save two copies of this file (File>Save As), one as MOCCA Arm FK and one as MOCCA Arm IK.

MOCCA Tools For Soft IK

MOCCA's Soft IK tools add a natural "stretchability" and more control to character rigs. Get to know MOCCA Soft IK by rigging this handy set of legs. Later you can expand them into a full figure, or attach them to any objects that might suddenly decide to run off. Be forewarned! This is a fairly tedious process. One small detail left out or in the wrong place can stop the whole rig in its tracks. Do this exercise when you are unhurried and feeling patient.

Step 1   Navigate to Chapter 09>C4D Files>Legs.c4d. Save a working copy to your Models folder (File>Save As). Open the MOCCA Layout.

When the file opens, the HyperNURBS object is on so you can see the form. Before you begin to work, click the green checkmark next to the HyperNURBS to red so it won't bog down your work. Claude Bonet maps have already been painted. If you want to look them over, choose the Claude Bonet tool and select each bone.

Step 2   Make sure Use IK is not on in the Plugins>MOCCA menu. Choose the Move tool.

Step 3   Command-click (right-click) on the Left Thigh Null Bone and choose New Tag>Soft IK Tag from the contextual menu.

Step 4   Command-click (right-click) on the Left Thigh Null Bone's Soft IK tag and choose Copy Tag to Children from the contextual menu.

Step 5   Cmd-click (Ctrl-click) on the Pelvis Bone (not on its children) and choose New Tag>Stop Tag from the contextual menu. In the Attributes Manager Tag Properties, check Stop Generators. This tag will prevent the Hyper-NURBS from smoothing anything beyond the hierarchal level of the tag.

Step 6   Delete the Soft IK tags from the Left Suction Foot and from its children.

Step 7   Cmd-click (Ctrl-click) on the Left Suction Foot and choose New Tag> Stop Tag. In Tag Properties, check Stop Deformer. (This will prevent the bones from affecting the parts of the Suction Foot.)

Figure 9.16 Birthday Cake Legs

Figure 9.17 Set Chain Rest Position and Set Chain Rest Rotation Icons

Figure 9.18 Add Root Goal Icon (and Add Tip Goal, Add UpVector)

Figure 9.19 Leg Hierarchy

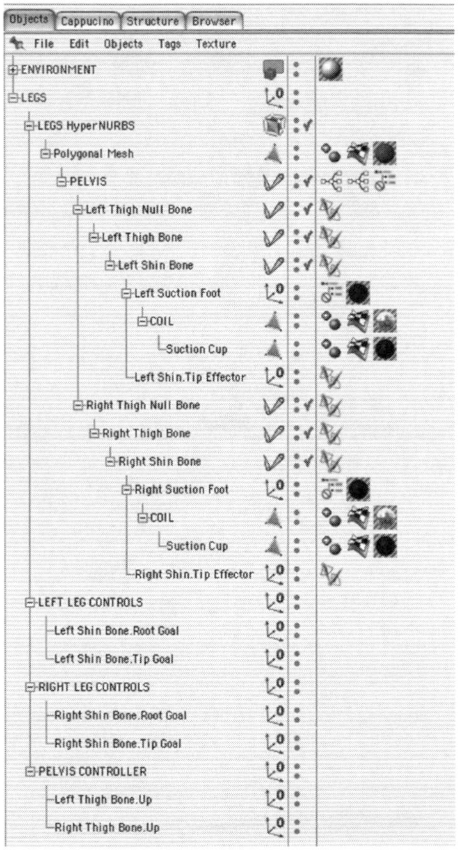

The Suction Feet will not be in the IK Chain, but because they will be children of the Left and Right Shin Bones, they will inherit the motion of the shins.

Step 8 Select the Soft IK tag for the Left Thigh Null Bone. On the Tag Properties Pane in the Attributes Manager, check the check box for Anchor.

Step 9 Making sure the Soft IK tag for the Left Thigh Null Bone is no longer selected, Shift-click the Soft IK tags for Left Thigh Bone and Left Shin Bone. In the Attributes Manager Rest panel, check Force Position. In the MOCCA Palette, click on Set Chain Rest Position and Set Chain Rest Rotation. (Use the cue at the bottom of the page until you get to know the MOCCA palette icons.)

Later, after moving the character around you can reset the IK chain back to these original states. Just choose the uppermost bone that had Rest Position and Rotation set originally, (in this case Left Thigh Bone) and click on the Soft IK Tag. In the Attributes Manager Rest panel, click the button for Reset to Rest State.

Step 10 Select the Left Shin Bone and click on the Add Root Goal button in the MOCCA Palette.

Step 11 Drag the new Left Shin Bone.Root Goal object out of the hierarchy and place it at the top of the Objects Manager list.

Step 12 Click on Left Shin Bone, and choose Add Tip Goal (a secondary choice under the Add Root Goal Button). Drag the the Left Shin Bone. Tip Goal to the top of the list also.

Step 13 From the top menu, choose Objects>Null Object. Choose the Model and Move tools. In the Editor window, position the null at the tip of the Left Shin Bone, checking it in the Front and Side views. (Choose Edit>Frame Scene if you can't see it.) Rename the Null Object as LEFT LEG CONTROLS.

Step 14 Drop both the Left Shin Bone.Root Goal and the Left Shin Bone. Tip Goal into the LEFT LEG CONTROLS object as its children.

These goals will pull the root (Root Goal) and tip (Tip Goal) of the Shin Bone towards them with the amount of strength you specify. An IK setup is a delicate balance of tensions and counter-tensions. For example, if you move the Pelvis upward, the Tip Goal will exert pull on the tip of the shin bone. The bone tip will always strive to reach its goal. If the Pelvis is lowered, the Shin Bone's Root Goal (which is positioned below and out in front of the knee) will work to keep the knee pointing toward it.

Step 15 Select the Left Thigh Bone (Be sure not to choose the Left Thigh Null Bone by mistake) and choose Add UpVector. (Again, this a secondary choice under the Add Root Goal Button.)

Step 16 In the Editor window, use the Move tool to position the Left Thigh Bone.Up out in front of and slightly above the Thigh Bone's root. (The Root is the original point of the bone where it is widest.)

UpVectors provide more influence over the rotation of bones, as the bone's Y axis (by default, unless you change it to X) will strive to face the direction of the UpVector.

Step 17 Click on the Left Shin Bone Soft IK tag, and in the Attributes Manager constraint pane set the Goal strength percent to 25. Select the Left Shin Bone.Root Goal in the Objects Manager, and in the Editor window move it slightly below and out in front of the knee. Select the Soft IK tag for the Left Thigh Bone. On the Constraint pane, set the strength for Up-Vector to 75 percent.

Step 18 Cmd-click (right click) on the Left Thigh Null Bone and choose Fix Bones, clicking the Yes button for Subobjects.

Fix Bones establishes the relationship of the bones to the mesh. If you want to reposition the bones later, select the topmost bone and choose Reset Bones before you adjust the bones. Then choose Fix Bones again when the adjustments are complete.

In the Objects Manager, it's critical that characters with multiple parts have a correct Hierarchal order or the HyperNURBS object will be making unnecessary deformations. By using Null Objects and Stop Tags, the function of the Hyper-NURBS object can be controlled correctly.

Now is a good time to see if things are working. First, *save the file* so you can use *File>Revert to Saved* in case things get disasterous while you are experimenting.

In the MOCCA menu, turn on Use Soft IK. In the Perspective view, use the Move tool to move the Left Leg Controls around. If your rig is not working, one of those little details is afoul! Open the LegsRigged.c4d in the Ch09>Examples folder on the DVD and compare your rig item for item to find the culprit! After you have finished experimenting, choose *File>Revert to Saved* to finish the rig.

Mirroring Bones

Step 1 Select the Left Thigh Null Bone in the Objects Manager, and choose Objects>Reset Bones. (This will prevent the existing fixation values from being mirrored to bones on the opposite side.)

Click the Bone Mirror tool from the MOCCA Palette.

Step 2 In the Dialog box, set the Origin to Parent.

Step 3 Clear the text from the input box for Prefix.

Step 4 In the Replace input box, type Left and in the With box, type Right.

Step 5 Check the Auto Find Center box. In the Match Search box, a larger value (try 75 and experiment from there) will mirror the Claude Bonet maps when a low value will not.

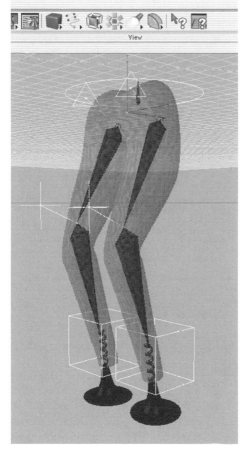

Figure 9.20 IK Leg Rig

Figure 9.21 Bone Mirror Tool

Step 6 Click Mirror. Mirroring will take a few seconds. Click the Mirror button only once. After you see the mirrored bones appear, close the Mirror Box.

Step 7 After mirroring the bones, select the Right Thigh Null Bone and choose Objects>Fix Bones.

Step 8 Create a new Null Object and move it to the tip of the Right Shin Bone (Check Front and Side views). Name it RIGHT LEG CONTROLS and drop Right Shin Bone.Root Goal and Right Shin Bone. Tip Goal and (both currently inside the LEFT LEG CONTROLS hierarchy) into it.

Step 9 Select the Right Thigh Null Bone and in the MOCCA palette, click Set Chain Rest Position and Set Chain Rest Rotation.

Step 10 Save the File (File>Save or Cmd+S/Ctrl+S).

Creating a Pelvis Controller and Display Objects

Step 1 Choose a Null Object and place it at the position of the Pelvis Object. (Functions>Transfer). Name the Null Object PELVIS CONTROLLER.

Step 2 With the PELVIS CONTROLLER selected, Command-click (right-click) any of the letters P in the Attributes Manager Coordinates (in the left-hand Position column) and drag down to Animation>Set Driver.

Select the Pelvis object, and Command-click (right-click) on any of the letters P (same column, Attributes Manager Coordinates panel) and drag to Animation>Set Driven (Relative).

Step 3 Select the PELVIS CONTROLLER again. Command-click (right-click) any of the letters R in the Attributes Manager Coordinates (Rotation column) and drag down to Animation>Set Driver.

Select the Pelvis object, and Command-click (right-click) on any of the letters R (same column, Attributes Manager Coordinates panel) and drag to Animation>Set Driven (Relative).

Step 4 Drop the Thigh UpVectors for both legs (Left Thigh Bone.Up and Right Thigh Bone.Up) as children of the PELVIS CONTROLLER object.

Step 5 By changing the display of some of these tiny objects, you can make them easier to see and set up a system of symbols for the kind of objects they are. Shift-click the LEFT LEG CONTROLS and RIGHT LEG CONTROLS null objects. In the Attributes Manager Object Properties, choose Cube from the Display pull-down menu. Increase the Radius to *150* and the Orientation to *ZY*. In the Basic Properties panel, choose Always from the Use Color pull-down and choose a color that will show up well against your background.

See the example file LegsRigged.c4d in Chapter 09>EXAMPLES for the colors and shapes applied to the Left Shin Bone. Root Goal and Left Thigh Bone.Up or make up your own system. In the Front view, check to make sure that the Goals and UpVectors are lined up over the leg properly.

Choose the PELVIS CONTROLLER and create a display object. The example file uses an (XZ plane) circle around the hips.

Test Drive The Rig

In the MOCCA Palette or Plugins>MOCCA menu, choose Use Soft IK. Use the Move tool to experiment with moving the LEFT and RIGHT LEG CONTROLS and the PELVIS CONTROLLER. After you've finished, choose File>Revert to Saved. You'll animate this file in Chapter 10.

Figure 9.22 Use Soft IK

◆ *Tips:*
- IK not working? Make sure Use IK is on, then check each IK *tag (Attributes Manager Tag Properties)* to be sure Use IK has not become unchecked. Certain actions (like clicking the "Reset to Rest State" button in an IK Tag's Rest panel) will uncheck a Tag's Use IK checkbox. An individual tag's checkbox overrides Use IK in the MOCCA tool panel.
- Bones in a twist? When you are learning, the bones you work so hard to get set up right have a way of ending up out of alignment. If you need to adjust the position and/or rotation of bones, select the uppermost bone and choose Reset Bones. When everything looks right, click Set Position and Set Rotation again, then choose Fix Bones.
- Turn on Auto Redraw to keep the IK updating as you work.
- With Auto Redraw on, experiment with increasing the Rest Rotation strength in the Tag Properties Rest pane. This value interacts with the force of Goals and UpVectors to influence the behavior of the chain.
- The Soft IK chain in this example was set up manually, but the Soft IK tags for the bones of a particular hierarchy (along with the Tip Goal needed to move the chain) can be created by choosing Plugins>MOCCA>SetupIKChain. In this example, if you select the Left Thigh Null and choose Plugins>MOCCA>SetupIKChain, the Thigh Null will be the anchor and a Tip Goal will be automatically added to the end of the chain.

Figure 9.23 Auto Redraw

Setting Up A Posemixer Hand

In Chapter 8, you learned how to "morph" from one facial expression to another using PoseMixer.

To create a PoseMixer hand, create a boned hand and save the file as "Hand Generator." Position the Object Axis at the base of the wrist or wrist bone. Keep this file around to use later for making other poses. There's a low poly "starter hand" in Chapter 09>C4D Files if you haven't made your own.

Step 1 Navigate to Chapter 09>C4D Files>*Hand Generator* file. Choose Save As. Click the New Folder button and create a HANDS folder. Enter CUBE in the title box and click *Save* to to save one unposed copy of the hand. Again, use Save As to save another copy named *Base Pose*.

Step 2 Repeat the Save As process with as many different poses as you want. Close the Hand Generator file.

Step 3 Open the Cube file. Select only the polygonal mesh inside the Hyper-NURBS object and choose Functions>Current State to Object. Drag the newly generated Cube polygonal mesh up out of the original Hierarchy. Throw away everything else in the file except the polygonal mesh you just created (including the bones). The polygonal object will be at the bottom of the Hierarchy and will have a blue triangle icon to the right of its name. All you will need in the PoseMixer file is the polygonal version of the hand, as the PoseMixer file will have its own HyperNURBS object. Save the file.

◆ *Tips:*

- PoseMixer cares deeply about the position and rotation of object axes. If posed objects have axes in different positions and various rotations, you'll get overall object movement and other weird behaviors when you use the sliders. By creating all the poses from a Hand Generator file, all the copies will have common axis placement. If hands which have been created in separate files start moving around in the PoseMixer file, enter coordinates of 0,0,0 (zero-ing out the axes) for everything in the file and then group all the components into a Null that you can move anywhere.

- It's easy for your PoseMixer Attributes to disappear as you go back to the Objects Manager to select poses. The lock on the upper right of the Attributes Window will freeze the Attributes for one object as you select others.

Figure 9.24 Hierarchy for PoseMixer Hand

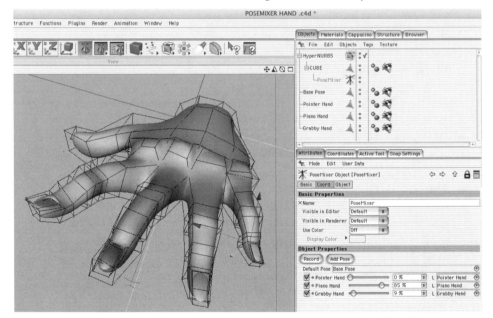

Figure 9.25 Hand Poses

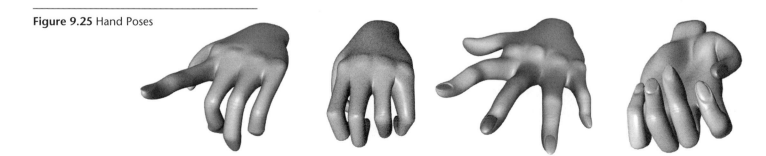

Step 4   Repeat Step 3 with the Base Pose, and rename the Cube in Base Pose as *Base Pose*.

Step 5   Open each pose file and use the bones to "strike the pose" before selecting the Cube and choosing Current State to Object as in Step 3. Name the Cube in each pose with a name describing the pose. Save each file.

Step 6   Create a new file and name it PoseMixer Hand. Choose File>Merge and import the Cube, Base Pose, and all the poses into this new file.

Step 7   Choose a HyperNURBS object and drop the Cube object as its child.

Step 8   *Turn off* both visibility switches for the *Base Pose* and all the other manipulated poses, but leave visibility of the *Cube* object on.

Step 9   From the MOCCA menu, choose PoseMixer. Make the PoseMixer object a child of the Cube. Select the PoseMixer object and in the Attributes Manager, drag the name *Base Pose* from the Objects Manager into the *Default Pose* box.

Step 10   Click the Add Pose button to add as many boxes as you need for the poses you created, and drop the names of the poses into the boxes.

Experiment with adjusting the sliders with different combinations, and save the file.

As alternate methods, the hand poses can be created in one file and objects with bones intact can be used. PoseMixer can also be used to morph Hierarchies for even more complex control of the hand. There is an excellent tutorial on this at www.maxoncomputer.com in the Support section. Also, the MOCCA manual has a more complex tutorial for a PoseMixer hand.

Character Shortcuts

If you made it through the Character.pdf, you may be in a state of shock over how much is involved in making a full Character rig. It does get better. Not only does it get easier every time you go through the process, but also you will find ways to take shortcuts. For example, with similar characters you can make a copy of the file and edit the character, using the same rig. There are some great plugins that provide a ready-made rig that will slide right into your character, saving tons of setup time. Check out Bonderland and Little Cup of MOCCA in Chapter 13>Plugins. There are example files of these on the DVD also. Paul Everett's Visual Selector plugin adds ease to the rigging process.

Multiple Versions and States of Characters

A finished animation may appear to have one character, but behind the scenes there may be hiding "multiple personalities." For example, the main "medium poly," fully rigged character with bones may be backed up by other versions that function better in specific situations. A much lower poly version will work better

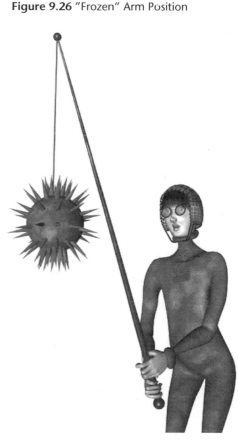

Figure 9.26 "Frozen" Arm Position

in complex scenes, in which extra polys won't be missed when seen from a distance. Often a low poly "stand in" is used while still working on the scene, with the high-poly version inserted for final rendering. On the opposite end, there may be a waist-up section of the character with many more polys for extreme close-ups when the camera's eye will be more critical.

3D Famous Saying

"In modeling, proportion is everything." *–Jim McCampbell*

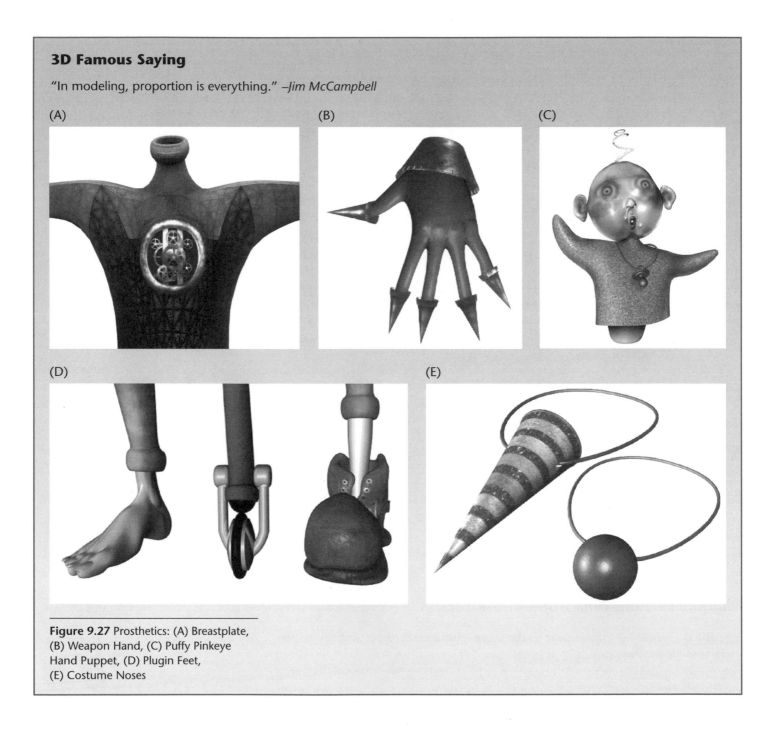

(A)   (B)   (C)

(D)   (E)

Figure 9.27 Prosthetics: (A) Breastplate, (B) Weapon Hand, (C) Puffy Pinkeye Hand Puppet, (D) Plugin Feet, (E) Costume Noses

In certain poses in which parts of the figure will never move, the bones can be used to nudge the pose into place, then frozen (current state to object) and the bones removed. There's no need for the computer to keep up with bones that will never be used.

Doing Your Character Homework

Let's leave the technical behind for a while. With enough time and patience, anyone can learn the mechanics of animating a character. Even if a character has achieved technical perfection, if it is one of an army of look-alike clones it will bring you little attention. Thinly disguised rip-offs of movie characters seen by all, or the same generic 3D face are simply not worth the trouble. Once again, it's here that sketchbook and pencil are more important than terabytes and megahertz.

Character Creativity

So, how do you come up with ideas? Chapter 20 is about making creative leaps.

Here are a few tips specific to Character Animation.

- Make time to observe people (or animals). Make mental notes about all their characteristics, differences and habits.

- Collect details from life in your sketchbook—pages of mouth expressions, funny ears, hands, noses from life, or a memory of someone you saw on the subway.

- Steal and incorporate. For example, go to nonhuman systems for details and forms, then brainstorm on ways to use them in your character. Coiling tubes from the inside of an airplane might become a prosthetic leg, fill a chestplate, or protrude from the top of a head.

- Invent! Fill your sketchbook with forms that you've never seen before.

Figure 9.28 Prosthetic Wings

Practice in drawing from life is a tremendous asset to your character skills. Many community art centers have "model nights" when you can draw from the model for a small fee. Study human and animal proportion generally and individually, then explore ways to exaggerate proportions into your own style.

Take time to study fields and subsystems that will add variety and believability to your character work. Investigate things like makeup, symbols, hair design, accessories, decorative elements from other cultures and times, old medical tools, clockworks and machinery, even science and math.

Google Image will come in handy for research. Type in sunglasses, and peruse the 50,000 styles. Explore crossover from field to field and system to system. Tattoo a microscopic diatom or celestial map on your character's chest.

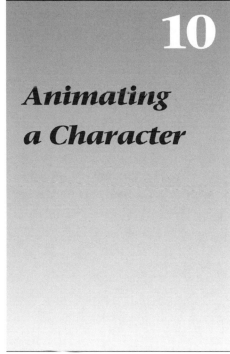

Figure 10.1

Figure 10.2 Jumpsuit with Prosthetics and Accessories

A part from the complex technical workings of rigging and animating a character is the even larger aesthetic life of animation with its rich past and unimaginable future. Day by day, new technological advances redefine what is possible. Once you have mastered the physical aspects of making a rig do what you want it to, there still remains much to be absorbed and explored. By reaching back into the history of animation and putting the time-tested principles of the art to use in exciting new ways, you'll enjoy a pursuit that is constantly redefining itself.

On the DVD: See Chapter 09>EXTRA!EXTRA!>InDepth for the Character..pdf. Also see Chapter 10>EXTRA!EXTRA! for references on Character Animation. Don't pass up building the character. It's a unisex jumpsuit with a trunkload of prosthetic heads, hands, feet, breastplates, and funky accessories. Once you have the jumpsuit jumping, you'll have tons of creative fun designing your own interchangeable parts.

Animating the Skeleton

If your character has a skeleton, you'll be animating it with Forward Kinematics (FK), Inverse Kinematics (IK), or a combination of both. In addition, there may be subroutines of other animation activity going on in the character, such as PLA animation of facial expression, deformers that wiggle part of the skin, or Posemixer keys controlling specific areas like hands.

Animating FK

When animating Forward Kinematics, joints are manually rotated and then keyframed.

When moving an arm for instance, you can rotate bones from the uppermost joint down, keyframing each rotated joint as you go. If you have an arm and hand with continuous bones that will all move in one frame, you may work from the shoulder down, rotating shoulder, elbow, wrist, down to the outermost finger joints. Once all the moving joints are rotated, you can then select the uppermost joint, choose the Select Children command and click the red Record button to keyframe them simultaneously. AutoKeyframing can also be used to record keys for FK. Remember the importance of setting starting state keys for everything that will be moving. Let's try out FK.

Step 1   Open the file Fortuneteller.c4d (Chapter 10>C4D Files). Save a working copy to your Models folder (File>Save As). Open the Crystal Ball object and turn off the visibility on the Hardware object for now.

Step 2   Before we animate the LEFT ARM with FK, we'll flip-copy it to make the RIGHT ARM, which we will animate with a different technique.

Step 3   In the Objects Manager, control-drag a copy of the LEFT ARM object.

Step 4   Choose Objects>Null Object. Drop the LEFT ARM copy into the Null Object as its child.

Step 5   Select the Null Object and in the Attributes Manager Coordinates panel, enter a value of – (minus) 1 for S.X (X Scale) and press return.

Step 6   Drag the LEFT ARM copy out of the Null Object and rename it RIGHT ARM. (You can throw the null away.)

Step 7   Open the RIGHT ARM Hierarchy and change all the "L"s to "R"s.

Step 8   Make both the LEFT AND RIGHT ARM objects children of the Manikin object.

Scrub through the Timeline, and notice what the hands are doing. They wiggle casually and then at the end (200 frames), they spread out more dramatically. We want the arms to begin with the hands resting (actually they will be tapping) on the table in front of the manikin, then passing over the crystal ball, and ending in the air as if revealing some mystery. There are two ways you can go about animating an arm with FK. For the LEFT ARM, you will hand-rotate and set a keyframe for every joint manually. With the RIGHT ARM, you will set starting keyframes for all the joints, and then turn on Auto Keyframing so that a change in any joint at any point in time will be recorded.

The fact is, you will probably have to try this out several times to get the hang of it. Experiment with timing and combining different rotations on different joints for elegant motion. At this point, use the File>Save As command to save several

■ **Shortcut:** The Select Children command is a great candidate for a custom shortcut key, (such as Opt-C or Alt-C). See the Appendix for instructions on using the Command Manager to set custom Shortcuts.

versions so you can start over without having to remove keyframes. Have the Animation Layout open, so it's easy to pop down and remove keys that don't seem to be working. If you do want to erase all the keys and start over, you can do so in the Timeline.

◆ *Tips:*

- Sometimes animation keyframes play hide and seek! Just when you think you've removed all the offending keys and are ready to start over, *some* key *somewhere* is making *something* move! If the Timeline is in *Automatic Mode* (when the padlock is *unlocked*), *Command-A* and *Delete* will clear the animation. When the padlock symbol on the upper right side of the Timeline is *locked*, (Manual Mode) only the keys for objects that have been placed in the Timeline will respond to Timeline commands like *Command-A* and *Delete*. Choosing *Show All Animated* from the Timeline Edit menu will place all keys in the Timeline, and Command-A followed by the Delete key will remove all animation.
- If your mesh is problematic around the elbows, you can always go back and adjust the bone functions, weight maps or work with the mesh itself until it looks good!
- The axes of the sections of the arm are already placed at the proper points of rotation for you. It's important to know that if you create your own jointed figures, you'll need to make each section editable and move each axis to the point on which you want it to rotate. You'll also need to make each section a child of the object above it. The figure in the Primitive menu is already set up, so open it up and study its hierarchy and axis placement as an example. It will also come in handy for more animation practice.
- As your animation skills progress, you'll want to explore advanced techniques such as using Xpresso to control FK animation.

Step 9 Open the LEFT ARM hierarchy, and select L Upper Arm Bone, L Lower Arm Bone, and L Wrist.

Step 10 On the right of the Animation Timeline, make sure Rotation is the only type of animation enabled.

Step 11 Making sure the current time is a 0 frames, click the Record button.

Step 12 Forward the current time to 25 frames, and working from the top bone (L Upper Arm Bone) down, rotate the joints into a position similar to Figure 10.3 B. Once you are happy with the pose, make sure you select all joints that were rotated and record keyframes for each. (You can either Shift-select all the rotated bones, or select the uppermost bone, choose Objects>Select Children and then click the Record button for all at once.)

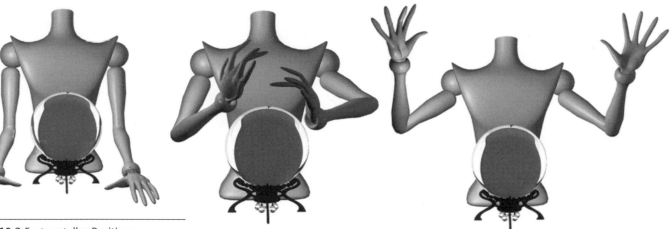

Figure 10.3 Fortuneteller Positions:
A) Starting Position, B) Second Position and
C) Ending Position

Figure 10.4. Automatic Keyframing Button

Step 13 At Frame 100, rotate the joints so that the hand is passing over the crystal ball. You'll have to rotate the top joint outward, not just up, for this to happen. Every time you change the pose, select any joints that were changed and record keyframes.

Step 10 At Frame 180, pose the figure so that the spread hands have their palms forward. As you get more accomplished at getting the movement you want, try keyframing the hand in an arch at the end for a little added magic. (See the Example movie in Chapter 10>MOVIES/STILLS>Fortuneteller.)

Ready to try another method on the right side? Let the arm move basically the same but with some subtle differences in the motion.

Step 11 Close the LEFT ARM hierarchy, and open the RIGHT ARM hierarchy. Select the R Upper Arm Bone, R Lower Arm Bone, and R Wrist. Only Rotation should still be enabled, so go ahead and click the Record button to set a starting state key for all the joints at 0 frames.

Step 12 Forward the Timeline to 15 frames. Here we'll turn on Autokeyframing so that anything that changes at any point in time will be keyframed.

Step 13 Create basically the same motion that you did before so that there will be a general symmetry of the hands rising, but let the right arm and hand have some subtle differences from the left side.

All you have to do is move to a new point in time and make changes, repeating those steps to the end of the Timeline. The red line around the editor window reminds you that Autokeyframing is on. Be sure to turn it off when you are finished. The frames you create can still be tweaked on the Timeline or in the F-Curve window.

There is a lot to be said for some planned asymmetry in animation. For example, you can see the movement you already created on the left arm as you work. Stagger the times slightly where important things are happening. Notice we started the right arm upward a touch later than the left arm. Barely noticable differences like this add believability to the motion.

The concept of asymmetry also applies across time. Rather than rotating all the joints at one frame in time, "roll up" or "roll down" the motion by rotating joints at slightly trailing times. In other words, instead of rotating the shoulder, elbow and hand on the same frame, rotate the shoulder first, the elbow a few frames later and in a few more frames follow with the hand.

Animate the Bubblegum

Figure 10.5 Bubblegum

Step 1   Navigate to Chapter 10>C4D Files> Bubblegum.c4d. Save a working copy to your Models folder (File>Save As).

Step 2   Enable only Position Animation on the right of the Animation Timeline.

Step 3   Using the Move tool, drag the Goal to different positions, setting position keyframes as you go.

Animating Soft IK

The Character PDF on the DVD has more advanced details about rigging and animating a whole character. Explore your MOCCA manual for more information on working with Selection objects and efficient ways to organize all the many pieces and parts in the rig. Compared to the complexity of creating a rig, animating one is fairly simple. As opposed to FK animation in which rotations of each joint are keyframed, animating an IK rig is about keyframing the position and rotation of the control objects. In some ways, it's like manipulating a string puppet. In addition, you'll animate the hand motions by recording states of the Posemixer sliders.

You'll work from the broader motions down to the details. In some cases, you may want to keyframe the broad directional motion of a Null containing the entire object across the space before you start animating smaller detail. For example, a fish (with body twists and flippy fins going on) will need to move as a whole from here to there in the ocean. In this case, we'll be moving the Pelvis (the object's center of gravity) along the path of movement to create the overall change in position. The best way to learn is to jump in and animate one character after another, so save plenty of practice copies of your rig.

Step 1   Open the file LegsRigged.C4D in the Chapter 10<C4D Files folder on the DVD. Save a working copy to your Models folder. Turn the green checkbox of the HyperNURBS object to red. When you start getting serious about a walk cycle, you'll want to create a floor and work in side view.

Step 2   Make sure the current time is 0 frames. Shift-click on the RIGHT LEG CONTROLS, LEFT LEG CONTROLS AND PELVIS CONTROLLER. (Notice these objects, the main ones you will be animating, are in caps so they are more easily seen.) Enable Position and Rotation animation and record a keyframe.

Step 3 Move the current time to frame 5. Turn on the Automatic Keyframing button.

You don't have to use Automatic Keyframing. The Record button can be clicked every time an object is moved or rotated at a new point in time. It's just so easy to forget! Also, the number of frames between keys determines how fast the steps are. These can be spread out or crunched together later as you adjust the timing.

Step 4 Select the RIGHT LEG CONTROLS, and choose the Move and Object tools. Click the Use Soft IK button in the MOCCA palette. Drag the mouse in the Editor window to move the right leg slightly up and forward. Don't go overboard with the motion for now. (Motions that push the chain beyond a certain rotation will require other adjustments we want to avoid for now).

Step 5 Set the Current time to 10 frames. Select the PELVIS CONTROLLER and move it forward with the green Move handle. Every time you plant a foot, the PELVIS CONTROLLER will need to be forwarded so that the center of weight stays over the planted foot.

◆ *Tips:*
- Using the green, red and blue handles when positioning or rotating LEG CONTROLS and PELVIS CONTROLLER can help you avoid some unplanned bone rotations.
- Remember that animating IK is not just about animating one object, but achieving a working tension between all the forces in the chain. As you start working with rigs and see bones start to flip in unexpected ways, another object in the rig may need adjusting to allow the motion to occur without unwanted spins. Spins and flips usually mean the chain is being pushed too far, so something has to give. That may mean changing the *strength* values of one force, or adjusting the position or rotation of a Goal or UpVector. The Strength of Rest Rotations on the Soft IK Tag's Rest panel also interact with the other forces and can be adjusted.

Step 6 At 15 frames, select the RIGHT LEG CONTROLS and plant the foot on the floor. Move the PELVIS CONTROLLER forward to maintain the weight over the foot. The PELVIS CONTROLLER can also be lowered on the Y axis when a foot plants to enhance the feeling of weight on the foot.

Step 7 Once the right foot is firmly planted and the weight is centered over it, the left leg can be lifted slightly to the back (in the same frame or a few frames afterward).

Step 8 At this point, select the LEFT LEG CONTROLS and repeat the same steps: left leg up and forward, PELVIS CONTROLLER forward, right leg lifting to the back, left leg plants, PELVIS CONTROLLER rolls forward.

● ***Springboard:*** From here, the way to success is "try, try again!" Every time the LegsRigged.c4d file is opened for a fresh start, use Save As to save a new working copy. After a smooth babystep walk is achieved, try adding more personality to the movement by adding some side movement or rotation to the PELVIS CONTROLLER. From there move on to hops, jumps, stair climbs, turnarounds (the rotation of the LEG CONTROLS and even the Shin Root goals and Thigh UpVectors may have to be animated for that one), hip-twisting boogies, slides and other increasingly interesting and difficult motion! Before you know it, your characters will be turning flips!

Figure 10.6 Animated Legs

To add further realism to the Suction feet, animate Bend deformers to curl their front edges as they roll up off the floor.

On the DVD: For a truly authentic walk cycle, study stop frames photos of walking bipeds and check out some of the excellent resource books on Character Animation (Chapter 10>EXTRA!EXTRA!>References).

Using Set Driven Key to Bulge a Muscle

Navigate to the Chapter 10>EXAMPLES>Muscle.c4d. Click the Play button and watch how the muscle "bulks up" when the elbow bends. After the rotation (Rotation on the H or Heading) is keyframed, Command-click (right-click) on the letter H in R.H in the Coordinates panel and drag over to Animation>Set Driver.

Figure 10.7 Bulging Muscle

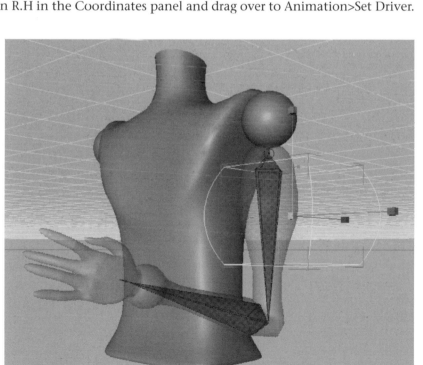

Knife a few extra cuts in the muscle area. Position the Bulge deformer on the arm and in the Objects Manager, and make the deformer a child of the arm. Then in Attributes Manager Object Properties, Command-click (right-click) on the word Strength and slide over to Animation>Set Driven (Absolute). The degree of H rotation on the joint will control the size of the muscle.

Putting Animation Principles To Work

You'll see these time-tested concepts hard at work in any kind of animation—2D, 3D or stop-frame.

- **Readability** What is behind your animated character? Is there a strong silhouette so the audience can clearly read the shape and action? Uncluttered backgrounds in a contrasting value are best.

- **Exaggeration** Animation is Art. Therefore, you have a license to exaggerate. As a matter of fact, animation happens so fast that exaggeration is often necessary for motion to be comprehended as normal.

- **Clear Motivation** Is the reason for an action clear? Think through what your character is feeling and thinking, so his or her actions appear to come from within rather than from the character being shuffled around by an animator.

- **Arcs** Watch some animation in slow motion. Notice that everything moves on arcs rather than straight lines.

- **Overlap** In complex animation, one action doesn't completely stop before another starts, and stops and starts happen at different times. The F-Curve window is extremely helpful in comparing the timing of different animated elements.

- **Asymmetry** Edit pairs or groups of matching objects for nuance. Throw the composition off balance. If you can find a pair of eyeballs the same size in a cartoon animation, you get the prize.

- **Secondary Action** Smaller actions that underscore a message. An expectant father pacing back and forth (primary) bites his nails (secondary).

- **Anticipation** A preliminary occurance that gets the viewer primed for the main action. Tippi Hedron hears the flapping of bird wings—in itself not a bad thing, but a precursor of something scarier to come.

- **Squash and Stretch** When a character is squashed, the opposing dimensions are stretched so that volume is maintained.

- **Overshoot** Most motion reads better if it goes past its destination and recoils.

- **Follow-through** The golf club doesn't stop dead when it hits the ball but continues on in an arc. Apply the concept to character motion. When your character stops in his or her tracks, the hair keeps going.

- **Continuing Motion** Nothing is completely still. Even a character listening to another more active one will be displaying subtle body language.

Animating with Posemixer

This one is easy. Select the Posemixer object in the Objects Manager. In Object Properties, just slide the sliders until you get the combination that creates the pose you want at a given point in time. Click the Record button. Go to the next place on the Timeline you want to set keys, and repeat the process.

Figure 10.8 PoseMixer Hand Poses

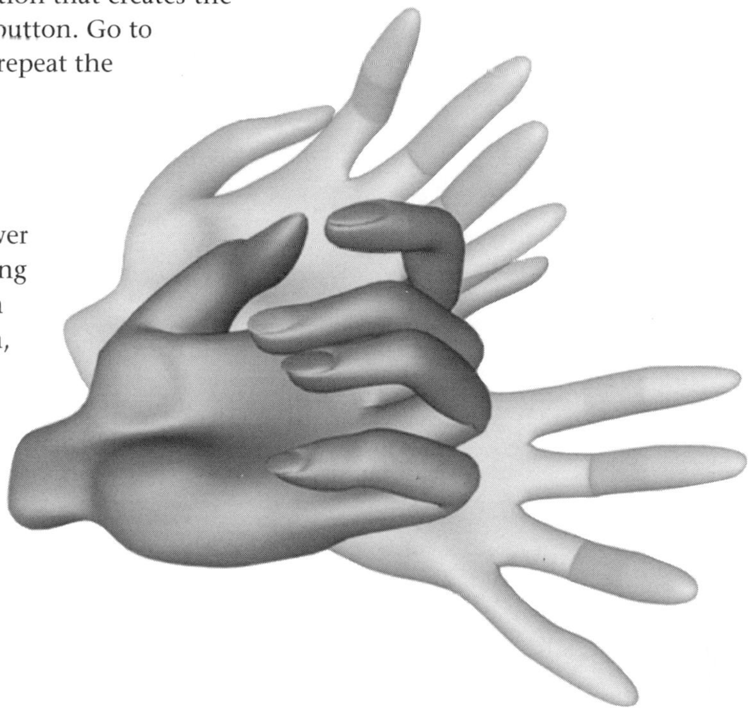

Using F-Curves with Character Motion

Once your basic movement is in place, remember the power of F-Curves. Many of the Animation Principles (see "Putting Animation Principles to Work") can be directly affected in the F-Curve window. Ease Ins and Ease Outs, exaggeration, arcs, timing, and other tweaks that make motion more believable can be controlled easily in this powerful window.

Connect: Planting the Feet In Chapter 14 "A Jolt of Xpresso," there is an expression for preventing your character's feet from going through the floor.

Planning Motion

Getting a feel for timing and motion is one of the aspects of animation that may or may not come intuitively. You may have to work at it. Being an animator is like being an actor, but with using a puppet.

Figure 10.9 Stopwatch

Studying acting, dance, and choreography will add depth and excitement to your work. Buy a stopwatch, and walk through motions, timing them for a rough idea of how long things take in real life. While you've been learning CINEMA 4D, your timeline has probably stayed on 90 frames most of the time. It's time to stretch that out so there is ample room for more manipulation of timing. After you have mastered the technicalities of making characters move, your next stop should be *Acting for Animators: A Complete Guide to Performance Animation*, by Ed Hooks

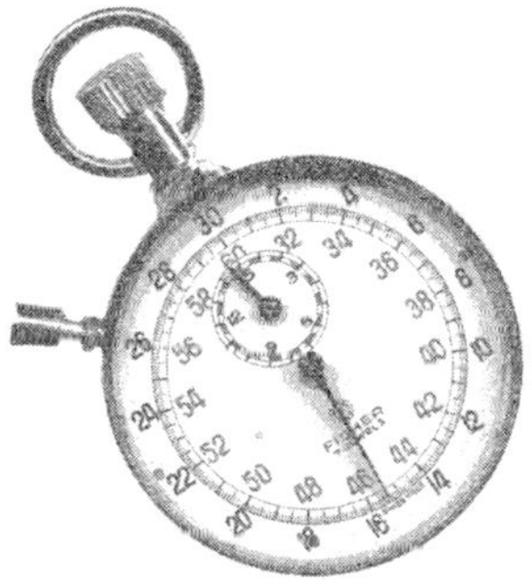

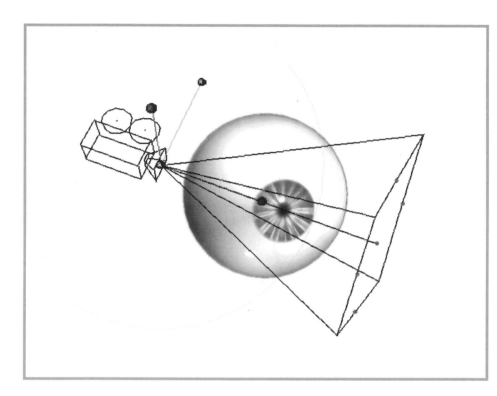

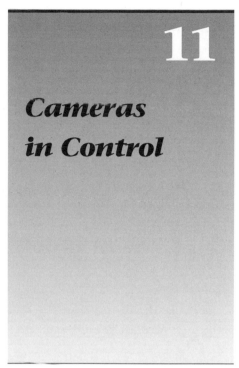

Figure 1.11

I t's probably clear to you by now that the creation of a 3D world involves many integrated skills. You have already been trying on the roles of painter, sculptor, lighting director, and animator. Now it's time to explore the work of director and cinematographer. So far most of your work has been viewed through the Editor camera, a default view of the 3D space as seen in CINEMA 4D's editor window. Since you didn't have to create that camera, there was probably not even much awareness about the role of the camera in the moviemaking process. You can create as many cameras as you need in C4D, and animate their position or rotations like any other 3D object. These virtual cameras have the same features as their real-world counterparts, and those parameters (like focal length or depth of field) can be animated as well.

Artistically, the camera through which the scene is viewed is the ultimate control over what your audience perceives. The virtual camera you create is the critical eye, and therefore, it's a good idea to set up cameras early in the process and edit everything in the scene to that camera's eye. As the director, you are using the camera as a tool, influencing your audience to regard the scene in a particular way and feel a specific emotion. Ask yourself this important question before you begin: What is it I want my audience to see and feel?

3D Famous Saying

"If it looks right, it is right."
—*Jim McCampbell*

Looking through a Camera

When you choose a Camera from the Lighting Menu, a new camera appears in the editor. If you are in the Perspective view when you create the camera, it will

The Camera Object

When you create a camera, the physical location and orientation is represented by a camera symbol. The X and Y axes of the camera correspond to the film plane and the Z axis is the direction in which the camera is pointing. The pyramid of lines indicates the camera's field of view, and the orange handles let you make adjustments to the camera interactively.

Figure 11.2 Camera Icons

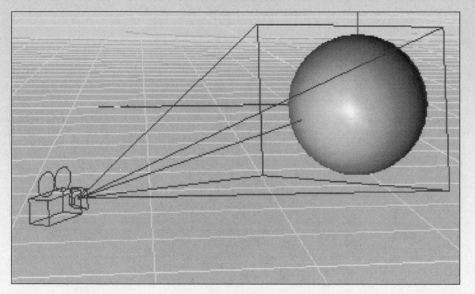

Figure 11.3 A Camera Object

be aligned the same as the Editor camera, and at that moment you are viewing the scene from the camera's view. However, if you choose Edit>Frame Scene or otherwise manipulate the editor view, you will no longer be looking through that new camera and will actually be able to look at it as an object in the scene. In this exercise, you'll set up the view so you are looking through the camera you create.

Create the Camera Object

Step 1   Open the file Poppers.c4d from the Chapter 11>C4D Files folder on the DVD. Save it as Poppers.c4d to your Models folder (File>Save As).

Step 2   From the top menu, choose Camera Object from the Lighting palette. Then choose Edit>Frame Scene from the View Menu. Use the mouse with the 2 and 3 keys to get a feel for the camera's orientation in space and an understanding that you are not looking through the camera you created, but at it.

Step 3   Double-click the Camera object in the Objects Manager and rename it MAIN CAMERA.

Set Up the View through the Camera

Step 1   Choose View>All Views (F5). The blue line around the edge of the upper left view tells you it will be the rendered view.

Step 2   From the menu of that view, choose Cameras>Scene Camera>Main Camera. Now that view is equivalent to the viewfinder of MAIN CAMERA and is what the audience will see. Any changes you make to the position or other parameters of the camera in any other window will affect this view.

To animate the camera, you will scrub through the animation and set keyframes for the camera at key positions. Just like any other animation, the movement of the camera will be interpolated between these keys. Make sure the MAIN CAMERA object is selected and then try out all these ways to change the position of the camera:

- Use the Camera Move, Scale, and Rotate tools at the top right of the upper left view.

- Manually move or rotate the camera in any of the orthographic views, top, side, or front.

- Drag the small black arrows to the right of the values in the Attributes Manager Coordinates panel.

- "Drive" the camera in the upper left view with the Move tool. Drag the mouse left and right or up and down (left-mouse), the Command-drag (right-mouse) to move in and out. The coolest way to drive the camera is with a multiple-button mouse. A mouse drag holding down the righthand button will move the camera in and out. (Spinning the wheel on a wheel mouse is an even easier way.)

Figure 11.4 Upper Left View as Camera Viewfinder

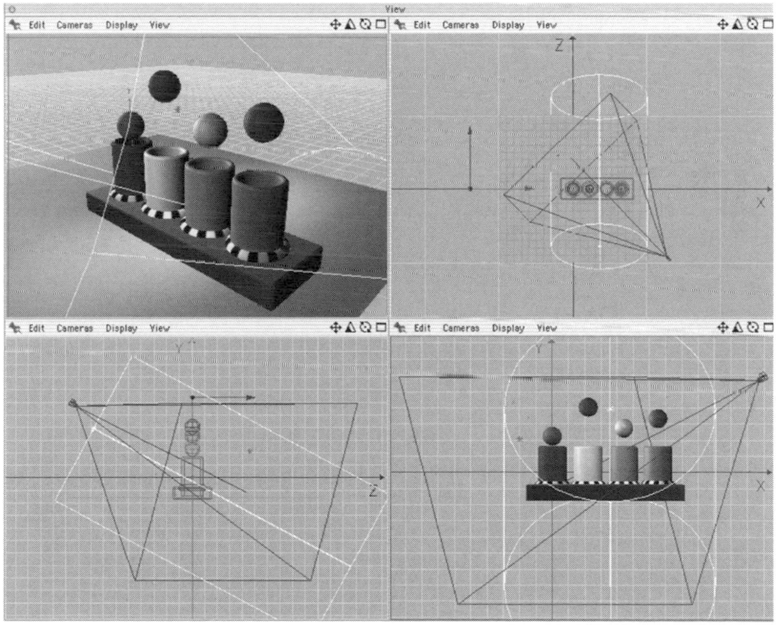

◆ ***Tip:*** Carsickness, Anyone? Keep in mind that the camera is essentially the eyes of your viewer; it's generally a good idea to keep camera movement simple and smooth, so that viewers are not distracted (or sickened) by its movement as they focus on the subject. If your viewer is experiencing the scene from a rollercoaster car, then go ahead and animate that camera with lots of loop de loops. Otherwise, avoid jerky camera movements by keeping keys to a minimum, placing keys far enough apart in time and space, and using tangent handles to create elegant arcs of motion.

Step 2 At Frame 0, drive the camera (using any of the methods listed above) to the beginning view you want. Remember, it's the upper left view that counts. Enable Position and Rotation animation, and click the Record button. Or, animate the camera using the Attributes Manager Coordinates panel. Click any of the Ps and right- or Command-click to set a keyframe. Click any of the Rs and set a keyframe for Rotation also. The settings for Frame 0 in the example movie are: P.X 200, P.Y 1300, P.Z 1400, R.H –132, R.P –30, and R.B left at 0.

Step 3 At Frame 90, adjust the camera in position and rotation for the ending view and set keyframes. (The example movie settings are P.X –700, P.Y 700, P.Z 2000, R.H –175, R.P –45 and R.B 3.) Be sure to save (File> Save or Cmd+S/Ctrl+S).

Step 4 Look at the animation path in the top view. Holding down the 2 key, drag the mouse right to left so you can see the entire path. Ouch—that straight line is a classic no-no in animation. In the Animation Layout, click the F-Curve tab. Drag the MAIN CAMERA object into the F-Curve window, choose Frame All, and select MAIN CAMERA>Position Z. Select the key at Frame 0, then Command-click (right-click) on it and choose Custom Tangents>Soft Interpolation from the contextual menu. Raise the right tangent handle so that the path is curved slightly, as in Figure 11.5. Notice how the animation path is now an arc.

Figure 11.5 Position Z F-Curve

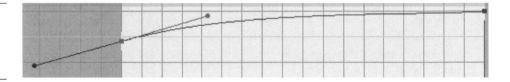

Figure 11.6 Arc in Animation Path, Top View

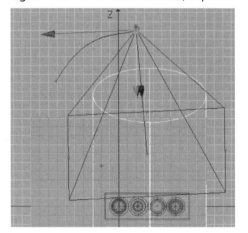

Step 5 What if the colored balls were popping up out of the view, and you needed to back up and take in more of the scene? The orange handles can be used to adjust the focal length to a wider angle so they will be included in the scene. Or, you could drag keys to new positions in the F-Curve window while keeping an eye on the scene in the editor window.

The interactive orange handles of the camera object can be used to adjust focal length to a wider or narrower angle of view, affecting how much is included in the scene. Changes in Focal length will distort perspective, while moving the camera object keeps the perspective "normal" (or whatever perspective it is currently set to).

To animate focal length on a selected camera, scrub through the animation and set keyframes for the focal length at key positions. Click the Object panel in the Attributes Manager, and click on the object Focal Length. Drag the black arrows and watch the editor window to see the value changes in action. Set keyframes where changes are necessary. Again, widely spaced, gradual changes are more effective than too many sudden in and out movements.

An Easier Way: Target Cameras

In the example above, you animated the position and rotation of the camera to keep the subject in the view. Here's a much easier way:

Figure 11.7 Target Cam

Step 1   Open the file StringofHands.c4d from the Chapter 11>C4D Files folder on the DVD. Save it as HandsCam.c4d to your models folder (File>Save As).

Step 2   Select a Target Camera from the Lighting Palette.

Step 3   Click the Target tag to the right of the Camera object. In the Attributes Manager, click the Tag panel and drag the object HAND 3 from the Objects Manager into the box for Target Object. Choose View>All Views.

Step 4   In the upper left view, choose Camera>Scene Cameras>Camera. Choose the Model tool and Move tool. In the orthographic views, use the blue and red Move handles to position the camera out in space and to the right, as in Figure 11.8. Set a keyframe for Position X, Y, and Z only.

Figure 11.8 Starting Position

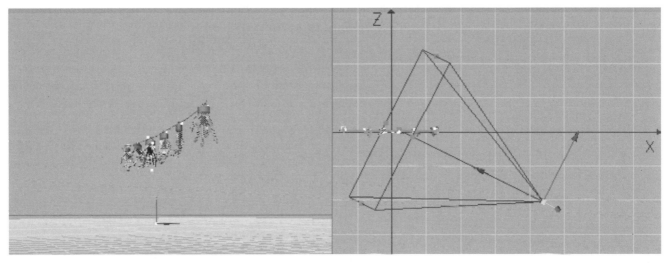

Because rotation is determined by the camera's relationship to the target object, it isn't necessary to keyframe rotation.

Figure 11.9 Axis Too High

Step 5   At Frame 200, working in the top view, use the red handle to swing the Camera around toward the Z axis and the blue handle to move the camera in close to the object.

Curses, foiled again! The target camera points specifically to the axis of the target object, which was placed at the top of the hanger so the hand could swing correctly from the string. To make the Target Camera head for a more central location on the hand, use this work-around.

Step 6 Choose Objects>Null Object. Place the Null object in the middle of the hand's palm, checking its position in several views, or use Functions> Transfer to get to the general vicinity, then adjust the position from there. Reselect the Target tag, and drag the Null Object into the Target Object box. Now set a keyframe for a close-up of the hand.

Animating a Camera on a Spline Path

In this exercise, the camera will be placed on a spline path to move through an environment.

Step 1 Open the file MasterEnvironment.c4d from the Chapter 11>C4D Files folder on the DVD. Save it as Joyride.c4d to your Models folder. Work in All Views.

Step 2 Select a Camera from the Lighting Palette. In the View menu, choose Cameras>Scene Camera>Camera.

Step 3 Control-drag a copy of the Tunnel Path Spline object in the Objects Manager. Rename the copy Cam Spline.

Step 4 Command-click (right-click) on the Camera object and drag to New Expression>Align to Spline expression. Select the Align to Spline tag, and in the Attributes Manager drag the object Cam Spline into the box for Spline Path. Check the check box for Tangential.

Step 5 With the current time at 0 Frames, click on the word Position in the Attributes manager and enter 0 percent as the value. Command-click (right-click) to set a keyframe. Around Frame 2500, keyframe the Position value as 100 percent.

Step 6 Scrub though the animation and watch the upper left view. You'll see places where the spline path needs to be adjusted. Select the Cam Path and the Points tool. Work with the motion of the camera in the orthographic views by tweaking the position of points, converting hard points to soft, and adjusting tangent handles. Start with a close-up of the current camera position in the Top view to get a clear picture of how the camera movement needs smoothing out, then go back and work in the other views if necessary.

A More Complex Camera Movement

The fly-through created above is fine for a quick joyride. Since the plan is to add interesting objects to this museumlike space, the camera will need to slow down or look sideways occasionally. The viewer will need time to study objects in the alcoves lining the tunnel. This method offers more control over what the camera is looking at and for how long.

Step 1 Open the file MasterEnvironment.c4d in the Chapter 11>C4D Files folder. Save a working copy to your Models folder (File>Save As). Choose Animation Layout.

Step 2 Choose a Target Camera from the Lighting palette.

Step 3 Set up the upper left view to be the "viewfinder" of the scene camera, and place the camera in a starting position at the entrace of the environment.

Step 4 Choose Objects>Null Object and drag the Camera's target as a child of the Null. Place the Null where you want the camera to be looking first.

Figure 11.10 18mm Camera on a Spline Path

Step 5 Scrub through the scene, keyframing the position of both the camera and the Null Object. (The Keys for the Null will be the points that you want the camera to stop and look at.) As you keyframe, you'll be working with the relationship between camera and target, moving both forward in a leapfrog fashion. The rotation of the camera will be determined by its fixation on the Null Object, so no Rotation keyframing is necessary.

Figure 11.11
50mm
Camera on a
Spline Path

◆ *Tips:*

- Set up the scene camera in the upper left view to use as a guide.
- Work in All Views.
- Choose a brightly colored and enlarged Display object for the Null Object, making it easier to see as you work. (In the Attributes Manager: Basic Tab>Use Color Always and Object>Display.)
- To drive the camera forward, use the Move tool with the Command-key (right-mouse) or try using the wheel on a wheel mouse.
- Drop the Camera and the Null Object into the F-Curve window for fine tuning of timing.

Focal Length

Open the file BatInCave.c4d from the Chapter 11>C4D Files folder on the DVD. Select the Camera object. In the Attributes Manager Object Properties experiment with different values in the box for Focal Length (just drag on the black arrows). A value of 50–52 is the equivalent of a normal lens on a real camera. Lower values, 45 and under, are in the Wide Angle range. A wide angle shot can distort slightly, adding a strange and dramatic feeling to the scene. Because the wide angle shot takes more in, it can also do more to establish a sense of place. Larger values are in the Telephoto range. They can create a sense of intimacy by filling the frame with the subject, and they flatten perspective.

Animating a Camera on a Helix Spline Path

Here's the easy way to circle an object, pulling the camera in tighter as you go.

Step 1 Open the file AlienPrincess.c4d from the Chapter 11>C4D Files folder on the DVD. Save a working copy to your Models folder (File>Save As).

Step 2 Select a Helix Spline from the Spline palette. Rotate the Helix 90º in Pitch.

Step 3 In the Attributes Manager, enter a Start Radius of 500.

Step 4 Create a Target Camera. Click the Target tag and and drag the Head into the Target Object box.

Step 5 Command-click (right-click) on the Camera object and drag to New Expression>Align to Spline expression. Select the Align to Spline tag, and in the Attributes Manager drag the object Helix into the box for Spline Path.

Step 6 With the current time at 0 Frames, click on Position in the Attributes Manager and enter 0 percent as the value. Command-click (right-click) to set a keyframe. At Frame 350, keyframe the Position value as 100 percent.

Step 7 Set the focal length of the camera to 22.

Step 8 Set up the camera as the scene camera in the upper left view; choose Window>New View Panel and in that Editor View, rotate the Helix Spline so that the last frame is a frontal close-up of the face. Adjust the height of the Helix to get the look you want.

Step 9 Open the F-Curve Manager. Drag the Align to Spline tag into the F-Curve window. Choose View>Frame All. Press Cmd+A (Ctrl+A) to select both points, and choose Custom Tangents>Soft Interpolation and Custom Tangents>Flat to create an Ease Out and Ease In.

Figure 11.12 Camera on a Helix Spline Path

Animating a Camera to Follow a Moving Object

Step 1   Create a Target Camera and set up the Object as the Target.

Step 2   Position the camera in the general relationship to the object and make the Camera a child of the object so it will follow it.

You can still go back and keyframe changes in the position of the camera in relation to the object it is following.

Placing a Camera inside a Null Object

A camera attached to a Spline path with an Align to Spline expression can't be rotated. If a Null Object "container" is attached to the path, a camera placed inside the Null can then be rotated independently.

Step 1:   Open the File Chapter 11>C4D Files>NullCamContainer.c4d. The Null Object (with the camera as its child) is placed on the spline with an Align to Spline tag, and the Functions>Transfer>(Position and Rotation) was used to give the camera the same starting position and rotation as the Null.

Step 2:   Scrub through the animation and in the top view, watch how the camera is behaving.
        The direction of the spline is controlling the Null rotation (and the camera rotation).

Step 3: Scrub back through the animation and keyframe independent rotations for the camera object. Enable Rotation Animation. At Frame 40, click the Record button to set a starting key. At Frame 35, adjust the R.H value so the camera turns its gaze to the blue cube. Record a key.

Using Depth of Field

Photographers often blur the foreground and background to focus attention on a specific object.

This shallow depth of field can calso be created with a virtual camera in CINEMA 4D.

Step 1 Open the file DOFPoppers.c4d from the Chapter 11>C4D Files folder on the DVD. Save a working copy to your Models folder (File>Save As).

Step 2 The camera has already been created, placed, and chosen as the scene camera in the top left view. Select DOF Camera in the Objects Manager.

Step 3 Select the DOF Camera in the Objects Manager. In the Attributes Manager, click the panel for Depth. Check the check boxes for Front and Rear Blur. Leave the Start value at 0 and enter an End value of 2000 for both Front and Rear.

Step 4 Open the Render Settings. Click the Effects page, and check Depth of Field. Make sure Enable Post Effects is checked. Click Depth of Field to bring up the pages for editing.

Step 5 Click on the Basic panel. Enter a value of 30 percent for Blur Strength. Check on Use Distance Blur and enter a value of 20 percent. Close the Render Settings and render a movie.

Figure 11.13 Camera Set for Shallow Depth of Field

◆ *Tip:* Depth of Field is a postrendering effect and will be added after the initial rendering of each frame.

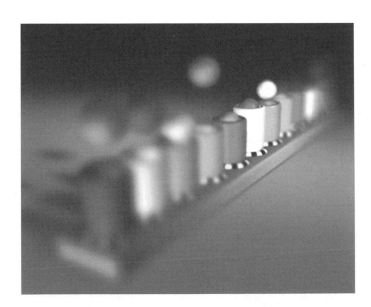

Virtual Lens and Filter Effects

The virtual counterparts of diffusers, fisheye lenses, vignettes, and just about any other real-life lens or filter effect can be easily emulated in 3D. Just make a lens from a primitive, apply a material that copies the properties of the real thing, and place the object in front of the virtual camera. For a vignette, use an alpha channel. A fisheye lens has a high refraction that can be emulated with a material. Although they are much easier to accomplish in AfterEffects, even *transitions* could be faked by animating materials or lights between scenes.

Switching Cameras in CINEMA 4D

To be honest, most people create different camera renderings and then composite them with sound and effects in a compositing application. You'll learn more about compositing in Chapter 19. You can switch from camera to camera in a single CINEMA file. Here's how:

Step 1 Open the file Switching Cameras.c4d from the Chapter 11>C4D Files folder on the DVD. Save a working copy to your Models folder (File>Save As).

Step 2 Choose Objects>Scene>Stage. In the Attributes Manager, click the Object panel.

Step 3 At Frame 0, drag the Floor Level Cam into the Camera box. Click the word Camera and set a keyframe.

Step 4 At Frame 50, drag the Low, Close Cam into the Camera box and set a keyframe. Scrub the Timeline to see the cameras change.

You can add as many cameras as you want. You can also use the Stage Object to switch Skies, Backgrounds, Foregrounds, and Environments.

A Critical Distinction

Remember there is an important difference between moving a camera in relation to the subject and zooming the camera by changing its focal length. Moving the mouse while holding down the 2 key now moves the camera while Cmd+2 and moving the mouse changes the focal length. While moving a camera closer and zooming in may look very

Figure 11.14 Zoomed Views

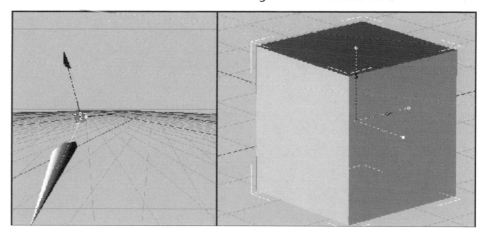

much the same through the camera viewfinder, there is an artistic difference. Moving the camera does not distort perspective. A camera zoomed back from a subject creates emphasized perspective, while zooming into telephoto range also distorts with an overly flattened effect. Either extreme can be used to create a unique look for a shot.

Looking through Other Objects

Occasionally it can be helpful to look at the scene from the point of view of an object or light. Select the object you want to look through, and choose Cameras>Link Active Object from the View menu.

On the DVD: Check the Chapter 11>EXTRA!EXTRA! folder for other resources on camera work and filmmaking.

The Art of Rendering

Figure 12.1

T he worlds you have created in a virtual 3D space and framed in the eye of a camera must now be rendered to create a final product. In layman's language, the computer paints a picture of the view through the camera for a still image or each sequential frame of a movie. The rendering can aim to simulate the look of the real world with photographic clarity, taking into account lighting, reflections, shadows, and all the other influences of the environment. Alternately, the scene can be rendered with sytlistic or even painterly strokes. The process of rendering is a delicate balance of the quality you must have with the time it takes to render the project. By getting to know render settings, you can make the best use of your time and achieve the level of quality appropriate for your project.

Rather than restating the manual on the specifics of every setting, this section will explore some of the most helpful uses of basic settings for the right balance of productivity and quality. In addition, it will focus on rendering methods that enhance the artistry of your work in CINEMA 4D.

On the DVD: Projects that require the installation of the optional Advanced Render module are on the DVD. See the Chapter 12>EXTRA!EXTRA!>InDepth>ADVANCED RENDERING folder for the PDF files.

Figure 12.2 Rendering Icons: Render Active View, Render in Picture Viewer and Render Settings

■ *Shortcut:* To access the Render Settings from the keyboard, press Ctrl+B.

Investigating Render Settings

When you click the Render Settings Icon, a dialog box with ten tabs appears. Let's look at the significance of the most commonly used settings.

The General Tab

Antialiasing

With this setting on None, the corners of pixels on the edges of objects will be noticable as "the jaggies." When you are test-rendering, None is fine and will save time. Depending on your need for smooth edges in the final rendering of the project, you may want to choose Better quality of Geometry or highest quality of Best. These settings oversample, or make more (and smaller) pixels for a smoother edge. Naturally, the higher quality settings take longer to render.

Check the Filter pulldown menu. If you are rendering a still, choose the Still Image filter for a cleaner edge. For movie frames, choose the Animation filter, which will yield a softer edge less prone to flickering. For even more control, click the Antialiasing tab.

Figure 12.3 Antialiasing , None (L) and Best (R)

Render As Editor

When test-rendering animation, you are often more concerned with how the motion looks as opposed to the quality of the surfaces or the effects of lighting. By checking the Render As Editor box, you can rapidly render one of the less time-intensive editor displays (Isoparm, for example) and still have all the information you need about the animation.

Transparency, Reflection, Shadow

These pulldown menus allow you to turn off or limit the rendering of these time-intensive features. When you are test-rendering, seeing these may not be critical and turning them off temporarily can speed up the rendering process.

Figure 12.4 Render As Editor

The Output Tab

Resolution

It is here that you tell CINEMA 4D the size of your still or frames in pixels. The default, 320x240, is fine for movies that you'll view on your computer or put on the web. But if you want your movie to look good on a TV screen, more pixels (640x480 NTSC) are required. If you are headed toward Apple Final Cut Pro with your movie, enter a custom size of 720x480. Enter 10 in the first Pixel box and 11 in the second, as Final Cut uses rectangular pixels. The CINEMA 4D manual has a comprehensive chart for resolution settings for various computer, TV, and film media.

Rendering for print output is a little trickier. The values in the resolution box are not dots per inch (dpi), but the exact number of pixels in the image. To get the proper number of pixels for a printed piece that will be 3x5 inches, multiply the desired dpi times the number of inches for each dimension. In the custom input boxes, you can let CINEMA do the math by typing 3*300 in the first box and 5*300 in the second.

Film Format

These are really presets for resolution that correspond to common X:Y format ratios in the film and video industry. Naturally, choosing one of these will change the Resolution setting above it.

Frame

The default of current frame renders only the frame of the current position of the time slider. If you want to render an animation, it's here that you'll need to drag down to All Frames to render the entire timeline. The Manual setting lets you enter any beginning and ending frame numbers in boxes to the right. Preview Range renders only the frames defined with the green preview slider across the Timeline ruler. Use one of these two options to zero in on the specific part of the animation you are currently tweaking to save lots of rendering time.

Field Rendering

To be safe, check with your client about their requirements. Also, stay away from compression that might destroy field-rendered images.

The Save Tab

Path

Click the Path button and navigate to the location where you want to save the file. If you want to create a folder as a container for frames, click the New Folder button and name the folder. Sometimes, however, it you are working on a project that is requiring lots of tests, it may be more efficient to create a template file (place it into the same folder with the C4D application) with a default title of test and default location of Desktop. Continue to replace that test file on the desktop until you get a keeper, then just rename and file the final file.

Format

The default format is TIFF. When you are rendering an animation, it is important that you either 1. create a folder (see Path above) for the TIFF frames, or 2. drag down to one of the QuickTime choices. If you fail to do so, you'll be doing some serious housekeeping with all the TIFFs that get splattered all over your desktop. QuickTime movie renders an acceptably compressed movie, QuickTime Small uses more compression for the web (with significant quality loss) and QuickTime Big has no compression. Note that CINEMA 4D offers an impressive list of formats for stills and still frames. If you create a template c4d file, (as discussed previously under Path), you could choose QuicktTime format as permanent insurance against forgetting to set the format for an animation and littering the desktop with TIFFs.

Name

This option offers numbering styles for numbered sequences.

Alpha

Click this check box to render a file with a clear background. This file will pop right into a compositing program like Adobe After Effects, or other applications like Apple Final Cut Pro and Adobe Photoshop. The model will have perfectly clean edges and slide right in over other layers placed in the composite. The After Effects Project File option will be covered in Chapter 19. The Save button at the bottom refers to saving an After Effects file and is not required to save the general render settings! The Radiosity and Caustics tabs will be covered in PDFs on Advanced Rendering on the DVD.

Artistic Rendering Effects

The Effects Tab

Click the Effects tab. Click the Post Effect button at the upper right of the window and choose the effect you want.

Object Motion Blur

Motion blur can be applied to a specific object or objects in a scene. This type of blur won't blur shadows and reflections associated with an object, but it emphasizes motion for the object that has a Motion Blur tag while the rest of the scene stays sharp.

Figure 12.5 Object Motion Blur

Step 1   Open the file Object Motion Blur.c4d from the Chapter 12>C4D Files folder on the DVD. Save a working copy into your Models folder (File> Save As).

Step 2   Command-click (right-click) on Tic Toc Stick and drag to New Tag>Motion Blur Tag. Leave the value at 100 percent.

Step 3   In Render Settings, click the Effects tab and choose Object Motion Blur from the Post Effect menu. Render a movie to see the effect.

Scene Motion Blur

An entire scene can be blurred, faking the look of a real camera being moved quickly across the scene. This type of blur does blur shadows and reflections and takes much longer to render.

Step 1   Open the file Scene Motion Blur.c4d from the Chapter 12>C4D Files folder on the DVD. Save a working copy into your Models folder (File>Save As).

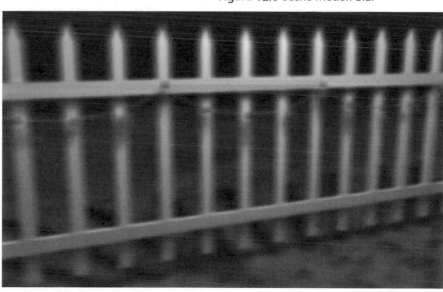

Figure 12.6 Scene Motion Blur

Step 2   In Render Settings, click the Effects tab and check the check box for Scene Motion Blur.

Step 3   In the box for Samples, leave 16 times as the value. This means each frame will be rendered 16 times, offsetting and blending the image to create the blur. Yes! The rendering will take 16 times as long. Remember the batch render queue? Stacking up a renders like this to happen while you are sleeping is a great idea.

Figure 12.7 Cel Rendering 1

Figure 12.8 Cel Rendering 2

Figure 12.9 Cel Rendering 3

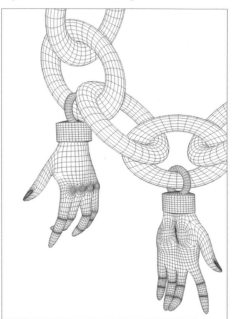

Cel Rendering

The cel rendering options in the Effect tab offer some interesting graphic interpretations of your scene. Click the Effects tab and Choose Cel Rendering from Post Effects. Open any of your previous files and experiment with different settings in the Basic Properties Settings.

Multipass Rendering

This option is a powertool if you are compositing your CINEMA 4D renderings in applications such as Adobe Photoshop or After Effects. Multipass allows you to render different artistic possibilities at one time, and then have more control over the separated layers in the compositing program. This opens up so many creative possibilities, it can make your head spin.

Figure 12.10 Multipass

Step 1 Open the file Multipass.c4d from the Chapter 12>C4D Files folder on the DVD.

Step 2 In Render Settings, click the Multipass page.

Step 3 Study the settings. Channels for Specular, Material Color, and Reflection have been enabled. Also, All is chosen in the Separate Lights menu. The format is Photoshop.

Step 4 Now, if you have Photoshop, open Multipass Render.psd from the Chapter 12>STILLS/MOVIES folder. Everything is neatly separated in your Layers palette. It would be easy to omit a light or apply a Hue change or Photoshop Layer Styles to any of the layers.

Rendering a QuickTime VR Movie

A QuickTime VR is a movie that the viewer can explore interactively with a mouse.

Step 1   Open the file QuickTime VR.c4d from the Chapter 12>C4D Files folder on the DVD. Press F5 for all views and notice the placement of the camera.

Step 2   In Render Settings, click the Save tab. Click the Path tab and set up the location for the rendered file.

Step 3   In the Format pull down menu, drag down to QuickTime VR Object. Press Shift+R to render the frames. (It's normal that the first frames of the rendering will be all black.)

Step 4   When you play the movie in QuickTime, drag the hand to navigate through the space.

On the DVD: If you have the Advanced Rendering Module installed, be sure to check the Chapter 11>EXTRA!EXTRA!>InDepth>ADVANCED RENDERING folder for projects that explore Radiosity, Caustics, Glows and Highlights, and HDRI. Even if you don't have the module, look at the examples of the kinds of things can be done with this powerful option.

Figure 12.11 Fives Rendered with Radiosity

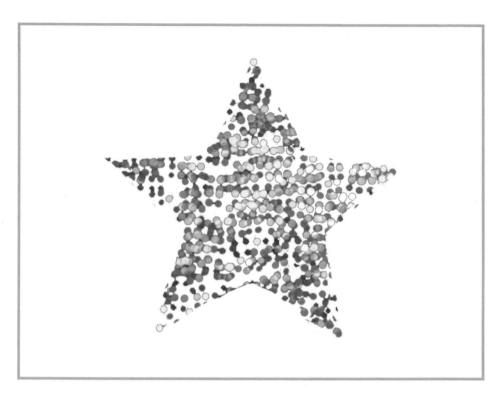

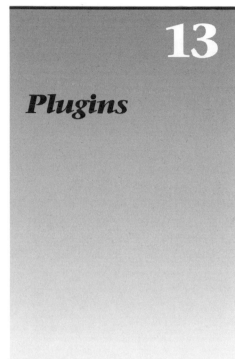

13

Plugins

Figure 13.1

When an application as solid, intuitive, and powerful as CINEMA 4D has a user community rich with talented and generous third-party programmers, it's a win-win situation for all. Support these individuals by paying them for their reasonably priced commercial wares, and reward their freeware with thank-yous, attaboys, and donations. Plugins are snippets of programming, minitools that do specific jobs and infuse new creative ideas. Most often instantly downloadable, CINEMA 4D plugins range from free to reasonably priced. Some of the add-ons discussed in this chapter are not actually plugins, but modules or standalone helper applications. After reading these descriptions of what you can do artistically with these, check the DVD for tutorials, example files, and a URL list of resources. Be sure to visit the Plugin Café at www.maxoncomputer.com, the motherlode for C4D plugins and other resources.

Installing Plugins

- Quit CINEMA 4D before installing plugins.
- Review the Read Me file for any specific instructions. The usual procedure for installing plugins is to drop the entire folder holding the plugin and its accompanying files into the Plugins folder (inside the folder for your current version of C4D).

- The plugin should then appear in the C4D Plugins pulldown from the top menu. Yet another reason to read the Read Me file is that some plugins have features in additional locations, so you may need some directions to those locations.

Figure 13.2 Scapel Example

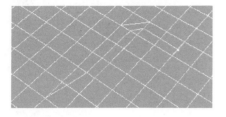

Figure 13.3 Katana

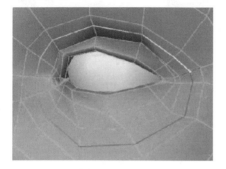

Figure 13.4 Superflange

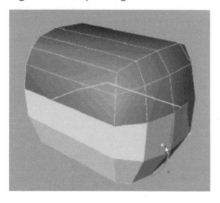

Figure 13.5 Hinge Extrude

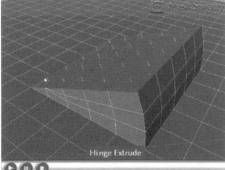

Commercial Plugins

Mesh Surgery

Mesh Surgery from Paul Everett and Per-Anders Edwards never fails to make any must-have C4D plugins list. This turbocharged suite of modeling tools empowers the crafting of meshes in ways you haven't even dreamed of. Mesh Surgery is packed with tools that can subdivide and manipulate the mesh in innovative ways. Be sure to check out the PDF, and then head over to www.tools4d.com for the grand tour, including excellent manuals and videos of the plugin in action. Here's a quick peek at just a few of the many features:

- **The Scapel.** Here's something everyone has wished for—you can use the Scalpel to cut through visible polys without affecting the surrounding mesh.
- **Katana.** With this tool you can create Edge Loops, a modeling technique that provides more naturally movable polygonal structure around organic forms.
- **Superflange.** This feature allows you to subdivide a HyperNURBS mesh while keeping a rounded quality in the form. (If you knife a HyperNURBS object close to the edge it flattens out the form requiring you to go back and push in the points to round off the shape.) With Katana and Superflange, you can quickly create cuts around the mesh and pull them out to round out the form on the fly.
- **Hinge tools.** These tools provide numerous ways to transform polygons. For example, you can rotate a selection of polys on one edge and extrude them upward.
- **Soft Selections.** Soft selections apply a falloff to the edge of selected polys you are transforming so the mesh can be pushed and pulled much more organically.

Figure 13.6 Mesh Brush" Clay Sculpted"

Figure 13.7 Mesh Brush" Hair Brush"

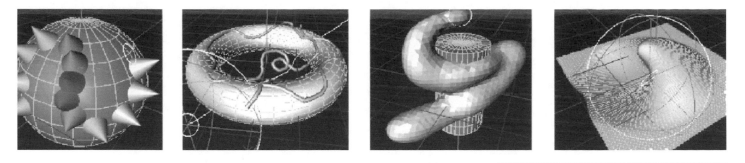

Figure 13.8 Scripted Brushes (Objectpaint, Splinepaint, Liquidpaint, Pinch Twirl)

- **Mesh Brush.** This unbelievably versatile tool is a fast, scriptable brush for interactively painting the push and pull of the mesh or applying behaviors and additions to the mesh. This super tool comes with a wide choice of scripts for brush behaviors, and you can download others and create your own. Combined with Soft Selection, this tool emulates the feel of sculpting clay. Scripts that come with the brush tool give it a staggering number of talents.

It should be said that you'll begin to notice a lot of overlap in the functions of plugins. For example, the Mesh Brush does some of the same things that other plugins do. Before you buy, check out as many demos as you can in order to make the most of your plugin dollars.

The added value of clear documentation and downloadable scripts for brushes makes this massive set of tools worth far more that the modest price.

Jenna

If you thrive on artistic experimentation, David Farmer at Cidertank has made you a happy camper. Jenna is a massive collection of tools for creating and animating complex objects and fascinating deformations. Here's a quick tip-of-the-iceberg look at some of the tools. Visit the galleries at www.cidertank.com for mind-boggling insight into the creative possibilities of Jenna.

- **Iterator.** Remember the first time you used C4D's Duplicate and Randomize function and a little voice said "Ah HAH!"? With animatable settings that go beyond basic duplication and randomization, Iterator lets you animate more complex transformations on your multiples and animate them along paths (yes, even text splines). By using Jenna's Multiple Source object, more than one different object can be mixed together in the group of iterated objects. The multiple objects can be anything, models or even lights. Time to buy more RAM.
- **Tweener.** This tool is a generator that interpolates between different states of two like objects. Place two copies of an object as children of a Tweener

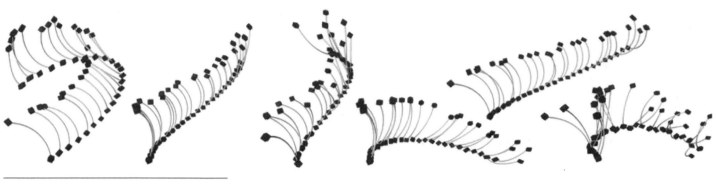

Figure 13.9 False Eyelashes Made with Iterator

Figure 13.10 Tweener

Figure 13.11 Tweener and Nickl

Figure 13.12 Nickl'd Sticks

object, and then experiment with changing any transform values on one of them. This also works with, for instance, colors of lights. Whoa!

- **DisplaceVIEW.** A DisplaceVIEW object placed as a child of an object with a displacement material gives you unlimited editor feedback on the displacement. In addition, this plugin finds bent quadrilateral polygons and convert them to triangles.

- **Nickl.** Nickl deforms objects with all kinds of organic and gelatinous wiggly motions. The nature of the deformation can be generated from math formulas or from materials.

- **GridArray.** GridArray is great for filling a 3D space with objects. Settings allow you to randomize the structure, rotation, and size of the objects in the space, or design precisely aligned arrangements.

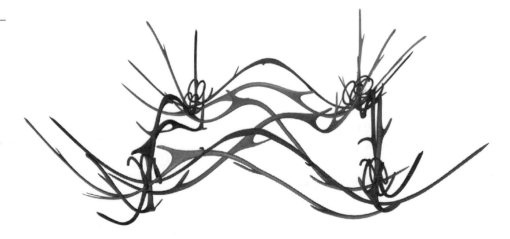

Figure 13.13 GridArray, More Random

Figure 13.14 GridArray , More Structured

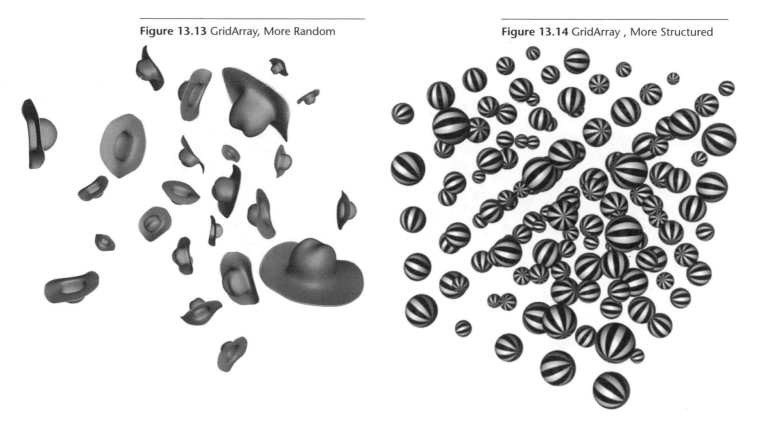

- **MeshArray.** This tool generates complex objects based on a source hier-archy or instanced hierarchy, with further opportunity for affecting the object and properties related to it with materials.

- **Allie.** This powerful complex object generator can apply animated materi-als to influence the behavior of characteristics of the object.

Figure 13.15 Allie with Jshader

- **JShader in conjunction with the Jtag.** Together, these faciliti-ate the placement of varied colors on instances in a complex object.

Loco

From the same source (www.cidertank. com), Loco is available as a beta down-load, and promises to be the ultimate hypertoy for creating particles on ste-roids. Loaded with playful potential (can you say, "Sleep deprivation"?), Loco is a drop-dead professional tool. This suite enables incredible ebbs, flows, tracing

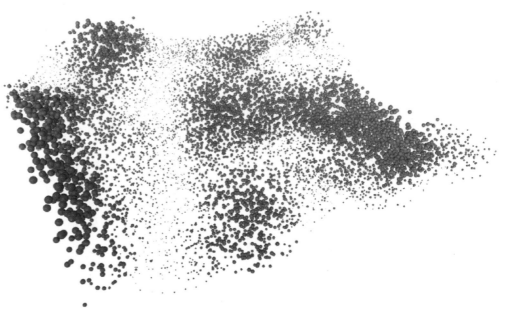

Figure 13.16 Loco Example, Courtesy of Joel Dubin

Figure 13.17 Sniper Pro

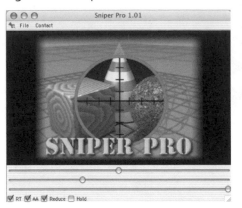

Figure 13.18 Surface Painter

Figure 13.19 Shave and a Haircut

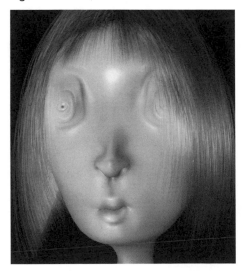

behaviors, animation driven by a sound object, and infinite out-there organic behaviors with particles.

On the DVD: See example movies for Jenna and Loco in Chapter 13>MOVIES/ STILLS>Movies.

Sniper Pro and Surface Painter

Paul Everett's Sniper Pro delivers superfast preview renders in a scalable window. The window has sliders that allow you to choose between levels of quality and rendering speed by selecting pixel resolution, level of detail, and the window's zoom factor. Further choices include check boxes for RT (real-time refresh of the window while you adjust settings), antialiasing, and reduction in the number of rays. This plugin is worth its weight in gold when you are in those endless tweak/test render cycles.

Paul Everett's Surface Painter allows you to paint small objects onto the surface of an active polygonal mesh. From the plugin's dialog box you can choose the paint objects, which are stored in the Presets folder. (As you can imagine, the real artistic power comes from creating your own paint objects and placing them in the Presets folder.) Surface Painter also paints splines (they can have gravity) for "hairy" or "grassy" objects and point clouds. Surface Painter's dialog boxes have input boxes for varying parameters of paint objects for a more random application.

Browse all Paul Everett's plugins at www.tools4d.com.

Shave and a Haircut

Shave and a Haircut is a comprehensive application for making all kinds of hair and hairstyles, including braids. Remember that Shave can also be used for other applications that call for multiples, like grass. "Shave and a Haircut" is available from the Plugin Café at www.maxoncomputer.com.

Figure 13.20 Sketch and Toon

Figure 13.21 Hatch Shader, Sketch and Toon

Sketch and Toon

Sketch and Toon is a remarkable rendering module that transforms 3D models into imagery more akin to illustration, drawing, and painting. A wide variety of shading engines which you can tweak until you drop will keep you busy with creative experimentation. If you are an artist coming from the world of traditional media or want to explore stylistic variety for cartoon animation, this add-on is a must. Find it at www.maxoncomputer.com, take the Highlights Tour, and explore the gallery of stylistic possibilities. Sketch and Toon has its own introductory PDF on the DVD in Chapter 13>EXTRA!EXTRA!>InDepth>SketchAndToon.

DiTOOLS 1.1

The commercial version of DiTOOLS is available from www.remotion.de.vu. Some of the DiTools are introduced in the Free Plugins section later in this chapter. Of course, the commercial version has many more tools and settings and is well worth the upgrade investment!

Figure 13.22 Tessa and DiCloner

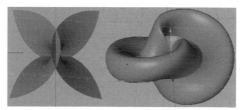

Figure13.23 DiTOOLS Parametrics

Figure13.24 DiTOOLS DiCloner/Parametric Combination

Figure 13.25 MSA

SpeeDisplay, and Find and Replace

From Rui Batista, SpeeDisplay adds get-up-and-go to your editor display by letting you dynamically choose the level of detail. Find and Replace is a more sophisticated tool for finding, replacing, and otherwise managing objects in complex scenes. Visit www.ruimac.com for these and other great utility plugins.

Multiple Spline Attach and HELIX

Mikael Stern at www.xlentplugs.com is the creator of these long-time favorite plugins for C4D. Multiple Spline Attach provides a variety of useful tools for working with splines such as animatable chains and tank treads. HELIX creates coiled forms along a spline. In addition to being indespensible for everyday tasks, these plugins are capable of oodles of creative fun far beyond their utilitarian appearance.

Figure 13.26 Helix

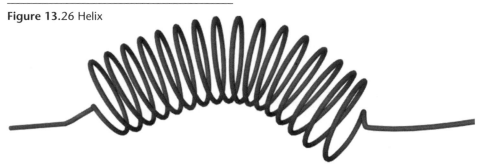

OnyxTREE

If you want believable trees, bushes, or foliage in your 3D world, OnyxTREE delivers superb results. This standalone package is not a CINEMA 4D plugin but will save models created in it as C4D files. The OnyxTREE 6 Suite has a quickly mastered interface and offers a deep level of customization. The materials within OnyxTREE nicely support foliage that looks like the real thing, but if you wanted a glass tree you could also apply C4D materials once the model opens in CINEMA 4D. The OnyxTREE 6 Suite is available from www.onyxtree.com.

Figure 13.27 OnyxTREE

Figure 13.28 Ozone

Ozone

Ozone is a powerful solution for creating animated atmospheric effects in CINEMA 4D. The package includes two plugins, two atmospheric models, and tons of presets for atmospheres and cloud forms. Ozone will let you create any approximation of nature or go out there on the horizon and invent never before seen environments. Weather presets, fogs, haze, customized lighting, infinite cloud design, and extra goodies like rainbows and ice rings are all part of this highly productive and definitely "worth-it" tool available from www.e-onsoftware.com.

Figure 13.30 Xfrog Plant Library

Xfrog

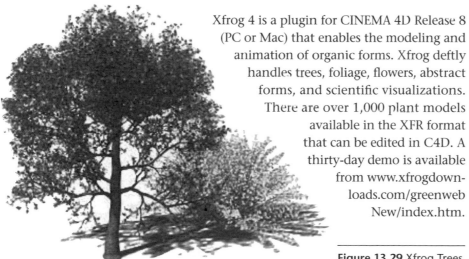

Xfrog 4 is a plugin for CINEMA 4D Release 8 (PC or Mac) that enables the modeling and animation of organic forms. Xfrog deftly handles trees, foliage, flowers, abstract forms, and scientific visualizations. There are over 1,000 plant models available in the XFR format that can be edited in C4D. A thirty-day demo is available from www.xfrogdown-loads.com/greenweb New/index.htm.

Figure 13.31 Xfrog Abstract Form

Figure 13.29 Xfrog Trees

Add-the-Sea

This C4D plugin from www.motion-gimmick.de/a-t-s-e.htm cranks up C4D's moving water capabilities quite a notch. You'll also find the Pleasantville video-post plugin and others worth checking out.

Character Animation Helpers

Bonderland (c4dplugins.idea-graphics.de/BL/BL_docs.php) and Little Cup of MOC-CA (www.studio-fabian.de) are rigs that can be fit to your character design. Both include readymade rigs (with all the tedious set-up work done for you) Bonderland (a commercial product) provides rigs for Bipeds, Quadrapeds and even Centipedes, along with a host of other awesome tools for rigging and animating characters in C4D. "Little Cup of MOCCA" is a plugin (with an accompanying rig which can be fit to your Biped) and can be downloaded free.

Visual Selector (Paul Everett strikes again) simplifies the selection of elements in a Character Animation rig. A character rig can be a sticky wicket, with many pieces and parts of varied functionality buried deep in hierarchies. This plugin makes elements more apparent and their selection more intuitive.

MAXON'S Modules

Add-on Modules from MAXON are discussed in the appropriate chapters. Go to www.maxoncomputer.com to learn more about modules for CINEMA 4D. The Dynamics module handles physics simulation, allowing you to introduce natural forces such as gravity, collision, and springs. The NET Render module is necessary for setting up distributed rendering over many machines in a lab. (This is especially great for schools. Go home and leave the render farm chugging away on a lab full of student renderings all night.)

Shareware and Freeware

DiTOOLS

DiTOOLS 0.892, available as a free download from www.remotion.de.vu is a suite of tools that deform and generate ultracool models. These tools are especially exciting for the invention of original animated forms for motion graphics or abstract web imagery, but you can also use them for the creation of representational multiples like grass or spines. Many hours can be spent experimenting with the art potential of these tools. In a typical DiTOOLS maneuver the DiTOOLS object would have two children, a base object whose points would determine the positions of cloned copies of the second child object. Furthermore, the behavior or parameters of the clones can be controlled with settings or affected by shaders or textures. When the clones are being affected by an animated shader, the animation possibilities start to get exciting. Here are just a few of the tools:

- **DiCloner.** The DiCloner has two children. The first must have points which will define the origin points of the clones. The child that represents the object to be cloned can be anything. Think lights!

- **DiSplinegen.** The DiSplinegen generates multiple splines with the ability to control the length of the splines with a texture. (It could be animated.)

- **Parametric Generators.** These provide settings for tweaking an awesome collection of mathematically defined parametric objects, making it a quick trip away from the same old models.

- **DiFormer and DiShaper.** The DiFormer and DiShaper deform a mesh based on a texture. Use these to make landscapes more bumpy.

- **Tessa.** This tool offers interesting interpretations on the surface structure of polygonal objects such as wire shaders.

Other DiTOOLS animate colors based on formulas, translate textures to vertex maps, and generate a material with numbers.

Figure 13.32 DiTOOLS Examples

Hair Department

Hair Department makes terrific hair, fur, or grass, and the price is so right. Download it from www.bgs-group.de. Click English, then choose Service>Plugins. You can also download an English manual from this site (Figure 13.33).

Fizz

Figure 13.33 Mrs. Bobblehead

While Fizz has not been officially updated for versions 8.2 and higher, it seems to work in most cases. Fizz is a set of add-on tools for particles that enables more complicated particle behavior, including the control of collisions, rolling, and friction. It can be used to make particles bounce off of polygonal surfaces or off of other particles—very cool! Available from the Plugin Cafe at www.maxon-computer.com.

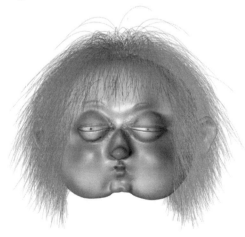

Stitch & Sew

One of several great plugins at Aquarius Graphic Wave (homepage2.nifty.com/aquawave) is Stitch & Sew. As the name implies, the plugin a useful tool for patching together sections of mesh.

Time Frequency

Rui Mac's Time Frequency plugin, provided for free at www.ruimac.com. is an easy way to make twitchy color changes. This plugin works best in version 8.5, where the plugin is accessed at the bottom of the Shader (texture) list in each channel. (It isn't in the top Plugins list.) Enter the starting and ending frames in the first start and end boxes, select two colors in the next Start and End boxes, and enter a frequency to determine how fast the colors change. Experiment with the curves to further design the nature of the "jumpiness" of the color.

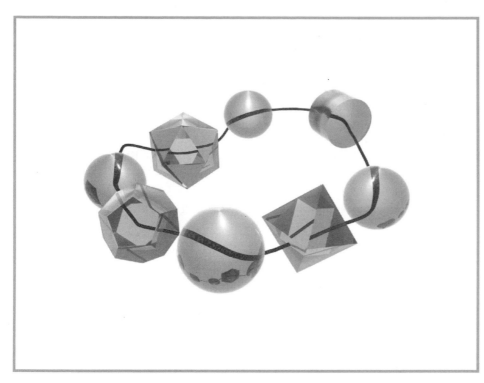

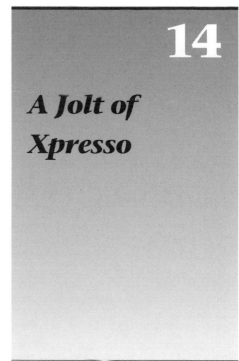

Figure 14.1

C4D users with programming skills have long been able to code minitools and bits of magic as add-ons to CINEMA 4D using C.O.F.F.E.E. This ability to get under the hood is a huge advantage and greatly multiplies the power of the basic application. The CINEMA community owes a great debt to the third-party programmers who share their talents in the Plugin Café (www.maxoncomputer.com) and at other sites. Support them! For the rest of us, the more recent addition of a visual interface called Xpresso lets nonprogrammers play too.

This chapter introduces the process of using the Xpresso Editor, and provides practice with some simple expressions. Realizing the full potential of Xpresso will be an ongoing process. The best way to learn Xpresso is to analyze example expressions (there are some on the DVD and links to many more) and read the comments. By all means, do read the manual and work through the tutorials for creating Xpresso expressions. When the need for an expression arises in your own work, you should be able to customize just the right helper.

What Is Xpresso?

The Xpresso Editor is a graphical environment for building expressions. Expressions are snippets of programming in which complex relationships between objects can be created and controlled. Expressions often streamline or automate interactions, allowing you to bypass time-consuming and repetitive keyframing. In the Xpresso Editor, visual building blocks called Nodes, representing objects or actions, are connected with wires into working relationships. The visual nature of Xpresso makes it easy to understand the mechanics of the expression.

Xpresso: Basic Anatomy

An Xpresso expression is created by Command-clicking (right-clicking) on an object in the Objects Manager and dragging to New Expression>Xpresso Expression. In the Xpresso Editor that opens, you will create Nodes and establish relationships between them.

Step 1 Choose File>New and save the file as OrbitHandle in your Models folder (File>Save As).

Step 2 Choose a Cube Primitive and a Sphere Primitive. In the editor window, move the Sphere out to the side of the Cube. With the Sphere selected, press the C key. Choose the Object Axis tool and move the Sphere's axis back to 0, 0, 0 inside the Cube.

Figure 14.2 Primitives Positioned

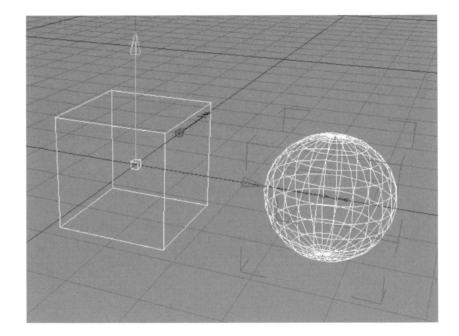

Step 3 Command-click (right-click) on the Cube and drag to NewExpression> Xpresso Expression. The Xpresso Editor window opens. If you want to bring it back up later for editing, just double-click the Xpresso Expression tag.

Step 4 Drag the objects Cube and Sphere from the Objects Manager into the Xpresso Editor window.

Step 5 Practice editing the physical appearance of a Node. Move the mouse on the red outlines around the selected Node to change the its size. Double-click the name to expand and minimize the window. To rename it, Command-click (right-click) the name and drag down to Rename. Move the mouse down on the white title bar to move the Node elsewhere in the Editor.

Step 6 Double-click the name Xgroup in the left column of the Xpresso Editor and rename it Orbit Handle.

The Nodes you just made represents the Cube and Sphere in the expression. Nodes can also house information coming in to affect an object and going out from the object to affect something else. On the upper left of the box, the blue square represents incoming information. The red square on the upper right is outgoing information. An X-Group is a container for a related set of Nodes and Wires.

Step 7 Click on the Cube Node's red square and drag to Coordinates>Global Position>Global Position.Y so that the vertical position of the Cube will be the outgoing information.

Information is passed from Node to Node via Ports and Wires. The red circle you just created is a port that communicates the position of the Cube.

Step 8 Now click on the Sphere Node's Blue input square and drag to Coordinates>Global Rotation>Global Rotation.H.

Step 9 Move the mouse down on the Square's Global Position.Y port (the red circle) and drag to the Sphere's Global Rotation.H input port (the blue circle). The wire is a connector between the ports. (If you wanted to remove the wire you would click on it and drag it away.)

Step 10 Return to the Editor window and use the 3 key to tilt the view so you are looking down over the top of the objects. Use the green handle of the Move tool to drag the cube up and down.

You are using one type of information (cube position) to affect another type (sphere rotation). The vertical motion of the cube is driving the orbit of the sphere.

Figure 14.3 The Xpresso Editor

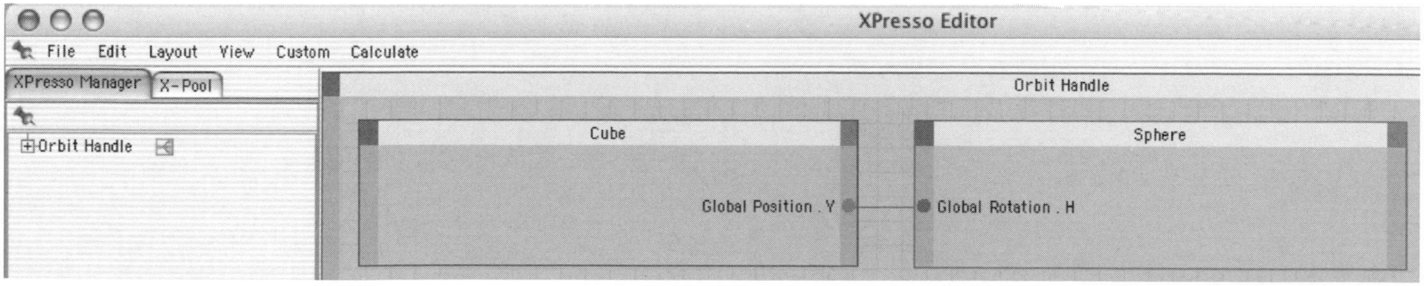

Figure 14.4 OrbitHandle

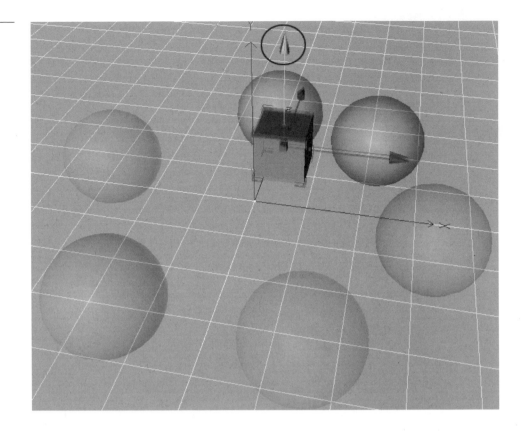

What's in a Node?

Nodes, the basic building blocks of Xpresso expressions, fall into groups:

- The General group includes nodes that provide access to information or affect information. For example, an Object node represents a specific object, material, or tag and can gather and output information about the object. Point or Polygon nodes provide access to specific under-the-hood elements. A Constant node allows you to input a numeric value into the mix from the Attributes Manager. Other general nodes like Random, Freeze, or Iterate affect the behavior of incoming information.

- The Adaptor group converts values from one kind of data to another. The Bool group nodes generate true or false states, and the Calculate group nodes apply math operations, manipulations, and constraints to input values.

- The Logic group includes nodes that make comparisons or assess conditions which will determine further actions.

The Sticking Place

This simple expression will stick an object to a specific point on an animated spline. (A similar expression could be used to stick an object to a particular polygon on a surface. See StickyTooth.c4d in the Chapter 14>EXTRA!EXTRA!>In-Depth folder on the DVD.)

Step 1 Open the file DieNotStuck.c4d from the Chapter 14>C4D Files folder on the DVD. Look at the hierarchy and notice that the Die is a child of the String. Note that at Frame 0 the Die seems to be positioned just fine on the String. Play the animation. When the Spline is PLA animated, the Die does not follow along.

Step 2 Choose File>Save As and save a working copy of the file as DieStuck. Now we will create an expression to stick the Die to a permanent spot on the string.

Step 3 Command-click (right-click) on the Die object in the Objects Manager. Drag to New Expression>Xpresso Expression. Drag the Path Spline and the DIE into the Xpresso Editor window and enlarge their windows.

Step 4 In the Path Spline Node, drag on the red output square down to Object to create a port.

Step 5 In the Die Node, drag on the blue square down to Coordinates>Global Position>GlobalPosition.

Step 6 We need a new Node that will allow us to define the position of a specific point. Command-click (right-click) on the gray area of the Xpresso Editor window and drag down to New Node>Xpresso>General>Point.

Step 7 Now we will create a new Node that will define which point the Die should stick to. Command-click (right-click) on the gray area of the Xpresso Editor window and drag down to New Node>Xpresso>General>Constant. In the Attributes Manager, you can input the number of the point in the Value box.

How do you know the value of a point? Choose the Points tool and make sure Path Spline is selected. Click the Structure tab next to the Objects tab at the top of the screen. In the Points column, click 0, 1, 2, and 3 and watch the spline in the editor window to see how the points are identified.

Step 8 Select the Constant Node and enter 0 in the Value box (in the Attributes Manager) so the Die will stick to the point on the right side of the string.

Step 9 Connect the red Object output of the Path Spline Node to the blue Object input on the Point Node. Then connect the red Real (0) output of the Constant node to the blue Point Index input on the Point node.

Figure 14.5 Structure Manager

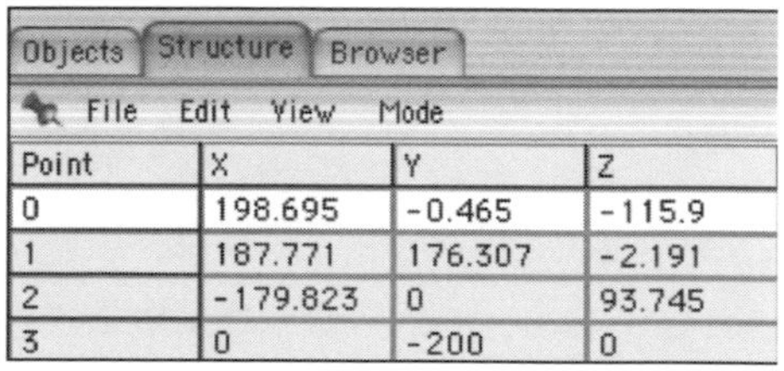

Objects	Structure	Browser	
File	Edit	View	Mode
Point	X	Y	Z
0	198.695	-0.465	-115.9
1	187.771	176.307	-2.191
2	-179.823	0	93.745
3	0	-200	0

Figure 14.6 DieXpresso Editor

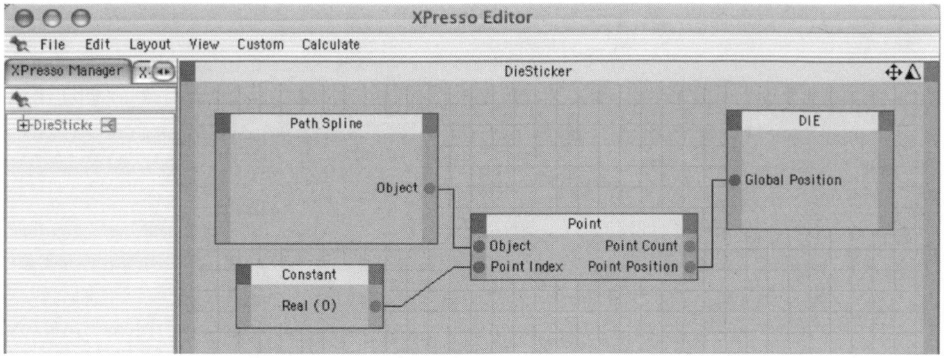

Figure 14.7 Die Stuck

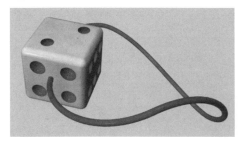

◆ *Tip:* The familiar navigation tools at the top right of the Xpresso Editor window can be used to move around the Xpresso window. The 1 and 2 keys work too.

Those last two steps are informing the Point node that this specific point on this spline is the point in question (in this case, the one you will be sticking the Die to).

Step 10 Now all that remains is to forward the position of the point that was fed into the Point Node onward to the Die Node. Connect the red Point Position port of the Point Node to the blue Global Position input on the Die Node.

Play the animation and watch the Die stick to the sticking place!

● *Springboard!* Want a whole string of dice? Just Control-drag three copies of the Die, then select the Constant Nodes and edit their values to be 1, 2, and 3. Make sure all the Die are children of the String object.

Stop Right There!

Did you ever want to stop a character's foot from going through the floor without having to pay constant attention to the Y position? Here's a simple, classic expression to make your floor behave like a real floor instead of a virtual floor.

Step 1 Open the file Footstopper.c4d from the Chapter 14>C4D Files folder on the DVD. Notice that the axis of the foot has been moved to the bottom of the foot.

Step 2 Command-click (right-click) on the FOOT object and drag to New Expression>Xpresso Expression.

Step 3 Drag the FOOT object and the FLOORTILE object into the Xpresso Editor.

Step 4 Create a new Node by Command-clicking (right-clicking) in the Xpresso Editor window and choose New Node>Xpresso>Calculate>Clamp.

Step 5 In both the FOOT and FLOORTILE nodes, click on the red output squares and choose Coordinates>Global Position>Global Position.Y.

Step 6 Draw a Wire connector from the FLOORTILE Node to the Clamp Node's Min input port.

Step 7 Make another connection from the FOOT output node to the Clamp Node's Max input port.

Step 8 Now connect another Wire from the FOOT output node to the Clamp Node's Value input port.

Step 9 Again, drag the name FOOT from the Objects Manager into the Xpresso Editor window.

Click the blue input square and drag to Coordinates>Global Position>Global Position.Y.

Step 10 Draw a Wire from the Clamp output port to the Global Position.Y input port on the new FOOT Node.

In the editor window, use the green Move handle to move the Foot up and down.

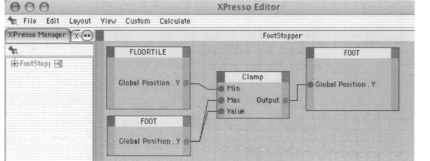

Figure 14.8 Footstopper Expression

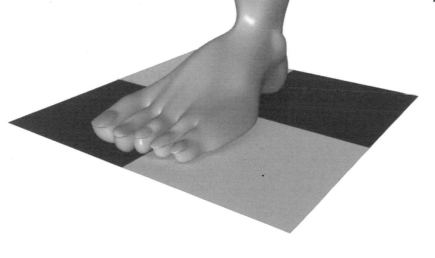

Figure 14.9 Foot on Tile

What Else Can Be Done with Xpresso?

The possibilities are endless. Just to name a few, expressions can be designed that offset or randomize attributes and animation or that trigger events based on compared attributes or times. All kinds of math operations may be input to affect objects and their motion. The best way to get a feel for the possibilities when you're beginning is to look through the descriptions of nodes in the CINEMA manual. We'll be using more complex Xpresso expressions in Chapter 15 when we work with Thinking Particles and PyroCluster.

On the DVD: See Chapter 14>EXTRA!EXTRA! for more examples of expressions that use other variables like time.

Connect: A Google search of "CINEMA 4D Expressions" should bring up examples. The Plugin Café at www.maxoncomputer.com also has an Expressions section.

15

Environment, Mood, and Magic

Figure 15.1

A girl named Alice once said, "If I had a world of my own . . . ." In this chapter, we'll build an interior structure with connected rooms nestled in an outdoor environment. Throughout the chapter, the emphasis will be on illusion. Much of what we create will be in the viewer's mind, since we'll use façades, lighting, and other kinds of theatrical fakery to present an enchanted world to the camera's eye. It's all a sham. Have you ever found yourself behind the scenes of a theme park in the glaring light of morning, wondering what happened to the magic of the night before? Who knew that the starlit outdoor cafe in old Mexico was only paint and cracked plaster in a prefab metal building?

These projects will introduce skills for creating environments. This 3D world will function as a final project and be a place to showcase some of the things you made as you worked through the book. The exact design or theme of your world is up to you. Because it is open-ended, you could apply your original touches to this personal space and use it as a demo piece. The example environment on the DVD, Eyefly, is a cross between a House of Mystery carnival ride and an art museum. It's a place where art, whimsy, and twisted funhouse collide and physics doesn't live any more.

On the DVD: See sections of an example Eyefly project in Chapter 15>EXAMPLES and MOVIES/STILLS.

In the EXTRA!EXTRA! folder be sure to check out References.pdf. In the GOODIES folder, there are materials you may want to use or edit for your environment.

The Interior Environment

Building the Basic Structure

We'll start out with a simple tunnel structure. Later, if you want to remodel, infinite rooms can be added. Chapter 15>EXAMPLES>EYEFLY has examples of more complex versions.

Step 1   Working in the Top view, use the Bezier Spline tool to draw a path spline similar to the one in Figure 15.2.

Step 2   Working in the Front View, choose Spline>Rectangle Spline. Scale the rectangle to be more in proportion with the spline, as in Figure 15.2.

Step 3   Choose NURBS>Sweep NURBS and drop the path spline in first, followed by the Rectangular cross section. (The cross-section profile could be another shape, such as the palladian shape in the example file.)

Step 4   Press the C key to make the Sweep NURBS editable.

Step 5   Choose Structure>Subdivide and enter a value of 2.

Step 6   Select and delete both caps inside the Sweep NURBS. Rename Sweep NURBS as Basic Structure.

Figure 15.2 Splines for Structure

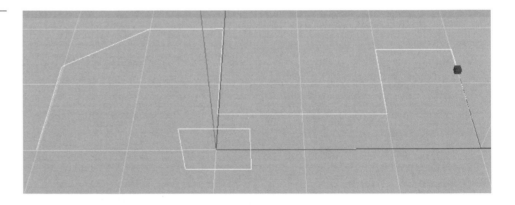

Figure 15.3 The Basic Structure

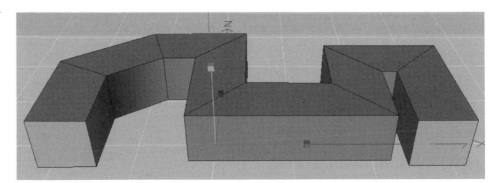

Adding on or Remodeling

Select any group of polys and use the Extrude tool to pull out side rooms. If you have plenty of computer power, you should be able to keep everything in one file. Just make selection sets and hide the ones you aren't working on at the time.

As plan B, you could build a room in a separate file and choose File>Merge to merge the room. Then delete polys from the basic structure and use Edit Surface> Weld to join together the two sections. Remember they will have to have the same number of points if you plan to weld them together. It's not really necessary that you weld them, as long as the rooms appear joined to the camera's view.

And as plan C, you could build all the rooms in the basic structure file, then use Structure>Edit Surface>Disconnect to disconnect each room. Use File>Save As to save a copy of the file for each room, and delete the polys you aren't working on from each file. When all the details are finished, just merge them back into a master file and place them in adjoining positions, or weld the rooms back on with Edit Surface>Weld.

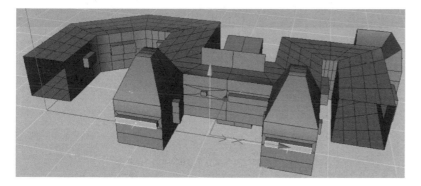

Figure 15.4 A More Complex Structure

On the DVD: See Chapter 11 for tips on animating a camera though the environment.

◆ *Tip:* Go ahead and create a camera, setting up the viewfinder in the upper left window. Then you can go inside your rooms to work. You can always switch back to the Editor camera by choosing Cameras>Editor Camera.

Handling the Huge Environment

If you attempted to build a large, complex world in a single file, your CPU would quickly bog down. Even if you use wireframe display, backface culling, temporarily turning off generators and HyperNURBS, and other efficiency methods, eventually there is a limit to how many polys can be stuffed into one file before the CPU shows signs of stress. With a little planning, the size of the world you can deliver to your audience can be infinite. Once the basic structure has been built, make copies of the file for individual scenes. In each scene file, delete everything outside the view of the camera. How much you can place in each of these smaller sections of camera animation will depend on your computer resources. By matching the coordinates of the camera from scene to scene, rendered separately, these sections can easily be pieced together later into complex animations.

Your other best friend for building incredibly rich environments is compositing (see Chapter 19).

"Render-heavy" elements such as volumetric lights or bits of magic from your library such as raining glitter can be layered in the post-production process. Even models can be rendered in separate scenes and later composited, although other factors like common directions of lights and shadows will need attention.

Fun with Architectural Detail

As you design your 3D world, think about how you can use architectural detail to introduce surprise and layered dimensions into the viewer's experience of the space. Select smaller polys and extrude them back out of the structure to create nooks and crannies. Some might have doors (that can be animated to creak open), some might be covered with glass (like an aquarium), still others may be mysteriously lit alcoves for showcasing interesting models.

Figure 15.5 Alcove Doors

Figure 15.6 Hinges: (L>R) Pointy Hinge, Mustardseed Hinge, Double Hinge , and Clover Hinge,

Figure 15.7 Aquarium Insert

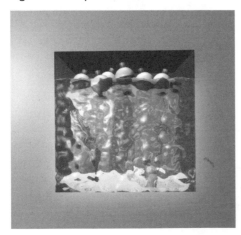

After creating some details that sink back into the wall, try making some elements that jut out of the wall into the space. The cloud in Figure 15.8 is flat for a cartoon look, but you could make a 3D, puffy one with a Metaball object. (You have already made the spline for this cloud in Chapter 2, so all you have to do is drop the cloud spline in an Extrude NURBS object.)

You can also add some elements that hang down, span the space, or add detail to edges and corners. The garland of flowers is a color and alpha map on a plane, intersected with a 3D pole. Check out the file in GOODIES>LIBRARIES> FLORAL TRIMS.

Relish lots of detail attention on your wall, ceiling, and floor surfaces. Play solid color against polished woodgrains, thickly painted white bricks against rusty beams. Add decorative elements like decoupaged pictures, graffitti, hooks with hanging objects, wallpapers and wallpaper borders, numbers, letters, symbols, or esoterica. Add

Figure 15.8 Cloud

Figure 15.9 Hanging Things

Figure 15.10 Elements Invading the Space

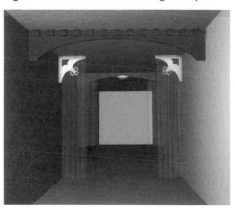

bump maps to emulate the textures of lumpy, flaking plaster or dripping thick paint. Rich surfaces and layers of dirt and cracks, deep wall colors, molding, and digital architectural "antiques" will enhance your space and make it believable. Research architectural details and interior design, and keep a sketchbook of traditional and invented elements for use in your 3D spaces.

Mixing Lights in an Interior Space

Nothing will add more depth, sense of place, and drama to your space than well-crafted lighting. Here are some general tips for orchestrating lighting in your rooms. Study the example files for various set-ups of mixed lighting. Look at the placement of the lights, the attributes for each light, and the materials placed on Light Fixtures.

- Compositionally speaking, it's usually best to have one main direction of shadow-casting light. This could be the Main (Key) light in the scene or light coming in from a window. Add to that any necessary Fill light (with little or no shadow), and then place smaller lights that gently illuminate the dark corners or function only as compositional interest (Radiation turned off).

- The collection of rooms in the final project will give you a chance to experiment with illumination. Use lighting purposefully to underscore the personality of each room. The spooky room might use a single, harsh light for a dramatic shadow, while a nostalgic room combine several lights for a soft, warm and comfy feeling.

- Use opposing color temperature with Main and Fill lights to create depth in the space, or assign colors to lights to attact attention or balance the composition. If a sky blue light is coming in the window, the shadows cast will be warm. A low, direct sun through a window will cast cool shadows.

- Create selection sets of lights for easy adjustment (see the Appendix).

- In this project with multiple rooms, think about shifting the light temperature from room to room as the kind of light fixtures change.

On the DVD: Don't miss Frederic Berti's scene file for "Something" in Chapter 15>EXTRA!EXTRA!>InDepth. This scene from the C4D Masters Gallery (in the Color section) is a great example of complex lighting.

The World Outside: Skies, Backgrounds, and Cycloramas

Let's make some daylight skies. The first sky will use the Sky object, a sphere infinite in size and centered on 0, 0, 0. If you want to, make a skylight in your structure to show off the sky.

Step 1   Choose Objects>Scene>Sky. Create a new material and click the color channel. Use a BhodiNUT Fusion shader in the Image box.

Step 2   Click the Edit button and place a BhodiNUT 3D Noise shader in the Blend Channel Image box. Check the Edit button for this shader and choose Turbulence as the noise. Change the global Scale to 300 and the X scale to 300.

Step 3 Click OK and in the editor window for the Fusion shader, place a Bhod-iNut Gradient shader with colors ranging from deep blue to light blue.

Step 4 Change the mode in the left panel of the Fusion editing window to Overlay. Place the new material on the Sky object, and click the Texture tag. There is an example of this sky in Goodies>Materials>Nature Materials Library if you want to check all those settings.

Step 5 Check Seamless in the Attributes, and adjust the X and Y tiling values to get the effect you want. The projection should be spherical or cubic. Upward camera angles will show a polar effect of the cloud shader, which can be fixed by choosing Shrink-wrapping projection for those camera shots. Save this generic sky to your Models folder if you want to keep it for future use (File>Save As).

8.5 Update The (BhodiNUT) Fusion Shader is now found by going to Shader>Fusion. The former BhodiNUT 3D Noise is now called Noise in the Shader list. Click the word Fusion in the elongated box to edit the Blend and Base channels. Use the navigation arrows at the top of the Material Editor to return to the Fusion pane where you can adjust the interaction of the layers.

Now for a second way to make a sky:

In a new file, experiment with making a sky with floor objects. Choose File>Objects>Scene>Floor Object and make two copies of the floor. Separate these floors on the Y so they float one over the other. Also infinite in size, the Floor object is a plane and can be used for anything that stretches to infinity (such as skies or bodies of water). Note that in the editor display it has a representative plane which does not look infinite, but it will be infinite when rendered.

Multiple floor objects can be layered with semitransparent cloud shaders and turbulence or noise materials animated in different speeds and directions. Make some materials that combine the colors found in stormy skies (warm and cold greys, blues and unexpected colors like ochres and creamy yellows) with noise and turbulence shaders. Experiment with increasing the size of turbulence shaders for interesting cloudy skies. Animate subtle rotations of the floors, too.

Here's the night version of the sky:

Step 1 Choose File>ObjectsScene>Sky Object. Create a new material and choose the Starfield Shader.

Step 2 Create a few Omni lights with various small visibility distances and barely there tints of warm and cool colors. Place them randomly in the sky. Animate some on and off visibility and visibility size to simulate twinkling. For added realism you could animate an occasional shooting star, some fireflies, or a blinking airplane light.

Figure 15.11 Clouds on a Floor Object

Figure 15.12 Night Sky

Figure 15.13 Sky Made with the Ozone Plugin

Using Backgrounds and Foregrounds

Background and Foreground objects allow you to place images, colors, or textures in front of or behind the models in a scene. Choose Objects>Scene>Background and assign any material to it.

You can use a solid color like white if you are tired of the default black background or a photographic image such as a city, landscape, or aerial view. You can also place a movie sequence on the background. Choose a Foreground object for anything you want to appear in front of the rest of the scene, such as the dashboard of a car driving through the scene.

Backdrops, False Façades, and Cycloramas

As opposed to a background, a backdrop is an actual 3D object that you place into the scene. Usually a plane, it uses materials to fake the presence of objects

Figure 15.14 Distant Trees and Alpha on a Cyclorama

Figure 15.15 False Facades

farback in space. The Alpha channel can be used to drop out the plane around the outline of objects. You can also construct backdrops like an actual theatre flat, (complete with canvas stretchers, rough wooden props and graffiti scrawled on the back) for an intriguing "fake, but real" element in your scene. A cyclorama, another crossover from the world of theater, is a plane or Bezier object placed outside a window or other viewport to provide bogus scenery only where it's needed. The material placed on the cyclorama could be a photograph, illustration, or again a movie.

The Outdoor Environment

We won't build all of the great outdoors for our environment, just enough to give the illusion of an outside world.

Nature: Realistic or Stylized

Making a Landscape

Step 1 In a new file choose Primitive>Landscape Object. In the Attributes Manager, enter Sizes of X 10,000, Y 500, and Z 10,000. Alternately, use a very large plane, subdivide if necessary, and push the mesh polys into a land form you like.

Step 2 Press the C key to make the object editable, and choose Structure>Magnet. In the Active tool tab, enter a Radius of 150. Nudge a small pond in the middle of the landscape. If the landscape needs to be smoother, drop the Landscape object into a HyperNURBS.

Figure 15.16 Landscape and Pond

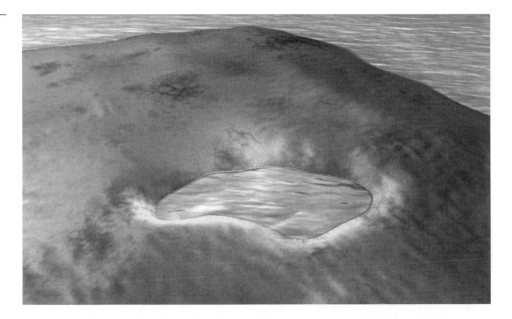

Step 3   Create your own Material, or choose a ground material from GOODIES>
MATERIALS>Environment/Nature>NATURE MATERIALS.c4d. If you
wanted a more cartoonlike material, you could use a BhodiNUT Cheen
shader or hand-paint a stylized surface in BodyPaint. The free DiTOOLS
Plugins available at www.remotion.de.vu have great tools for using materials to displace surfaces into very organic landscapes.

Helper Apps for Natural Environments

While models straight from Bryce may have a canned, predictable look, you may
find an occasional use for them in your digital toolbox. Nothing is more boring
than "already done for you" models, and using premade models will get you little
respect in the 3D community. However, on occasion you might incorporate elements created in these applications into your C4D worlds. You can find information on and support for Bryce at www.corel.com. Other applications for scenery
generation are Vue d'Esprit and Vue 4 Professional, in which natural environments
with advanced wind silumation can be animated. Check out their features at www.
e-onsoftware.com. Terregen (www.terregen.com) is a free scenery generation application. Ozone creates awesome atmospheres (www.e-onsoftware.com), and Add-
the-Sea (www.motion-gimmick.com) is a flowing water solution.

Connect: See Chapter 13 for information about environment plugins.

Water, Water Everywhere

The Pond in our project is still water, rippled by a light touch of wind.

Step 1   Choose Objects>Floor Object. (Note that you could use a plane instead
if you want to deform the surface more. The Formula Deformer or Struc-
ture>Edit Surface>Crumple will deform a plane, but not a Floor object.
For this still water, the shader will be enough to suggest water.)

Step 2   Create a new material and place the water shader in the color channel and
bump channel. Layer semitransparent water or turbulence shaders on
multiple Floor objects (using the same process as the sky made with multiple Floors earlier). Don't forget that the water and turbulence shaders
can be animated. Open the water material in GOODIES>MATERIALS>En-
vironment/Nature>NATURE MATERIALS.c4d and study the settings.

Step 3   Save the Landscape and Pond to be merged later with the Indoor structure (File>Save or Cmd+S/Ctrl+S).

You can create dripping or slowly rolling puddles of water with a Metaball
object:

Step 1   Choose a Metaball object from the Array palette. In the Attributes
Manager, try a hull value of 40 percent, and 5 Subdivisons for Editor
and Render.

Step 2 Choose Objects>Spline Object. Make sure the Move tool and the Points tool are selected, and Control-click some points in a long line across the screen.

Step 3 Enable PLA Animation, and animate the points to move in the general direction you want the puddle to move.

Step 4 Make the Spline Object a child of the Metaball object.

Step 5 To make the puddle appear flatter, sink the metaball down under the floor or surface it's sitting on.

Figure 15.17 Fountain

● ***Springboard!*** Take the Metaball object a step farther and make a fountain. Open the file Fountain.c4d in the Chapter 15>EXAMPLES>Fountain folder. Study the set-up of the Particle Emitter inside the Metaball object. Then check out the settings in the Attributes Manager for Particle, Emitter, and the Metaball itself. You can copy the material from this file for making your own fountain.

Connect: Want to make an underwater scene? The Advanced Render PDF in the Chapter 12>EXTRA!EXTRA!>InDepth on the DVD shows how to use Caustics to create the undersea illusion. If you think the next step is the making of surging ocean waves splashing on rocks, hold that thought—that is one thing that won't happen easily in C4D, and not without special plugins. See Chapter 13.

Trees

A decent, distant realistic tree can be made with this manual method. The secret to this manual method is the alpha material. Navigate to Chapter 15>EXAMPLES>Tree.

The groups of leaves are placed on single polygons that were duplicated (20 instances) and then randomized in position, scale, and rotation. The resulting Null Object can be copied several times for more thickness, and a copy can be scaled down and placed in the center of the tree for more density.

From the Chapter 15>EXAMPLES>Tree folder, open the Tex folder and look at the materials for the Color and Alpha channels.

For a distant tree, a cylinder made editable and bent in a few places using the Magnet tool will do fine for the trunk. The limbs are multiples of Stick 1 in GOODIES>LIBRARIES>Sticks and Weeds>Stick Library. Once the wood material is placed on the truck and limbs, it works visually as a unit.

After you place your tree in a scene, you may need to rotate some of the "leafy" polys for more randomization, better angles, or more specific placement. Just click on the offending polys in the editor window and use the Move and Rotate tools to adjust them, or select Null groups in the Objects Manager to rotate so they look better from the camera angle. If it's a close-in tree shot you need, a more specific image

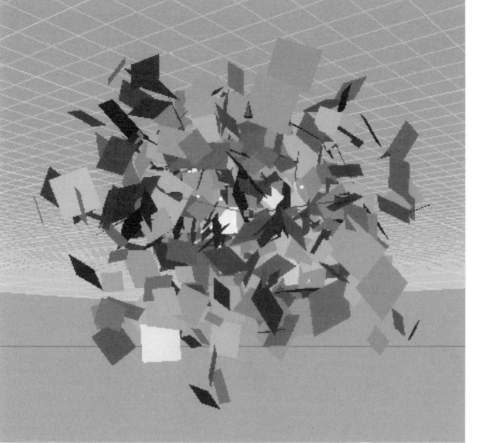

Figure 15.18 Tree Top Polys

Figure 15.19 Tree

map with actual leaves may be required. If the tree is in a background seen from one angle, that angle is all that matters. Naturally, if a camera will be flying around the tree, there will be much more work involved in placing the polys so they look good from all angles.

Helper Apps for Trees

If you expect trees and foliage to be showing up regularly in your 3D worlds, you'll need a specialty application. Xfrog and OnyxTREE are two good ones discussed in Chapter 13.

Grass

Here are a few of many ways to make grass, from the most robust to the most primitive.

For limited amounts of grass in close-ups:

- Use a Hair Plugin.
- Use DiTOOLS, Jenna, Mesh Surgery, or Surface Painter Plugins.

- Use Edit Surface>Matrix Extrude.
- Create a single grass blade model, Duplicate Instances, and then randomize.

For large, distant grassy surfaces, rely on materials placed on the surface to fake the look of grass.

How's the Weather?

To make some simple rain or snow, we'll use the Particle Emitter. In the next section, we'll move up a notch and use the Thinking Particles module to create Particle Systems with much more control.

Step 1 Make a single weather particle model. Depending on the style of your animation, it could be a long and very skinny cube for more realistic rain, a sphere for realistic snow, or a teardrop or snowflake for more cartoon-like precipitation. Whatever it is, make it small. A 2m sphere would be fine.

Step 2 Experiment with your own materials or use the ones in GOODIES>MATERIALS>Weather. Place some kind of turbulence into the alpha of the material to keep the model from looking too hard-edged.

Figure 15.20 Weather Models

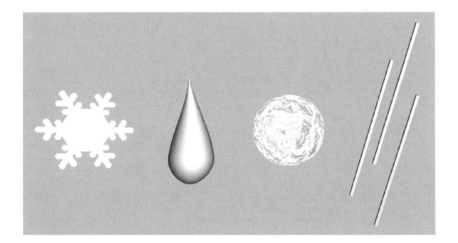

Step 3 Choose Objects>Particles>Emitter to create an Emitter object. Rotate the emitter so that its Z axis is pointing downward and move it to the top of the screen.

Step 4 Make your weather particle a child of the Emitter object. Select the Emitter.

Step 5 In the Attributes Manager, click the Emitter tab. For a weather system you'll need the X value to stretch all the way across the screen. It can be as deep or as shallow on the Y as you need it to be for the level of realism desired.

Step 6   Try changing the Horizontal and Vertical Angle values to create narrower and wider sprays. A value of 360 on both would will spew particles out in all directions. For our weather system, we don't really need any angle settings as we want the precipitation to fall straight down.

Step 7   Click the Particle tab. Enter the number of particles you want in the editor and the render. Enter a value for scale variation if you want the particles to vary in size. If the check box for show objects is unchecked, a representative tic will appear in the editor. If you want to see the particles, check the box. Having done that, you can now see the results of your variation settings better. Just be sure to scrub all the way to the beginning of the animation for an accurate preview.

Step 8   To make your weather a little more blustery, choose Objects>Particles>Wind and place the new object on the same hierarchical level with the Emitter. Scale and position the modifier so that it encloses the particles you want to affect. Try some of the other tools in the particle menu. You can stack up multiple modifiers for some interesting custom effects.

A cool thing about emitters is that you can put more than one object in as a particle. In other words, you could put all the letters of the alphabet in the emitter at one time and rain alphabet soup.

Figure 15.21 Cartoon Snowflakes in an Emitter

Here Comes the Glitz

A Little Light Magic

Step 1 Create an Omni light and leave the color white. Check the check box for No Light Radiation. Make it visible and in the Visibility pane, give it an Outer Distance value of 3. In the Objects Manager, Control-drag a copy of the light but change the color of this one to light blue.

Step 2 From the top menu, choose Objects>Particle>Emitter. In the Attributes Manager Emitter panel, give it an X and Y Size of 0, but both Horizontal and Vertical Angles of 30º.

Step 3 Drop both lights into the Emitter.

Step 4 Enter –90 in the Pitch value for the Emitter. Look at the Little Emitters.c4d example movie in Chapter 15>MOVIE/STILLS folder on the DVD to see how the rotation of the Rotation Modifier affects the particles.

● ***Springboard!*** Render that one again with a larger outer distance on the visible lights. What if you put the emitter in an array object? Try stacking on the particle modifiers in different orders. The possibilities never end with RAM, or lack thereof, as your only limit.

Pixie Dust

Pixie dust power is best realized with the Thinking Particles module. The Pixiedust.pdf in Chapter 15>EXTRA!EXTRA!>InDepth introduces Thinking Particles expressions in combination with PyroCluster. However, PyroCluster (also a separate module) can also be applied to regular emitters.

Smoke and Fire

Step 1 Use the rotating emitter you just made in the above project and save a working copy (File>Save As), or create a new emitter just like it. Edit the Emitter to be X-Size and Y-Size of 25m and have both Horizontal and Vertical Angles of 100º.

Step 2 Remove the lights as particles.

Step 3 From the top menu, choose Objects>Scene>Environment.

Step 4 In the Materials Manager, choose File>PyroCluster>PyroCluster Volumetracer.

Step 5 Again in the Materials Manager, choose File>PyroCluster>PyroCluster.

Step 6 Drop the PyroCluster Volumetracer material on the Environment object.

Step 7 Drop the PyroCluster material on the Emitter.

Test-rendering all the different settings for the PyroCluster material in the Attributes Manager will take up a few rainy afternoons. That's the best way to really get to know PyroCluster. For your first efforts, click the Pyrocluster Material thumb-

Figure 15.22 Smoke Emitter: Lamp

Figure 15.23 Smoke Emitter: Spinnercraft

nail and edit the settings in the Attributes Manager, using the Preview button to see the effects. The Noise types on the Fractal panel will give you an idea of the wide variety of things you can do with PyroCluster. In the Applications>MAXON>CINEMA R8>Features>PyroCluster folder, there are plenty of starter examples.

Connect: As you begin to craft more complex worlds, connect to these skills from other chapters. They are major players for adding magic to your environments.

- Strings of Lights and other twinkling lighting. Use those F-Curves to randomize light visibility for twinkling effects (Chapter 6).
- "Painted" atmospheres or blinking puffs of colored visible lights (Chapter 6).
- Highlights and Glow (Chapter 12).
- Hand-painting decorative elements (Chapter 16).
- Glitter Materials, (Chapter 5),

On the DVD: See the Chapter 15>MOVIE/STILLS folder for examples of sparkle, magical lighting, decorative painting, and fun with architectural details.

The Importance of Music and Sound

The process for placing sound into CINEMA 4D for preview is discussed in Chapter 7, Animation ABCs. So, just a word about sound. Appropriate music and timely sound effects can make or break your project. And don't neglect the layers of secondary ambient noise that can add realism to your world. It would be well worth your while to master some kind of sound mixing application if you plan on hanging around the world of 3D.

● ***Springboard!*** Now that you have the basic idea of how to create the structure of a world, you are ready to fill it with objects, textures, colors, and sounds. It's a good time to go back and review all the things you've learned in other chapters and to think about how you can incorporate those elements into a finished project.

On the DVD: If you have the Thinking Particles module and are ready to start toward poweruser status, be sure to work through the Pixiedust.pdf in Chapter 15>EXTRA!EXTRA!>InDepth.

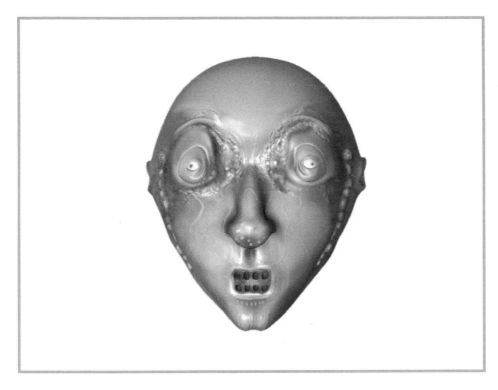

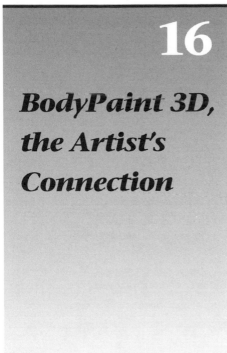

Figure 16.1

Getting to Know BodyPaint

If you like 3D but miss the intuitive hands-on surfacing of 2D painting and drawing, get ready to love 3D. BodyPaint makes the connection between the constructive ways of creating 3D objects and the placement of designed materials on those objects with the 2D methods artists have used for centuries to lovingly craft surfaces. With BodyPaint, the artist can apply familiar 2D drawing and painting skills directly onto the 3D model. In addition, many of the features of your favorite digital imaging applications are right there in BodyPaint, ready to go to work. With BodyPaint's Raybrush Render View, rendering is going on while you paint, so you have real-time feedback on the painting process. Rarely does an application make the leap that has been made from the initial version of BodyPaint to BodyPaint 3D v2, which allows artists to work more intuitively without tangling up in the digital tools. In BPv2 resides a Wizard ready to whisk you past the complication of UVW mapping and get you right to work doing what artists do best.

Painting a Simple Model

In this first project, we'll work with color palettes and brushes, paint in single and multiple channels, learn how to create Wallpapers, and explore other BodyPaint basics.

Figure 16.2 Painted Prop

16

BodyPaint 3D, the Artist's Connection

Setting up with the BodyPaint Set-up Wizard

Step 1 Open the file PaintedProp.c4d from the Chapter 16>C4D Files folder on the DVD. Save a working copy to your Models folder (File>Save As).

Step 2 Select the Lathe Object in the Objects Manager, and turn off all other objects in the scene except the Light. Press the C key to make the object editable. (It is necessary to make parametrics editable before UVs can be recalculated.)

Figure 16.3 Layout Icon

Step 3 Select the BP 3D Paint Layout from the Layout Icon (the top icon on the Left Palette).

Step 4 Click on the Paint Set-up Wizard. On the first page of the Wizard (Step 1), make sure only the Lathe Object has a green check mark. Click on the names of the other objects so the green check marks turn to red. Click Next.

Figure 16.4 Paint Setup Wizard Icon

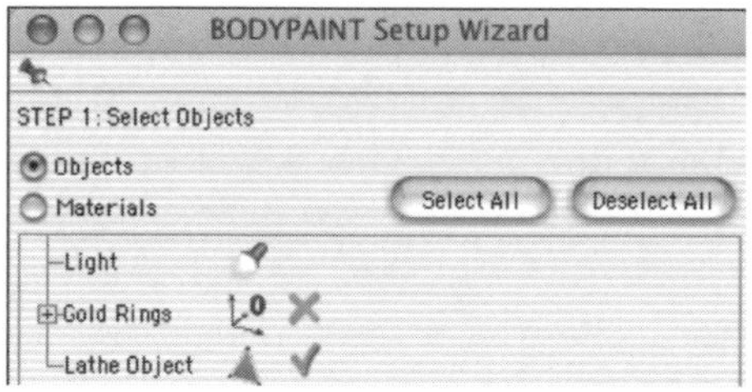

Step 5 On the Step 2 page, accept the default choices by clicking the Next button. (If you had a file with separate objects and wanted to create separate textures for each rather than painting across all the objects with one texture, you would uncheck Single Material Mode.)

Figure 16.5 Wizard Page One

Step 6 On the Step 3 page, check the boxes for Color and Bump. Click the box next to color and edit the color to be a pale gold-orange. Leave the Bump color gray and click the Finish button. Wait for the Wizard to make its calculations (Set-up Wizard End will be the last line in the list) and click the Close button. You're ready to paint.

The Basic Tools

Step 1 Click the Colors tab in the upper right of the screen, then click on the Channels panel. You'll see Co for Color and B for Bump, corresponding to the two channels you created in the Wizard. To the left of those, there is a box with a pencil and a green check mark or red cross mark.

If the green check is showing, multichannel mode is enabled and you can paint in both channels (or more if you originally set them up in the Wizard) simultaneously. If the red cross mark is showing, you will only be painting in the active channel with pencil showing and a red line around it. You can click the red line to enable either for painting, but only one will be active at a time until Multichannel mode is enabled again.

Take a moment to stop and absorb this one, as it is a critical concept of how BodyPaint works. Even after you understand it, you'll still have to concentrate to be sure you are assigning a color to the channel you intend to paint in. Notice that either Color or Bump will have a red line around it at any given time. The channel with the red line is the one for which you are choosing a color and/or wallpaper. The color chosen for the color channel will paint that color or wallpaper.

However, choices for the Bump channel (or any other channel you may later activate) will only be seen as grayscale values, determining where and to what degree that channel is active. In the case of Bump, degrees of whiteness or blackness (value) determine height or depth, and the pattern of values determines texture.

◆ *Tips:*

- The Color tab can actually deliver more than just color. By choosing the Wallpaper panel and then clicking the tiny black arrow to the right of the sample rectangle, you can choose from an astounding array of patterns and textures to integrate with the color. As a matter of fact, those wallpapers can be used in any of the channels.
- To make your own wallpaper available in the list, place any TIFF, BMP, PSD or JPG into BodyPaint 3D's Library>Pattern directory. The Eyedropper tool may be used to sample a pattern or painted area created in BodyPaint.
- To make things even more interesting, in the upper left of the Active Tool tab there are Brush Presets that already have their own Color and Bump attributes. You can change the Bump or Color by clicking either and choosing a new color.

Step 2 Choose the Active Tool tab, click on the sample square in the upper left corner and drag down to the Reptilian Skin 4 preset (from the top left, two over and five down). Now choose the Colors tab again, clicking Channels. Notice the reptilian texture appears in both Color and Bump. Click Color so that it has the red line around it. Now click the rectangle with the reptilian pattern at the top left of the Colors Page and drag down to choose a light green solid. Now the color will be green, but the reptilian pattern will remain in the bump channel to define the highs, lows, and texture.

Step 3 Paint on the Lathe Object. Use the 3 key and the mouse to rotate around the object.

Step 4 Notice the circle that appears on the surface when you touch it with the brush. You can change the brush size in the Active Tool>Settings panel.

Step 5 If you are using a graphics tablet and the pressure sensitivity is active, you will have some control over density of the painting. You can also change the opacity of the paint in the Blending panel. Click Blending and use the slider to try out some different transparency levels. There are also modes similar to those in image editing applications to the right of the slider.

Step 6 Click the Color tab and choose Channels. Click Color so it has the red line around it, and drag on the sample rectangle in the upper left to

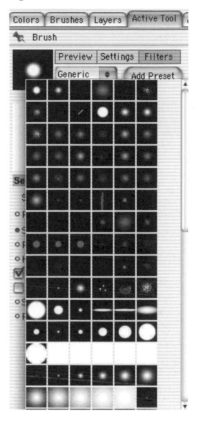

Figure 16.6 Brush Presets in Active Tool Tab

■ *Shortcut:* [and] decrease and increase the size of the brush. Opt+[and] rotate the brush counterclockwise and clockwise.

◆ *Tip:* A color preset can be edited for more individualized color by clicking the Color (panel) under the Colors tab.

Figure 16.7 Wallpapers

None
Load From Disc ...
Reload Directory
A004.TIF
A004BM.TIF
Bark_04b.jpg
Bark_04c.jpg
Bark_04s.jpg
C019_b.jpg
C019_c.jpg
C019_s.jpg
C053_b.jpg
C053_c.jpg
C053_s.jpg
C088_b.jpg
C088_c.jpg
C144_b.jpg
C144_c.jpg
chalk.jpg
chalk_chunky.jpg
chalk_oil_pastel.jpg
chalk_sharp.jpg
chalk_soft.jpg
chalk_square.jpg
charcoal.jpg
charcoal_chunky.jpg
charcoal_coarse.jpg
charcoal_soft.jpg
crayon_dull.jpg
crayon_sharp.jpg
crayon_waxy.jpg
Dirtg02b.jpg
Dirtg02c.jpg
Dirtg02s.jpg
eyebrow1.jpg
eyebrow2.jpg
flesh1.jpg
flesh2.jpg
flesh3.jpg
freckle.psd
Glitter Star Bump .jpg
Granite.tif
hair.tif
hair2.tif
half_moon.jpg
lava_b.tif
lava_c.tif
lava_s.tif
lip2.jpg
metal.jpg
Nat513_b.jpg
Nat513_c.jpg
Nat513_s.jpg
Nat524_b.jpg

choose a bright orange solid color. Click the Bump channel so it now is surrounded by the red line. Now open the Wallpaper panel, and drag down on the tiny black arrow under the word Wallpaper to Dirtg02b.jpg. Paint with this new hybrid material on the Lathe Object, experimenting with different Blending modes.

Step 7 The result of your painting may be a little fuzzy and hard to see. Just turn on Raybrush Render View, and the painting will be rendered in real-time for a clear picture of your artistry.

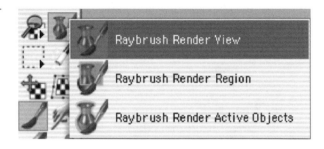

Figure 16.8 Raybrush Render View

Step 8 Want to work on your texture in a flat 2D state? Click the Texture tab on the upper left of the View. Click the View tab to return to painting on the model.

Step 9 Experiment with editing brushes in the Active Tool tab. Click Add Preset and enter a name for any brush design you want to keep.

Step 10 Now for some serious art fun! Choose Window>Brush Presets. Drag the pushpin from that window to the pushpin in the upper left of the Colors window to add it as a tab with the other important tabs. Click the Brushes tab. First, open some of those folders and check out how many brush presets you have (that's not even counting the ones you can make yourself). You can close your mouth now, and open the Oil folder. Choose Oil Round Wide.

Step 11 Paint on the Lathe Object. Notice how the brush is picking up the existing color, blending it into the new color like real oils.

■ *Shortcut:* Want to use the paint already on the surface as a palette? Hold down the Ctrl key and use the Eyedropper tool to sample any area, then paint with the sampled color.

Step 12 To keep a floating color palette more handy, choose Window>Color Presets. If you want to edit a preset and keep the new version, double-click the preset and edit it in the Color panel, then choose File>Add Single Color Preset from the Color Panel menu and give the new preset a name. If you want to replace an existing preset, choose File>Overwrite

Preset. Check the Colors>View menu for ways you can set up the palette. Sometimes, it is easier to identify a preset by name so viewing by list is helpful.

Finish painting the Lathe Object with abstractions of color and texture. Experiment with various combinations of color, blending, wallpapers, and brush styles for infinite possibilities. Do your own thing. There are examples on the DVD in the Chapter 16>EXTRA!EXTRA!>InDepth folder if you need inspiration.

Figure 16.9 Floating Color Palette

◆ *Tips:*

- Remember to use the 3 key and mouse to paint all the way around the object. On the other hand, if you are creating the object for a still seen from the front view only, no one needs to know you didn't waste your time painting a back that will never be seen.
- Ready to get rid of that Reptilian texture now? Any texture that was painted in the Bump channel can be erased (actually, flattened back to the original surface) by painting over the texture with a medium gray in the Bump channel.
- To paint a stroke with optimum lift up off the surface, choose white for the Bump color. For a stroke that digs down deep into the surface, the bump color should be black. A black and white texture in the Bump Channel will make the most obvious 3D textural surface.
- So many brush presets, colors, and wallpapers—here are some favorites to get you started: Watercolor Rough Brush Preset, Smear>Tri Smear Brush Preset, Brush Settings>Spacing and Jitter.

Figure 16.10 Painted Prop

- Troubleshooting: What if BodyPaint won't paint? Make sure the BodyPaint icon in the lefthand palette is depressed, the brush tool is chosen (also on the lefthand palette), and the object you want to paint on is selected.
- Don't neglect the power of stamping. Choose Brush Presets>Multi-brushes>Non-Organic and check out the rivets and screws. Then make your own stamps by placing grommets, symbols, and other artbits into the Library>Patterns folder.

Making a Weathered Sign

This project features Type, Layers, and Masks.

Painting the Sign Surface

Step 1   Open the file Old Sign.c4d from the Chapter 16>C4D Files folder and save a working copy (File>Save As).

Step 2   Choose the BP Paint layout. Run the BodyPaint Set-up Wizard and accept all the default settings, except on the Step 3 page where you will check the Bump channels. Edit the color for the color channel to be a slightly dirty red. (Note that the model was already made editable.)

Step 3   At the bottom right area of the screen, click the Materials tab and choose Texture>New Layer from the menu.

Step 4   Choose Window>Brush Presets. If the Brush Presets are not already in the Tab bar, drag and drop the Brushes Pushpin onto the Pushpin on the Colors tab. In Brush Presets, open Multibrushes>Non-Organic and choose Rust. Increase the size of the brush (Active Tool tab) and decrease the blend value (Colors tab). Paint some rust on the sign, especially around the edges and bullet holes. Also try out the Rust Scratches brushes. Use the Rivets brush to add rivets around the edges of the sign. (Any of these details could be placed on separate layers for more control with mode interaction later.) Many brushes, like Rivet, work better when you actually stamp (not moving the brush) rather than paint.

Figure 16.11 Rust

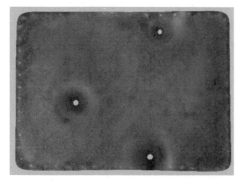

Step 5   Choose Window>Layer Manager. In this Manager, you can choose which layer you are working on (the one with the pencil) and control how the layers interact with each other. You can also create Layer Masks.

Step 6   After you have painted some rust, open the Layer Manager and experiment with the Opacity slider and modes to control how this layer interacts with layers beneath it.

Creating a Mask

Step 1   In the Layers Manager, select the red background layer. Undock the Layers Manager for easy access to it and the Colors tab at the same time.

Step 2   From the menu at the top of the Layers Manager, choose Functions>Duplicate Layer. From the same menu choose Functions>Add Layer Mask. Notice the Layer Mask Thumbnail in the Layer Manager. If it has a red line around it (click on it if it doesn't) anything you paint or draw will appear on the Mask. From the Colors tab, choose black as the color. From the left palette, choose the Paintbucket (Fill Bitmap) tool and click on the image to fill the Mask shape with black. Then change the color to white by choosing it from the Colors tab.

Step 3   From the Left Palette, choose the Draw Polygon Shape tool.

Step 4   Click the Active Tool tab on the upper right, and drag down to Star in the Shape pulldown menu. Click Edit and give the Star five points. Click in the center of the sign and drag a Star shape that works well with the bullet holes. Now in the Layers Manager, click back on the image thumbnail to the left of the mask thumbnail. Since you chose the Fill Bitmap tool (the Paintbucket) before, you will have to click back on the Brush tool to return to painting. Anything you paint on the image now will be blocked by the mask.

Step 5   Choose Brush Presets>Multibrushes>Dosch Texture Brushes>Stone 3. Paint inside the Star.

Step 6   After you paint the Star, return to the Layer Manager and use the Opacity slider and the modes pull-down menu to make the star look more like faded paint.

Figure 16.12 Fill Bitmap Tool

Figure 16.13 Draw Polygon Shape

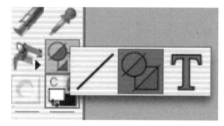

Making the Sign Letters

Step 1   Click the Colors tab and activate the Color channel. In the Layers Manager, choose Functions>New Layer. Choose a color and brush style.

Step 2   From the Left Palette, choose the Draw Text tool. In the Active Tool tab, type A R T in the text box. Click the Select button to choose a font. Enter a size of 200 and choose Align>Center. Enter a Feather value of 2.

Step 3   Click the I-beam to place the text on the surface. If you miss, just press Cmd+Z (Ctrl+Z) and try again.

Step 4   Create another New Layer and repeat the text creation above, except enter a size of 125 for the word "AHEAD."

Step 5   Select each layer and experiment with the opacity slider and modes.

Figure 16.14 Draw Text Tool

Figure 16.15 Old Sign

Step 6 The type on each layer needs to be dirtied up a bit. Return to the Brush icon on the left palette. Choose a Charcoal Chunky from the Brush Presets, and in the Active Tool tab click the Filters panel. Play back and forth on the letters with the Dodge and Burn filters. You may want to add some touches of migrant color to the letters also.

Painting a Head with BodyPaint

To be a spooky Wizard, Mr. Bobblehead needs some surface interest. In this project, we'll use the color and bump channels to create dry scaly skin, wrinkles, veins, scars, warts, and other lovely details.

Preparing the Head for Painting

Be sure to save frequently and say yes when BodyPaint asks if you want to save the textures, which must be saved in a separate file and kept with the .c4d file. If you use Save Project, the BodyPaint files will be in the right place.

Step 1 Open the file Mr.Bobblehead.c4d from the Chapter 16>C4D Files folder on the DVD. Save a working copy to your Models folder (File>Save As). Choose the BP 3D Paint Layout.

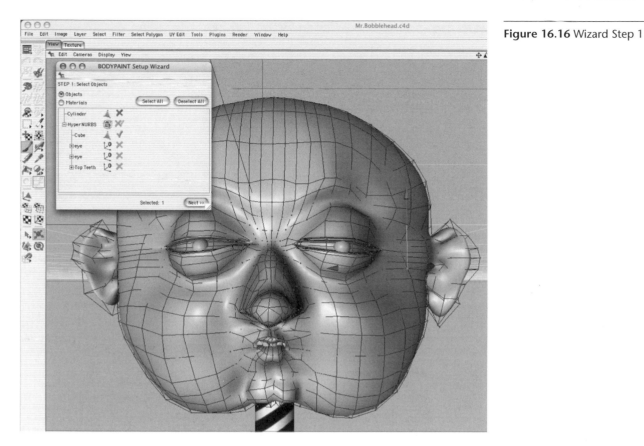

Figure 16.16 Wizard Step 1

Step 2 Click the Paint Set-up Wizard. On the Step 1 page, check Deselect All and then click the red checkmark next to the Cube so it turns green. On the Step 3 page, check Color and Bump. Edit the Color channel to be a sickly pale skin base color. Click Finish and Close.

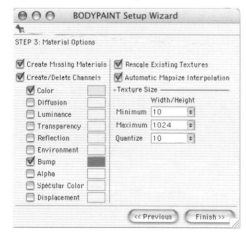

Figure 16.17 Wizard Step 3

Projection Painting

Take advantage of BodyPaint's Projection Painting mode. This lays the paint onto an invisible plane floating parallel to the screen and then drops it onto the model. The advantage of this mode is that brush strokes are more true and undistorted. If you change views or click the Apply Projection Paint icon, the paint will be applied to the surface. To continue painting on other sides of the model, rotate the view and projection paint in that view. If you click the Discard Projection Paint, the painting will not be applied. To activate Projection Paint, click the Enable Projection Paint icon.

Figure 16.18 L>R, 3DPaint Enable, Projection Paint Enable, Apply and Discard

Putting a Variety of Brushes to Work

◆ *Tips:* If you lay in too much color, it's easy to work back and forth from the original light skin color and the new tones by using the Ctrl key to sample the original color. Don't feel like you have to paint all over the head. Some well-placed tone and detail around the features will carry a lot of weight when the head is part of an overall scene.

Figure 16.19 First Colorings

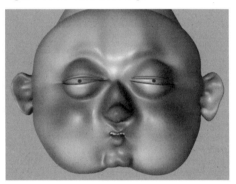

Step 1   Activate Projection Paint by clicking the Enable Projection Paint icon. You can choose Raybrush Render View also. Paint the broadest areas first, working down to the finer and finer detail. In the Colors tab under Channels, turn Multibrushing off (It should have a red checkmark, not green). Start by choosing Brush Presets>Standard Tools>Airbrush. Click the Active Tool tab and give the Airbrush a size of around 100. Choose a more colorful peach skintone for the color and set the blending to 15. Lay in broad areas of soft color. Check the color example in Chapter 16>EXAMPLES>InDepth on the DVD for reference. Again, it helps to choose Window>Color Presets and keep a floating palette of colors at your fingertips.

Step 2   Now click on the Channels panel in the Colors Tab. With Multibrushing still off, click on the Bump Channel. Click the Wallpaper panel and drag down to Dirtg02b.jpg. Paint over some of the areas of the face with this crackled dry skin bump.

Step 3   Now select Brush Presets>Multibrushes>Dosch Texture Brushes>Skin 4. Then choose a darker skin color solid for the Color channel under the Colors tab. Adjust the brush size if necessary, and turn down the blending value to 25 percent.

Step 4   Paint some scales around Mr. Bobblehead's eyes. Turning the blend value down low, choose some different colors in the color channel to introduce some variations of color into the scales. The Skin4 texture has a "canned" look, but by overlapping several wallpapers (or better yet making your own scales wallpaper) you'll get great results.

Step 5   From here, experiment with presets and brushes of your own design to create detail for the Bobblehead Wizard. Try out some of the effects in Brush Presets>Multibrushes>Organic. For a natural-looking "popping" veins, use a soft-edged brush and a blue color with a very low blend value, and choose white as the bump color.

What's a Wizard without a wart? Choose a low blend value and a reddish brown color. Choose white as the Bump color. Use a small brush in a circular motion to build up warts. Build up the color more dark and dense toward the middle.

◆ *Tips:*
- If you own BodyPAINT, a graphics tablet is a necessity. Trying to paint with a mouse is much worse than typing text with one finger.
- It's important to remember that you can use any color with any wallpaper in unexpected ways to get an effect. For example, the Stone 3 preset edited to a flesh color is great for adding grungy shadows to skin crevices.
- To escape the canned look of the presets, overlap several layers of wall-

paper textures or, better yet, place your own textures in the Library>Patterns folder.

- Flesh tones aren't just peach-colored. Add more interest to your flesh tone with earth colors and whispery shadows of blues, greens, and violets.
- Keeping the Blend level down is important for natural-looking application of color, especially when the color is working in conjunction with a Bump Channel.
- When adding last minute bump detail, disable Multibrushing and just use white and black in the Bump channel. To erase, just switch to middle gray and brush over the offending Bump.
- If you decide to go back and edit the BodyPaint work at another time, don't run the wizard again, just click the BodyPaint icon. (The palette and brush to the left of the Projection Paint Icon.)
- You can access most Adobe Photoshop plugins in BodyPaint if you have Photoshop installed on your computer. Go to Edit>Preferences>BodyPaint>BitmapFilter, and check Use Photoshop Filters. Then use the pulldown menu to navigate to the Photoshop Plugins folder in your Photoshop Folder. Any filter in the Filter menu at the top with a PS is a Photoshop Plugin. Many third-party Photoshop filters work too.

Pasting on a Tattoo

Step 1   Open the file Mr.Bobblehead.c4d from the Chapter 16>C4D Files folder and save a working copy as Tattoo.c4d (File>Save As). Choose the BP Paint Layout and run the Wizard on the Cube. On the Step 1 page, Deselect All and then check only the Cube. Check the Color and Bump channels and assign a flesh color to the Color channel.

Step 2   From the top menu, choose File>Open and open the file Tattoo 1.psd. This file is located on the DVD in the GOODIES>LIBRARIES>Tattoos folder.

Step 3   When the file opens in the Texture view, notice the Layers Manager. The two layers of the file as it was created in Photoshop are still separate in BodyPaint. That is a good thing to remember, as later you may want separate parts. For now though, choose Functions>Merge Layer Down from the Layer Manager menu to combine the two layers into one. If you want to edit the image on this layer, the Filter menu at the top has some familiar image-editing tools. For example, experiment with the sliders in Color Correction>Gamma Correction for different looks for the Tattoo.

Step 4   Press Cmd+A (Ctrl+A) to select the image and Cmd+C (Ctrl+C) to copy the image.

Figure 16.20 Mr.Bobblehead Tattoo

Step 5 Click the View tab to return to the 3D view, and make sure Gouraud shading is active.

Step 6 Press Cmd+V (Ctrl+V) to paste. Notice that Projection Painting has activated.

Step 7 Move the mouse anywhere inside the box to move the tattoo into a more centered position, then work with the handles to size it.

Step 8 Turn off Projection Painting by rotating the view or clicking the Apply Projection Painting icon. Of course you can continue to paint on top of the image.

This technique can be an end it itself, allowing you to add art from any other source to the surface. Or, you can use photos or art made in other programs as a start for drawing or painting in BodyPaint.

Figure 16.21 Mr. Bobblehead with a Crown of Stars

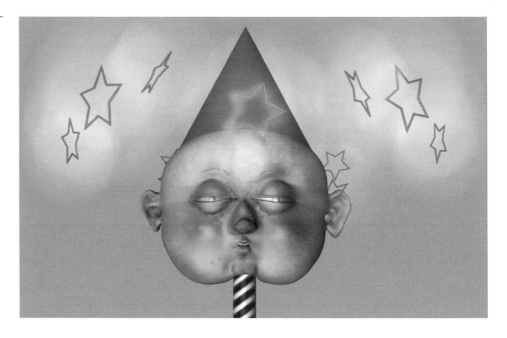

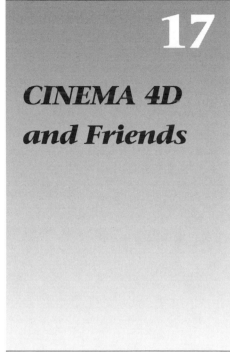

17

CINEMA 4D and Friends

Figure 17.1

As awesome as CINEMA 4D is, no application is an island. These digital wonders deserve special mention for their ability to partner with CINEMA 4D for exciting artistic results. Each of these programs is vast, but here are a few favorite examples of their supporting roles with C4D.

Figure 17.2 Image Maps

Adobe Photoshop

On the DVD: The PhotoshopSkills.PDF in Chapter 17>EXTRA!EXTRA!>InDepth on the DVD has step-by-step instructions for Adobe Photoshop tasks most often used in conjunction with CINEMA 4D.

Image editing skills are a necessity for the 3D artist. Especially if you don't have BodyPaint 3D, Photoshop's robust selection of tools, filters, and intuitive Layers make the creation of channel defining imagery a snap. Photoshop Layer Styles are important helpers when it's time to create believable graphics for 3D surfacing.

Figure 17.3 Custom Shapes and Layer Styles

Photoshop Custom Shapes come right into CINEMA 4D as splines. After creating the custom shape in Photoshop, choose File>Export>Paths To Illustrator. Open C4D, and choose Objects>Load Object. Choose Edit> Frame Selected Elements to find the spline in the 3D space.

Adobe Illustrator and Macromedia Freehand

You'll head for Adobe Illustrator (or its Macromedia counterpart, Freehand) when you need vector art. Intricate patterns, customized text, graphs, and complex splines that would be too clunky to tackle in CINEMA 4D are easily imported from these two applications into CINEMA 4D. Vectors created in Illustrator and Freehand can be imported into C4D for use as construction splines and motion paths, or they can be rasterized and imported into a raster program (or simply captured as a screen shot) to function as linear texture. If you are not very familiar with these applications, roll your mouse over the tools for a quick ID.

If you are one of those closet Bezier-phobics, it's time to bite the bullet and get over it. The lack of Bezier skills will make a gaping hole in your 3D repertoire, so take an afternoon to sit down with a good Bezier curve tutorial.

Things can get a little strange when importing elements from other programs. Remember that the other application has no idea what size your C4D world is. It may be totally normal that you have to scale elements drastically to make them proportionate to your world. Also, objects often come in way off base, so zeroing out the axes of the imported object (by entering 0, 0, 0 in the coordinates) to send it to the center of the world is usually a good idea. Often there will be maverick splines on import. Sometimes these can be taken care of by checking or unchecking Close Spline or by changing the Intermediate Points, but other times you'll have to do a little point editing on the spline.

Illustrator

Complex Splines

Complex vectors are easily generated in Illustrator. Here's an example:

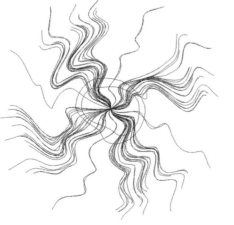

Figure 17.4 Flare tool and Warp tool

Step 1   Move the mouse down on the Rectangle tool and slide over to the Flare tool in the sidecar menu.

Step 2   Double-click the Flare tool to access the settings. The number of Rays may depend on what your CPU can handle. Drag the cursor in the work area to create a Flare.

Step 3   Use the Warp Tool (Shift+R) to make an organic version of the Flare.

Step 4   Save the file with Illustrator 8 compatibility (File>Save As), and in CINEMA 4D choose Objects>Load Object to import the outlines. Select the separate paths and choose Functions>Connect to create a single spline to be used in the usual ways in C4D.

Tech Graphics and Custom Type

These basic Illustrator skills will come in handy when you want to make Dials and Gauges.

Step 1 Move the mouse down on the Line tool and choose the Polar Grid tool (the last choice in the sidecar menu). Double-click the tool icon and custom edit the settings to create a polar grid. Hold down the Opt key (Alt) to draw the grid from the center and the Shift key to constrain it to a perfect circle and click-drag the mouse to make the grid.

Step 2 To make circular type or numbers, move the mouse on the Rectangle tool and drag to the Ellipse tool (third from the left). Holding down the Opt (Alt) and Shift keys again, click the mouse on the center of the grid and drag the mouse outside the grid to make a baseline for some text.

Step 3 Click on the Type tool and drag to the third Type tool from the left.

Step 4 Click the I-beam cursor on the circle path. When the cursor starts blinking, you can type the text. Drag the I-beam with the Selection tool (V) to move the position of the line of type along the track.

Any type can be placed on any Bezier curve with the Type Path Tool. Lines of text can also be placed inside Bezier shapes. Use the Ellipse tool to create another circle path and click on it with the Area Type tool to see how the text arranges itself within the shape.

While you could use these as splines for 3D forms, you'll probably want to rasterize these and layer them over some aged surfaces in Photoshop or BodyPaint.

Making Decorative Elements for Textures

Let's start out with the way-cool Symbol Sprayer.

Step 1 Use the Bezier Pen tool to draw a shape. Click, click, click and make the last click on the first point you started with.

Step 2 Choose Window>Symbols. With the shape selected,(click on it with Selection Tool) choose New Symbol from the small triangle menu on the right of the Symbol palette.

Step 3 Choose the Symbol Sprayer tool (Shift+S) and spray a complex shape or letterform.

Step 4 Choose Break Link to Symbol from the small black triangle to convert the symbols to outlines.

As with most tools in Illustrator or Freehand, double-click the tool to access specialized settings. Try adjusting the settings to vary the spray with a pressure-sensitive tablet.

Figure 17.5 Tech Graphics

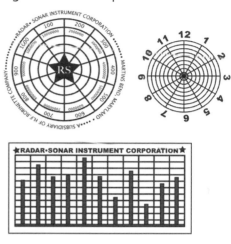

Figure 17.6 Gauge Layered

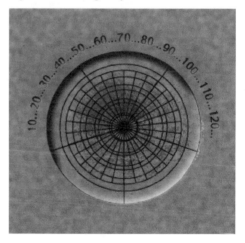

Figure 17.7 Symbol Sprayer

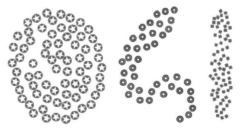

Making Repetitive Patterns

Step 1   Use the Bezier Pen tool to draw a shape and choose the stroke and fill colors from the Color palette (Window>Color).

Step 2   If the Pattern Piece you are building has more than one object, group them together with Cmd+G (Ctrl+G).

Step 3   Select the Pattern piece (or Group) and Opt-drag (Alt-drag) a first copy, dropping the copy with the desired spacing. Once that first copy is correctly positioned, you can press Cmd+D (Ctrl+D) for as many copies as you want. If you want to constrain the movement of the first copy on a level line, hold down the Shift key after you begin the Opt-drag (Alt-drag).

Step 4   Press Command-A to select the row of pattern pieces, and Command-G to group them.

Step 5   Repeat Step 3 to copy the rows vertically.

The Tile shader within CINEMA 4D will handle most patterning jobs, but your favorite vector application will help out when needs for more complex repetitive bump maps or surface designs arise.

The uses for Illustrator in creating imagery for surfacing are endless. Any forms you create can easily be used to create patterns. The Pathfinder (Effect> Pathfinder) is particularly useful for generating fresh forms for logos. The Paintbrush tool is great for adding custom decorative trims to your textures.

Figure 17.8 Repetitive Pattern

Figure 17.9 Shapes created with the Pathfinder

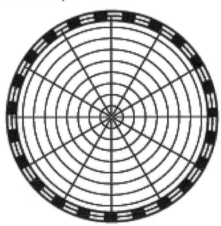

Figure 17.11 Decorative Edge Using an Illustrator Style

Figure 17.10 Decorative Trims Using Illustrator's Brush Tool

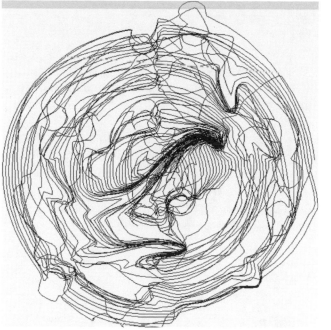

Figure 17.12 Radial Freeform Splines

Figure 17.13 Abstract Spline Shape

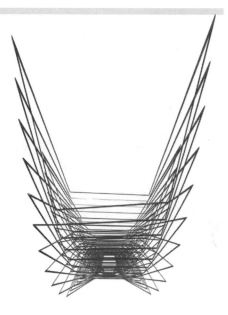

Freehand

These vector spirals (Spiral tool with 50) lines were manipulated into organic forms with the Freeform tool. From Macromedia Freehand, choose Export and choose Macintosh EPS as the format. In CINEMA 4D, choose Objects>Load Object.

These forms began with rectangles cloned in Freehand. The C4D Sweep NURBS objects were then deformed.

Pixologic Zbrush

Here is a horse of a different color. With it's 2.5D Pixols, Pixologic Zbrush (just like the name says) allows you to pull brush strokes out into the Z space. Truly one of a kind, Zbrush has a steep learning curve but is packed with artistic tools you haven't seen before. Zbrush is great for making unusual background elements for compositing with animated CINEMA 4D models. Models can be exported to and imported from C4D as .obj files. Download the free demo from www.pixologic.com.

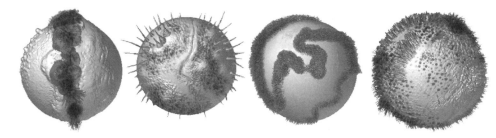

Figure 17.14 Zbrush Examples

Synthetik Studio Artist and Corel Painter

While Adobe Photoshop is the basic image-editing workhorse, two other applications are must-have if you lean toward the fine arts and natural media. These applications provide both unique elements for import into CINEMA 4D and creative possibilities for postproduction.

Corel Painter has long been a champion in the natural media arena, and the newest version has an improved interface. Painter's inventive tools offer exciting texturing possibilities for the CINEMA 4D artist. Painter's cool feature list includes watercolors that actually run down the page, believable impastos, nozzles that spray multiple images, and the best fur brush around. An extra plus for 3D: Painter has an editor for custom designing warps and wefts of fabrics.

Figure 17.15 Painter Nozzles

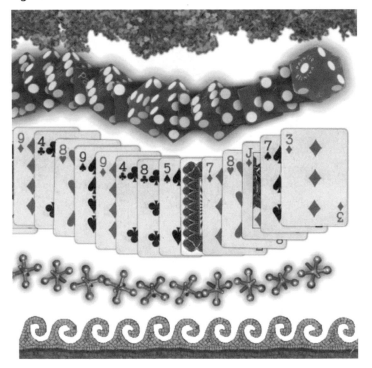

Figure 17.16 Fabric Patterns in Painter

Figure 17.17 Painter Impasto Surface

Synthetik Studio Artist, a graphics synthesizer, is a massive set of illustration and postproduction tools. If you want to create imaginative and original textures, this is your weapon of choice. Its massive palette of tools in the natural media genre is almost distracting. In addition, Studio Artist will use any of its tools to automatically generate markings over imported resource images. On the postproduction side, animations created in CINEMA 4D can be opened in Studio Artist and automatically processed with thousands of stylistic treatments for

Figure 17.18 Studio Artist Brushes

a myriad of new versions of the original. Mac users can download a free demo from www.synthetik.com.

Sources and Software for Splines

The web has many sources for free splines for vector and raster programs. Type "Free PS Custom Shapes" in a search engine such as Google. Free font dingbats are also plentiful. Adobe Streamline can be useful for converting any raster image into vectors. Illustrator and Freehand have trace functions also.

Sound Solutions

Apple Computer's Garageband and Soundtrack provide easy ways to make original sounds and background music for your animations. GarageBand comes with the economical iLife package. Soundtrack ships with Final Cut Pro or you can purchase it as a standalone application. Even if you have no music training, these amazing applications will let you produce just the right sound for your 3D projects.

GarageBand

With GarbageBand, you can connect your own keyboard or guitar inputs (with extra hardware) and mix the different tracks into a song. If you don't have your own music input, GarageBand includes a keyboard for inputing your original tunes with a mouse. In addition, GarageBand comes with a library of royalty-free loops that you can layer creatively. The loops include a wide choice of instruments and

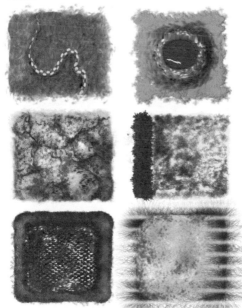

Figure 17.19 Textures Painted in Studio Artist

drums. Since the loops are searchable by keyword, it's easy to quickly find and mix appropriate sounds for your animation. For those who aren't ready to go into more complex sound editing but need copyright-free and inexpensive music, this is it.

Soundtrack

Soundtrack is similar to GarageBand, but has a video window so you can match the music tracks you are creating to a QuickTime movie.

Open Soundtrack, and choose Window>Media Manager. To build a soundtrack for your animation, drag the QuickTime you rendered out of CINEMA 4D into the upper left Video window. In the Media Manager, click any genre panel where you can choose the sounds to preview. When you find a sound you like, just drag and drop it into the soundtrack (Untitled Track 1). You can drag left or right to any starting point you like. (Hold down the Cmd key to bypass snapping for more accurate placement.) To loop the sound over and over, move the mouse on the right edge and drag out multiples of the sound. Change the key of the sound by dragging down to the desired key in the pulldown menu to the right of the record and playback controls at the top of the window. In that same window you can change the beats per minute, access the SMPTE timecode, control the play of the project, and even record sound.

Try it! Choose Synths>A Bleep Odessey.aiff in the first track. Add a new track with Cmd+T and choose Drums>Bass Drum Pattern. Now here's the ultimately cool thing about Soundtrack—it automatically matches the tempo of anything you add to the existing beat. Add some more tracks. When you are finished mixing, just choose File>Export to QuickTime to create the soundtrack intact in the original QuickTime or File>Export Mix to export a separate soundtrack.

To the Web with You, C4D!

Here are ways to show off your masterpieces on the web:

QuickTime

Choose QuickTime Movie Small from the Render Settings>Save panel for a variation on the Cinepak codec, which will produce a small time-compressed file of fair quality. For a more lossless version (and a larger file size) choose QuickTime Big. If you want to experiment with other choices that might work better with the color and detail in your animation, choose QuickTime Movie and use the Options button to access a pulldown menu of codecs. The Animation codec will usually work fine, but the color quality, detail quality, and motion quality that you require in a particular movie will vary and other compression styles might work better. Render out several different compression options and compare them. Compression applications like Sorensen Squeeze and Cleaner will be great helpers for efficiently compressing your movies for the web.

Using the FlashEx Plugin

FlashEx is a plugin that exports CINEMA 4D models as .swf files and even generates the HTML file.

Because these exports are vector graphics, raster textures are not exportable. But interesting models exported in a variety of rendering modes and line styles can add fresh looks for your Flash work.

Step 1 Place the FlashEx folder inside CINEMA 4D's Plugins folder. The plugin should show up in the Plugins list the next time you start CINEMA 4D.

Step 2 Choose the FlashEx plugin from the Plugins list.

Step 3 On the general page, click the Render button and the save location will appear in the File input box. Under Duration, enter the beginning and ending frames you want to export. Under Optimize For, enter the size you want the exported art to be. Choose a frame rate and a mode.

Step 4 Click the Background tab and set a background color.

Step 5 Click the Lines tab. In this page, you can experiment with different line widths and colors.

Step 6 Click OK, and the .swf file will be saved to the specified Save location.

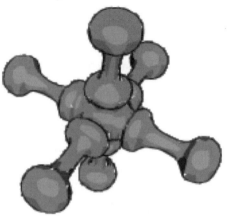

Figure 17.20 Web Element made with FlashEx Plugin

CINEMA 4D into Adobe ImageReady

Step 1 Make a folder on your desktop named Frames. In the Render Settings Output page, you might want to choose Manual to make a tiny movie. The example is 50 by 50. You'll end up with an animated GIF, so the Frame Rate needs to be very low (5–7).

Step 2 On the Save page, click Path and navigate to the Frames folder you made. Change the Format to Photoshop PSD. Check Alpha channel if you want to layer the image over other layers in Photoshop. Render the frames.

Step 3 Open Photoshop and click the Jump to ImageReady button at the bottom of the Toolbar. Choose File>Import>Folder as Frames and navigate to the Frames folder to import the rendered frames.

Step 4 Click the Play button if you want to preview the movie in ImageReady. To export the GIF, choose File>Save Optimized. In the dialog box, enter a title for the GIF and under Format, choose Images Only or HTML and Images.

On the DVD: Open "BodyPainted Gif" in the MOVIES/STILLS folder.

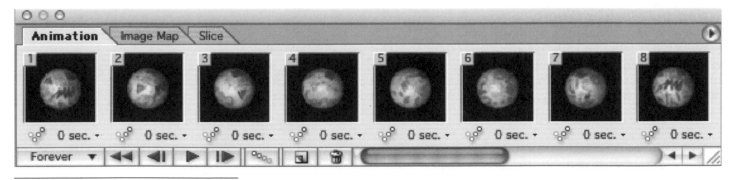

Figure 17.21 Sphere Painted in BodyPaint
and Imported into ImageReady

Figure 17.22 C4D Rendering in
Final Cut Pro

CINEMA 4D and Apple Final Cut Pro

CINEMA 4D animations are easily imported into Apple Final Cut Pro by choosing File>Import>Files. Just click the Alpha check box when rendering out of CINEMA 4D, and objects journey into Final Cut Pro with beautiful edges.

Organizing Libraries

After you get started in 3D, it won't be long before you are drowning in a sea of files. CINEMA 4D models, textures and image maps, sounds, fonts, and rendered projects will crowd your storage real estate.

Set up an organizational system now, and file faithfully after you finish a project. This little bit of forethought now will save hours of unnecessary searching in the future. Not only will organized libraries save lots of time but they are important for saving storage space. Huge libraries of rarely used files can be saved with a catalog to DVD.

The Browser

Place your models in a folder, and click the Browser tab in CINEMA 4D. Choose

Figure 17.23 Organization Example

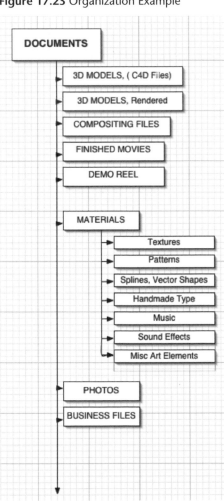

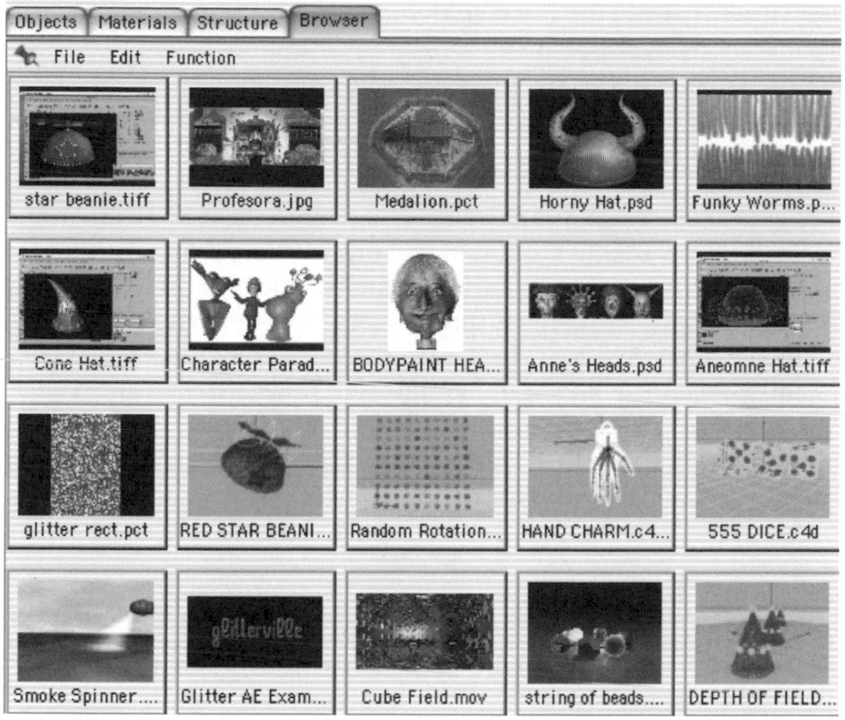

Figure 17.24 C4D Browser Catalog

Figure 17.25 Iview Catalog

File>Import Directory from the Browser Menu. This collection of models may also be saved as a Catalog (File>Save Catalog). Drag and drop models to the Editor window or materials to the Materials Manager.

iView Media Pro

Drag and drop a folder of (almost) any kind of files onto the iView icon on the dock, and you'll get a blazingly fast thumbnail preview. Image files, QuickTime movies, sound files, fonts, just to name a few, can be quickly browsed with this indespensible application. Not only is this program great for organization, it's a super tool for client presentations. Students or teachers can drop a folder containing an entire semester's work (random mixes of raster, vector, QuickTimes, even SWFs) into iView for quick and easy presentation or grading. (Note that iView does not preview CINEMA 4D files, only rendered models and scenes, but you have the CINEMA 4D Browser for that.)

Hardware Friends

There are catalogs full of hardware toys, but here are the digital artist's bare necessities:

- A decent digital camera.
- A scanner.
- A digital tablet.
- A stopwatch.

On the DVD: Chapter 17>EXTRA!EXTRA!>InDepth>More Tools and Toys.pdf for a list of cool toys that aren't necessary but add bells, whistles, and fun to the 3D process.

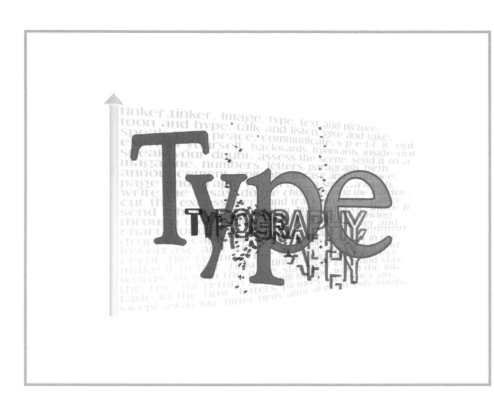

Tips on Type

Figure 18.1

After an introduction to making text objects in CINEMA 4D, this section will look at creative ways to glorify letters and numbers in 3D space and time. The names of comicbook superheros were extruded in space long before the age of the desktop designer. Enjoy those 3D Archi-Types, and then explore some new techniques for appropriate and inventive typography. Be sure to check out the resources on typography on the DVD. Building and animating 3D letters is one thing, but choosing type and applying the wonders of CINEMA 4D in regard to the design process is another. Not knowing the language of typography (with its foreign words like serif, kern, and counterspace) can cause the most clever 3D artist to lose credibility and clients in the professional world. You can never know enough about the communicative qualities of typestyles and the beauty of letterforms. If your work will involve typography, make it your business to learn about it. If you can't take design classes, there are many excellent, free Internet resources on designing with type.

On the DVD: See Chapter 18>EXTRA!EXTRA!>References for pointers to more information about designing with type.

The Basics of Text Splines

Step 1 Choose File>New and save the file as TextPlay in your Models folder (File>Save As).

◆ ***Tip:*** In these projects, you may or may not have the indicated fonts available on your system. If you don't have the specified fonts, choose a similar font. Naturally, your efforts may look different from the examples. The quality of the spline will determine the quality of the 3D Type, so be aware that some fonts (like some free handcrafted Internet offerings) may have troublesome splines. Among the many trustworthy typefaces and dingbats shared for free or nominal fees are those at www.larabiefonts.com. Some of them are used in these exercises if you want to download them.

Figure 18.2 Add Text Spline

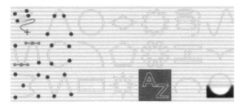

Figure 18.3 Attributes Manager Text

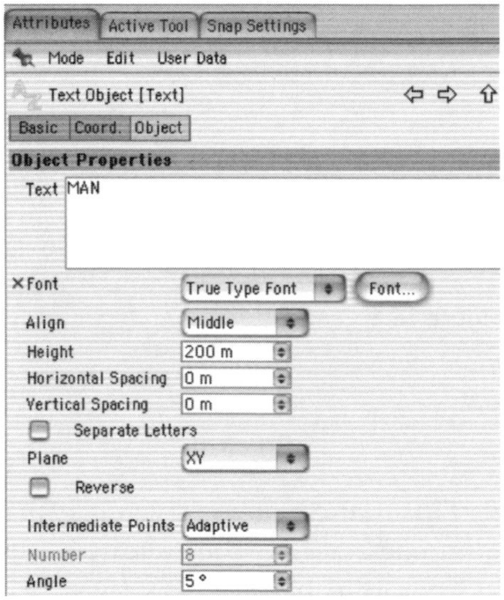

Step 2 Choose Add Text Spline from the Spline palette.

Step 3 In Attributes Manager Object Properties, type to replace the word Text in the Text input box with the word MAN in capitals. Notice that pressing Return (Enter) does not enter the text but returns to the left margin. Clicking anywhere outside the text input box will finalize the text change.

Step 4 Click the Font button to choose the font Times from the TrueType pull down menu. (You could also pull down the menu that says TrueType Font and choose Postscript, in which case clicking the Font button will allow you to navigate to wherever the Postscript fonts are stored.)

Step 5 Try all the choices in the Align menu and watch the position of the type spline in relation to the spline object's axis.

Step 6 Return to the Text input box and type the word MAN again underneath the first word. Now use the small black arrows to the right of Height, Horizontal Spacing, and Vertical Spacing to adjust those values on the fly. Remember that these values can be animated by Command-clicking (right-clicking) on the words.

Step 7 Click the word Text in the Objects Manager and press the C key. Notice that all the letters remain in the single Text Object. Press Cmd+Z (Ctrl+Z) to undo the Made Editable state. Now click the check box for Separate Letters and press the C key once again. Click the (+) to open the Text hierarchy. Each letter is a child of the Text Object and could be independently edited and animated.

Press Cmd+Z (Ctrl+Z) to undo the Made Editable state, as we want to continue looking at the Object Properties.

Step 8 The Plane pulldown menu may be used to orient the spline. If the Reverse check box is checked, the point order of the spline will be reversed. The Intermediate Points pulldown menu allows you to change the way points are interpolated. (We'll see this in action in the section on Deformable Type.)

Once text splines are made editable, they become regular splines like any other. You can no longer edit the words themselves by typing, but you can edit the points and tangents of the spline as you learned how to do in Chapter 2. Some text splines, like the ones in Figure 18.4, are naughty (in that their splines don't translate well to Cinema 4D) and may need to have points or tangent handles edited at this level. Another type issue involves the moving of a C4D file from machine to machine or platform to platform. A text spline not yet made editable will require the font to be installed on the target machine, whereas a text spline already converted to a standard spline will not.

On the DVD: For more Spline Editing tips, see Chapter 02>EXTRA!EXTRA!>In-Depth>More About Splines.pdf.

I Have No Words

Despite all that editing, a render at this point would look like a panther deep in a coal mine. Remember that splines are invisible and are used as elements to create geometry. For now, create an Extrude NURBS and drop the text spline into it. You may want to review the Extrude NURBS and Sweep NURBS tools in Chapter 3.

Making Text Behave in CINEMA 4D

Step 1 Return to the Text input box and replace the word Man with MOON (all caps). Change the Type to TrueType>Helvetica. Uh oh—looks like someone took a bite out of the Os.

Step 2 Make the Text Object Editable, select each O. Choose Structure>Edit Spline>Soft Interpolation. You will still need to tweak a few points and tangent handles. It is inevitable that you'll occasionally run into weird splines, but they can be manually adjusted.

Deformable Type

Study Figure 18.6. The first A on the left has no apparent problems since it is static and was never intended to bend. The second A from the left became rather cubist-style for lack of enough subdivisions when it was subjected to a bend deformer. Unfortunate. The third and fourth As are just right. First the Intermediate Points of the Text spline were changed to Natural. Then the Subdivision of the Extrude NURBS object was increased in Object Properties. In the Caps panel, Regular Grid was checked and the Width was increased. How much these values are increased depends on the letter itself and the degree of the bend, so you will have to experiment and test-render each situation.

Figure 18.4 Naughty Splines

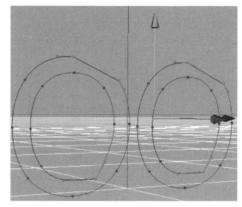

Figure 18.5 Fixed "O"s

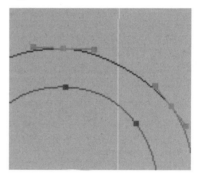

Figure 18.6 Not Deformed, Badly Deformed, Well Deformed

And Now, Some Creative Text Messaging

The whole point of typography is communication. In the 2D world, a single letter can speak volumes and send a message without even joining others in the spelling of a word. The typestyle itself—by virtue of its curves, overall shape, motion, or historical reference—may say seriously businesslike, funky, frivolous, or nostalgic. The 2D artist may add further communication value by rendering the type in colors, patterns, or stylistic treatments that remind the typographic audience of times, places, emotions, or attitudes.

In the CINEMA 4D environment, this ability to tell a story with letters increases exponentially. The capability to animate position, rotation, scale, color, transparency, and other attributes provides infinitely more ways to bring type to life. Letters can be made to twitch and wiggle, or flop over and die. So a word of warning is in order. It's not always about making type fancy but rather about using it to say what needs to be said. Sometimes a restrained motion of the most plain or traditional typestyle is called for. Some of your type may speak with quiet elegance, while other letters play boisteriously. Enjoy and explore the differences.

Sleek and Sophisticated

The strength of classic type and 3D tools are a powerful combination. Deceptively simple, this genre of 3D typography can take hours of tweaking before every material surface, highlight, and movement comes together in a perfect gestalt. Let's review basic Extrude NURBS skills with this corporate logotype.

Step 1   In a new C4D file, choose Spline>Add Text Spline and type CORPCO (all caps) in the Text input box. Choose the Charcoal TrueType font. (If you don't have Charcoal, choose a similar blocky, sans serif font.) Increase the Horizontal Spacing to 20m. (Any time type will be seen from side angles, increasing the horizontal spacing will help maintain readability.)

Step 2   Choose an Extrude NURBS object, and drop the text spline inside. Select the Extrude NURBS object and in the Attributes Manager, increase the Z Movement to 50.

Step 3   Click the Caps panel, and enter Fillet Caps with Steps 1, Radius 5 for both Start and End. Leave the Fillet Type on Convex.

Step 4   Create two silver metal materials, one leaning toward blue and one toward green. Make sure the blue material has a high, narrow Specular highlight and set the color to a bright blue. Turn on Reflection for the green material and leave the Brightness high. Turn on Environment and navigate to any file from GOODIES>MATERIALS>HDRIImages. Experiment with the Brightness and Mix sliders to get the right look. (Later if you want to render the animation with HDRI luminance, return to Chapter 12>EXTRA!EXTRA!>InDepth for a review on how to set that

Figure 18.7 CORPCO

up.) Place the blue material on the Extrude NURBS first, and place the green material on the Extrude Nurbs last. Select the green material tag, and in Tag Properties type C1 in the selection box.

Step 5 Using the skills you learned in Chapters 6 and 11, set up lights and a camera to fly up to the logo. (Turn on Title Safe in Preferences>Viewport and keep the type within those guidelines.) Set up basic Main/Fill lighting, and then add a light to animate across the top or bottom faceted edge of the letters. Experiment with highlights as finishing touches. If this is rendered out with an alpha channel, it can be layered over video footage. Don't be surprised if it takes a long time to get it right. Even the most simple logo can require numerous test renderings to balance the delicate interactions of surface, timing, camera, and lights.

On the DVD: See Chapter 18>MOVIES/STILLS for example movies.

◆ *Tips:*
- What about kerning in C4D? The spacing you made between letters in the Horizontal Spacing box is called tracking (equal space added between letters). What if you needed to kern, or independently adjust the space between any two letters? That must be done manually, which is another good reason to check Separate Letters when you make the text spline.
- While selecting objects in the editor window is usually OK, it's a bad idea with text objects. You'll probably end up with only a Cap selected instead of the entire 3D object.

> **Multiple Materials on Text**
>
> Drop the overall Material on the name of an Extrude NURBS object first. Then drop additional materials. (Materials without selections should go to the left of those with selections.) In the Tag Properties selection box, type R1 for Rounding 1 (the front), R2 for Rounding 2 (the back), C1 for Cap 1 (Front Cap), and C2 for Cap 2 (back cap). Once the Text object has been made editable by pressing the C key, you can also make polygonal selection sets and assign different materials to those.

Text on Illustrator Paths

Step 1 Create a new C4D file (File>New) and save it as TextSpiral.c4d into your Models folder (File>Save As). In the Objects Manager menu, choose File> Load Object. Navigate to LittleGirl.AI from the Chapter 18>C4D Files folder. It's important to note that this file was saved out of Adobe Illustrator with Illustrator 8 file compatibility. Also, in Illustrator, select any text you create and choose Type>Create Outlines so the type will appear in CINEMA 4D.

Figure 18.8 Illustrator Type on a BezierPath Imported into C4D

Step 2 After you see the text splines in CINEMA, click the (+) next to the Type object and note that every letter is a separate spline. If you wanted to manipulate each letter independently, each one would require its own Extrude NURBS. Since you don't need separate letters in this case, select all the text splines (drag over them with a selection rectangle and scroll down). Choose Functions>Connect to create an object that includes all the splines. After the new Path 1 object appears in the Objects Manager, you can throw away the separate splines unless you think you may need them later.

Step 3 Create an Extrude NURBS object and drop the new Path 1 object into it. Set the Z distance to 3 in the Object panel.

Step 4 Try placing some deformers on this object. From the Deformer palette, choose a Bend and Twist deformer. Make each of them a child of the Extrude NURBS object. Experiment with moving them in the editor window and reverse their order in the Hierarchy. Try other deformers too.

Using Text Splines in Other Ways

Most often, text splines are extruded to create a 3D form. Here are methods you may not have used before.

Making Text with a Sweep NURBS

Step 1 Create a new C4D file (File>New) and save it as SweepNURBS Text.c4d (File>Save As).

Step 2 Select Spline>Add Text Spline. Type a capital K in the Text box and choose Courier as the font.

Figure 18.9 SweepNURBS K

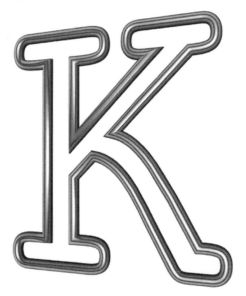

Step 3 Select Spline>Add Circle Spline. Give the Circle Spline a Radius of 2m.

Step 4 Choose NURBS>Sweep NURBS. Drop the Text Spline in first and then add the Circle Spline.

Step 5 Select the Sweep NURBS in the Objects Manager and go to frame 0.

Step 6 In the Attributes Manager Object panel, set the value for Growth to 0 and Command-click (right-click) on the word Growth. Slide to Animation>Add Keyframe to set a keyframe.

Step 7 Go to Frame 75. Change the value for Growth to 100 percent and set a keyframe.

Step 8 Create a new Material. In the Color channel, click on the small black triangle and choose Shader>Spectral. Place the material on the Sweep NURBS. Render a Movie.

Figure 18.10 SuperText

Try using a text spline as the profile for a Sweep NURBS (start with an Arc Spline as the path), and keyframe the Growth value.

On the DVD: See Chapter 18>MOVIES/STILLS for examples of these techniques.

Easily Animated Flat Letters

Text splines could also be placed in Loft NURBS object to create a totally flat letter. But, here's a more versatile way to make flat letters that can behave organically in the 3D space.

Step 1   Create a new C4D file (File>New) and save it as A_Flat_Letter.c4d (File>Save As).

Step 2   From the top menu, choose Primitive>Plane. In the Attributes Manager, change the Width to 300 and the Orientation to –Z.

Step 3   Press the C key to make the plane editable.

Step 4   In the Materials Manager, choose File>New Material. In the Color channel, navigate to GOODIES>MATERIALS>TYPEIMAGES>A_Color.psd. Activate the alpha channel and navigate to GOODIES>MATERIALS>TYPE IMAGES>A_Alpha.psd. Click the Invert check box on the Alpha page.
Place the material on the plane.

Step 5   With the plane still selected, choose the Use Polygons tool, and then choose Structure>Edit Surface>Crumple. Now animate some deformers

Figure 18.11 Wispy Floating Type

Figure 18.12 Deformed Type

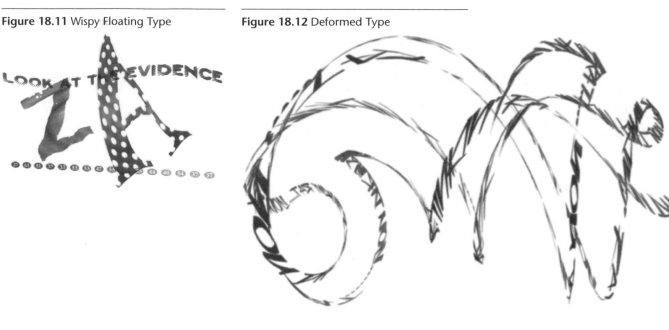

on the flat letter. If your edges begin to get too chunky, you can always drop the plane into a HyperNURBS for instant smoothing.

Step 6   Return to the material and place some patterns in the Transparency channel.

This technique offers some additional ways to play. Think about using Adobe Photoshop filters to create creative edges for the Alpha channel. (The Photoshop PDF on the DVD shows you how.) Revisit the Color channel and experiment with different tile patterns in the Transparency channel. This technique is great for creating wispy typographic floaters to invade your 3D space as secondary noise.

On the DVD: See Chapter 18>MOVIES/ STILLS for examples of these techniques and Chapter 17>EXTRA!EXTRA!>InDepth for a PDF on Photoshop Skills.

Type Forms: Finishing Touches and Creative Play

Beyond the choice of typestyle and modeling tool used to make a 3D type form, there are many ways to individualize type. When the situation calls for sophistication, you may be using simple, elegant materials and adjusting caps and rounding in subtle ways to catch the light in a scene. For more stylized or edgy type, you'll experiment with color, patterns, cap/rounding treatments, or radically distorted text meshes.

Study the files from the Chapter 18>C4DFiles>Typeplay folder. Study the Caps panel settings and Material settings. (There are two Caps_Rounding files: Caps_

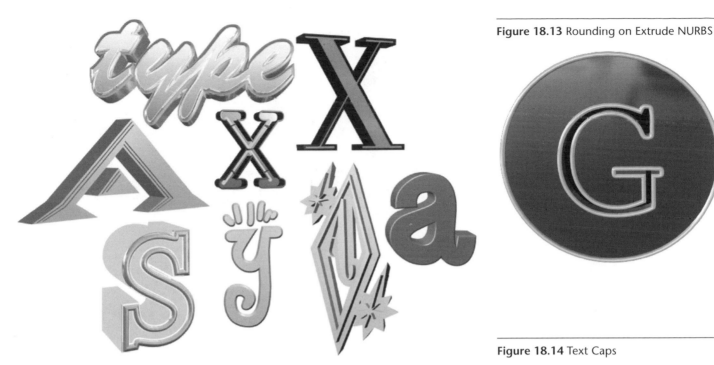

Figure 18.13 Rounding on Extrude NURBS

Figure 18.14 Text Caps

Figure 18.15 Text Materials

RoundMat.c4d has been made editable to maintain the typestyle, and Caps_Round Set.c4d has not been made editable so you can inspect the Caps and Rounding settings.)

Open the Chapter 18>C4DFiles>ComplexSplines folder. In the HD.c4d file, the object was created by first making the H and D splines editable and choosing Functions>Connect. The eight-pointed star was then created and made editable, and Function>Connect was chosen again. The text object inside the Extrude NURBS was selected and the top and bottom points of the star were moved with the green move handle. In the Five Fragments.c4d file, the text spline was made editable and the points and tangents adjusted to create the fragmented forms. CINEMA 4D does fine with these types of nonoverlapping splines.

To create complex spline combinations that involve combining shapes and joining points, you are better off creating the complex outline in Illustrator, saving the file as Illustrator 8, and choosing Objects>Load Object to import the new spline into C4D. FancyM.c4d started with a spline created by using the pathfinder tool in Illustrator.

Figure 18.16 HD, Splines Adjusted in CINEMA

Figure 18.17 Complex Splines in Illustrator

Figure 18.18 Complex Splines Loaded into C4D

Figure 18.19 Five Fragments, Splines Adjusted in CINEMA

Figure 18.20 Dragon Queen, Polys Extruded

Figure 18.21 Text Object, Manipulated and Objects Added (Toothy A)

Figure 18.22 Cheese Boolean

Figure 18.23 Numbers on a String

Figure 18.24 S Beads

In Chapter 18>C4Dfiles, open the Stylized Text folder. These letters are readable but manipulated as 3D objects for the sake of novelty.

Now open the Chapter 18>C4DFiles>TypeAsArt folder. There's a place out there on the edge where type is less concerned with readability of words but becomes more about communicating as an art element.

Even if they are not readable, typographical elements can still have much to say. At this point, play becomes the work of the most serious designer. Those who are willing to let go, take chances, and spend many hours experimenting will go far in this genre.

Figure 18.26 Moonman Duplication

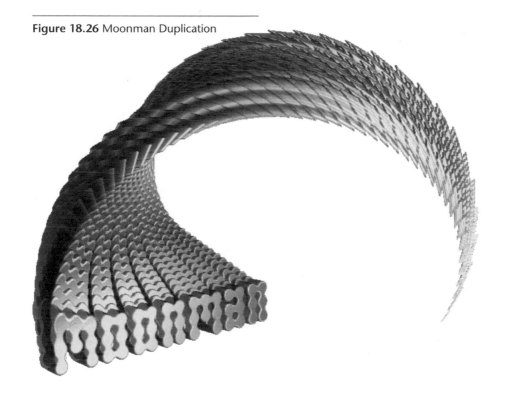

Figure 18.25 Flag for the Digital Age

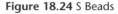

tinker.tinker. image. type. text and picture.
toon and hype. talk and listen. give and take.
speak your peace. communicate. s-p-e-l-l it out.
express yourself. backwards. frontwards. inside-out.
speak your doubt. assess the scene. send it to a
magazine. numbers. letters. paragraph. birth
announcement. epitaph. phrase and sentence.
page and graph. type a cry....a smile....a laugh.
write the essay. do the chore. letter to the edi-tor.
cut the excess. kern and track. proof the galley.
send it back. punctuation. hunt and peck. shove it
through the spelling check. illustration. flowing
chart. doodle on a broken heart. character and
dropping cap. mspace.nspace. tap.tap.tap!!!!!!!!!!!!
lowercase and superscript. drop the edits in the
crypt. file 13 and office shredder. cut the fat and
make it better. tinker. tinker.digital age. process
words. design the page. state your case and slay
the foe. hit return and spill the joe. watch the ink
fade in the flow. letters. pictures. there they go.
swept away like bitter birds. after all they're only words.

Figure 18.27 C Made Editable

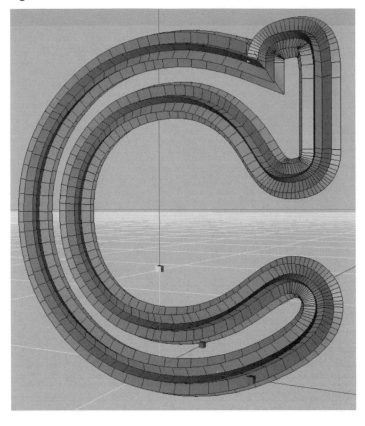

Figure 18.28 Festive C, Deformed type as Art Element

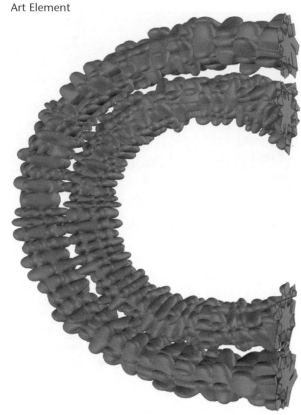

Figure 18.29 Exploded X

Once a text object has been made editable, or Functions>Current State to Object is performed on a NURBS object the text is a polygonal mesh and can be edited and deformed in many ways for out there on the edge letterforms. Also, don't overlook the possibilities of building letters from scratch for the creation of personal forms.

Figure 18.30 Cracked Glass

Animated Type Effects

Happy Trails to "U"

Step 1   Create a new C4D file (File>New) and save it as Trailing U.c4d (File> Save As). Set the project length to 200 frames.

Step 2   Select Spline>Add Text Spline. Type a capital U in the Text box and choose Impact or another chunky sans serif font.

Step 3   Choose NURBS>Extrude NURBS and drop the Text Spline inside. Name the Extrude NURBS object U DADDY.

Step 5   Control-drag 4 copies of U DADDY, naming them U CHILD 1, U CHILD 2, U CHILD 3, and U CHILD 4.

Step 6   Command-click (right-click) on U CHILD 1 and drag to New Expression> Xpresso Expression. Drag the names U DADDY and U CHILD 1 into the Xpresso Editor window. Enlarge the window of the U DADDY Node.

Step 7   Move the mouse to the blue input square of U DADDY and choose History Level. In the Attributes Manager, enter Relative Reference as Reference Mode, 10 as History Depth, and 10 as the History Level.

Step 8   Move the mouse to the red output square of U DADDY and choose Previous Position.

Step 9   Move the mouse on the blue input square of U CHILD 1 and choose Coordinates>Global Position>Global Position. With the U Child 1 Node selected, set the Reference Mode to Relative and enter 10 for History Depth. Draw a connector line from U DADDY's Previous Position port to U CHILD 1's Global Position port.

Step 10   Control-drag the Xpresso Expression tag from U CHILD 1 to U CHILD 2, U CHILD 3, and U CHILD 4.

Step 11   Use the Move tool to drag U DADDY around the screen, and you should see the U children follow. Animate U DADDY to move up and down across the screen. If you want the children to catch up with the daddy by the end of the animation, leave some frames at the end of the animation so there will be time for that to happen.

Step 12   Create a new material in a solid color. Make four copies of the material, and make each one increasingly transparent. Place the solid on U DADDY and the material copies on the U children, with U CHILD 1 being least transparent and U CHILD 4 being most transparent.

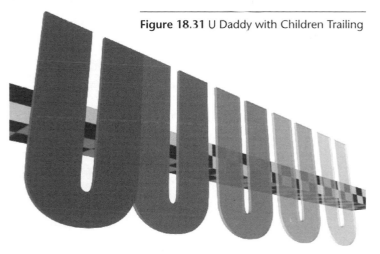

Figure 18.31 U Daddy with Children Trailing

■ *Springboard!* Make a more interesting version of this project by adding a Previous Rotation output port to the U DADDY Node. Then add an input port to the U CHILD 1 node for Coordinates>Global Rotation>Global Rotation. (If you make this addition to the initial Trailing U file, be sure to remove the tags previously copied to the children and copy the new edited tag so all the tags will be updated.) Any animation of position or rotation for U DADDY will be copied by the children as they follow along. See the examples on the DVD.

On the DVD: Don't miss the Chapter 18>EXTRA!EXTRA!>InDepth! folder. There are examples of creative type play, including Fun with Dingbats.

Figure 18.32 Dingbats1&2

Figure 18.33 Helvetica, reproduced by permission of Chris Cousins

19

Creating Elements for Motion Graphics

Figure 19.1

I f you said the words *motion graphics* a few years back, a flying logo for the nightly news or a sports spectacular might career across your mental TV screen. While those kinds of things are still a large part of the broad definition, motion graphics is becoming more inclusive, organic, and exciting minute by minute. Seen on a TV or movie screen, DVD, kiosk, or web site near you, these animations fill the viewing space with everything from type to video, stills and illustrated elements, 3D models and 2D layers, and bugs (a historical reference to the movie *Seven*, a fabulously rich example of movie title graphics). This chapter will emphasize making and animating interesting elements for motion graphics in CINEMA 4D.

A motion graphics animation can be done entirely in CINEMA 4D. The reality is, however, that compositing will usually be part of the process. What is compositing? It is the layering of imagery and sound into a finished movie. In the layering process are countless creative options for adding to, adjusting, and blending the original elements. The animation process is certainly a creative end in itself, but skillful compositing will showcase your 3D work even more. There are many excellent applications for compositing, but because there is a particularly well-developed partnership between CINEMA 4D and Adobe After Effects we'll use that to introduce compositing of 3D with other elements.

Design and Flow

Artistically, the same art elements and design principles used in fine art or graphic design apply to motion graphics. The difference is that these elements and principles now apply across time and interact with motion and sound. The design process has much more depth and complexity. As you begin to create motion graphics, these simple guidelines may help you create cohesive and interesting visuals.

- Variety and Contrast. Kindergarten art teachers sometimes tell their young artists to include something small, medium, and large in their designs. Look at motion graphics and you'll see the same principle at work. Variation of size, value, and other kinds of elements keep things interesting.

  You might ask yourself, "What kind of element do I need to contrast against what I already have?" For example, sharp, mechanical edges might be best showcased against soft, organic blur. Geometrics might call out for curvilinear elements, or large, slowly moving, heavy forms might need itchy-scratchy, rapidly twitching lines to complement them. In 3D animation, the word for variety is randomization.

- Unity. Repeating some kinds of elements across the frame and across time can act as "cosmic visual glue" to unify your design. Repeating typestyles, colors, shapes, sounds, and kinds of motion throughout the piece reinforces the sense of design purpose.

- Direction and Patterns of Flow. What directional paths or 3D forms will define the motion? Get out your real paper sketchbook. Use a real pencil and doodle rough storyboards, using little arrows and primitives to think about how things will move in space. Ask yourself the right questions before you begin, like "How will I use motion and speed to affect the viewer?" Think about how motion functions as a design element. Motion paths will serve as the structure of the design. Start analyzing motion graphics, and think about the implications of motion paths as they move across, toward you, and slowly away. Experiment with motion and countermotion. For example, if one type element enters from the left, another might enter from the right to meet it, but with slightly different timing or in a different color.

- Timing is everything. Listen to some jazz. Use your F-Curves to massage visual happenings over time. Syncopation, jitter, drumbeats, tension and repose, ebb, and smooth, slow flow are all inspiration for lively moving graphics.

- Stars, Supporting Cast, and Extras. Decide up front what elements will be the stars and secondary stars in your visual production. Then, find ways to "knock back" all the extras so that they provide richness, noise, and texture but don't compete with what you have to say. If all the colors in your design are intense, nothing will stand out. In motion graphics, an element floating almost transparently though the space can have much more artistic power than if all the elements are equally articulated. Use blur and transparency, dulling of color, and diminishing size to reduce the importance of subliminal layers.

- Purpose. Every element should have a reason to be in the space. It's tempting to throw in that cool 3D widget you just made. Even abstract objects or visual noise should contribute to the message. If not, use it another day when it is appropriate.

On the DVD: The C4D_AE.pdf in the Chapter 19>EXTRA!EXTRA!>InDepth will provide introductory After Effects skills to get you started with compositing.

The Rich 3D Space

Picture yourself on the ocean floor or far, far out in the universe. All the fish, sea-weed, and anemones (or stars, comets, and planets) don't exist on a plane at your fingertips, but randomly populate the Z space for as far as you can see. For the beginning motion graphics designer, that Z space can seem like an impossibly titanic space to fill. In this project, we'll look at ways to enhance the depth and richness of the 3D space.

Each of these short projects will create an element for the final piece named Planet Eternal. To make things challenging (and unified), let's limit our elements to spherical, circular, or round. Why challenging? The sphere is the ultimate over-used 3D symbol (in fact, one of the very first) so we'll be forced to give our C4D tools a creative workout and dig for ways to escape the cliché.

It helps our cause that the circle is a classic symbol for eternity, that circular motion evokes planetary orbit, and that the sphere (besides being obviously planetary) is a historical reference in computer-generated graphics.

Figure 19.2 Circa1982

Figure 19.3 Moved Clock Parts

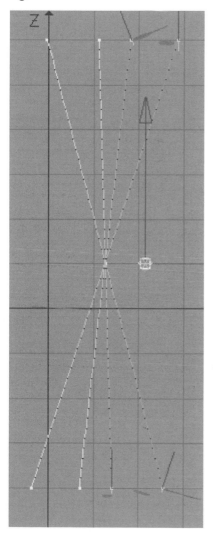

Clockworks

Step 1   Navigate to the folder Chapter 19>C4DFiles>Clockworks and open Clock-works.c4d. Save a working copy into your Models folder (File>Save As).

Step 2   In the top view, notice that two of the clock parts are far out in front of the Z space, –5000 and the other two are far back on the Z at 5000. At frame 0, set keyframes for these X and Z positions.

◆ *Tip:* You can set keyframes for all the clock parts at once. Shift-click to select all four clock parts inside CLOCKPARTS ONE, Command-click the X in P.X and the Z in P.Z, and drag to Animation>Add Keyframe.

Step 3   Go to frame 45, and move all the clock parts to opposite positions on the Z and X axes. In other words, the part that was at –5000 on the Z would move to 5000. (The easy way to do this is to delete the minus signs from in front of the originally minus values, and add minus signs to the originally positive values.) Set a keyframe for all the clock parts moved to their new opposing X and Z positions.

Step 4   In the Timeline, copy all the keys at frame 0 to frame 90 to create a back-and-forth motion.

Step 5   Now the fun begins. Change to View 1, and click the Play button. Make sure all the clock parts are showing in the F-Curve Manager, and tweak the curves to randomize the surging motions. If you want, animate some action on the Y axis, or add rotation to the clock parts.

Here's the truly cool thing. You can adjust the editor window view, the F-Curves, or the overall values of any attributes in the Attributes Coordinates on the fly while the animation is playing. Of course, if you want to keyframe changes over time, stop the play and set the current time for keyframing. While it's important that you know how to do this kind of thing manually, plugins like DiTOOLS, Jenna, and Loco are awesome tools for animating organic multiples in space.

On the DVD: Study the example file ClockParts.c4d in Chapter19>EXAMPLES and the movie ClockParts.mov in Chapter 19>MOVIES/STILLS.

Rendering a Single Layer for After Effects

All you have to do to render a single layer for After Effects compositing is check the Alpha check box on the Save page in Render Settings. The background will be clear, and the edges of the objects smooth. The Alpha checkbox creates a pre-multiplied alpha. In some video compositing situations antialiasing can cause an unexpected edge behavior, in which case you should choose Straight Alpha instead. Stay away from Floors, Skies, Backgrounds, or Foregrounds when rendering alpha channels, as these objects block out the entire channel.

Once you have a set of clock parts that has decent timing, render it with an alpha channel. If you want a more dense array of clock parts in the final After Effects composition, you could adjust the F-Curves and render several layers with differently timed files. In AE, you will be able to control the size and position of each set of clock parts but not the rotation of each individual object, so the rotation needs to be randomized in CINEMA 4D. If you wish, you can just make a copy of the clock parts and place a set on each side of the scene. Exactly where they are positioned is up to you. You'll need to be sure that the camera doesn't see one of the clock parts flying through the solid glass sphere we are about to add.

Figure 19.4 Spiny ClockPart's Axis Moved to Center

Creating the Centroid

Step 1   Continue working in the Clockworks file, but hide the CLOCKPARTS ONE objects by clicking the gray visibility dot to red.

Step 2   Choose a Sphere primitive, and give it a radius of 1000. Command-click on the Sphere and choose New Tag>Display Tag. In Tag Properties, choose Wireframe mode.

Step 3   Copy the the Spiny ClockPart object (inside CLOCKPARTS ONE) to the top of the list, make it editable by pressing the C key, and move its axis to its center. (You may need to use Frame Selected Elements to find it.)

Step 4   Select the Model tool, and enter 0, 0, 0 for the object's coordinates.

Step 5   Remove the object's animation tracks and keys in the timeline. (Make sure the Timeline lock is locked, and drag the Spiny Clockpart into the

Timeline. Drag a rectangular selection over the all the keys and type Delete.)

Step 6 Repeat Steps 3–5 with the Big Clock Part.

Step 7 Select the Sphere and choose Frame Selected Elements.

Step 8 Scale both elements so they fit the outside of the sphere, and rotate them as in Figure 19.5.

Step 9 Create a clear glass material with a refraction of 2 (the BhodiNUT Banji shader will do nicely), and place it on the Sphere.

Step 10 Make the two clockparts children of the Sphere.

Step 11 Animate the Sphere to rotate 360º on the H. Add some Pitch rotation if you like.

Step 12 Place a target camera in the scene and drag the central Sphere as the target. Set up the View in the upper left window, and position the camera so that everything looks good when you play the animation.

Step 13 Animate the camera to move in slowly so that the Centroid ends up being larger at the end of the animation.

Step 14 Go ahead and set up some basic lighting, and place a strong backlight behind the Centroid to show off the glass. You'll want to adjust the lighting after all the elements are placed and animated.

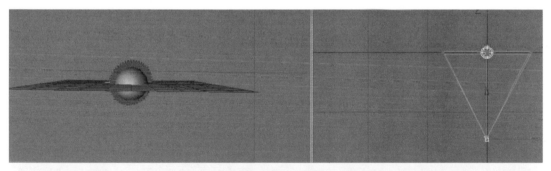

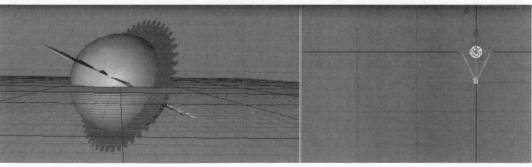

Figure 19.5 Target Camera's Starting (top) and Ending (bottom) Positions

Figure 19.6 Atom Array

Figure 19.7 Plane Position Behind the Atom Array

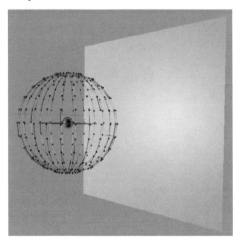

An Opposing Motion

Step 1 Choose another Sphere, and enter 12,000 for the radius. You may need to adjust the size depending on the position of your camera, which needs to be inside the outer sphere.

Step 2 Choose an Atom Array from the Array palette on the top menu. Drop the Sphere inside the Atom Array. With the Atom Array selected, enter a Cylinder Radius of 2, a Sphere Radius of 200, and Subdivisions of 15. Place the glass material on the Atom Array and animate it to rotate –720° on the H over the duration of the animation.

Step 3 Create a material with only the Luminance channel active. Edit the color to be a bright yellow green. Place it on the Atom Array.

Add More Depth

Step 1 Choose the top view and use the 2 key to back away from the outer Sphere. Let's create another visual layer behind the Atom Array using a plane that is 50,000m square. Place the plane as shown and rotate it 90° in pitch.

Step 2 In the Materials Manager, create a new Material and choose the Bhod-iNUT Tile shader. (In version 8.5 choose Texture>Surfaces>Tiles.) Choose the Spiral 1 tile. Edit it to be 20 percent global scale and only black and white. Edit the Color channel to be a light dull green and use multiply as the mix between the color and the Spiral shader. Turn on the Transparency channel and give it a high value of at least 90 percent. The background should be barely there.

Step 3 Place the material on the plane. If you need to, move the plane so that the spiral is well placed behind the Centroid.

Wrap Some Text

Step 1 If that rich 3D space is starting to get in your face, press Cmd+N (Ctrl+N) and create the type in a new, uncluttered file. Then copy it into the original file (Cmd+C/Ctrl+C then Cmd+V/Ctrl+V) and send it to 0, 0, 0.

Step 2 Create a text spline and choose a blocky, sans serif type. Type PLANET ETERNAL in caps three times, placing three or four bullets (Opt+8) between each set of letters.

Step 3 Create an Extrude NURBS object and place the text spline inside. Scale the text up so it fits across the screen.

Step 4 Choose a Wrap deformer and make it a child of the Extrude NURBS, placing it under the text spline in the hierarchy.

Step 5   Using the Scale tool, enlarge the Wrap Deformer object until all the type is visible. If necessary, further adjustments can be made with the deformer's orange interactive handles. The Text splines could also be scaled. Rename the Extrude NURBS as PLANET ETERNAL TEXT.

Step 6   You will also need to make the Extrude NURBS object editable and reposition it's axis in the center. In the Top view, use the grid to center the Extrude NURBS object around 0,0,0. Then use the Object Axis tool and the Move tool to center the axis. Choose the Object tool when you are finished. With the PLANET ETERNAL TEXT returned to the original file with the spheres, set all its coordinates to 0,0,0 and animate the type to rotate counterclockwise (-360) around the centroid.

Figure **19.8** Wrap Deformer on Text

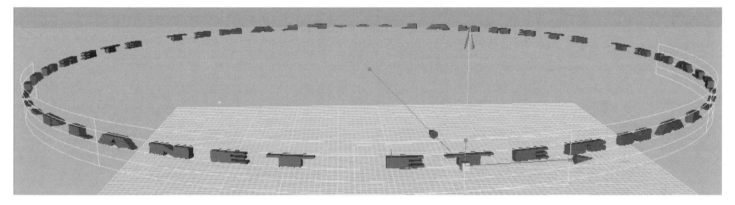

As your RAM allows, add a few more elements of your choice. See the example movie on the DVD in Chapter 19>MOVIES/STILLS>EternalPlanet.mov. In the example movie, two orbits of semitransparent clockparts (using the Arrange function) were added around the Centroid.

On the DVD: Study the example file EternalPlanet.c4d in Chapter 19>EXAMPLES.

The After Effects Plugin

The After Effects plugin is located in MAXON>CINEMA R8>ExchangePlugins> After Effects. You should install the proper version for your After Effects (5 or 5.5, Mac or PC). Run the .sit file and drop the plugin in your After Effects Plugins folder.

Setting Up A Multi-Pass Rendering

Step 1   In the Objects Manager, Shift-click to select the two clock parts that you used to make the metal rings around the Centroid sphere. Command-click (right-click) on one of them and drag down to New Tag>Compositing Tag. Click the Object tab, and select Object Buffer 1.

Step 2   In the Render Settings Save page, check the After Effects file check box.

Step 3   In the Render Settings, click Multi-Pass page. Use the Channels pull-down menu to the right to select which information you want rendered separately into AE. For this example, choose Object Buffer and click OK to Group ID 1, but notice all the other choices you have.

Step 4   Back on the Multi-Pass page, pull down to All in the Separate Lights menu, and 1 Channel in the Mode menu. Render the file.

Figure 19.9 The Multi-pass Page

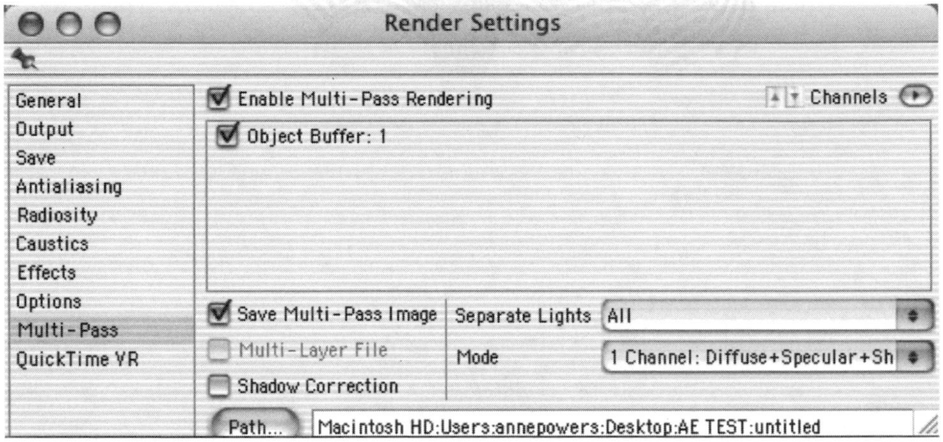

On the DVD: Working with Multi-Pass layers in After Effects is discussed in C4D_ AE.pdf in the Chapter 19>EXTRA!EXTRA!>InDepth folder on the DVD.

Explore the additional motion graphics projects in Chapter 19>EXTRA!EX- TRA!>InDepth. They contain embedded explanations in their Objects Managers or have accompanying instructional PDF files. The Planet Eternal project rotated elements in front of a stationary camera. The projects on the DVD use camera fly- throughs and other types of motion design.

20

The Creative Leap

Figure 20.1

This chapter is a collection of miscellany about becoming an artist using CINEMA 4D, leaving most of the technical how-to behind and going back to the jungle of digital art. Now that you are fairly comfortable with the toolset of C4D, it's time to address other parts of the process in becoming a 3D artist.

Finding Your Voice as an Artist

Here's some solid advice. Spend an afternoon surfing the web and visit as many 3D app user sites as you can. By typing 3D Animation and the names of 3D programs (including CINEMA 4D) in your favorite search engine you'll find plenty of user galleries. You may begin to notice that 95 percent of the work all looks alike. When you've grown tired of the same spaceships, generic models (that only show that someone learned to use a 3D tool), and lookalike characters, sit back and do some soul searching. The truth is, anyone with a lot of patience can learn to make 3D worlds and animate. Compelling 3D work is born only to those who push beyond technical skills. Why spin your wheels in the same rut with everyone else when you can make the creative leap into a personal vision?

Make your own list of the things that distinguished the truly memorable work, for example:

- Chances are that the artist was taking a quirky, offbeat look at the subject.

- The artist made an effort to escape the sameness. Models with a new stylistic twist, color schemes that inspire emotions, or a fresh look at an everyday story will stand out from the crowd.
- Often outstanding 3D work showcases beautiful texturing, coloring, or rendering algorithms that give the work a unique look or personal style. The artist may have put a lot of effort into escaping that too clean and perfect look so prevalent in beginners' 3D work.
- Even if they were very short, movies had compelling and well-articulated stories with good timing.
- The artist used psychological content. In animation, even a cube can have a psychological state and today's animation world is highly populated with interesting oddities of personality.

Then, as you aspire to break away from the pack, ask some questions of yourself:

- What subjects outside art and animation am I into? (Great animators are usually open-minded information sponges, interested in everything. Passion and knowledge about a subject or topic, well supported by art and application skills, is the formula for greatness in 3D.)
- What kind of art do I really enjoy? Do I like to construct geometrics, paint organically, or decorate with meticulous detail? (Find ways to incorporate the things you enjoy into your work.)
- How can I increase my observation of the world and personalities around me? (Take mental notes about the characters that you meet every day, and then transfer those characteristics to a cube.)

The World Outside the Realism Box

It's a buzzword already turned cliché, but thinking outside the box is still a good idea. Just because today's 3D tools enable us to closely approximate physical realism does not mean that in itself is the final goal. Think back to your tour of 3D user sites and you'll remember that many of artists seem satisfied to stop at making something look just like it looks in real life. That is an admirable technical skill that all modelers and animators should have, but just looking real doesn't necessarily give a model or scene artistic integrity and excitement.

Here are some ways to go beyond the technically correct model:

- Push the envelope when shaping models, making a conscious effort to create more inventive forms or add unusual details to the model.
- Combine forms and systems that don't normally live together in real life.
- Use BodyPaint (or another raster program) to create unexpected or more organic surfaces.

Figure 20.2 Resident Alien by Eni Oken

- Distort space and perspective by using small camera focal lengths or placing highly refractive transparent surfaces between the camera and the scene.

- Use rendering tools such as Cel Renders or Sketch and Toon to create new looks for a scene.

- Postprocess your animations in rotoscoping applications such as Studio Artist, or treat your animations to some filtering in a compositing program like After Effects.

- Layer your scenes in post processing to create new realities.

Figure 20.3 Tim Borgmann

Figure 20.4 Sketchbook Pages

Walk Away from Your Computer

Whaa? You heard right. Take a day (or even better a week) and meander, unplugged, through the rest of your world. It is there that you will find the inspiration, ideas, visual richness and content, which are the most important part of what you will ultimately do with 3D. Turn your eyeballs on high and get your sketchbook and #2 pencil out. Chase the dust bunnies out of the forgotten corners, and search high and low for a story. Sketch everyday scenes and objects, then brainstorm on what would happen if they came to life in a world that knows no boundaries . . . the world of animation.

Physics Doesn't Live Here Anymore

No boundaries. While lots of people develop some facility with the tools of 3D, not all have mentally escaped the real world. Surprise! The rules no longer apply. The laws of nature no longer demand to be obeyed and gravity has taken a vacation. In the 3D world, objects can pass through each other, float unsupported through space, or change form from solid to rubbery to gaseous in an instant. Linear perspective can be disregarded. Study Cubism, the impossible perspectives of Escher, and the dripping clocks of Salvador Dali for inspiration.

Challenge Reality and Play with Space

- Play with scale. Things no longer have to be the size they are in real life. Lilliputian figures can shuffle across a normal-sized coffee table.

- Rethink materials. Make a cup out of fur and ballet dancer out of glass. Animate native material into impossible mutations.

- Incorporate the pop-up book idea. Create walls in the 3D space, then punch holes for the camera to move through, or animate objects to pop out from behind the façade to surprise the viewer.

Figure 20.5 Floating Landscape 1

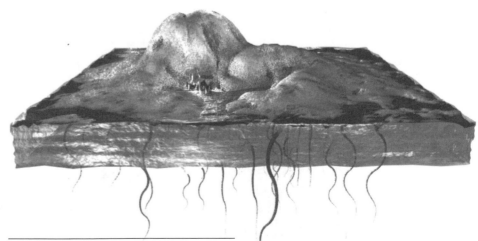

Figure 20.6 Floating Landscape 2

- Float landscapes in mid-air or saw blocky chunks out of bodies of water.
- Make books that have animated textures moving on their pages.

Objective or Subjective?

An objective treatment of the inhabitants in your world focuses on making them look as much as possible like they look in the real world. Line for line, freckle for freckle, the artist aims for detached representation. In a subjective approach, the artist takes liberties, adjusting or inventing forms, colors, and texturing to express feelings about the model as a subject. Whether you choose to model and texture objectively or subjectively, there are many ways to introduce the artistic twist. Surrealistic relationships of objects in your scene, the story itself, psychologically engaging personalities, humor, fascinating timing, and elegant staging are among many elements of art in the 3D world. Be sure to see the Chapter 20>EXTRA! EXTRA!>References folder for pointers to great examples of the animator's art.

Put Your E-Toys to Work

Keep a digital camera and/or a digital video camera with you whenever possible. Inspirations are out there for the taking. Become a surface collector, capturing cracked layers of faded paint, hardened drips of whitewash, sunbleached sign

Figure 20.7 Aqua Head Box

Figure 20.8 Digital Photos

Figure 20.9 Wood Type Digital Photo

Figure 20.11 Target Wall Texture

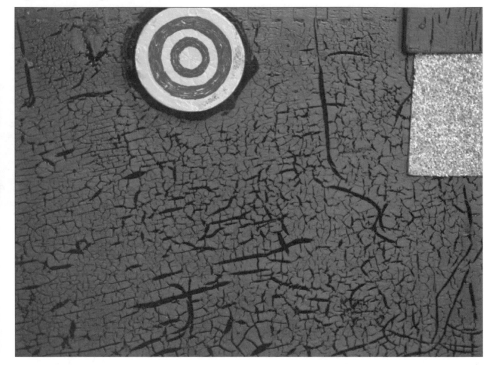

Figure 20.10 3D Texture Found on the Back of a Truck

letters, and any other details to add to your material layers. A small digital sound recorder is also a great traveling partner for capturing and creating sounds. A Proscope (available at www.apple.com) accesses unseen microscopic imagery and works on Mac or Windows.

Make Some Grunge

Get out your calendar and schedule a studio day. Gather real materials like paint, plaster, wallpaper paste, paints, glues, and sticks, and spend the day making thick and textural messes on surfaces. Scrape thick impastos and invade the surface with

Figure 20.12 Rough Paint

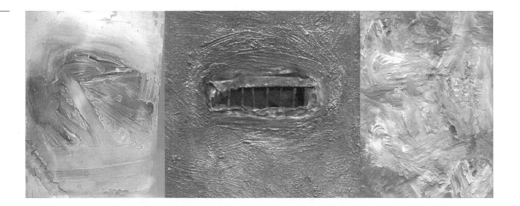

scratches and dents. Use paint and stains to intensify the textures. A few days later after the surfaces have dried (your scanner will love you for being patient), scan the surfaces. If you have a good digital camera you won't have to wait as long. Just light the surfaces from the side and shoot. Save these organic image maps in a Library.

Figure 20.13 Spray Insulation on Hardware Cloth

Famous 3d Saying: "It's All in the Details" —Anonymous

Photographing Existing Textures

- Make sure your shots are not out of focus from being too close. Use a Macro setting if you need to.

- Be sure there is plenty of illumination. Nothing degrades digital photography like a lack of light. Existing textures should be shot with side lighting, as frontal lighting would flatten them.

- Shoot 300 dpi TIFFs whenever possible, so you'll have adequate resolution for close-up textures.

- Try to face the surface flat-on, with as little perspective as possible. (If you can't escape the angled perspective you can use Adobe Photoshop's Crop tool to correct the perspective.)

Become a Scrap Rat

The current scrapbooking rage has a lot of crossover application to 3D. Go to a scrapbooking store and you'll be inspired. The collage mentality leads to rich textures and backgrounds for 3D. In a shoe box or filing cabinet, collect treasures—tags and torn papers, strings and ribbons, handwriting and doodles, stationery items, Want to create textures that have a genuine look? Stain papers in teabags. Think about how scrapbooking activities like punching decorative holes in paper, embossing, using decorative grommets, stitching, or staples, and dusting with glitters and metallics could translate into 3D forms and surfaces.

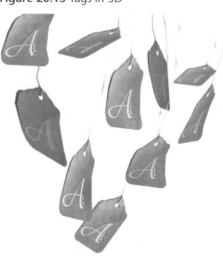

Figure 20.15 Tags in 3D

Figure 20.14 Scrapbook Examples

Create Libraries of Digital Details

The more collections of cool things you have already made, the faster your workflow will go.

Mechanical parts, splines, symbols, patterns, confetti, interesting small objects, light fixtures, architectural details, character accessories, face parts, colorful game pieces, letters, decorative 3D forms, color palettes, fonts, and materials in easily accessed and well organized Libraries will speed up your work and enable you to quickly add more interest to scenes.

On the DVD: See examples of these in GOODIES>LIBRARIES.

Figure 20.16 Charm Library

Figure 20.17 Flower Swag

The Holistic Artist

The best digital artists often make nonvirtual art too and find ways to integerate or cycle the nondigital into the digital (and vice versa). Bring that video, sculpture, painting, or drawing into your 3D world and use it as a background or wrap

Figure 20.18 Green Box

Figure 20.19 Baby Squares

Figure 20.20 Wall Piece 1

it around a model. Turning the process around, use a printout of your 3D scene as inspiration for a large painting or sculpture.

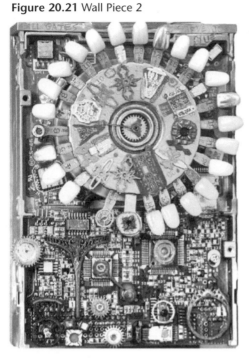

Figure 20.21 Wall Piece 2

Optimize Your Creative Time

Everyone has times when their mental wheels just won't stop spinning. For some, it's when they first wake up. Once you've identified your best creative time, don't sit down at the computer and get bogged down in process. Instead, crash in a comfortable place with your sketchbook and pencil. (Sometimes colored pencils, gel pens, or watercolors can add to the creative flow.) Let the personal brainstorming session happen away from the computer.

Become An Art Historian

On your way to finding your own style, it's helpful to study other artists, illustrators, filmmakers, and architects of the present and past. In analyzing the work of others, lessons about design and storytelling begin to sink in almost subconsciously. It's fun to add depth and interest to your work with historical references. You may find yourself developing affinities for stylistic flavors from the past that may weave themselves into the tapestry of your own style.

Cultivate Efficient Work Habits

- Back up animation projects often and in several different locations and volumes. Things happen.
- Create a structured organizational system for everything you use and create in 3D. (See Chapter 17.) You should be able to go right to Models, Sounds, Image Maps, Splines, Resources, Fonts, and all the other bits and pieces.
- Use logical titles that will be easy to find in a systemwide search later (for example, when you are trying to find a model rather than make it from scratch all over again). Titles like Number Two are as good as lost in space forever.
- Keep a Calendar and Task list to keep projects on track.
- Learn where to find references. The name of an object typed in Google Image will bring up thousands of visual references. These images are copyright protected, but you can check details like the colors of a parrot or the number of legs on a squid.

Storyboards, Thought Charts, Animatics

A storyboard is a collection of still sketches that show key stages in the development of a story. Ideally, the drawings communicate the feeling of the moment without being too labored over or sacred. The more time that is spent on a storyboard, the less willing one might be to rip it up and replace it with a better idea. Storyboards can be rather thumbnail in size, but in studios they are often letter size (8 1/2"x 11").

Thought Charts are verbal plans that state what each character is thinking in key frames. These are a valuable aid in creating characters that appear to be alive and acting out their own desires, rather than being puppeteered by an animator.

An Animatic is a rough approximation of the finished animation. It can begin as a slideshow of the storyboards, but can include sections of rough or close to finished animation as the process unfolds. The animatic is structured on the actual timeline of the finished piece, so the actual music and sound may be in the background.

Most animators keep some sort of Archive, that holds the collected notes, storyboards, and resource files for a single project and tells the story of the project's development. Be sure to write down important settings in case something has to be recreated.

Figure 20.22 Storyboards

3D as a Day Job

Figure 20.23 Cards

Every aspiring artist has surely been encouraged away from art and toward more "responsible" fields by a parent, relative, or friend who sees art and animation as immature play rather than legitimate work. Because the animation field is inherently fun and requires playful thought, it may appear to lack the seriousness of other grown-up careers. In fact, the vocation requires long hours, hard work, dedication, and mountains of academic study. If you find that you are so passionate about working in 3D that you can't wait to get up in the morning and begin again, there's a good chance it could be a viable career for you.

On the DVD: As your 3D skills grow, you'll be designing increasingly complex worlds. Without some basic understanding of color theory and the principles of design, you'll be creating with a limited set of tools. See Chapter 20>EXTRA!EXTRA!>References for resources to jump-start for your creativity and design skills. The more you learn about traditional art, film, and design, the more exciting and cohesive your work will be.

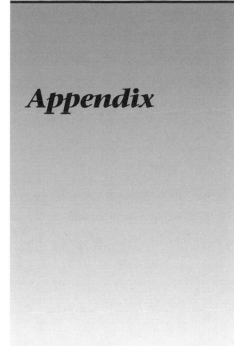

Appendix

Figure A.1

If you are new to CINEMA 4D, this reference section covers what you need to know now about general use of the application. As always, see the manual for details and further explanatory text. The documentation disk that shipped with your copy of C4D has the manual in PDF form. Install it if you want to have the manual always available under the Help menu.

Basics of the C4D Interface

Fire up your engines! Start CINEMA 4D by clicking the C4D icon in the dock or the original application icon. You can also drag a C4D file onto either icon. Although double-clicking a C4D file will *usually* open the application, there are times when that's not the best way. Quit with File>Quit or Command-Q, saving at that point if you need to. However, the best saving habit is to save immediately upon starting a project and update with a quick Command-S every time you stop to think. An important twist on saving is when you have any texture that you have imported (apart from the shaders inside CINEMA 4D, for example a photographic image map you imported). It is necessary to use *Save Project* if you want the textures to stay with the project so that it will render properly. (Save Project creates a nice folder for you and tucks everything inside.)

In the default layout, there is a main menu across the top, one down the left side of the main window, and another smaller menu at the top of each View Panel, sometimes called the Editor window (the one where you see the objects).

A new view panel can be added any time by choosing *Window>New View Panel* from the top menu. Each View window has a unique menu, so it can have separate settings for angle of view and display style. Go to *View>Panels* on at the top of each view for a variety of pre-designed panel layouts. If you want to view your scene from a different angle, or from *perspective, top, side and front simultaneously* use these key shortcuts to switch from view to view. (Or choose them from the View menu in each View.)

- **F1**   View 1 Perspective
- **F2**   View 2 Top
- **F3**   View 3 Right Side
- **F4**   View 4 Front
- **F5**   All Views

To change the way objects are drawn in a view, choose *Display* from that View's menu. Gouraud shading roughly previews the general effect textures and lighting, but Wireframe or Isoparm displays are much faster and may be all you need when modeling. When working with complex motion in animation, box display may be necessary. Wireframe and Isoparm displays let you see into or through the object, making it easier to select buried points. When modeling, it can be helpful to make a new View Window and set one window to Gouraud display (so you can clearly see the surface), but change the display of the other window to Wireframe or Isoparm (so you can easily see and select points on the mesh). You can also assign a specific display style to just one object in a scene by assigning a Display Tag (Right-click on the object, choose *NewTag>Display Tag*, click *Use Display Mode*, and choose the display style from the pull-down menu.)

The *Manager Windows* are specialized work areas that house the controls for the major processes in CINEMA 4D. Most manager windows have a menu specific to the work of that window. Be aware that for shortcuts (such as Command-A) to work in a Manager window, it must be the *active one*. It's a good habit to click on an empty area of a window to activate it before working.

Figure A.2 View Menu, View Window and Manager Windows

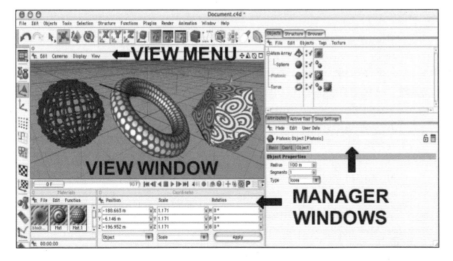

Changes in Version 8 from Previous Versions

Former CINEMA 4DXL users should note that it is no longer necessary to double click the *Edit Object Icon* to open a window for editing a new object. The information is now automatically available in the *Attributes Manager*, available by default underneath the Objects Manager. Objects can now be *Shift-selected* in the Editor or the Objects Manager, allowing for multiple selections to which settings or transformations can be applied simultaneously. For example, ten separate lights could be reduced in brightness at the same time by Shift-selecting (or dragging a rectangular marquis over) the lights and turning down the brightness of *one*. F-curves provide a more streamlined and powerful way to control animation keys. See the CINEMA 4D manual and the Addendum PDFs for a complete list of changes in versions 8 through 8.5.

The World Grid and 3D World Geography

In C4D, Y is up and is the vertical axis of the 3D world, or the height. X is the horizontal axis or width, and Z goes away from you into space representing the depth of the space. It will also help to memorize the colors of the axes in CINEMA 4D. You may get turned around at times and not be able to see the labels, and the colors may be your only signpost.

Successfully navigating the 3D world requires familiarity with the geography of the 3D space.

The world grid is a default construction plane, a subdivided grid that helps you get your bearings and imparts a sense of *where* you are placing objects. The green, red and blue arrows in the world grid represent the world axes. The position of any *object axis* or even *any single point* in the world can be defined by its coordinates, or *numeric values on each world axis*.

The origin of the world is where the X, Y and Z axes coincide; the location with coordinates of 0,0,0. The diagram in Figure A.3 shows the direction of positive and negative values for each axis. It may seem strange that negative Z (–Z) comes to the front and positive Z (+Z) goes to the back, but that's the way it is!

Figure A.3 The World Grid and World Axes

Figure A.4 XY, ZY and XZ Planes

In the modeling process, it may help to imagine the invisible planes defined by any two axes. For instance, the world's default construction plane lies on the XZ Plane.

There are several ways you can manipulate the camera through which you are viewing the 3D space. One way is to use these hotkeys to navigate the view.

1 + Mousedrag	*Moves* the camera from side to side or top to bottom
2 + Mousedrag	*Moves* the camera in and out

◆ *Tip:* You can use either the numbers on the regular keyboard or the numeric keyboard.

Figure A.5 Viewport Icons

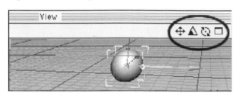

Figure A.6 Distorted Perspective

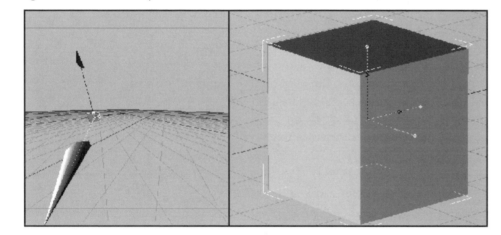

◆ *Tip:* If you are a former CINEMA 4DXL user, you may remember that the 2 key zoomed the camera and that Command-1 allowed you to move the camera in and out without perspective distortion. You can still use Command-1 in the same way until you break your old habit, but the 2 key will now move the camera in and out with normal perspective.

2 + Command Key+ Mousedrag	*Zooms* the camera (changes focal length)
3 + Mousedrag	*Rotates* the camera, or *tumbles* the view

To get back to where you started choose *Edit>Frame Default* from the menu over the view.

When using the 3 key to rotate the camera, it's important to note that the camera rotates around the 0,0,0 point in space. However, if an object is selected, the camera will rotate around that object. If a group of objects is selected, the camera will rotate around the axis of the group. The Command and 3 key maneuvers the view in a Dutch tilt.

The icons at the top right corner of the View correspond to the 1,2,3 and F5 keys. *Click and drag on* the first three symbols to see how they work.

It's easy to end up in a distorted perspective without knowing *how* you got there and *how* to get out! When *Command-2* is used to Zoom the camera, it doesn't *move* the camera up and back but changes the *focal length* of the camera lens. Just as a Telephoto or Wideangle Fisheye lens on a real camera exaggerates and bizarrely twists the scene, a virtual lens change will distort camera's perspective.

To maintain normal perspective, *move* the camera in and out by using the 2 key and dragging the mouse. For artistic purposes, you may *want* the distorted effects of a wide angle or telephoto lens like in Figure A.6. Use Command-2 and drag the mouse (or on a two button mouse Right-click with the 2 key and drag the mouse) to Zoom the lens for flattened or stretched perspective.

The Lost and Found Department!

When first learning CINEMA 4D, you will occasionally *lose things*. Some typical situations are listed below, with tips on how to get out of them!

• If manager windows or views disappear, or your layout is suddenly in general havoc, choose *Window>Layout>Reset Layout* to restore the default layout.

• It can be easy to get the 3D world twisted around into a weird and unwanted perspective. To start over at the default perspective view, choose Edit>Frame Default from the menu of that view.

• Occasionally objects are *completely* lost in space. If you see their name in the Objects Manager, they are probably still in there *somewhere*. Rather than hunt around in space manually, choose Edit>Frame Scene from the menu over the view.

The number of "undo levels" can be set in preferences. In C4D, *Command-Z* steps back as many levels as you have set, and the *Redo* command *Command-Y* steps forward. The default level is 10.

Working with Objects

Each Object created in C4D is "born" in the center of the 3D world where the X, Y and Z-axes coincide at coordinates 0, 0, and 0. Each object has its own set of axes, so if the object is *tilted* those axes are no longer oriented in space *as when they were born*, and no longer *match the world axes in orientation*.

To *select* an object for editing or transforming, you can click on the object itself in the Editor window. A better habit is to click on the name of the object in the Objects Manager. All the transform tools (Move, Scale and Rotate) can be used to select objects or their inner elements in the Editor window. For more complex selections, the selection tools in the top menu can be used.

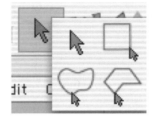

Figure A.7 Selection Tools

The Objects Manager

Welcome to Inventory Central! CINEMA 4D's Objects Manager is the bin where all the objects in your 3D world are listed by name. More importantly, objects are listed in a meaningful diagram called a *Hierarchy* that visually communicates the *relationship* of one object to another. It will be clear to you when objects are in Groups or Parent/Child relationships.

In the Objects Manager, object *names* are critically important for recognition, selection and organization. Taking the time to rename generic elements like splines and primitives is a necessary habit that will pay big dividends later when you attempt to manage large projects.

"Pool Ball 8," "Mars," and "Eyeball" will provide more information than "Sphere," "Sphere," and "Sphere."

Take a look at the dots and checks in the column to the right of the object names. When clicked twice to a red state, the top dot turns off the *visibility* of

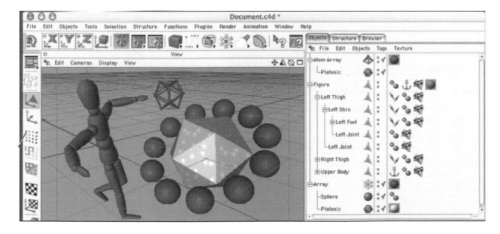

Figure A.8 A Hierarchy in the Objects Manager

an object in the Editor window. The bottom dot does the same thing for visibility in final rendering. The visibility will be that of the object's parent if the dots are gray. A green dot means the object will be visible even if its parent is *invisible*. The check marks activate and deactivate *deformers* and *generators*. (Deformers and Generators are tools you will use later to modify the shape and state of objects or primitives.)

Tags (including the tags for textures) have their own icons in the third column to the right of the object name. You can also drag and drop these from one object to another in the Objects Manager. To access a contextual menu of tags in the Objects Manager, Command-click (Or Right Mouse button) on the object and choose the tag you want from the New Tag sidecar menu.

The Attributes Manager

The *Attributes Manager* is where you will find all the editable characteristics about an object *currently selected* in the Objects Manager. It is here where you will go to enter or modify all information about an object. You can even set animation key frames in the Attributes Manager by Command-clicking the title word or letters next to a value and dragging over to Animation>Add Keyframe.

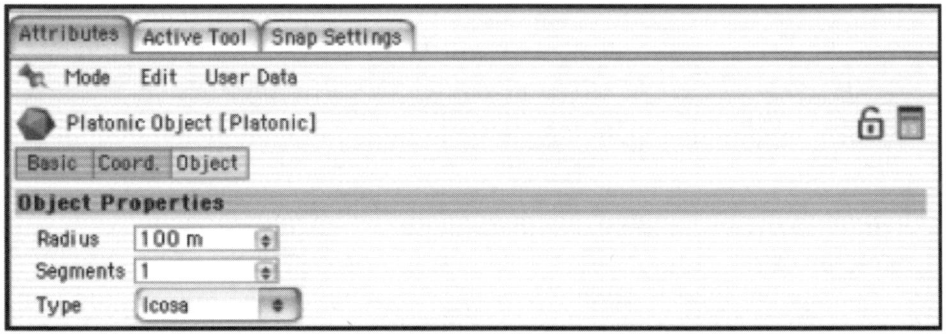

Figure A.9 The Attributes Manager

```
Attributes  Active Tool  Snap Settings
   Mode   Edit   User Data
   Platonic Object [Platonic]                    🔓 🖻
  Basic  Coord.  Object
  Object Properties
  Radius    100 m      ⊜
  Segments  1          ⊜
  Type      Icosa      ⊜
```

The Model and Object Tool

Figure A.10 L>R, Model, Points, Edge, Polygons, Object Axis, Texture and Make Editable Tools

Figure A.11 Model Tool, Object Tool

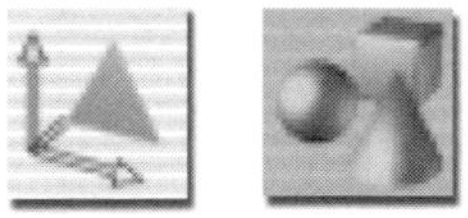

First let's talk about the Model tool in relation to the Points, Edges, Polygons, Axis and Texture tools. Use the Model tool when you want the action of the Move, Scale or Rotate tools to apply to the *Object as a whole*. However, if you want to *get under the hood* to edit elements that make up the object, switch to the Points, Edges, Polygons, Axis or Texture tool to use the Move, Scale or Rotate tools on those respective elements. You'll have to make the object editable (just type the "C" key!) before being able to access them!

Now for some discussion on using the Model tool versus the Object tool. Both of these will allow the moving, scaling and rotation of whole *objects*. When you are making models, *use the Model tool*. When animating though, *The Object tool* should be used to avoid problems, particularly with scaling. The Object tool scales an object's *Axes*, to which CINEMA 4D refers when animating.

Transform Tools

You will be reaching for these transform tools often to perform the most basic changes on objects in your 3D world. With them you can move, scale or rotate objects and limit those actions to happen on specific axes.

Hotkeys for basic transform tools: Move is the 4 key (no modifiers), Scale the 5 key and Rotate the 6 key. Hold down the Hotkey and *drag the mouse in the editor window*. (This is a temporary shortcut that works while the key is held down, so it does not change the tool in the palette.)

The action of a tool can be limited to one axis. The Move, Scale and Rotate tools have color coded X,Y and Z Axes. (X is red, Y is green, and Z is blue) Mouse on a single axis, and the manipulation will be constrained to that axis. (Figure A.14) For free manipulation, just drag your mouse in the gray area of the window. An alternate method for constraining movement is to use the X, Y and Z symbols

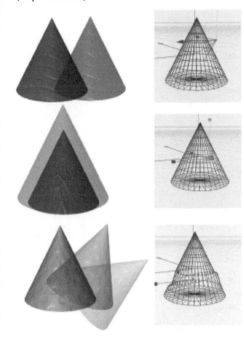

Figure A.12 Move, Scale, and Rotate (Top>Bottom)

Figure A.13 *Left:* Basic Transforms *Below:* Move, Scale, Rotate.

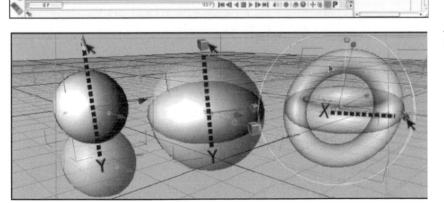

Figure A.14 Constraining Transform Tools

Figure A.15 Object Axis

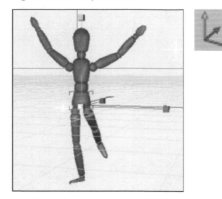

Figure A.17 Object Coordinates System Icon

Figure A.18 World Coordinates System Icon

Figure A.19 The Coordinates Manager

Figure A.20 HPB System

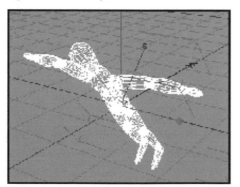

on the top palette. If one of these is *locked* (no line around it), the object will not be able to move on that axis. If you want to move the object only along one axis, then the symbol for that axis should unlocked. (It *should* have a line around it!)

Each object has its own system of axes placed by default in the center of the object when it is created. These axes are used as an orientation point by the Move, Scale and Rotate tools, and the coordinates of an object's axis define the single point on the object referred to in matters of positioning and

Figure A.16 Make Editable, Model and Object Axis Tools

movement. You will often need to move the object's axis either within or completely outside the object using the Object Axis Tool. For example, a planet rotating around the sun would have its axis, the point of rotation, at the center of the sun.

The object's axis is *independent* of the world axes, and you can decide which set of axes to use. Click the Object Axis icon to switch to the World axes.

The Coordinates Manager is where numeric values for position, size, scale, and rotation may be input. In addition to entering typed values, you can quickly change the values by dragging on the small black arrows by each input box (drag upward for larger increments and downward for smaller ones), or by single-clicking the arrows with the mouse to nudge tiny changes. If you have a wheel mouse you can spin the values. Don't confuse this separate manager with the Coordinates panel in the Attributes Manager, where you can Command- or right-click on the names of values and set key frames from the Contextual menu.

Rotation in the Coordinates Manager is entered in plus or minus values for H or Heading, P or Pitch, and B or Bank. Heading rotates around the Y axis, Pitch around the X axis and Bank around the Z axis. Visualizing those terms in relation to an airplane may help you get your bearings.

These are the basic working elements in CINEMA 4D:

- **Points are** also called control points or vertices, defined by their position in the X,Y,Z space.
- **Splines** are lines in space, series of points connected by lines that can be straight or curved. Splines are invisible in rendering.
- **Spline Primitives** are splines of various shapes available in the palette.

- **Edges** are single sides of a Polygon, each connected by two points.
- **Polygons** are closed planes formed by points connected by lines, usually connected in a mesh.
- **Parametric Primitives** are mathematically defined basic 3D forms.

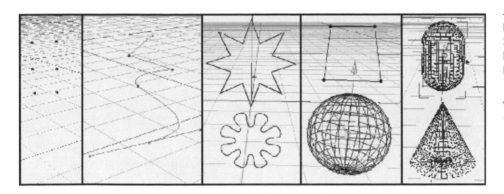

Figure A.21 Basic Elements: L>R Points, Spline, Spline Primitive, Polygon (and Edges), Spherical Polygon Mesh, Parametric Primitive

◆ *Tip:* Choose Selection>Convert Selection to switch a selection of one type of element to another. For example, convert a selection of Points to a selection of Edges, or a selection of Polygons into a selection of Points.

Rendering

- For a quick test render of the editor window, just type Control-R.
- If you want to render and save a still picture, type Shift-R. After the rendering is complete, in the Pictures Window choose File>Save Picture As>(format of your choice). Use the finder to title the file and navigate to where you want to save it. Click Save.
- If you want the picture to be bigger, choose Render>Render Settings and click on the Output tab. Drag down on the box next to Resolution and set the size to 640x480 NTSC or other desired size. Close the Render Settings Window and type Shift-R again to render.
- If the edges have the jaggies, choose Render>Render Settings and click on the General tab. Drag down the box next to Antialiasing and choose Best.

Rendering an Animation

- Choose Render>Render Settings, click on the General tab and choose Filter>Animation. Select the Output tab. Drag down on the box next to Frame and choose all frames.
- Still in Render Settings, click on Save in the left-hand column. Click the Path button and use the finder to title the movie and navigate to where you want to save it. Click Save. Under Format, choose QuickTime movie. Close the Render Settings Window.
- Type Shift-R on the keyboard to render the animation in the Picture Viewer. The animation will automatically be saved to the location you specified.

◆ *Tip:* Important! This is a definite gotcha! If you forget to set the Save/Format settings to QuickTime or set up navigation to a folder created for Individual frames, many annoying TIFF files will be piled on your desktop by default. This can be a real ordeal to clean up, so make a mental note to check those Save>Format settings every time you render an animation. Better yet, create a Template.c4d file with Render Settings set to output a QuickTime movie. Place the template in the same folder with the current version of C4D and it will open every time you work with those settings.

Previewing an Animation

From the top menu, select Render>Make Preview. In the input box, click your choices for the kind of preview you want. The progress box at the bottom left of the main window will show you the rendering progress, and then a QuickTime window will open. Click the Play button. Choose File>Save if you want to save the QuickTime preview movie.

Chose Preferences>Edit>Viewport to turn on Render Safe (the borders of your final rendering determined by the format choice in your render settings), Action Safe or Title Safe (for TV output) guidelines.

Customization

Figure A.22 Layout Icon

You can place any elements of the C4D interface anywhere you wish, and then save your redesigned workspace as a custom layout (Window>Layout>Save Layout As), and place the file inside the Library>Layout folder which resides in the current CINEMA 4D folder. It will then be accessible in the Layout icon at the top of the Left Palette.

If you want to float a window and be able to move it freely around the workspace, click the pushpin in the upper left corner of any window and drag over to choose Undock. If you click the red close button on the window, it will disappear from the interface. To bring it back, choose the name of the window from the Window menu.

If you want to make a Manager window share a space with another window, and reside as a tab in the same tab bar, drag the window's pushpin and drop it on the pushpin of the target window. Dragging a window's pushpin against the edge of another window will result in a new docking position. To change the height or width of a window, mouse on its border and drag with the double-sided cursor.

To restore the layout to the original layout, choose Window>Layout>Reset Layout.

Click on the top icon of the left-hand tools palette to choose a layout appropriate for the task at hand. CINEMA 4D has several already built in that are set up for specific tasks, like using MOCCA or BodyPaint 3D.

Right-click on a Palette to access a contextual menu for custom editing. Choose Edit Palettes and you will be able to drag and drop icons from one palette to another, or delete palettes.

Choose Window>Layout>Command Manager and you'll see a complete list of all CINEMA 4D's commands. Select the command for which you want to assign a key combination. Click in the Assign Text box and type the short-cut. Click the green check to the right of the text box and the new shortcut will appear in the *Current* box above. (You'll get a message if the key combination you requested is already in use.) As an example of how shortcuts can make your life easier, long-time Photoshop users might capitalize on their lifetime Command-D habit by assigning it to Deselect All.

Other Bits of Information

To restore CINEMA 4D to its original factory settings, throw away the CINEMA 4D.prf file in the current C4D Prefs folder. Don't be afraid! The next time you use CINEMA 4D, a clean prefs file will be created automatically. You can explore the deeper meaning of the many preferences settings in your manual. Preference settings will stay in place from file to file, until you change them or restore the original settings. One note: If you plan to use a Graphics Tablet (which is a must have if you plan to use BodyPaint 3D), better head right into Preferences and check the Graphics Tablet checkbox, or you'll see some strange cursor behavior.

Project Settings (Top Menu>Edit>Project Settings) apply only to the current scene. Here you can set a frame rate appropriate for your output, enter the first frame of the animation in the Minimum box and the last frame in the Maximum box.

If you are working on a Mac, buy a two-button wheel mouse if at all possible. Right-clicking will bring up contextual menus and streamline your workflow greatly! If you stick with the regular Mac mouse, holding down the Command (Apple) key does the same as right-button mousing. If your mouse has a wheel, use it to scroll sliders, enter values in numerical input boxes, and move in and out of the editor window.

CINEMA 4D plays cross-platform very nicely. With just the usual differences listed below, there is little difference between the Mac and PC versions of CINEMA 4D.

MAC	PC
Command	Control
Opt	Alt
Command-click	Right-click

The Selection Filter allows you to turn the *selectibility* of certain subcategories of objects on and off. This applies to the Editor window (and *not* the Objects Manager where all objects can always be selected). When scenes get very dense with objects, you can use this list to isolate the type of objects you're working on. Just Control-click on one object and all others will be disabled, or uncheck the objects you don't want to be selectable. You can also Shift-select objects and choose Create Selection Object from the Selection Filter list, creating a selection object in the Objects Manager. Later, if you click Restore in the Attributes Manager, all these objects will select at once for easy multiple editing.

Figure A.23 Selection Filter for Editor Selection

Figure A.24 Display Filter

Remember that in R8 you can Shift-select multiple objects (in either the Editor Window or the Objects Manager) and mass edit parameters, but there would be times when having a complex group of objects already saved would make things much easier.

The Display Filter works the same way, but determines which sets of objects will be *visible* in the editor window. You'll still see the axes of objects which have been made invisible. To return the objects to the view, just check the checkbox again.

◆ *Tip:* You can access a glossary of terms pertinent to CINEMA 4D at http://www.maxoncomputer.com.

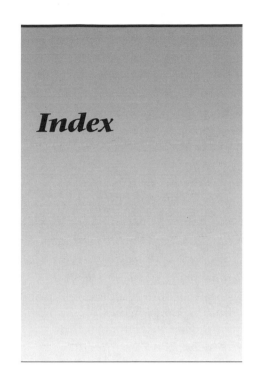

Index

DIGITAL MEDIA Academy

The **Digital Media Academy** is a premier technology training company offering a variety of courses in topics including Web design, video production, 3D, digital media for the classroom, motion graphics, and game design. Courses are open to educators, teens, and adult learners. DMA instructors include nationally recognized technology experts and award-winning teachers. All DMA courses are offered for optional Stanford University Continuing Studies credit.

DMA is best known for its summer programs at prestigious locations like Stanford University. Each summer, hundreds of teens and adults attend one or more five-day immersion courses. DMA summer programs feature optional on-campus housing and dining and state-of-the-art facilities, all in a relaxed, collaborative environment.

DMA also provides on-site training to educational institutions and companies through its DMA on the Road program. Courses are customizable and available in any length from one to five days or more.

For more information about DMA and to register, call (toll-free) 866-656-3342, visit www.digitalmediaacademy.org, or email info@digitalmediaacademy.org.

Digital Media in the Classroom
Gigi Carlson

Use digital media in the classroom to educate, engage, and motivate today's digital generation. K-12 educators learn how to use software, the Web, interactive games, desktop publishing, and digital accessories with everyday classroom lessons. This book's activities integrate professionally oriented software with academic lessons in math, physical and social sciences, language arts, and career development. You'll also discover ways to develop your own capabilities in designing dynamic classroom curricula using digital media.

Gigi Carlson combines years of educational theater and improv with her devotion to merge technology and creativity. In addition to teaching for the Digital Media Academy, she creates curricula and multimedia projects for students and educators.

$34.95, Softcover with DVD, 240pp, ISBN 1-57820-241-8, **August 2004**

Guide to the DVD

The gestalt of this book package is much more than the text, so remember to spend time with the DVD. It's literally loaded with instruction presented in alternate forms. Remember to browse through these folders as you read each chapter for a wealth of extra learning experiences.

Chapter Folders

With the exception of the Goodies Folder, which contains collections of models, materials, splines, and other freebies for overall use, materials related to specific chapters are in a folder named by the chapter number. For organizational purposes, the folder structure is identical from chapter to chapter, so don't be alarmed at the occasional empty folder. You may want to use the folders later as you generate your own examples. The structure within each chapter folder goes like this:

C4D Files: In this folder you'll find CINEMA 4D files necessary for projects. These are starter files that have materials or models already prepared so you can get right to work. Rarely, you may find an interloper, a non-C4D file (for example, an Illustrator file) that is necessary for the project.

EXAMPLES: Residing in this folder are finished versions of projects or other C4D example files that you can analyze and learn from.

EXTRA!EXTRA! Here you'll find the References folder (pointer lists to other information like books, magazines and multimedia, and web URLs) on the chapter topic.

In addition, here's where extra instruction lives. The In-Depth folder has extra project PDFs, Instructional Movies, supplementary instruction, explanatory information, and lists. Many of the C4D Files are annotated. When you see READ ME in the Objects Manager, just double-click the Xpresso tag on the right for notes on how the model was made. MOVIES/STILLS There are example C4D files and movies for animations on the DVD. Just look in the appropriate chapter folder for these helper files. Also inside this file are the Figures for each Chapter. In some cases, it may be important to see a figure in more detail, or in color. You'll find them here.

The Goodies Folder

LIBRARIES: There are example libraries of models, materials, sounds, and other elements for the C4D work process in these folders.

MATERIALS: This is a general bin of materials and other art elements for projects on the book (and for your use later).

View DVD

Click on this icon to view an interactive preview of book projects and guest artist galleries. If the interface doesn't appear, Command-click or Right-click on the icon and choose "Open with" Internet Explorer or Safari. Use the newest browser version for the best behavior.

INTRODUCTION: A short joyride through the kinds of things you'll learn how to make by working through this book.

MOVIES: QuickTime movies featuring Guest Artists and sample Book Projects.

CINEMA 4D GALLERY: A gallery of still images from C4D Artists around the world.

Updates

Want to receive e-mail updates for *CINEMA 4D: An Artist's Project Sourcebook*? Send a blank e-mail to cinema4d@news.cmpbooks.com. We'll do our best to keep you informed of software updates and enhancements, new tips, and other CINEMA 4D resources.